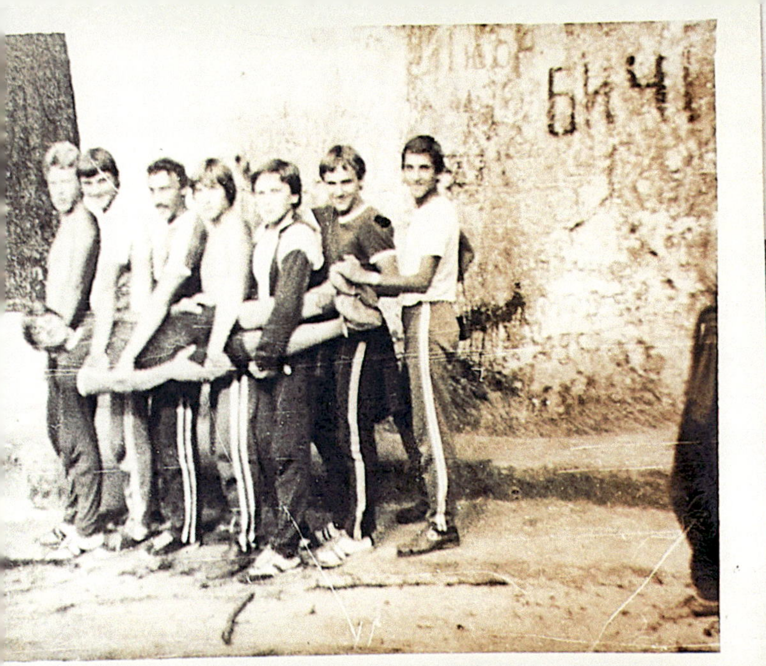

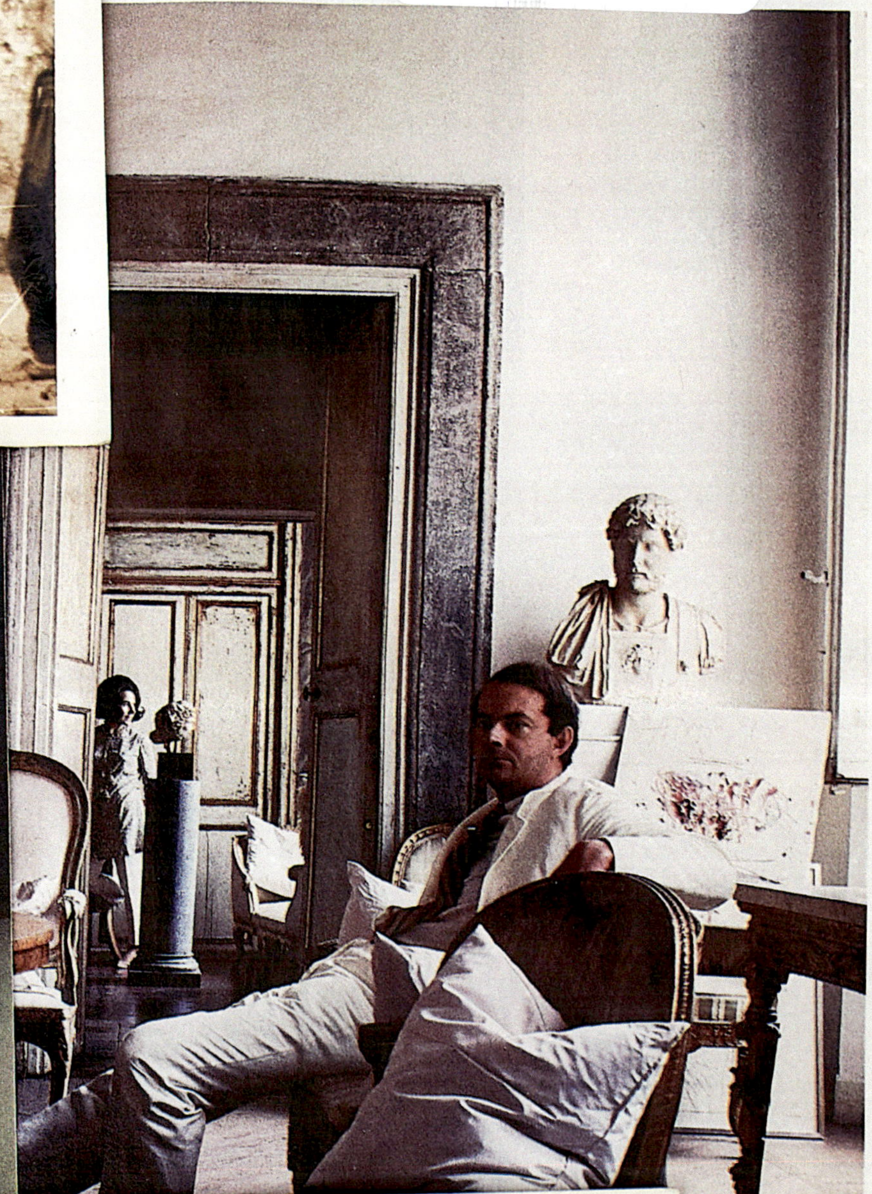

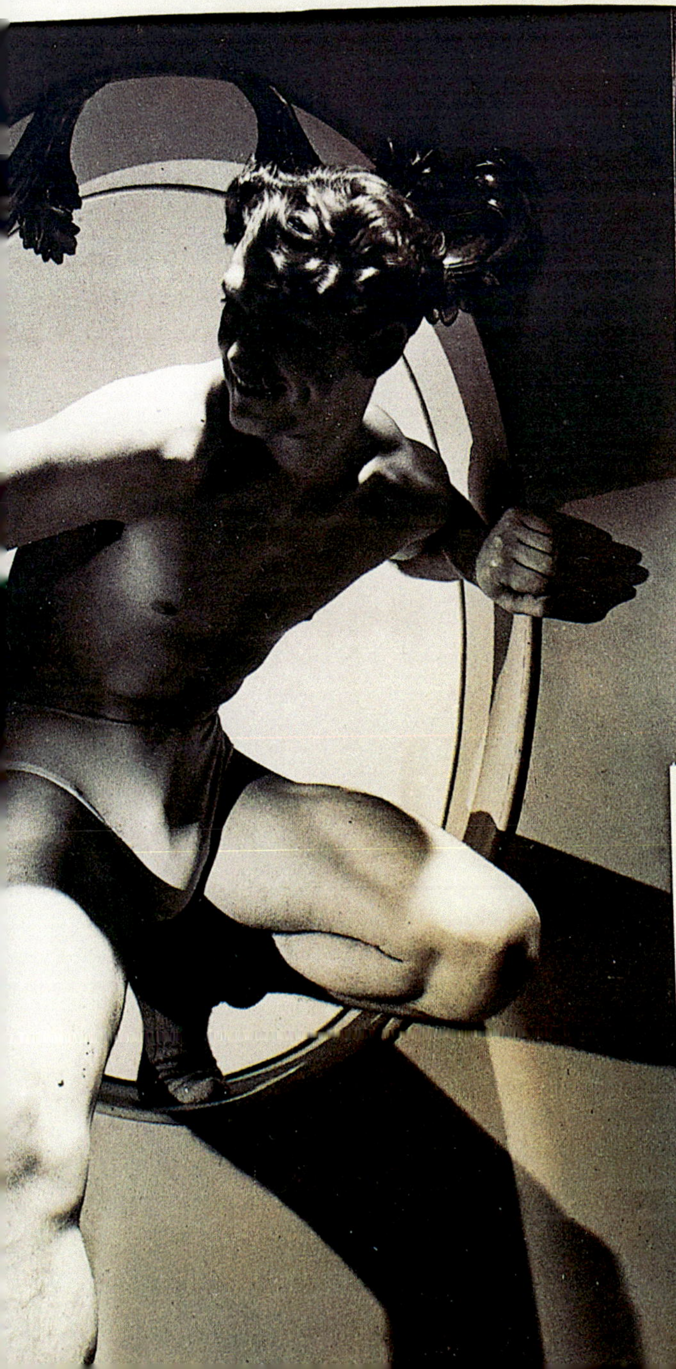

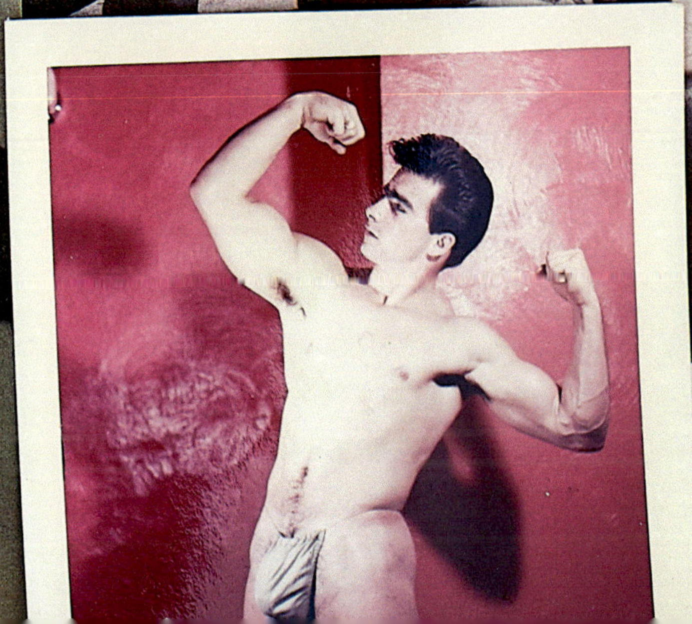

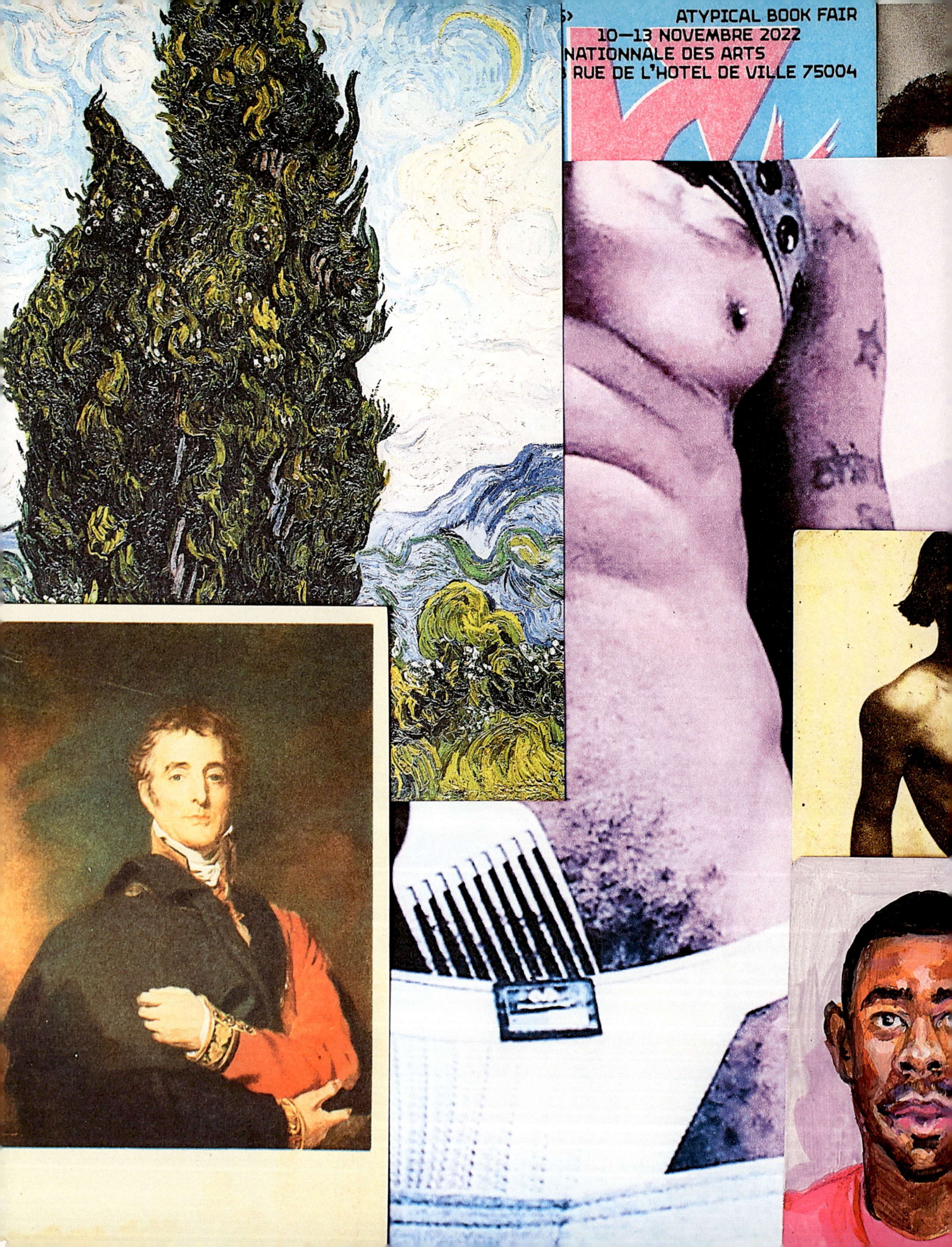
ATYPICAL BOOK FAIR
10—13 NOVEMBRE 2022
NATIONNALE DES ARTS
RUE DE L'HOTEL DE VILLE 75004

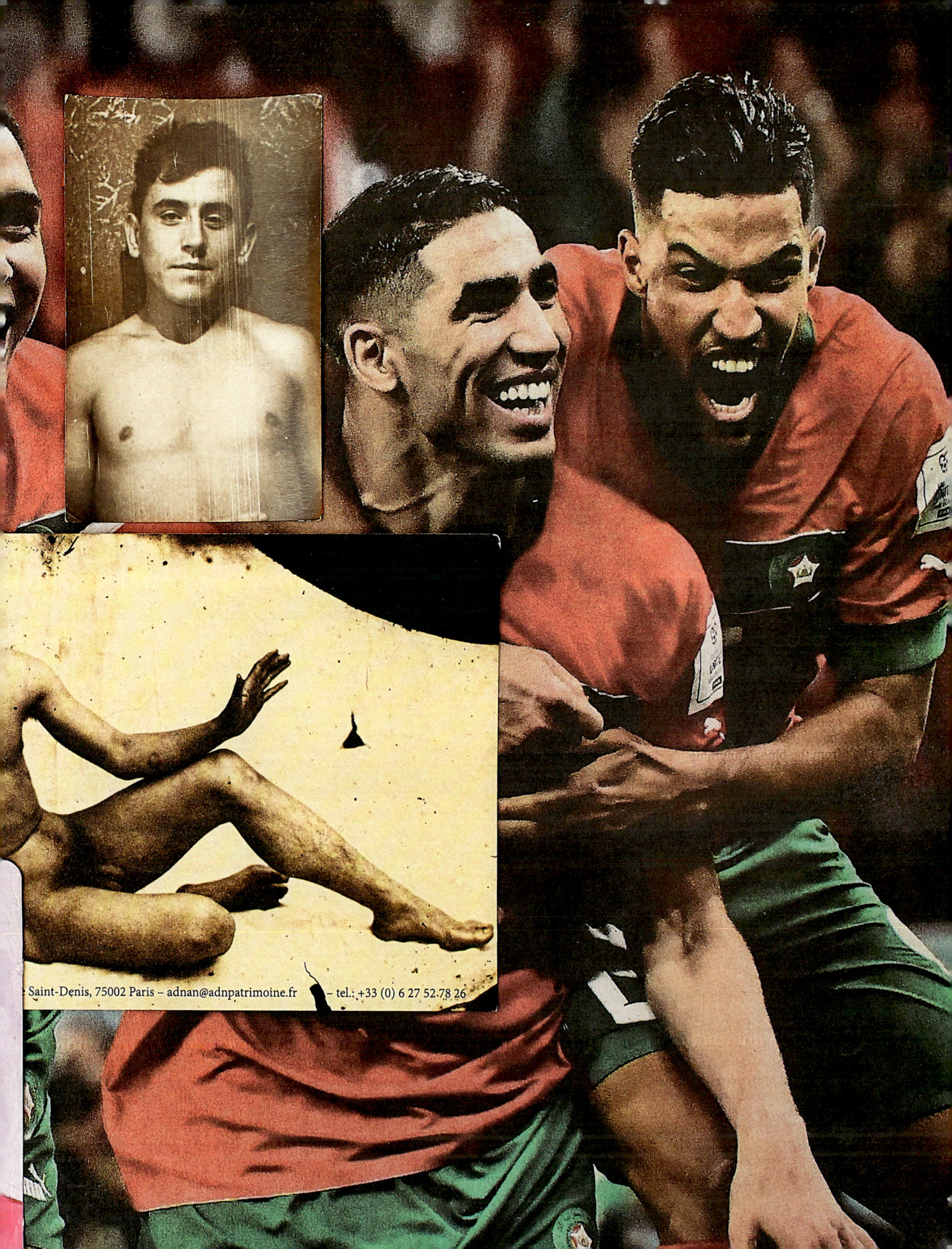
Saint-Denis, 75002 Paris – adnan@adnpatrimoine.fr – tel.: +33 (0) 6 27 52.78 26

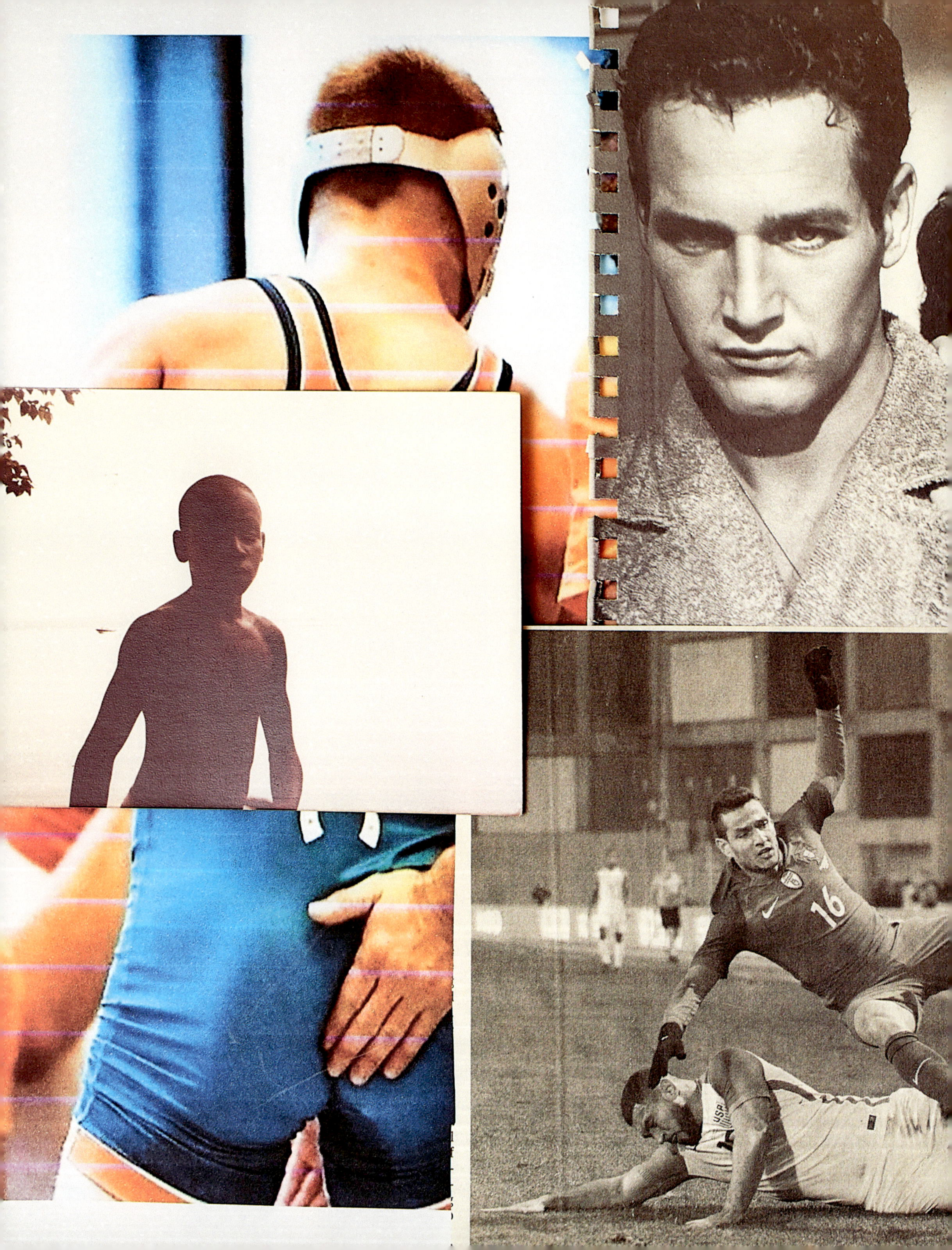

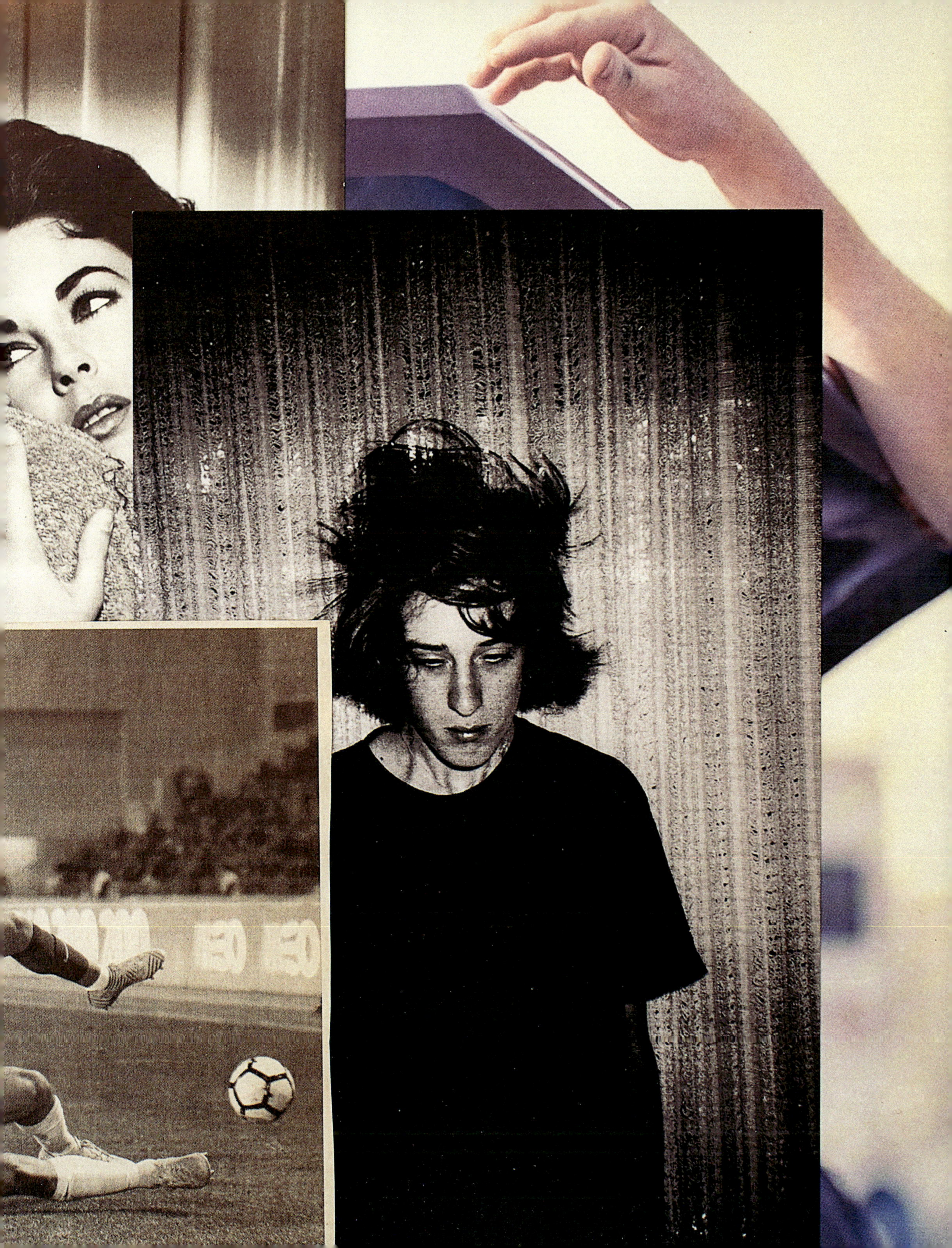

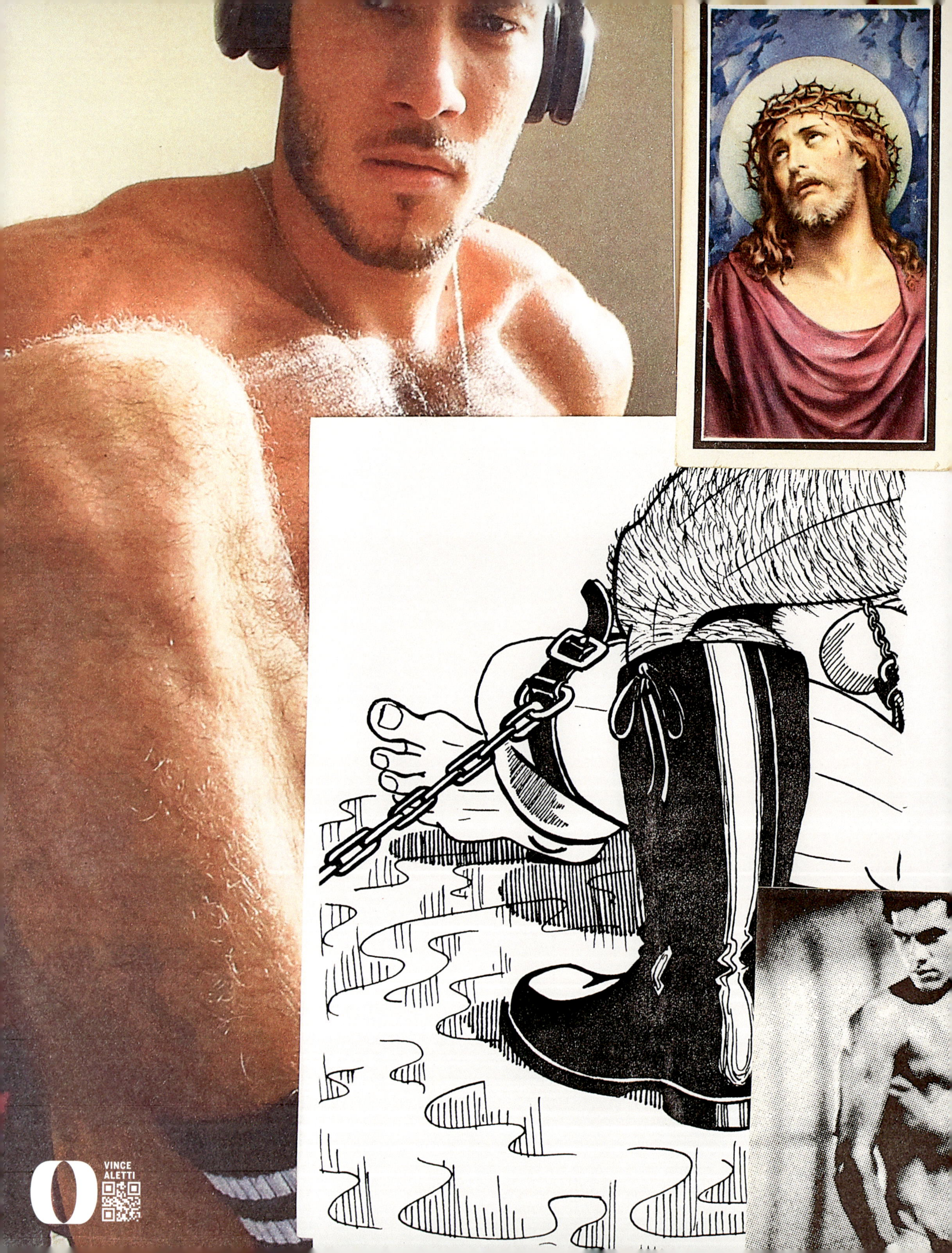
VINCE
ALETTI

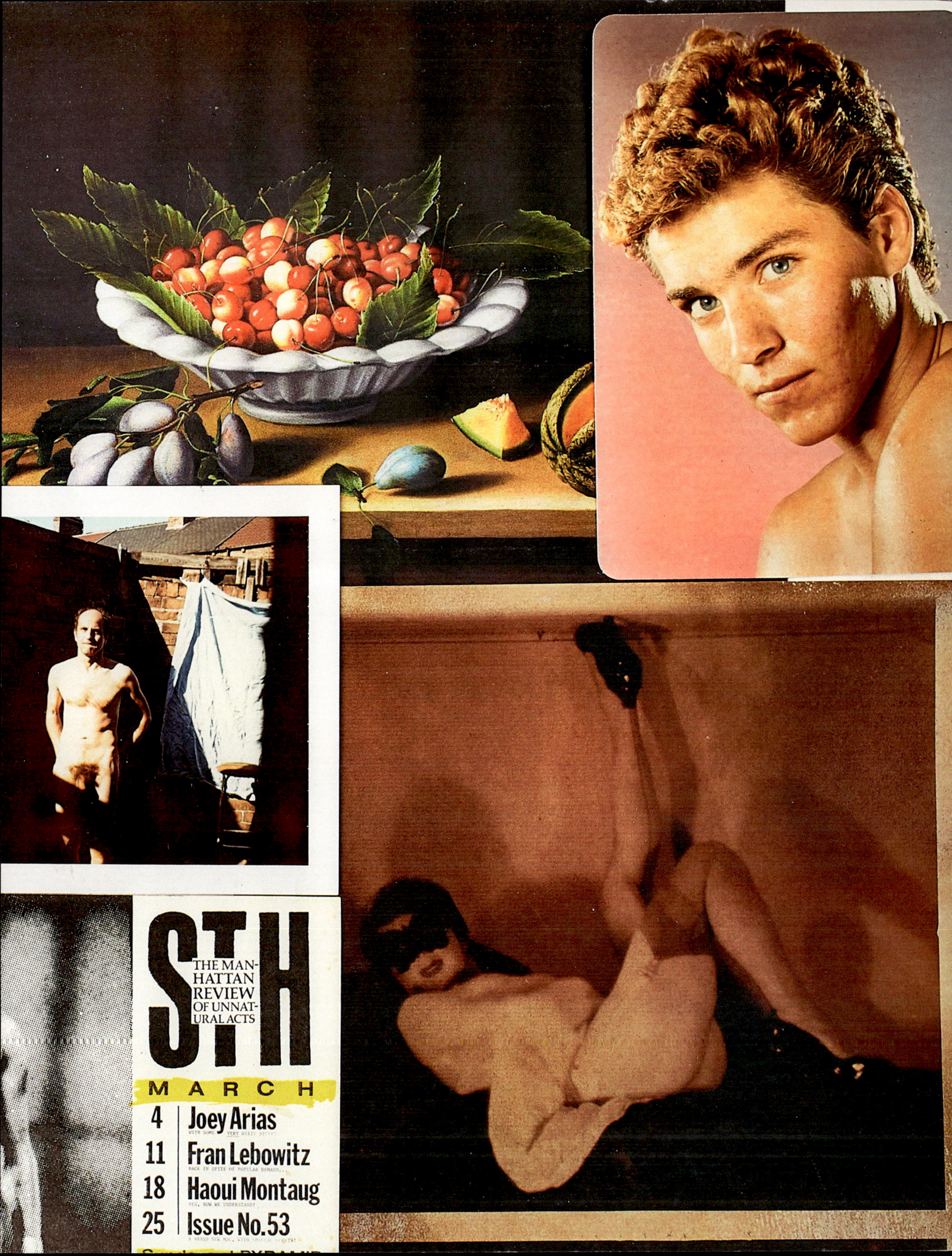
STH
THE MAN-
HATTAN
REVIEW
OF UNNAT-
URAL ACTS
MARCH
4 Joey Arias
11 Fran Lebowitz
18 Haoui Montaug
25 Issue No.53

EDITORS-IN-CHIEF
Charles Daigrepont Desselle EDITORIAL DIRECTOR & Phillip Bogart Duncan CREATIVE DIRECTOR

DESIGN & TYPOGRAPHY
Nobi Kashiwagi

CONTRIBUTORS
Jun Ahn, Vince Aletti, Mark Carrasquillo & Lucian Clifforth, Guido Ciompi, Hans Feurer, Thibaut Grevet, Shaniqwa Jarvis, Ron Jude, Emmy Rappe, Kuba Ryniewicz, Emma Summerton, Catherine Wagner, Eva Wang, Zeng Wu

CONTRIBUTING EDITOR
Alex Zafiris

IMAGE RESEARCH & RIGHTS CLARIFICATION
Maud Lomnitz, XY Zèbre

EDITORIAL ASSISTANT
Lucrezia Caracciolo

PRESS OFFICE
press@daisychainmagazine.com

ADVISORS
Vince Aletti, Anthony Bigazzi, Jen Ford, Vali Mahlouji, Emma Summerton, André Werther, Alex Zafiris

SPECIAL THANKS
Brent Adams, Mert Alas, Frederic Arnal, The John Baldessari Trust, Cheri Bowen, Stefanie Breslin, Dana Brockman, Chris Cassetti, Raj Debah, Julien Desselle, Jacob Daugherty, Karen Elson, Hans Feurer, Adeline Gault, David Gross, Harry Gruyaert, The Henri Matisse Estate, Mark Holgate, Jonathan Höglund, Katy Hundertmark, Carlijn Jacobs, Roch Jamelot, Alexander Kamnitsis, Miranda Kendrick, George Kocis, Nick & Charlotte Knight, Matthew Krejcarek, Ann Lee, Fanny Level, The Peter Lindbergh Foundation, Theresa Luisotti, Stacey Mark, Martha McClintock, Colin McIntosh, Christopher McCoy, Christopher Michael, Duane Michals, Alejandra Moros, Reina Nakagawa, Davide Nigrelli, Jonathan Doria Pamphilj, Matthew Pasterisa, The Irving Penn Foundation, Rachelle Pereira, Marcus Piggott, Steven Pranica, Chris Rawson, Philip Reeser, Sølve Sundsbø, Fanny Snijders, Bing Sokolsky, Eliott Soriano, The Staley-Wise Gallery, Anna Townsend, John Valdivia, Gwendoline Victoria, Martha Violante, Cassandra Victor, Shawn Waldron, Olliver Wang, The Estate of Tom Wesselmann, David Zwirner Gallery

PUBLISHED BY **DAMIANI**
info@damianieditore.com
www.damianieditore.com

PRINTED IN ITALY BY **ABC TIPOGRAFIA**
January 2023

64 Bleecker Street, #335
New York, NY 10012

ALL INQUIRIES
info@daisychainmagazine.com

© DAMIANI 2023
ISBN 9788862087940

1

PHOTOGRAPHY, FASHION, EPHEMERA
THE SPACE ISSUE:
SPRING / SUMMER 2023

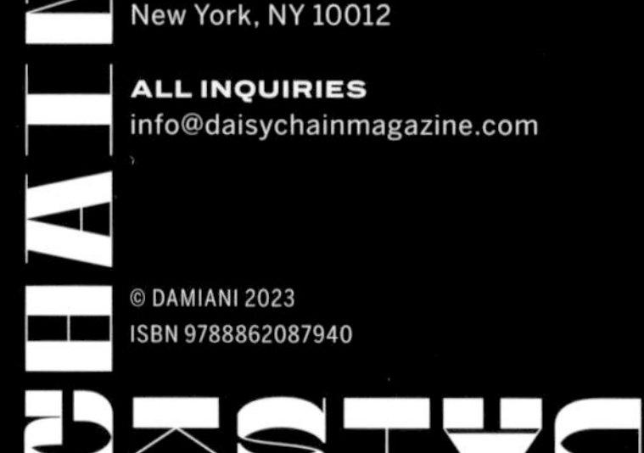

DAISYCHAINMAGAZINE.COM

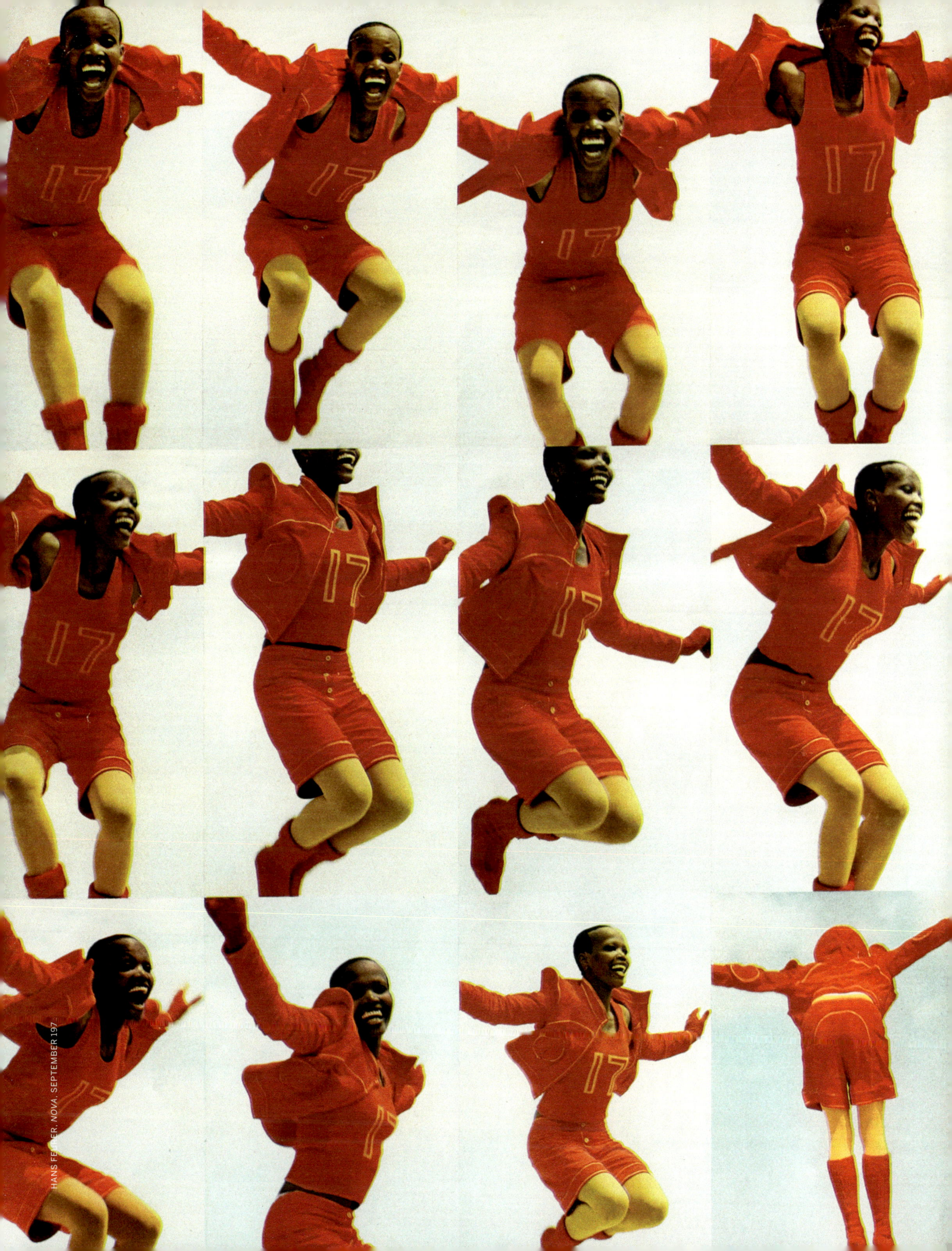

HANS FEURER. NOVA. SEPTEMBER 197

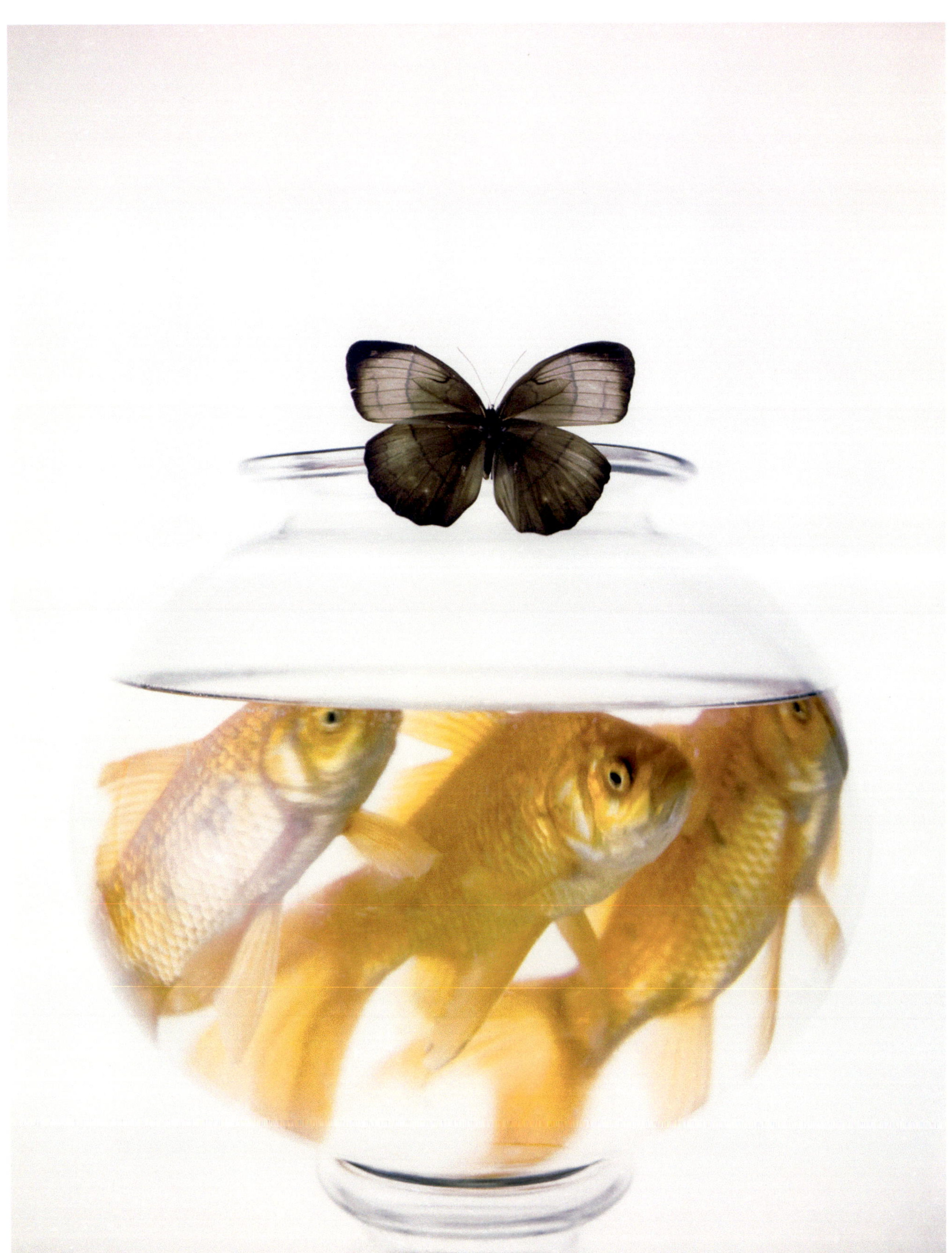

IRVING PENN, *GOLDFISH*, *VOGUE* COVER, APRIL 15, 1947 © CONDÉ NAST

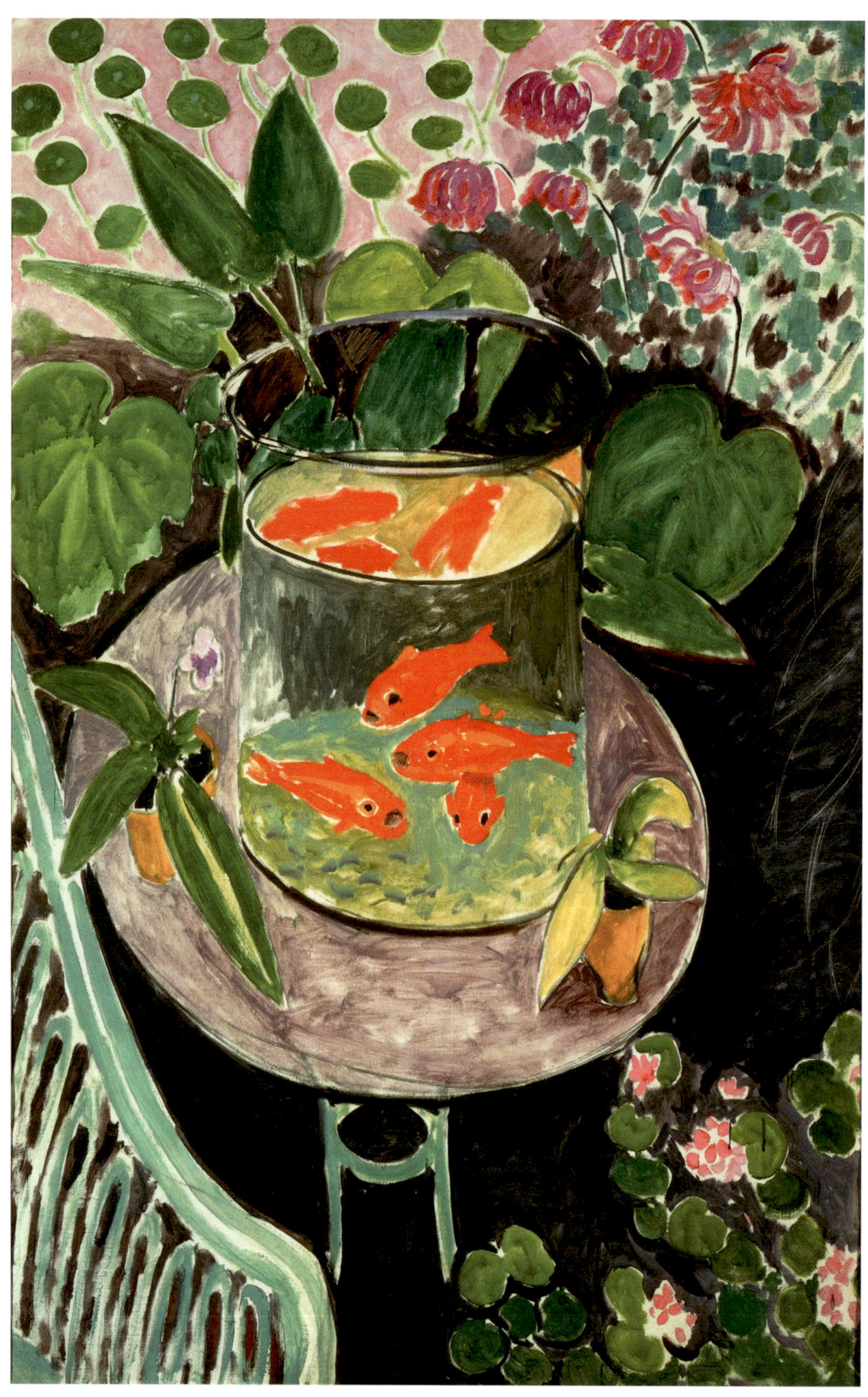

HENRI MATISSE, *GOLDFISH*, 1912

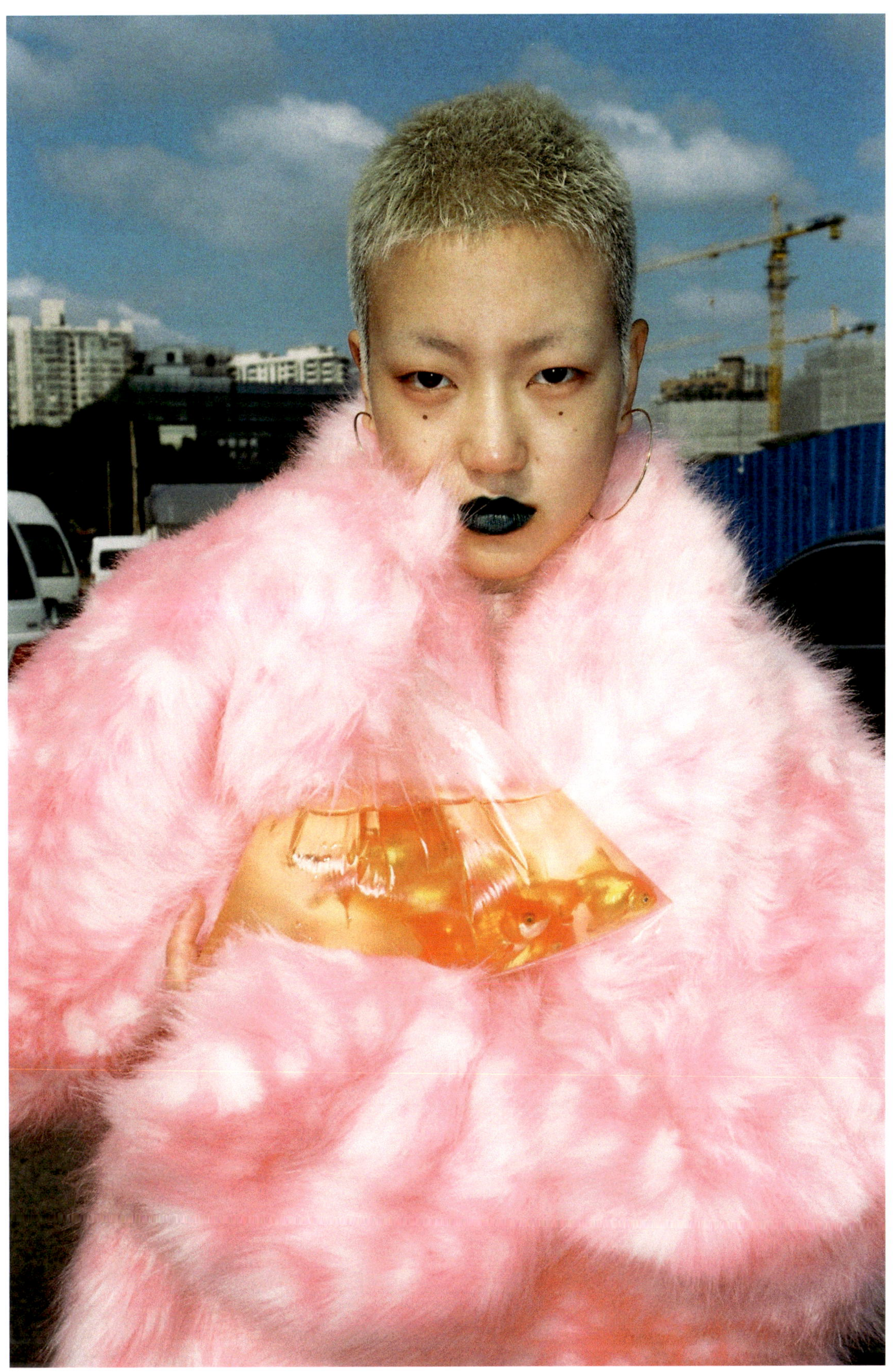

LUO YANG, *YAYA*, 2019

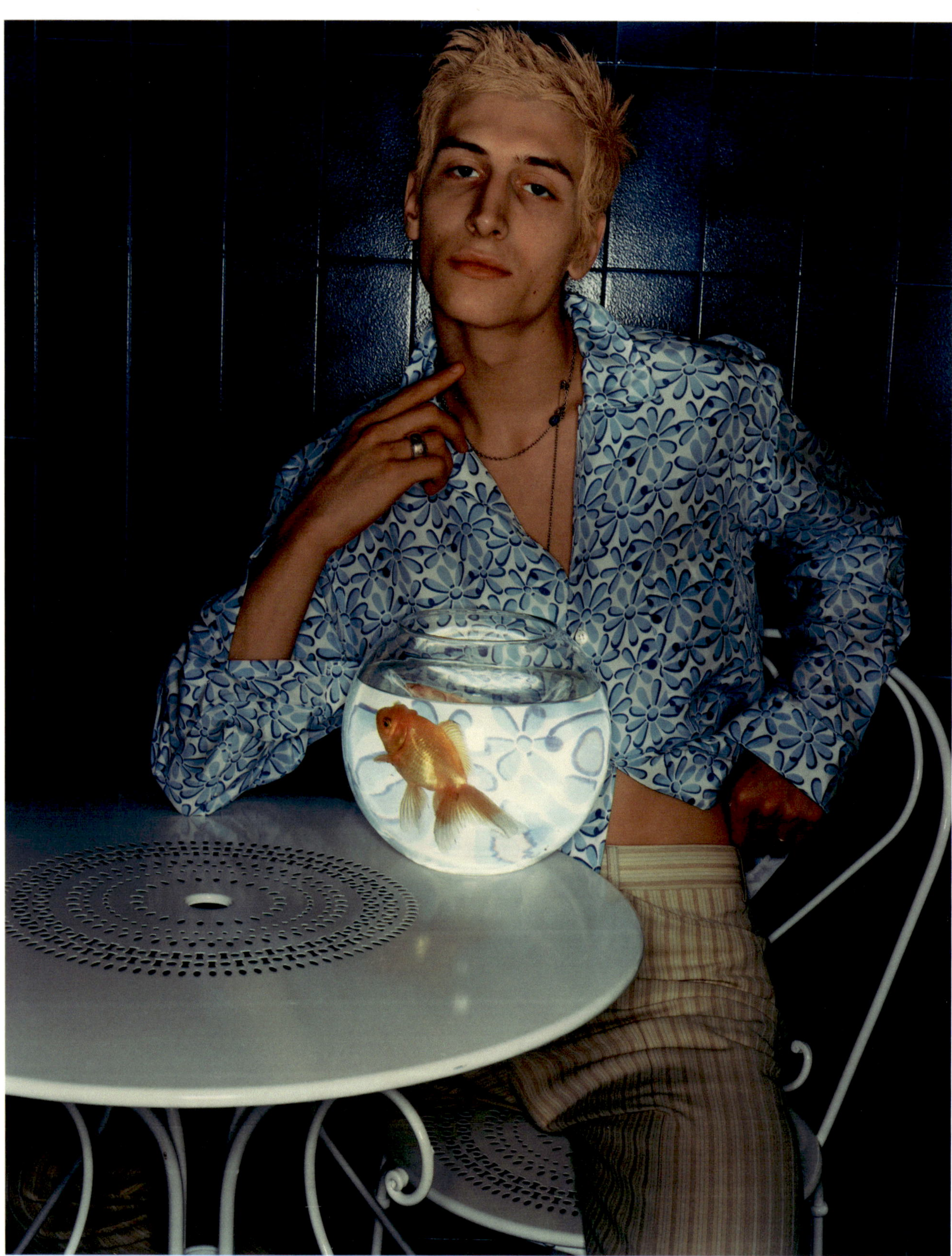

NICK KNIGHT, *JEROME WITH GOLDFISH*, 1994

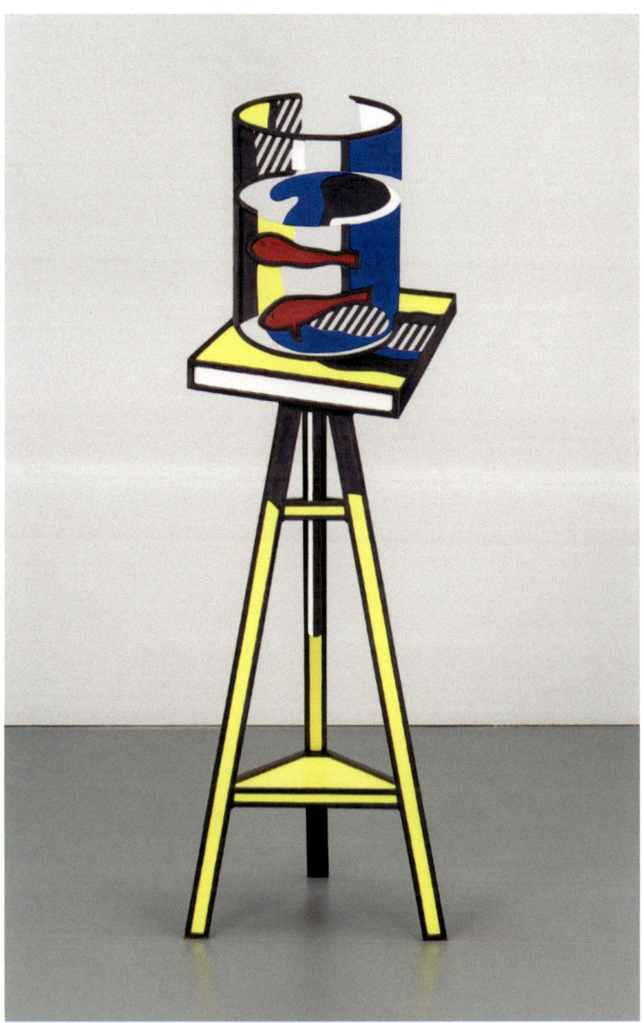

ROY LICHTENSTEIN, *GOLD FISH BOWL*, 1977

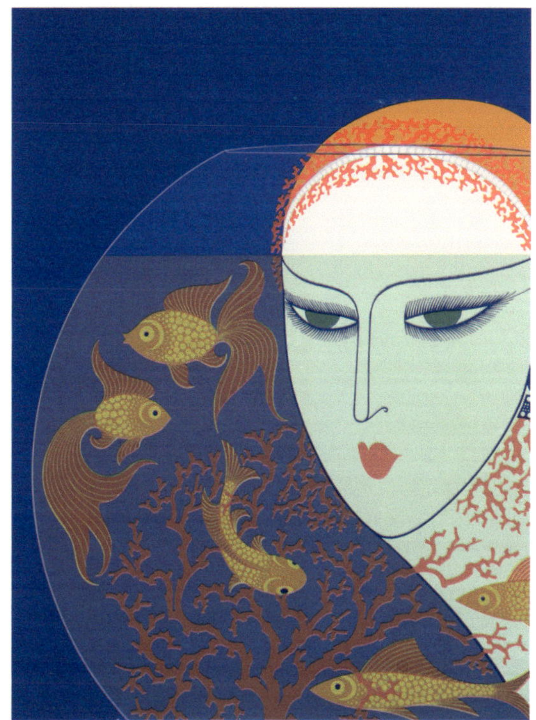

ERTÉ, *FISH BOWL*, *HARPER'S BAZAAR*, COVER, JUNE 1931

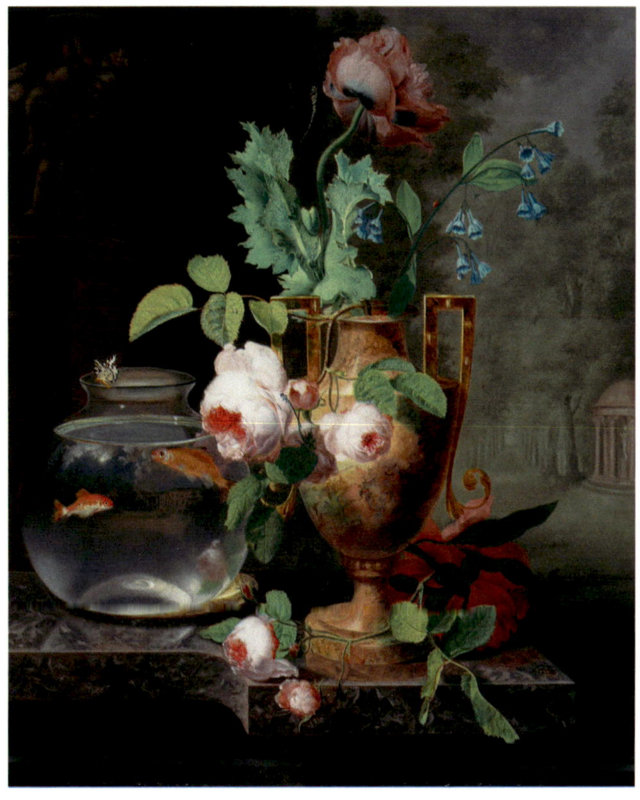

JEAN BAPTISTE BERRÉ, *STILL LIFE WITH FLOWERS IN A VASE AND GOLDFISH BOWL*, 1800

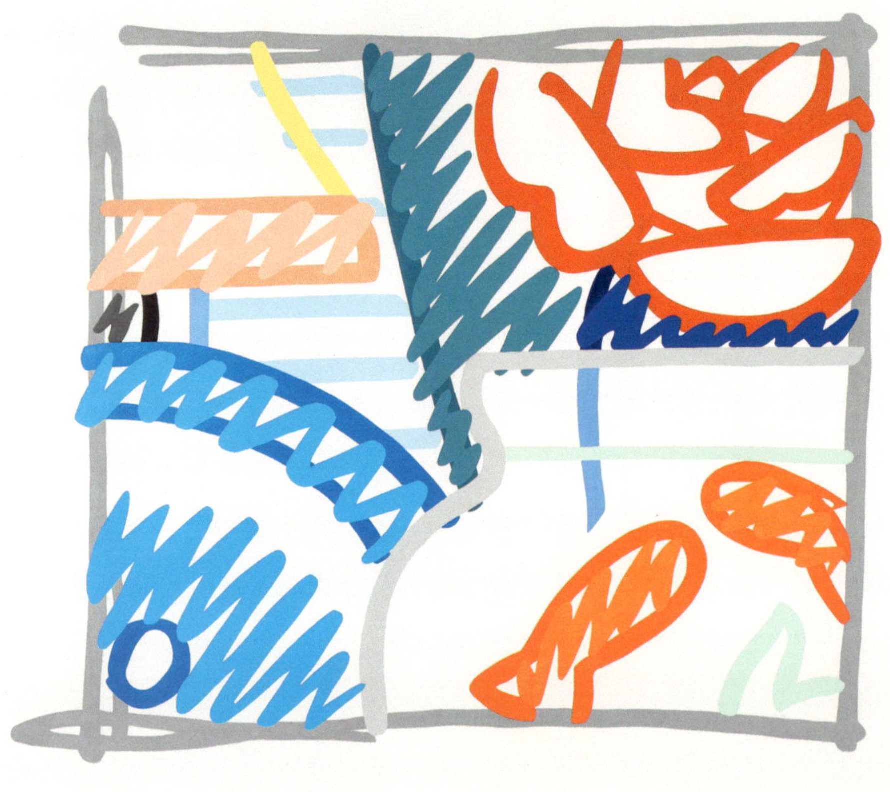

TOM WESSELMANN, *STILL LIFE WITH GOLDFISH AND ROSE*, 1984

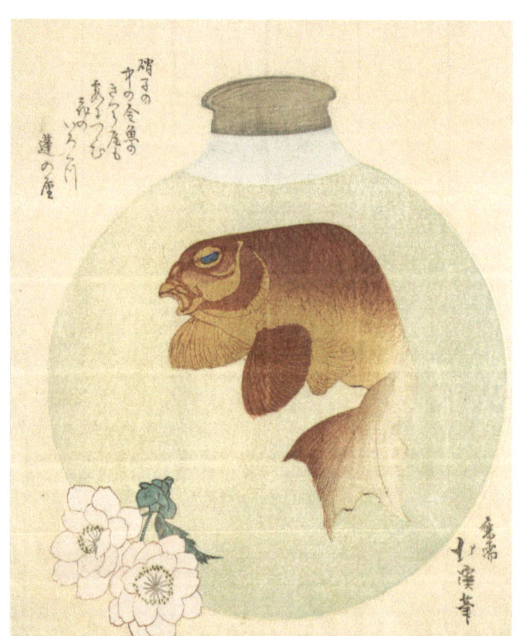

TOTOYA HOKKEI, *GOLD-FISH IN A GLASS BOTTLE*, 19TH CENTURY

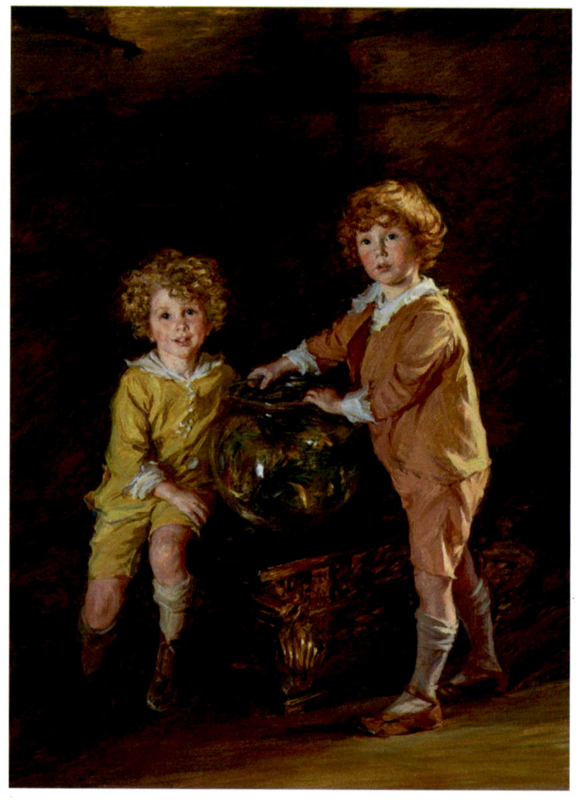

LYDIA FIELD EMMET, *GOLDFISH, A PORTRAIT OF ROLAND AND PETER HAZARD*, 1921

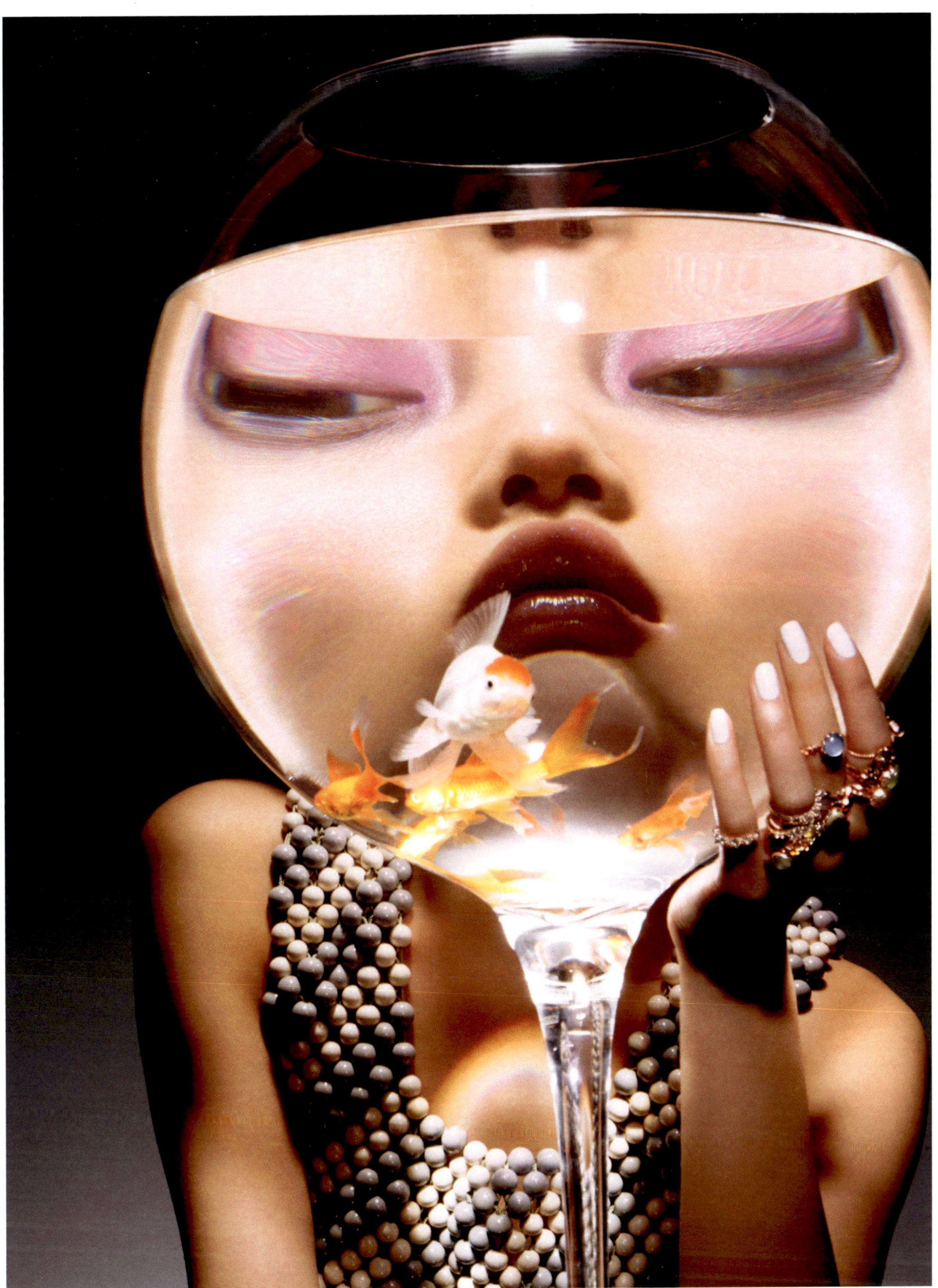

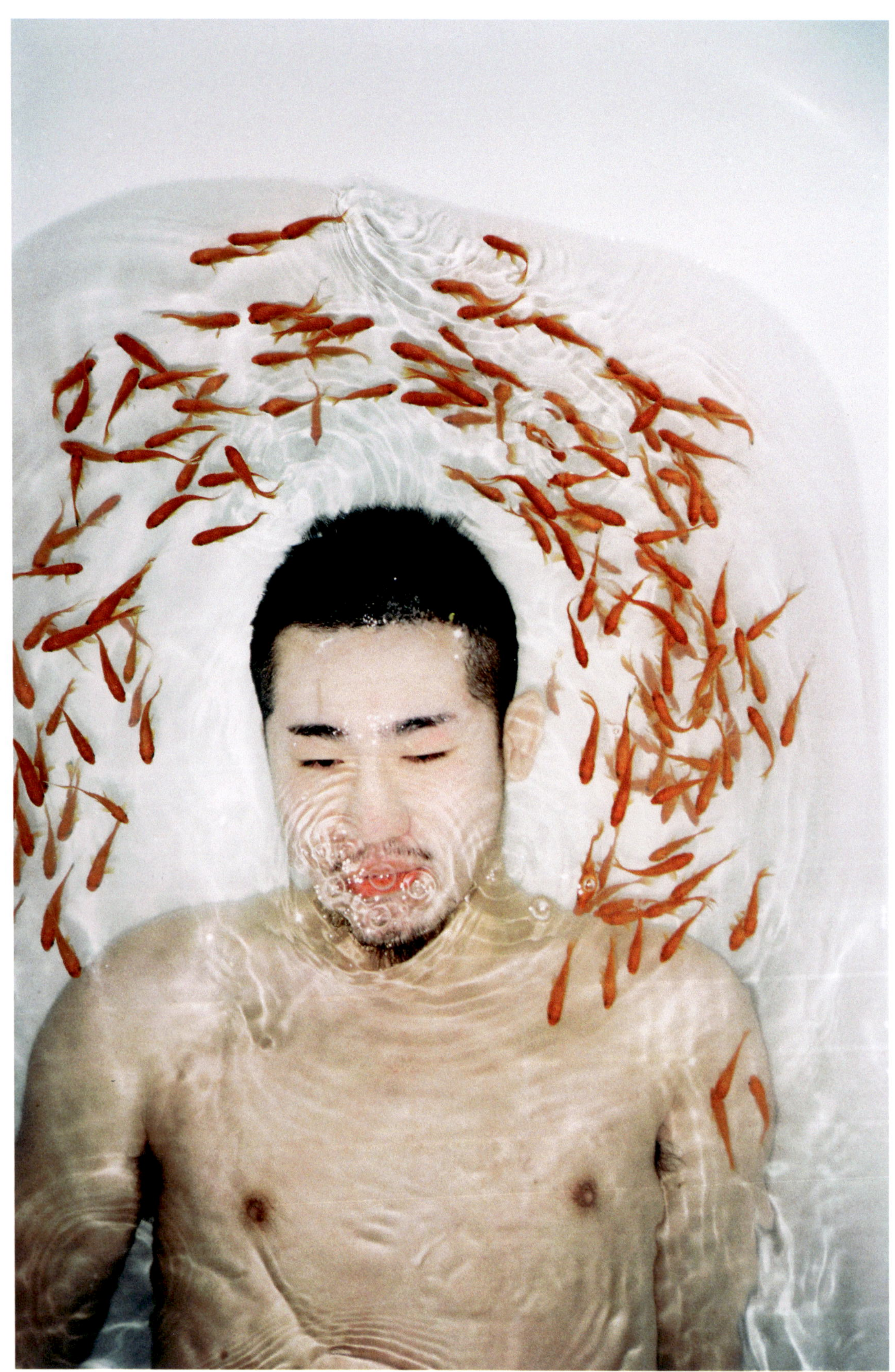

REN HANG, *UNTITLED*, 2012

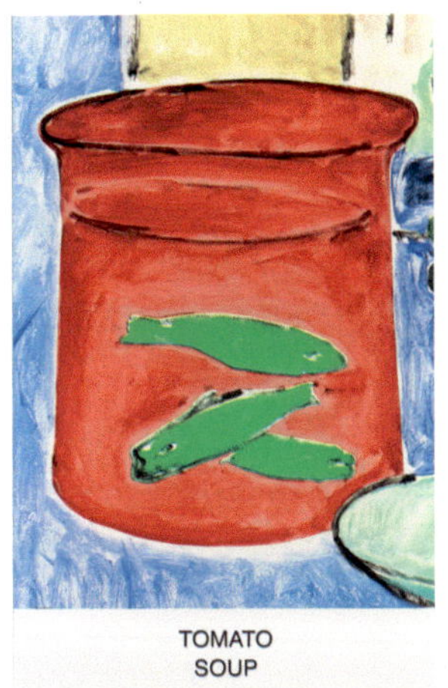

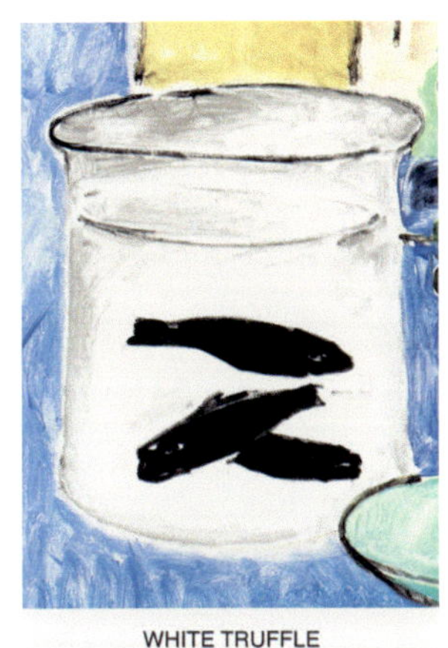

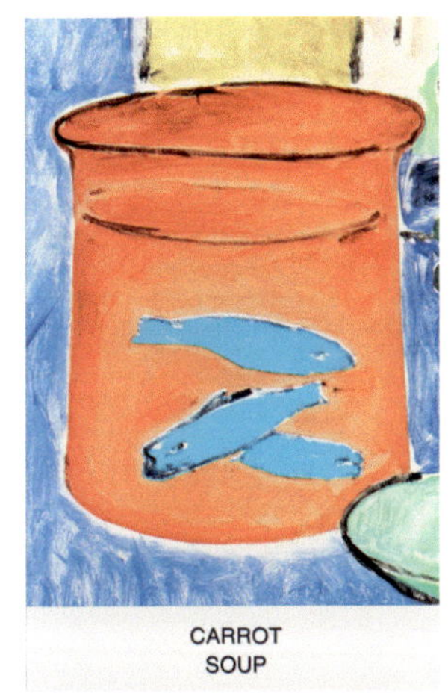

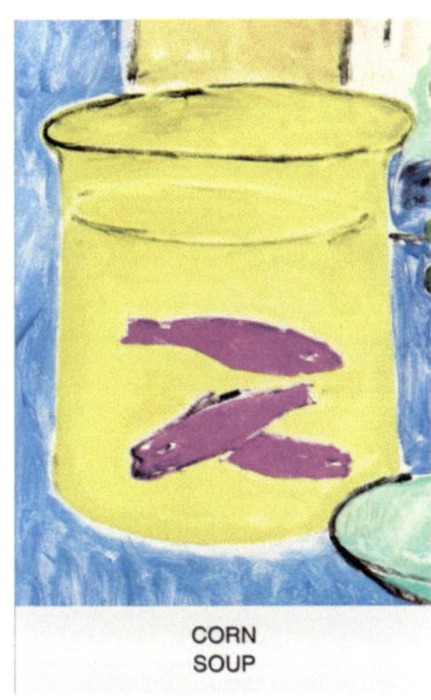

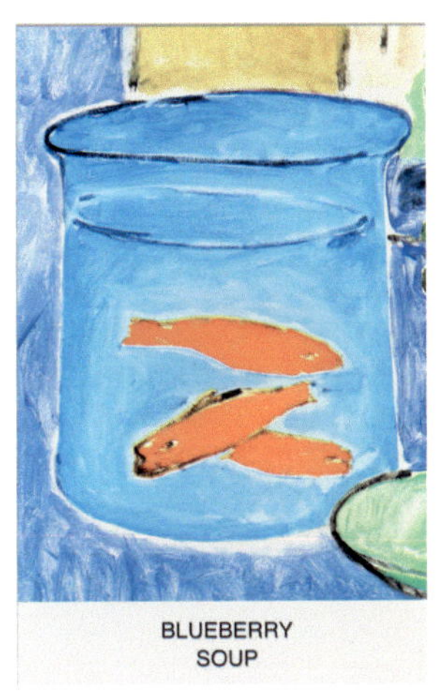

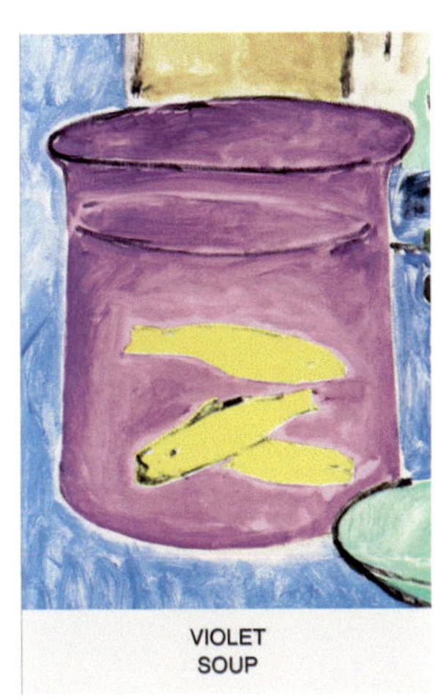

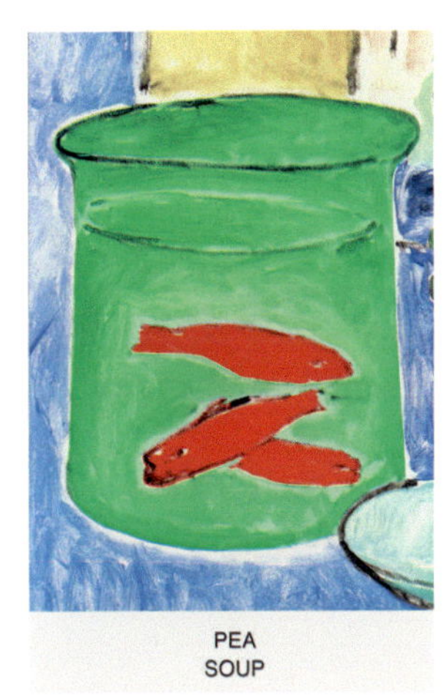

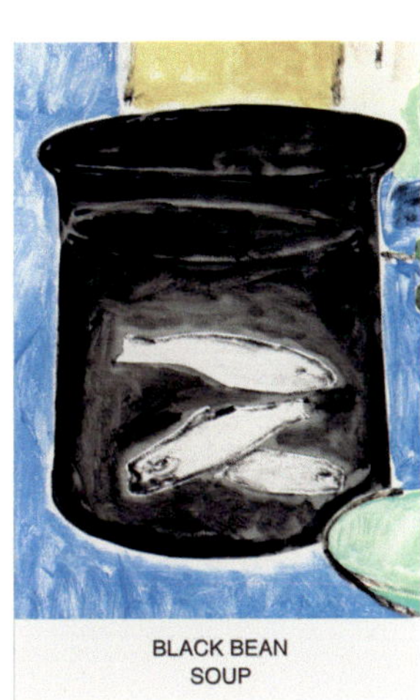

JOHN BALDESSARI, *SET OF EIGHT SOUPS*, 2012

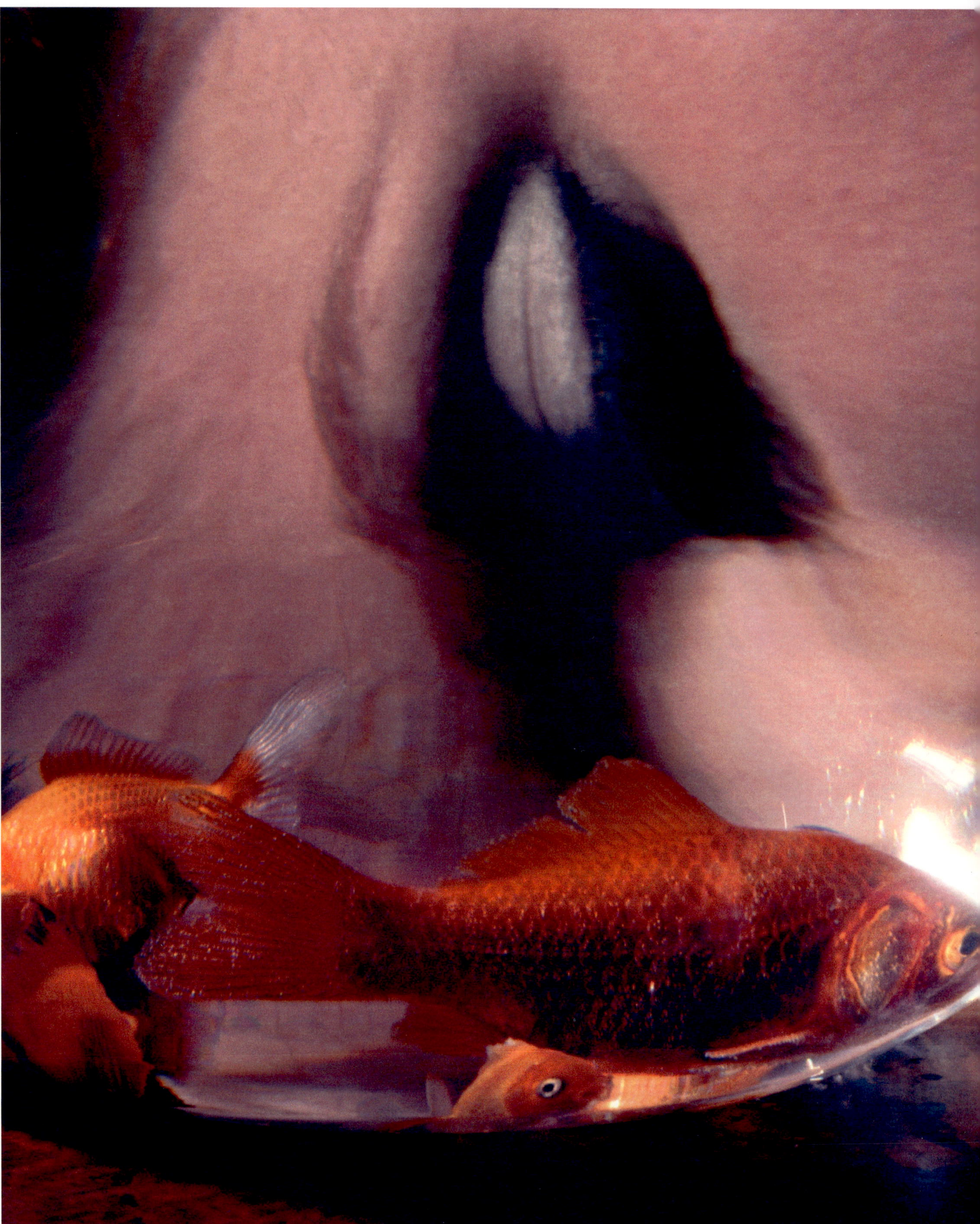

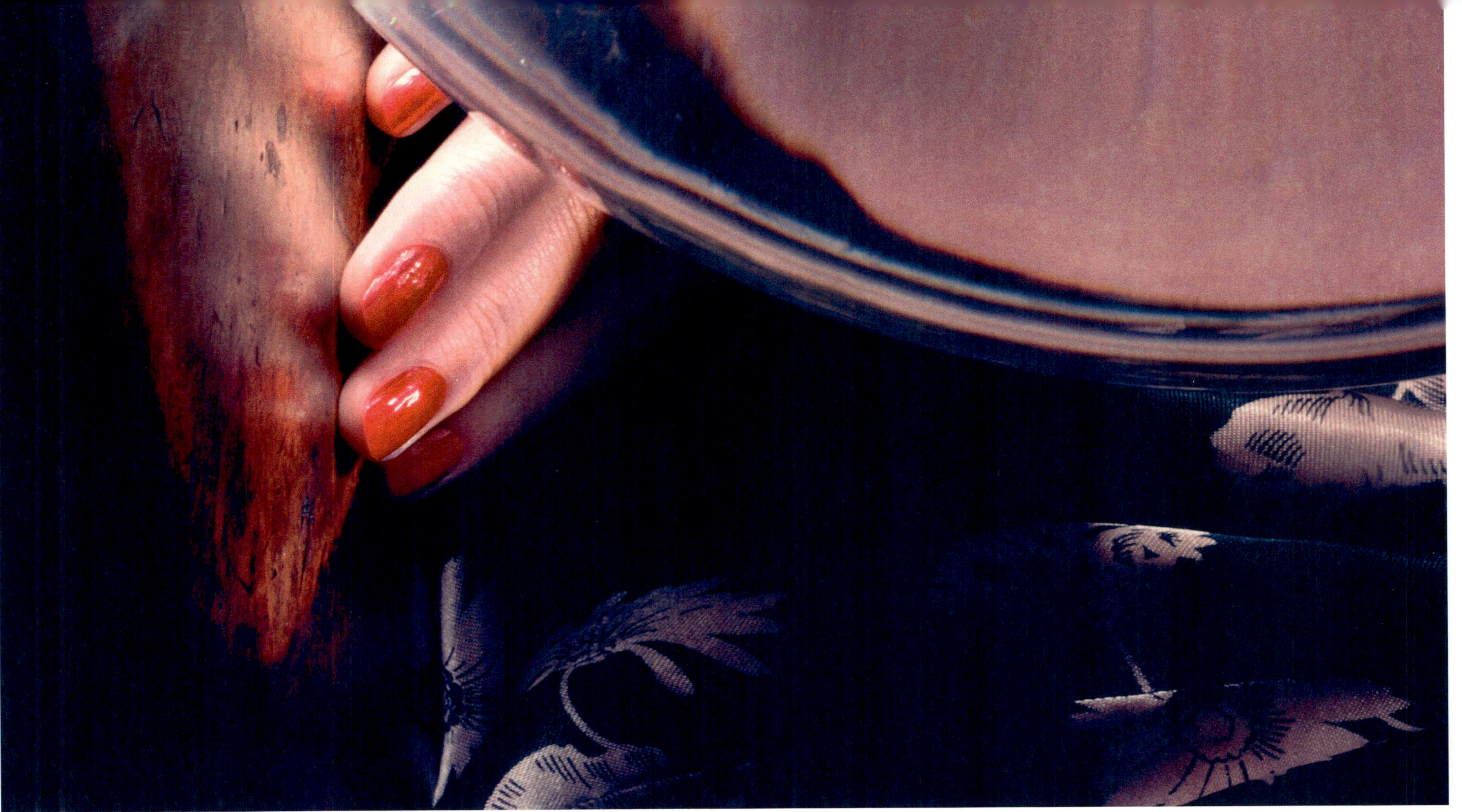

GUY BOURDIN, *GOLDFISH INCIDENT. VOGUE* PARIS, MAY 1977

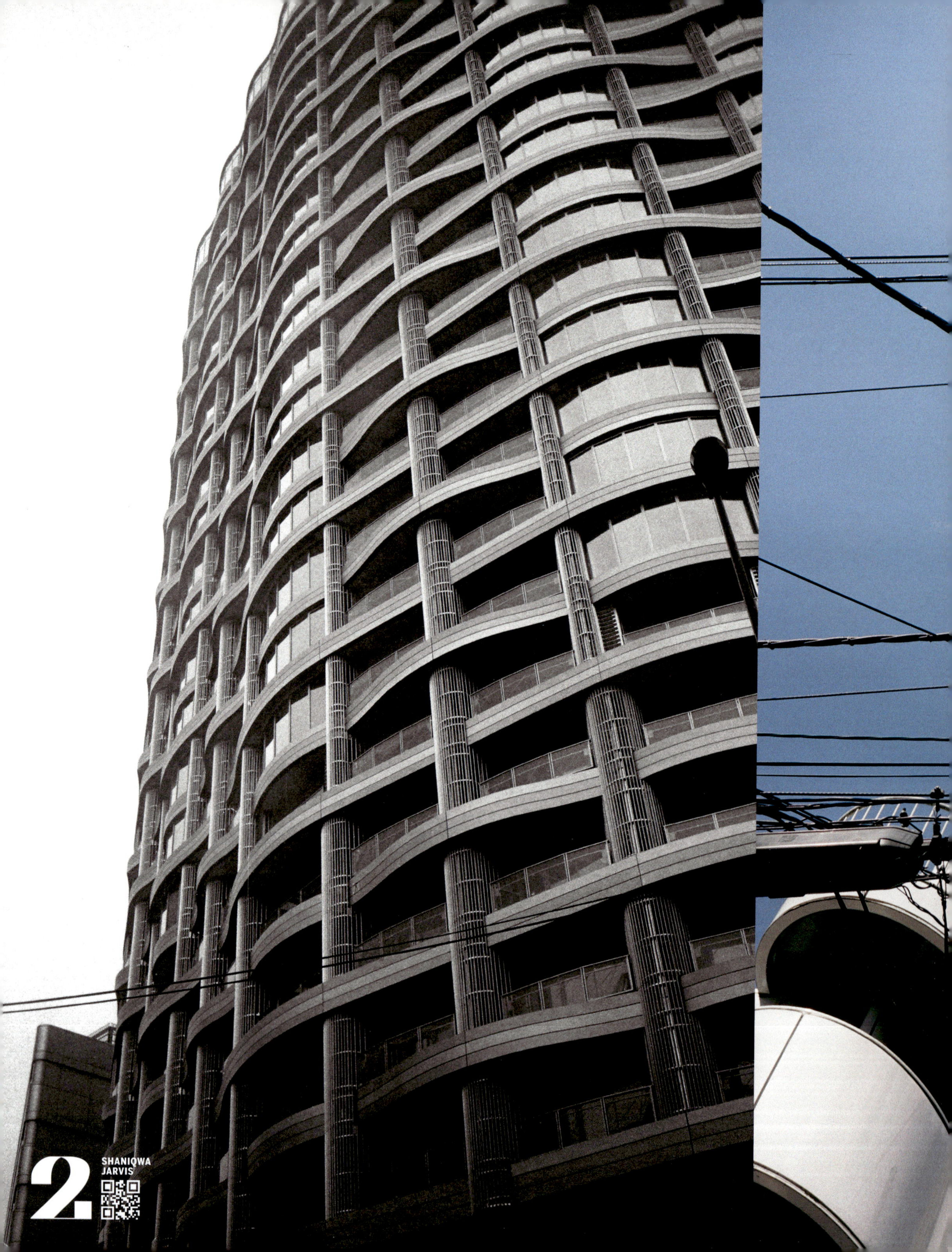
2.
SHANIQWA
JARVIS

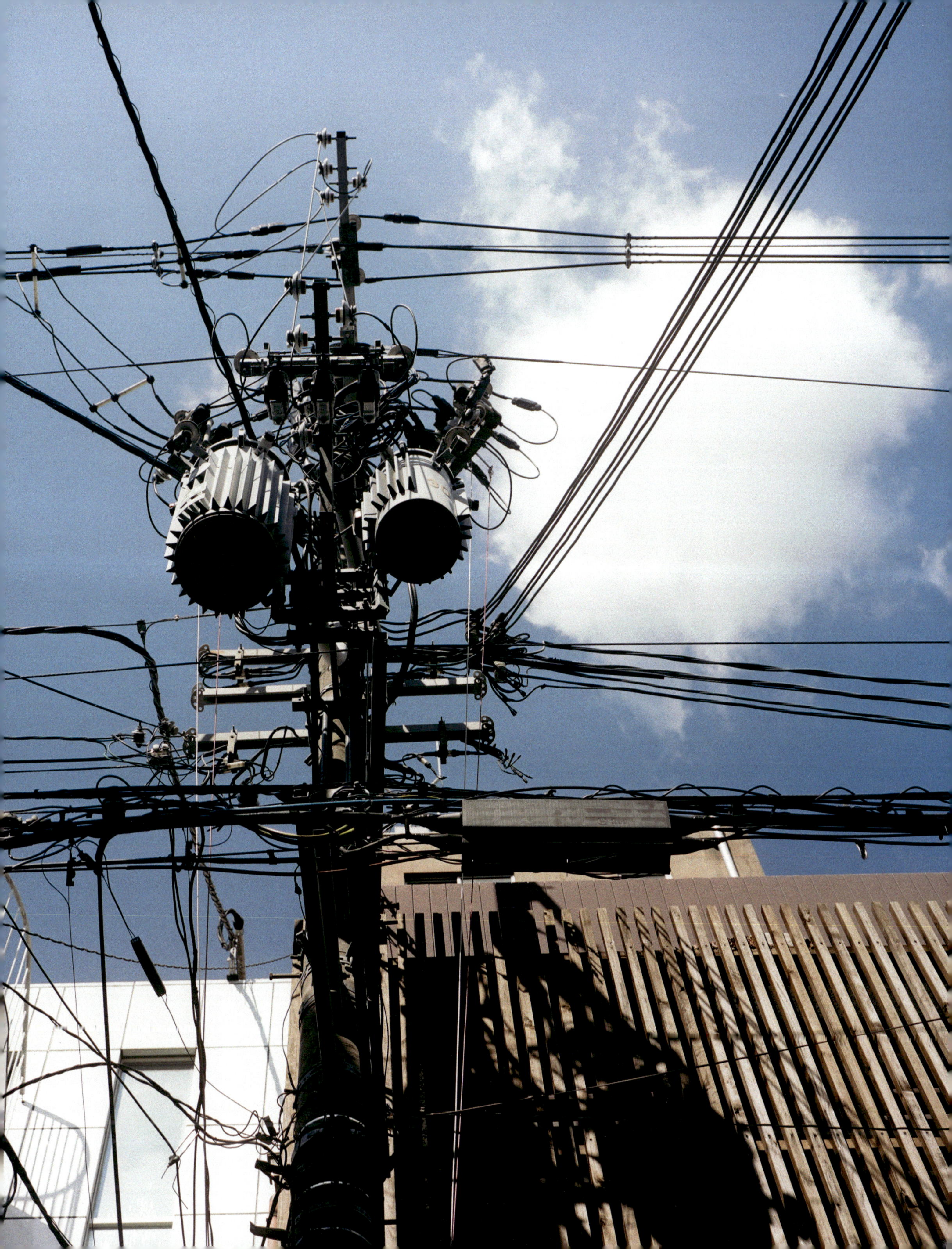

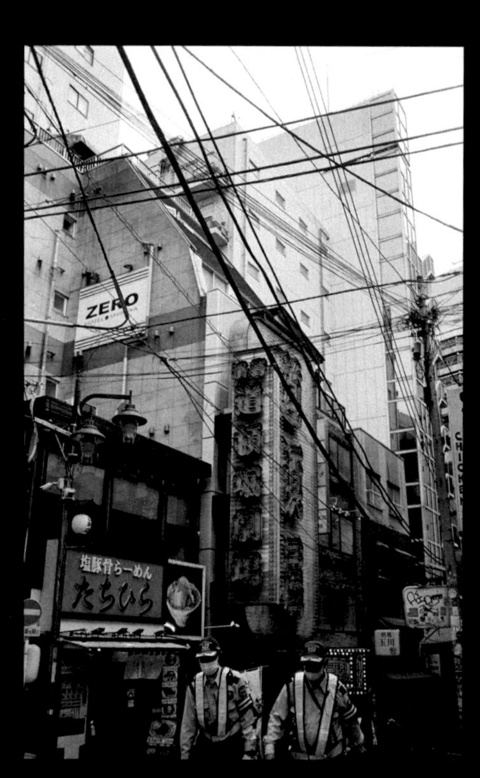

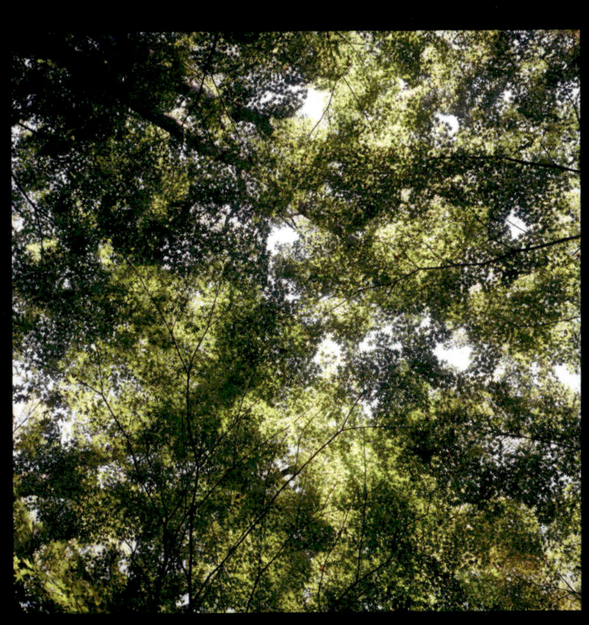

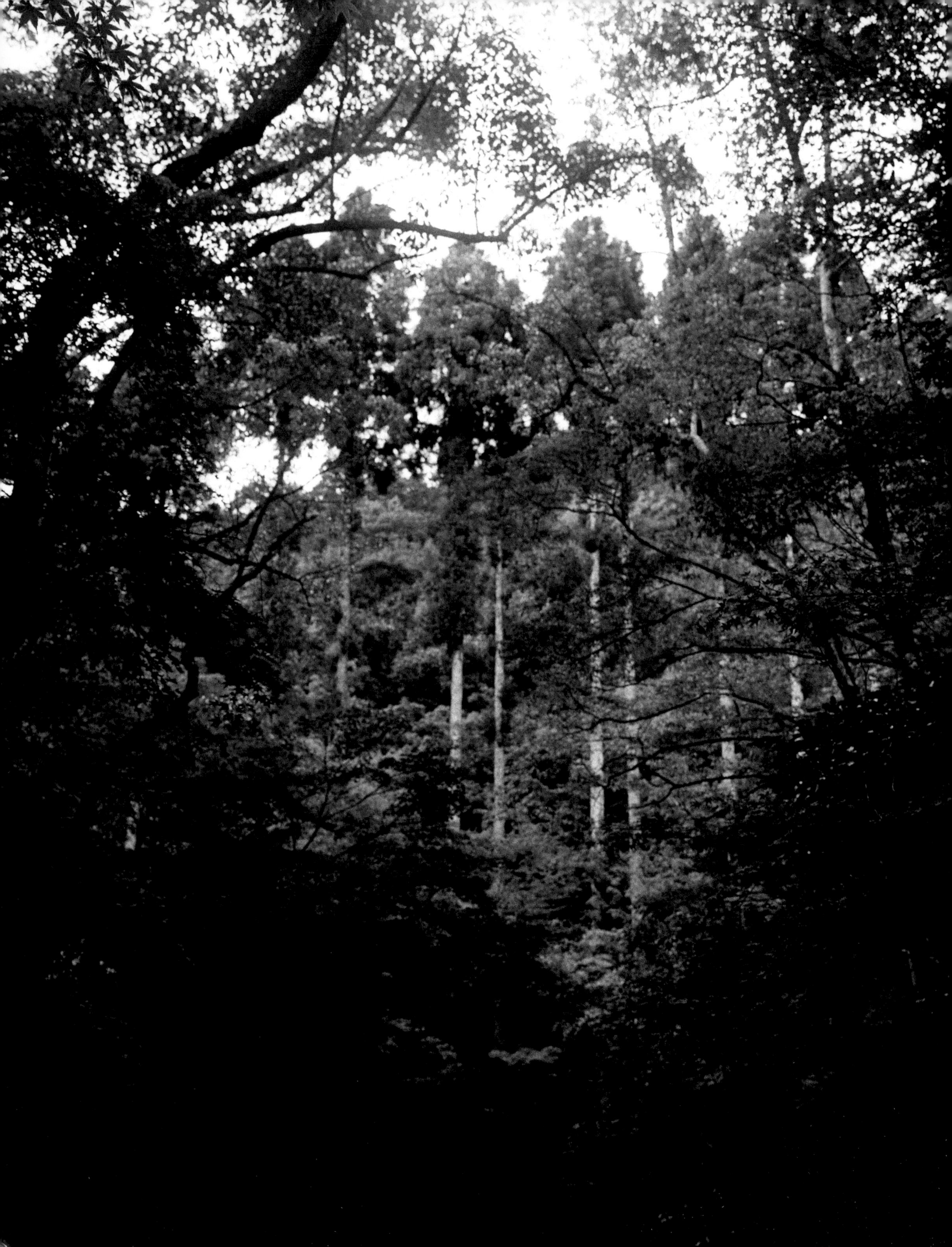

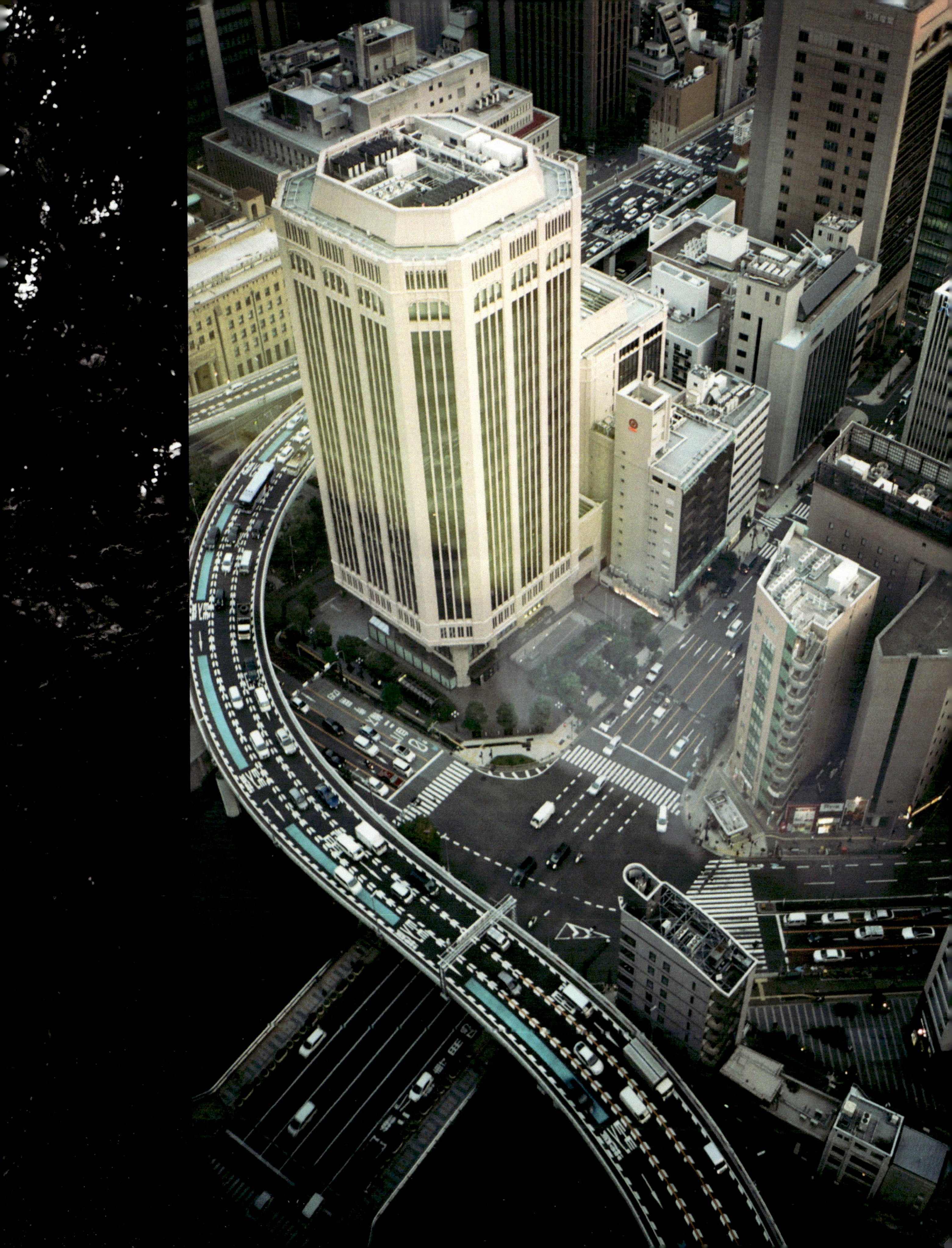

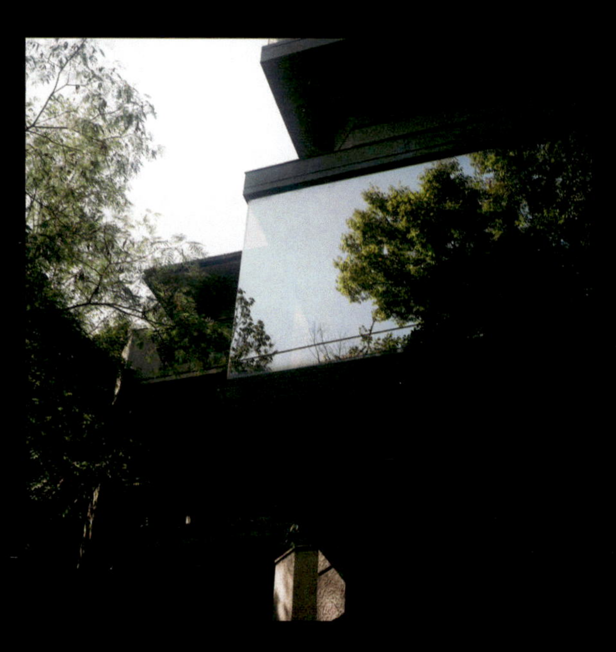

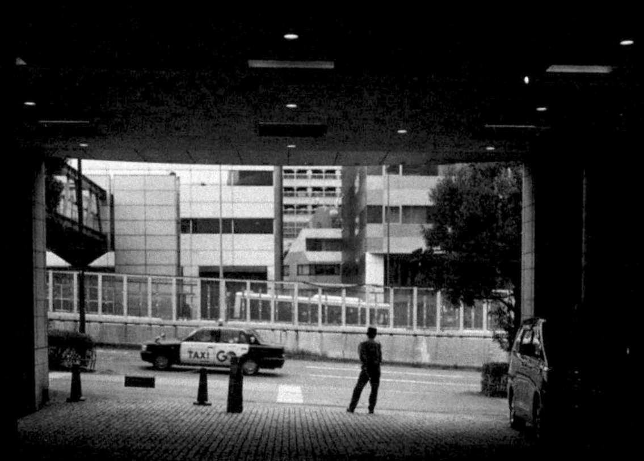

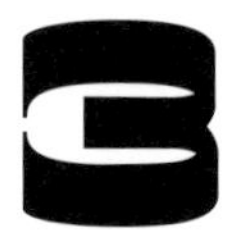

RON
JUDE

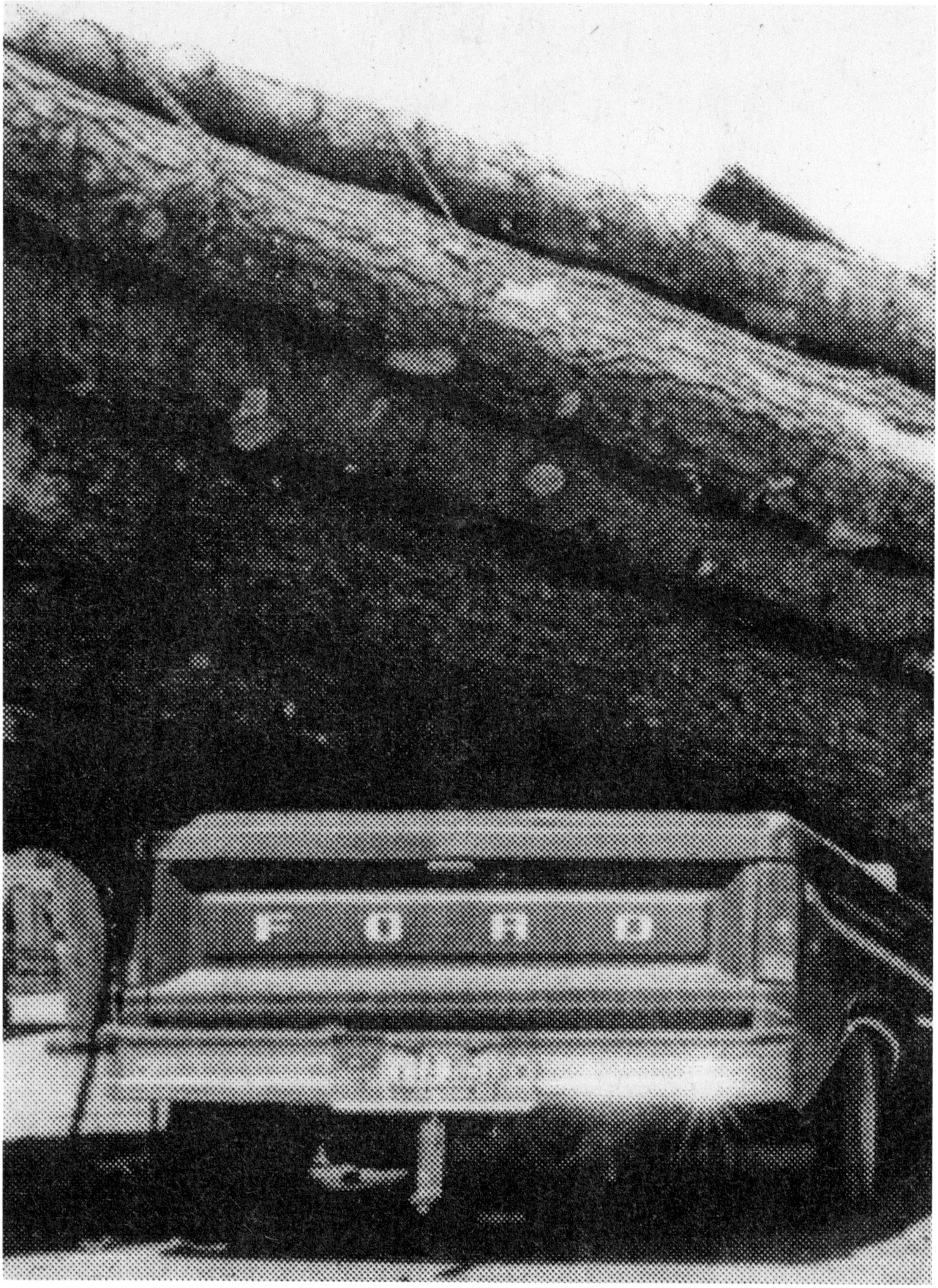

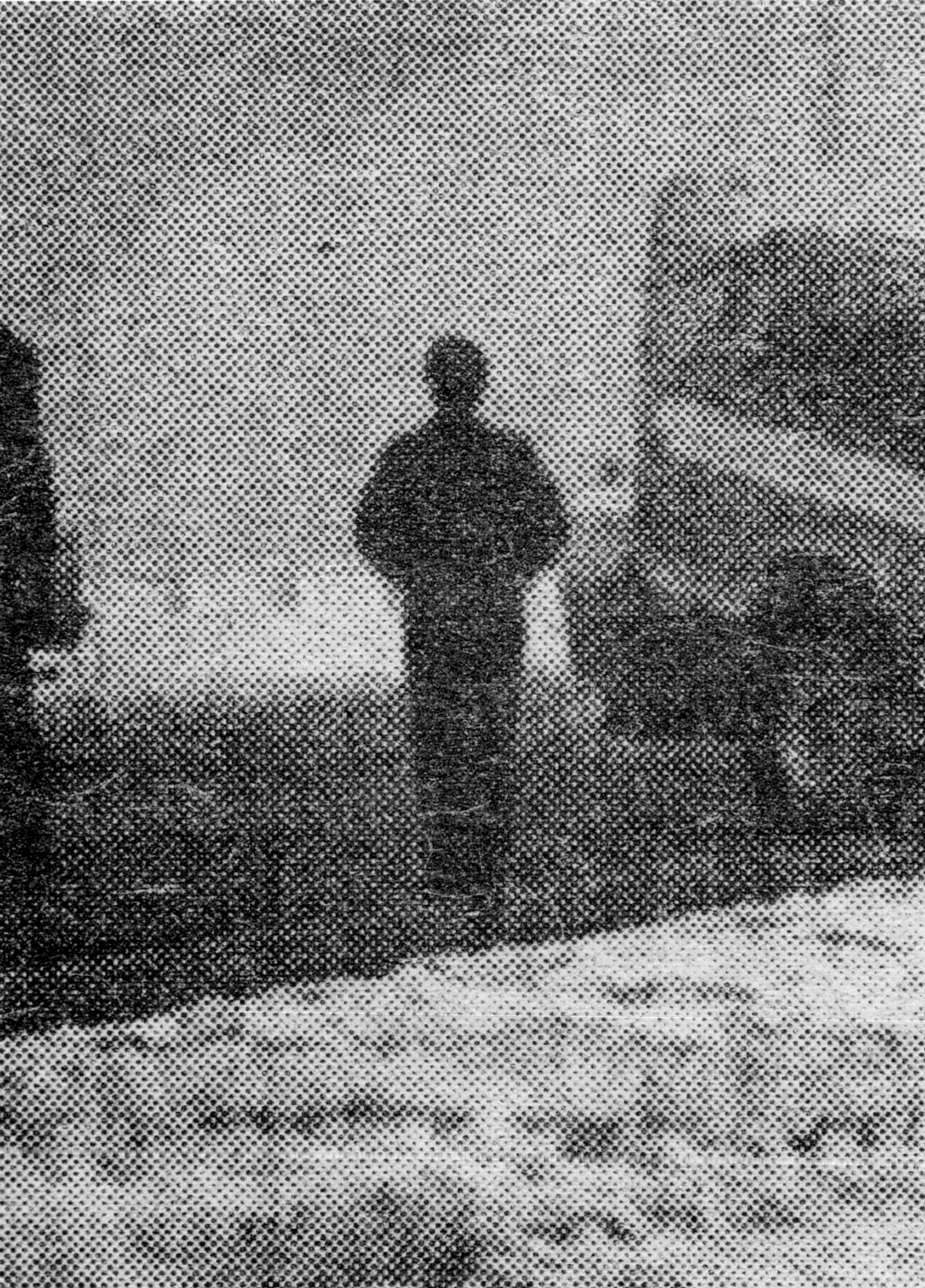

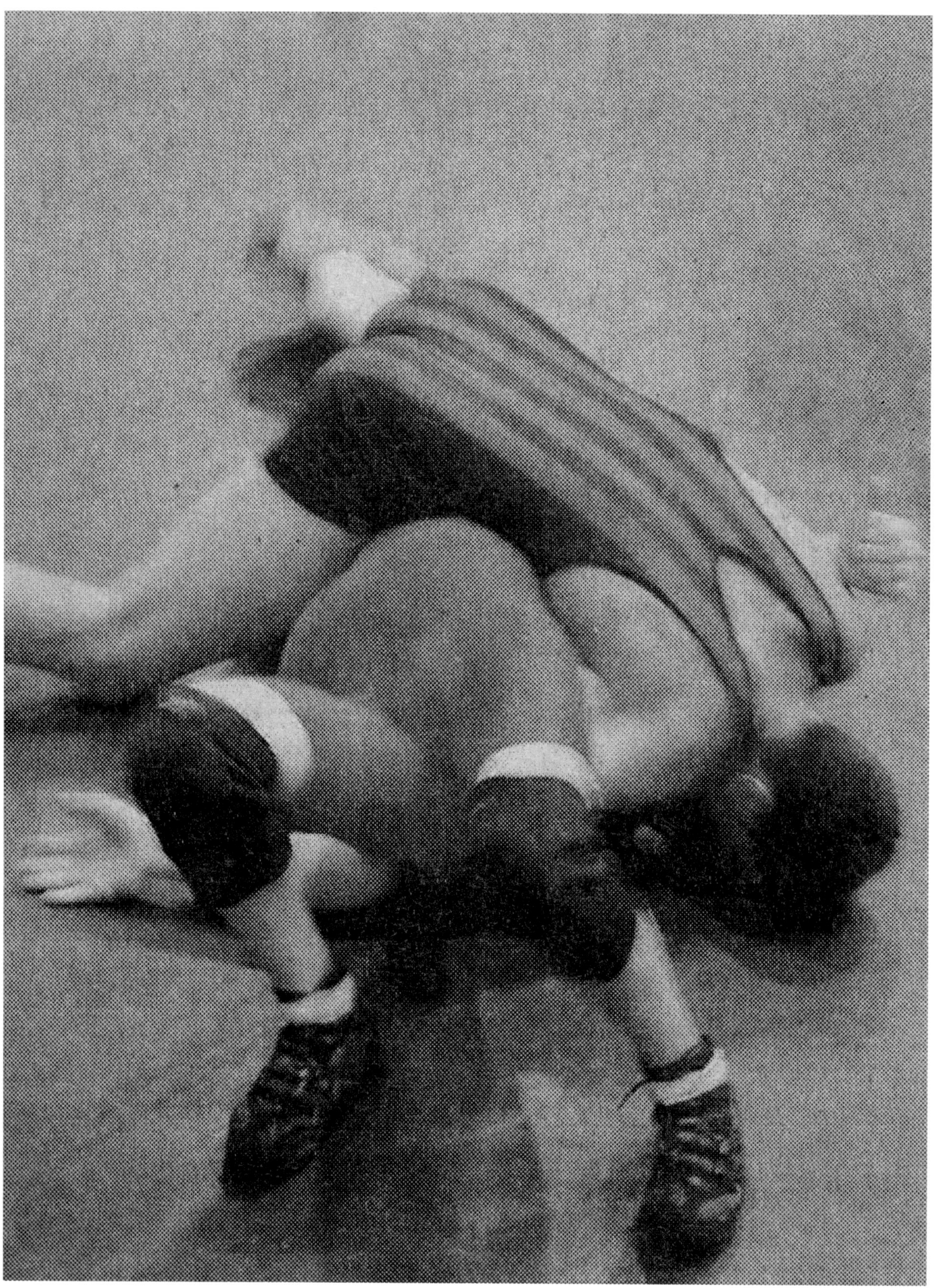

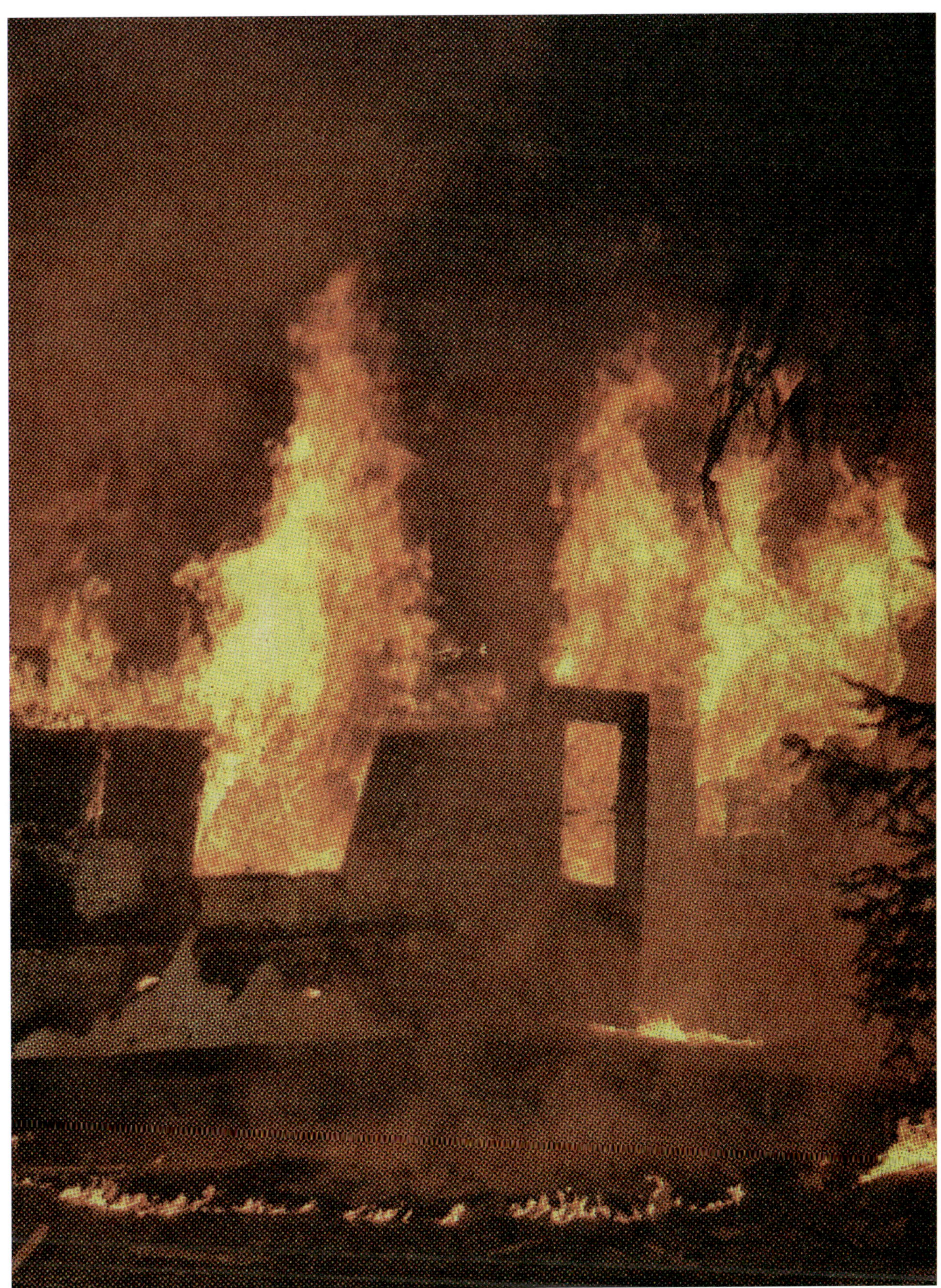

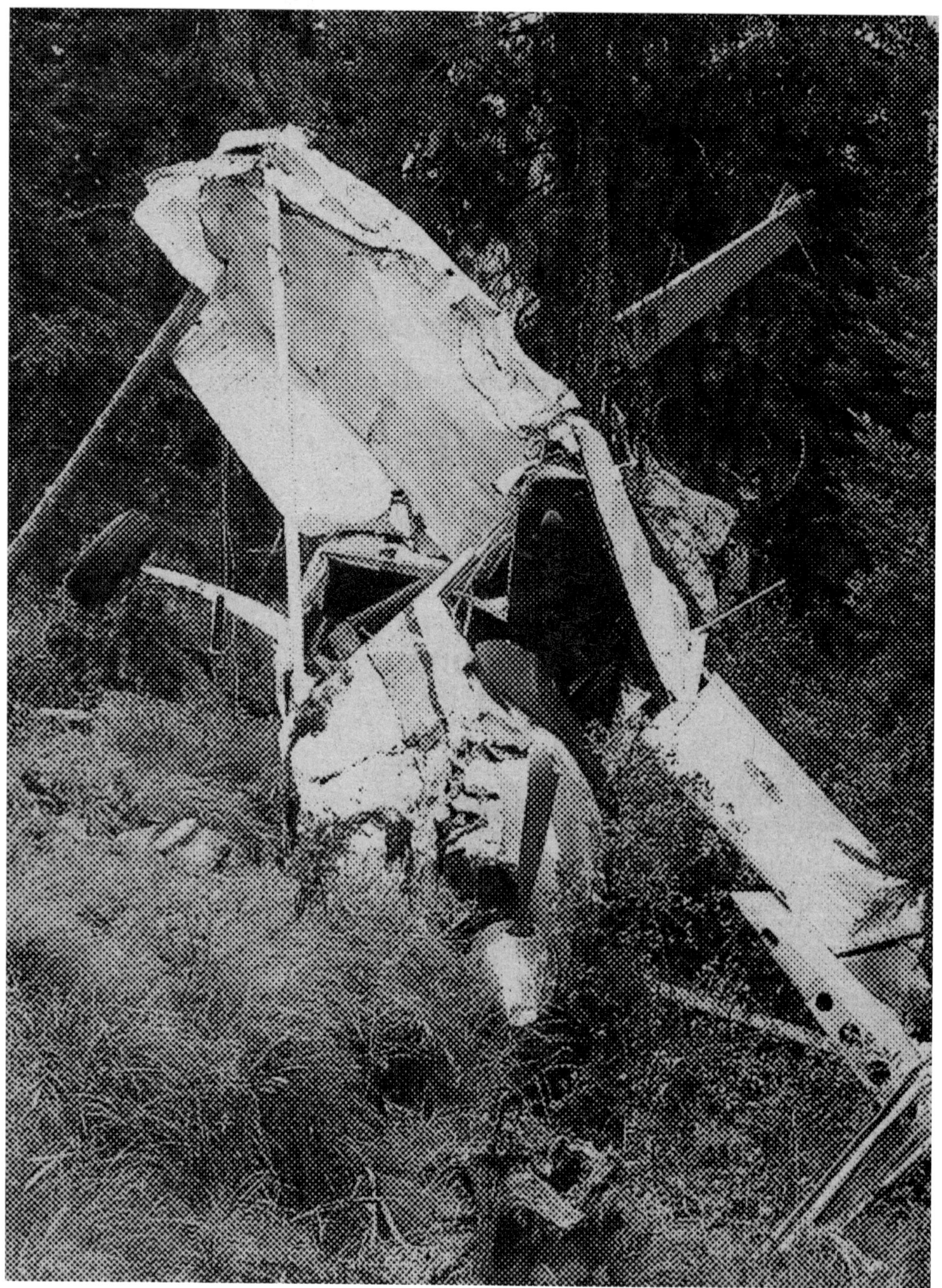

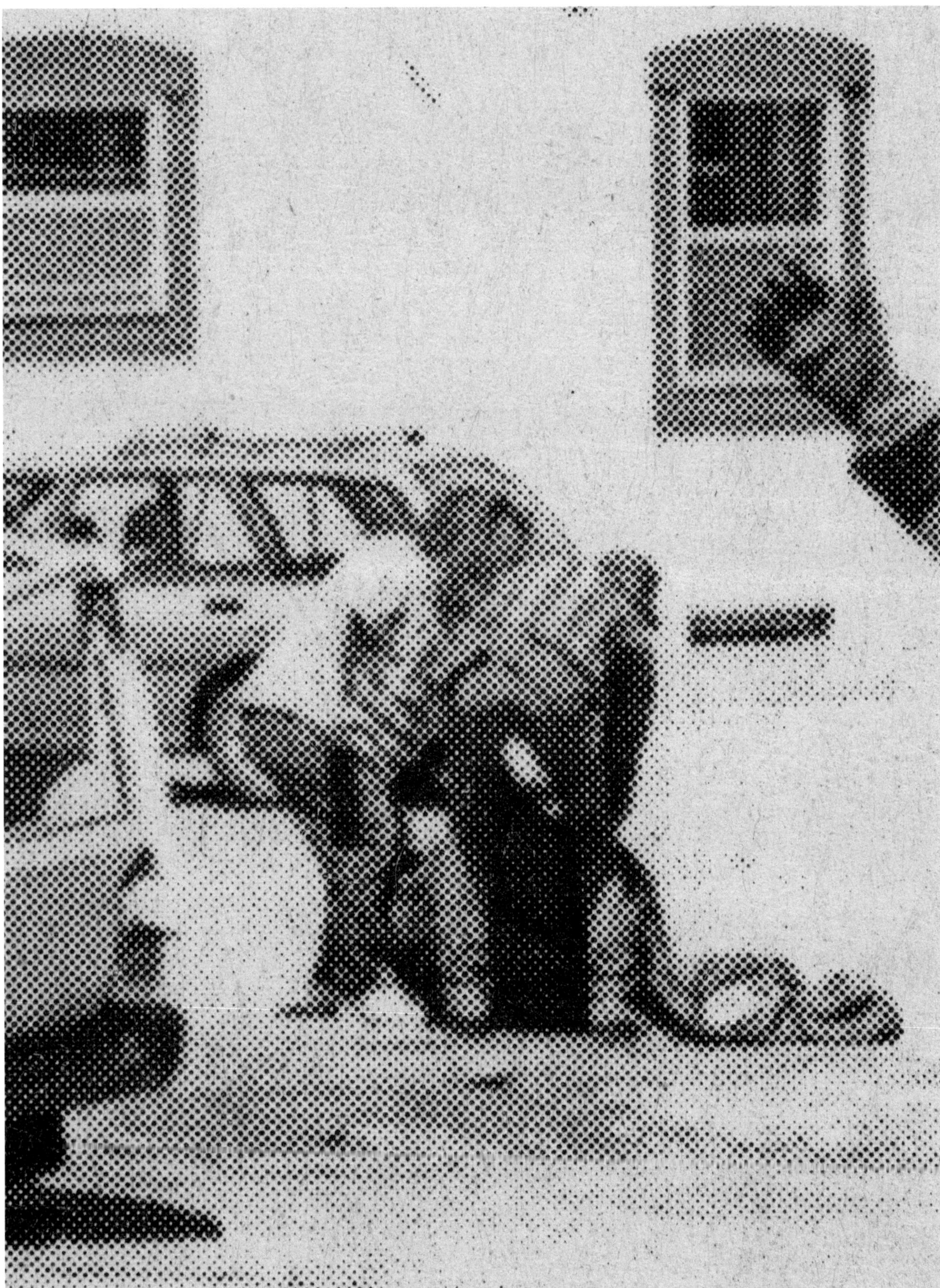

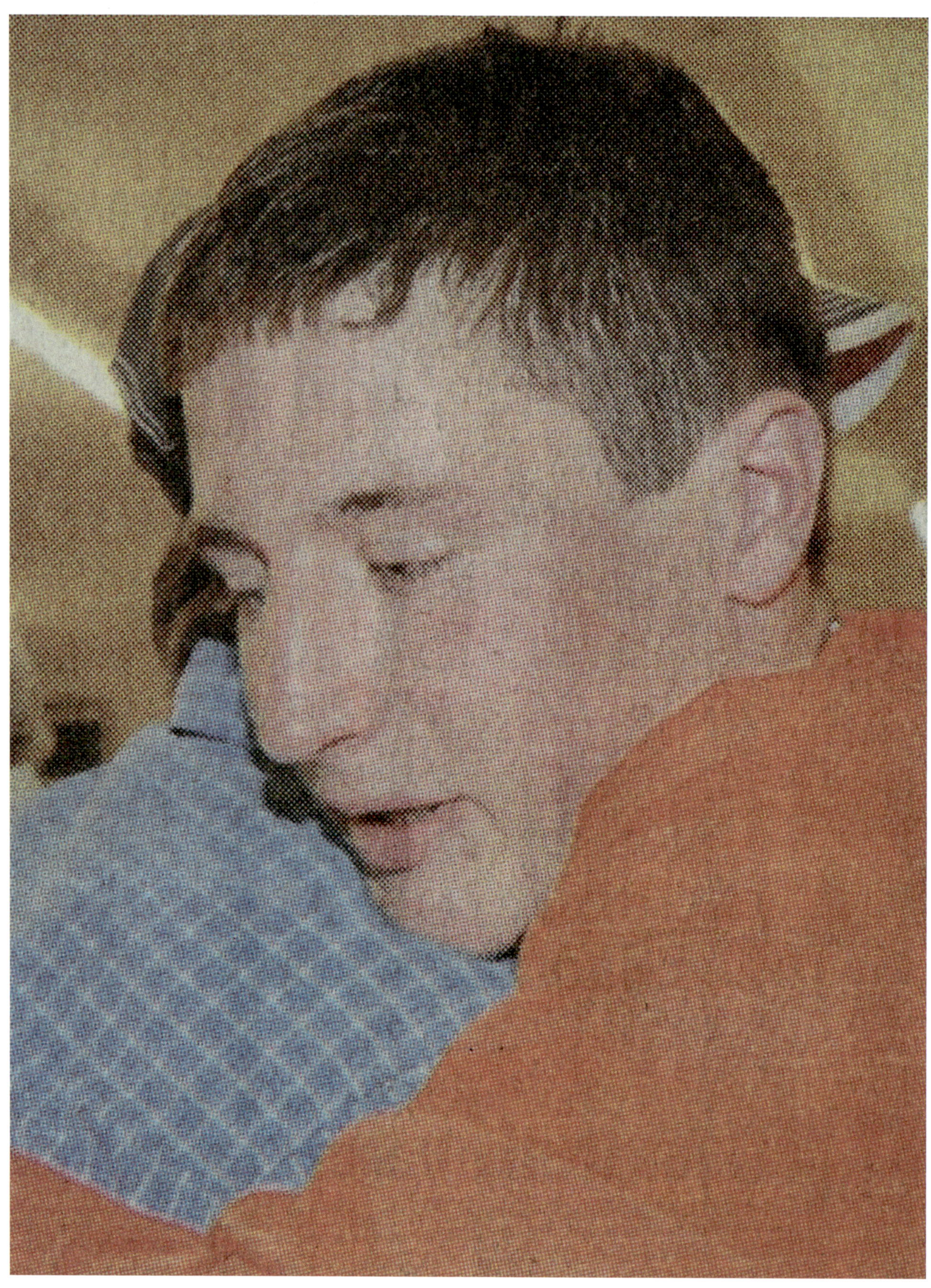

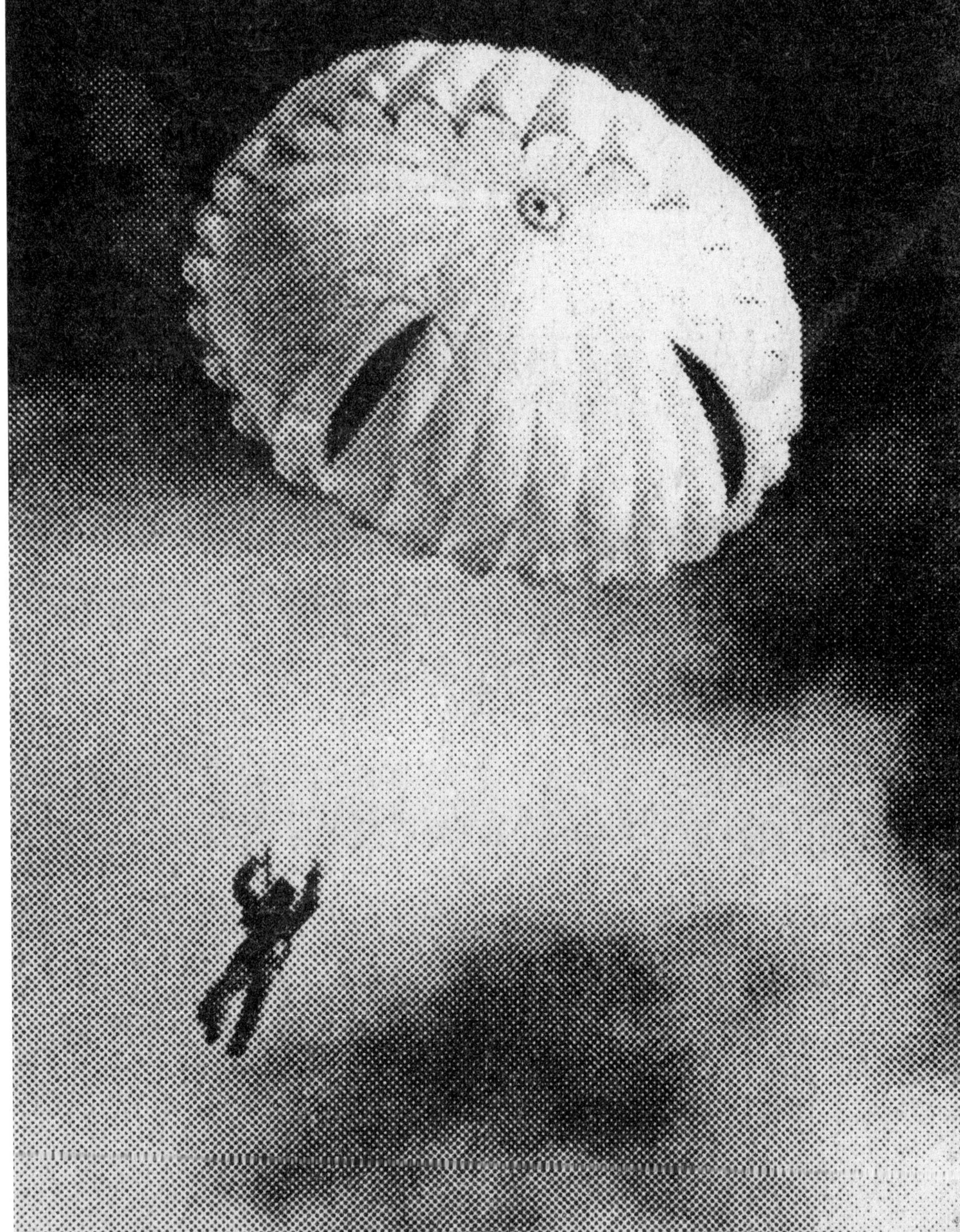

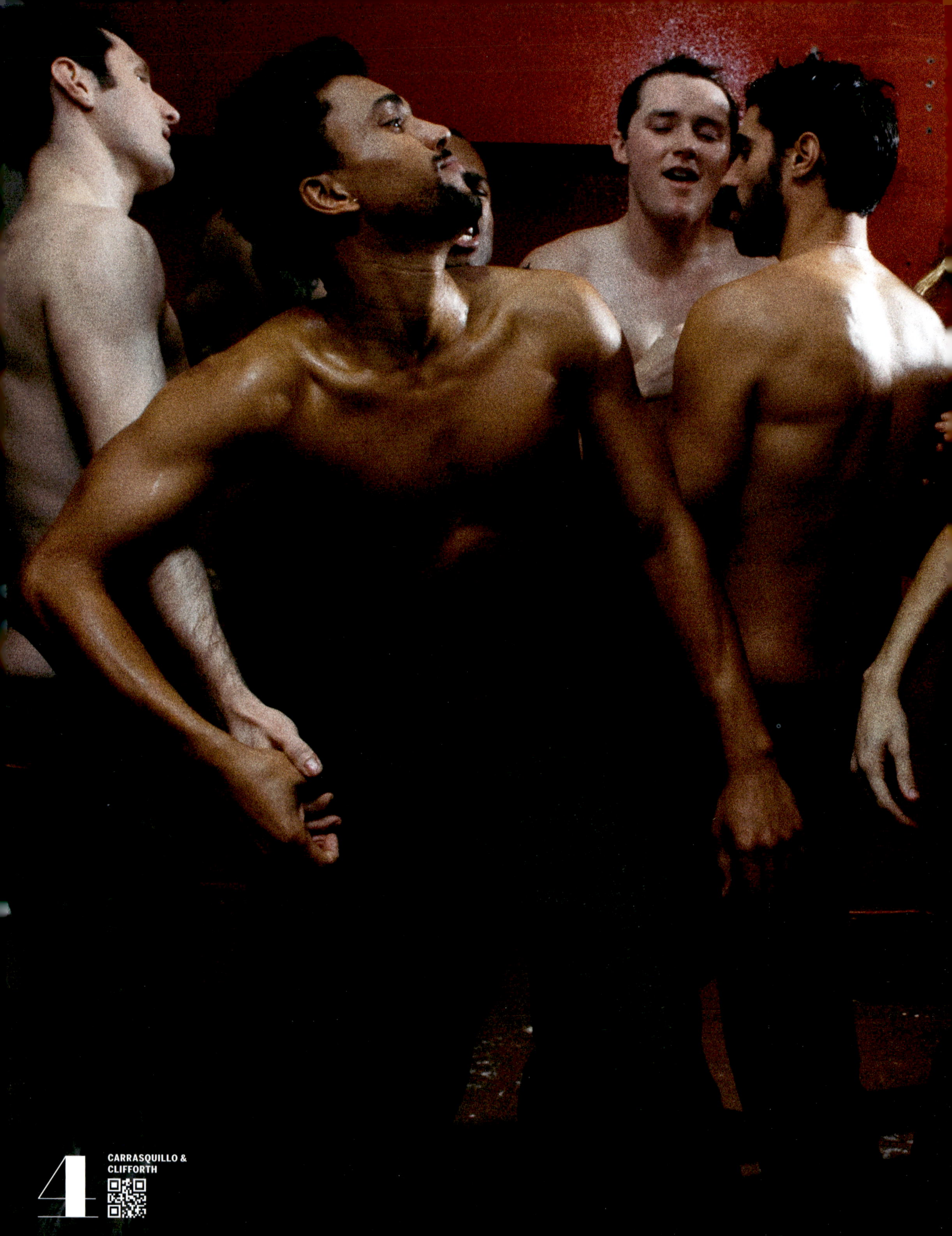

CARRASQUILLO &
CLIFFORTH

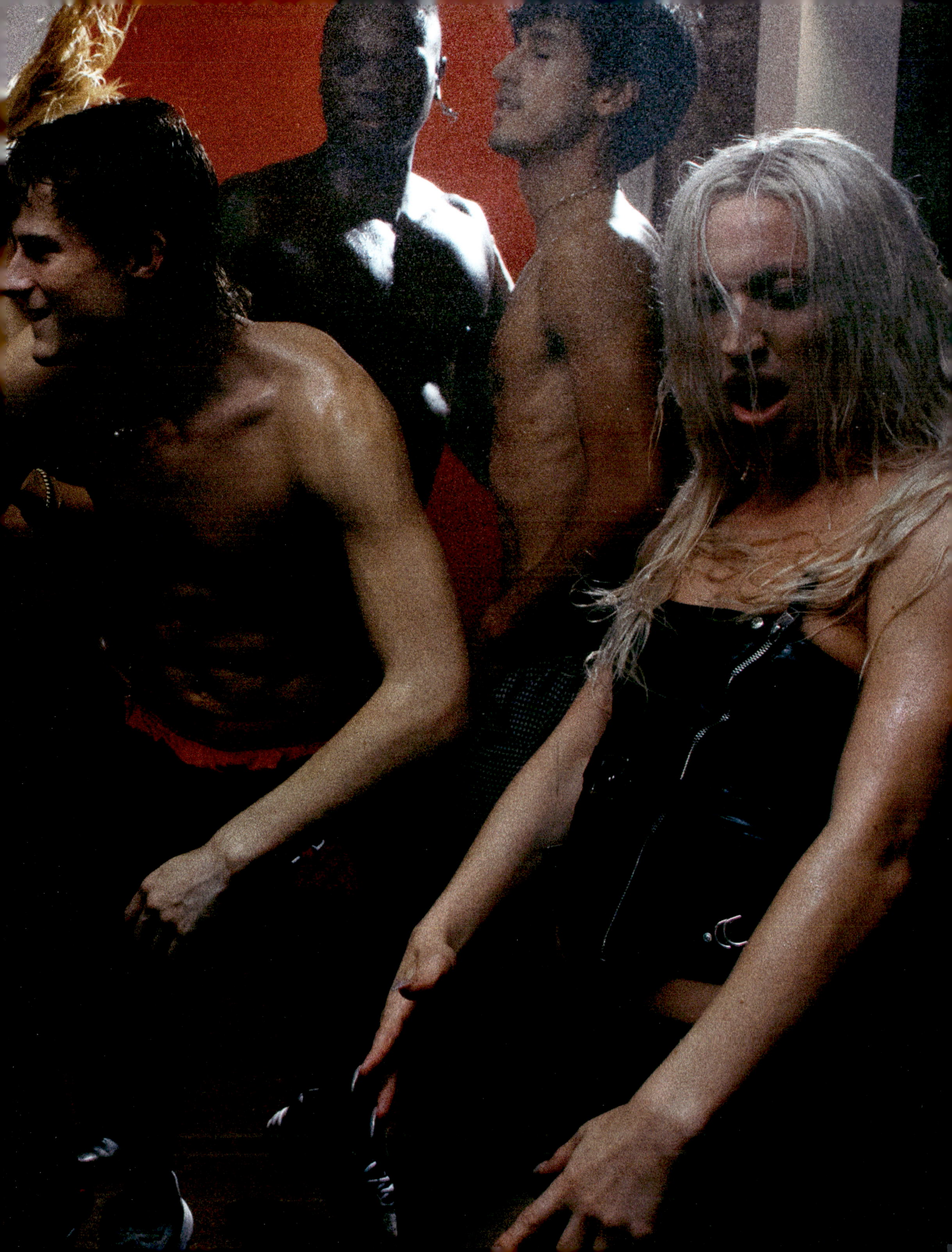

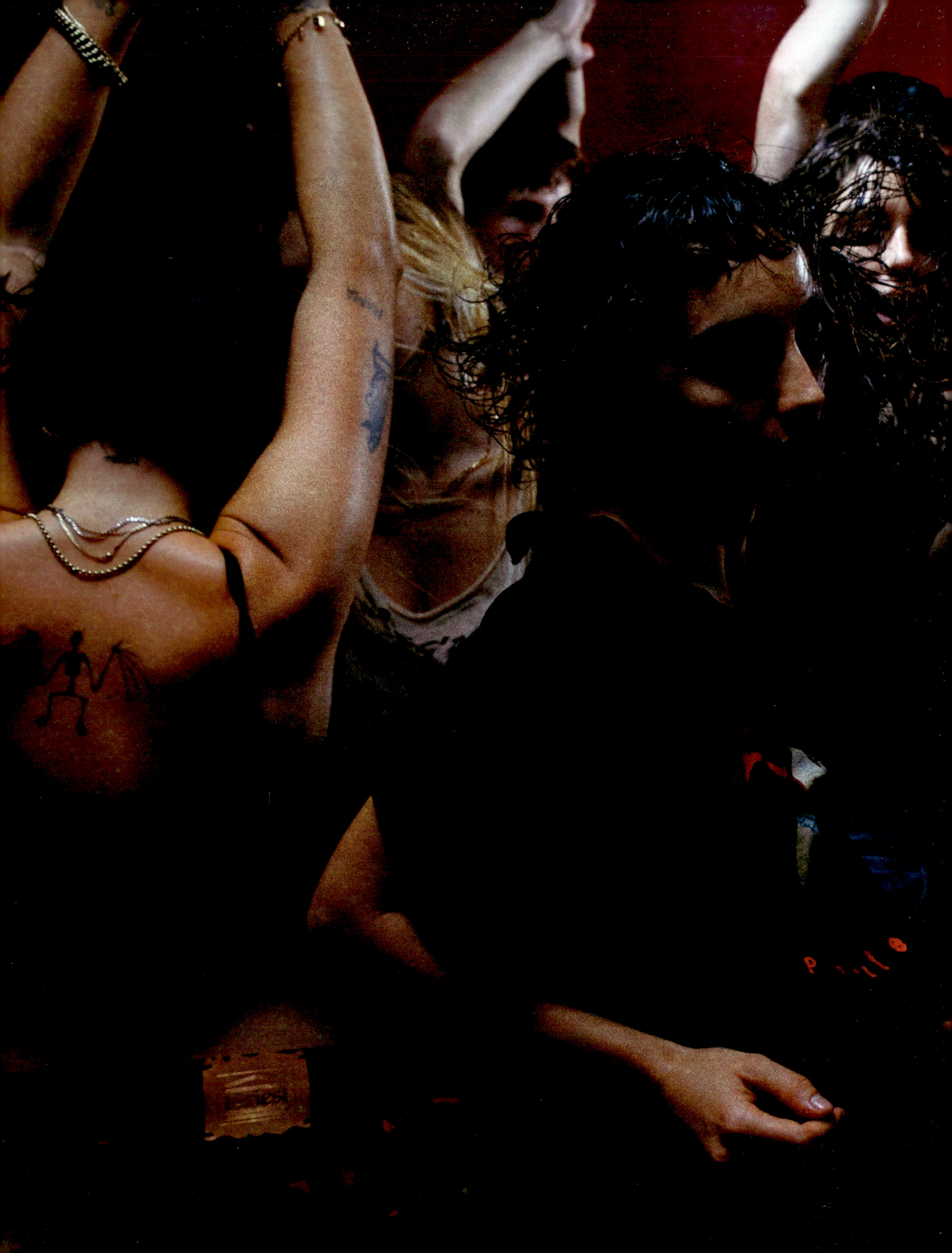

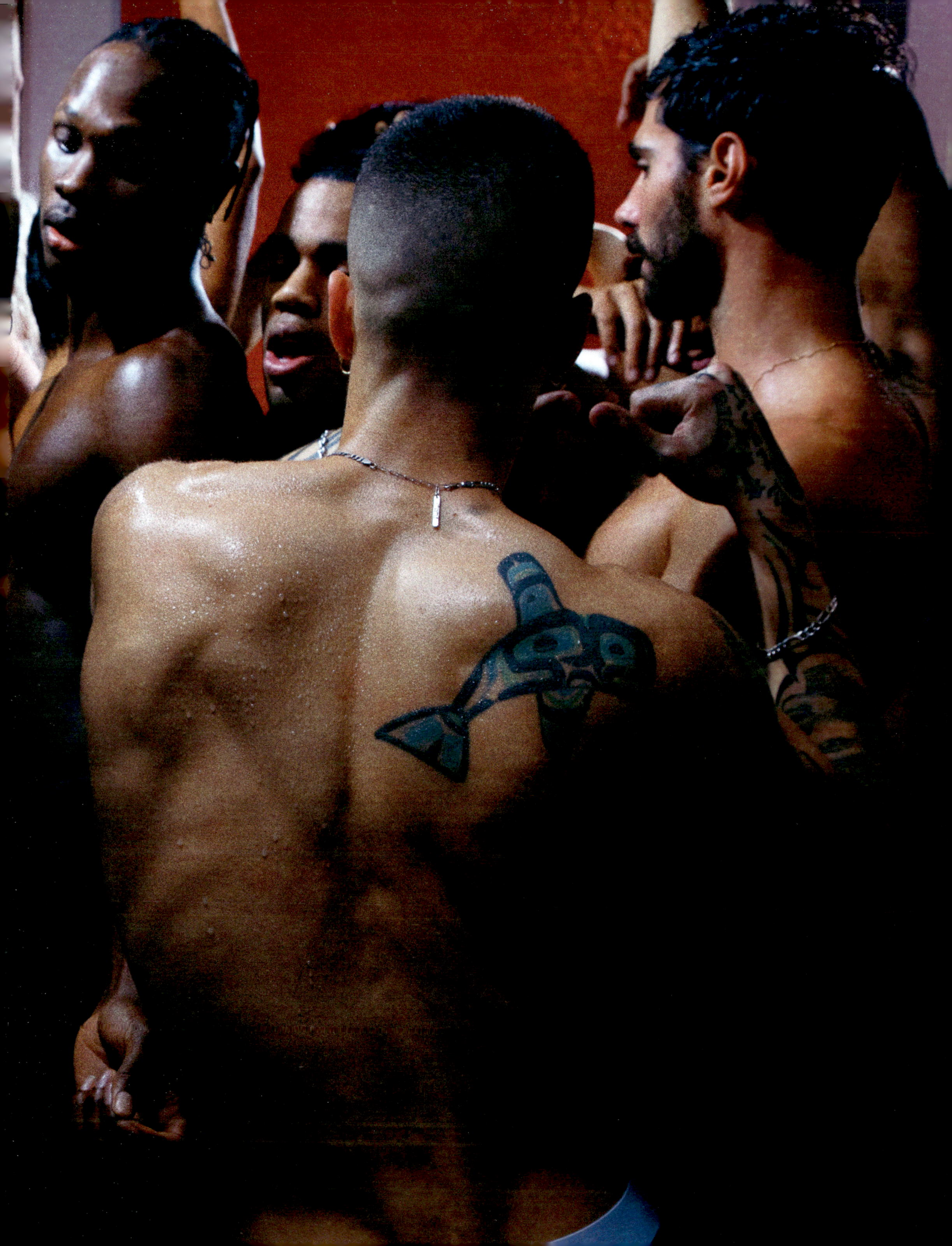

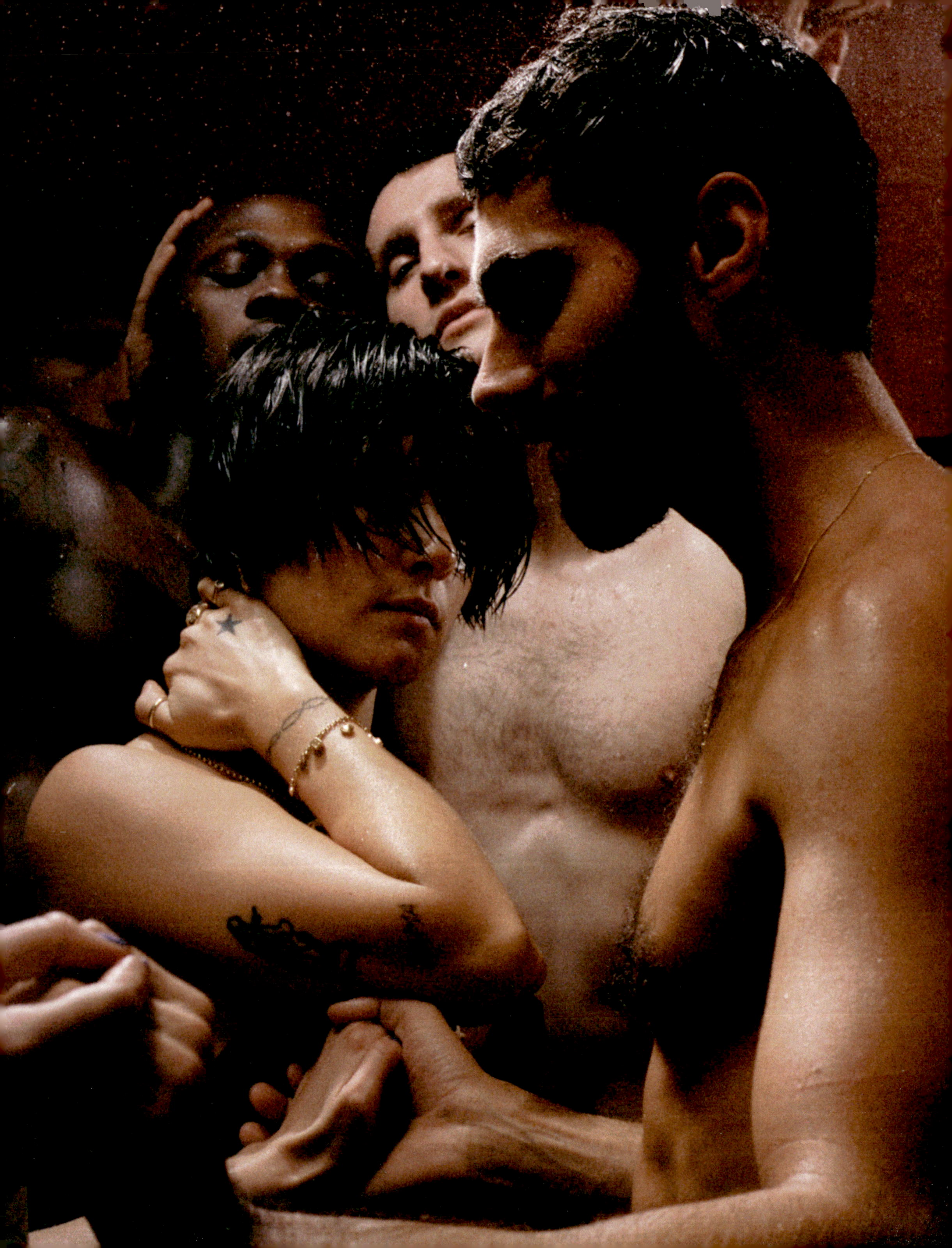

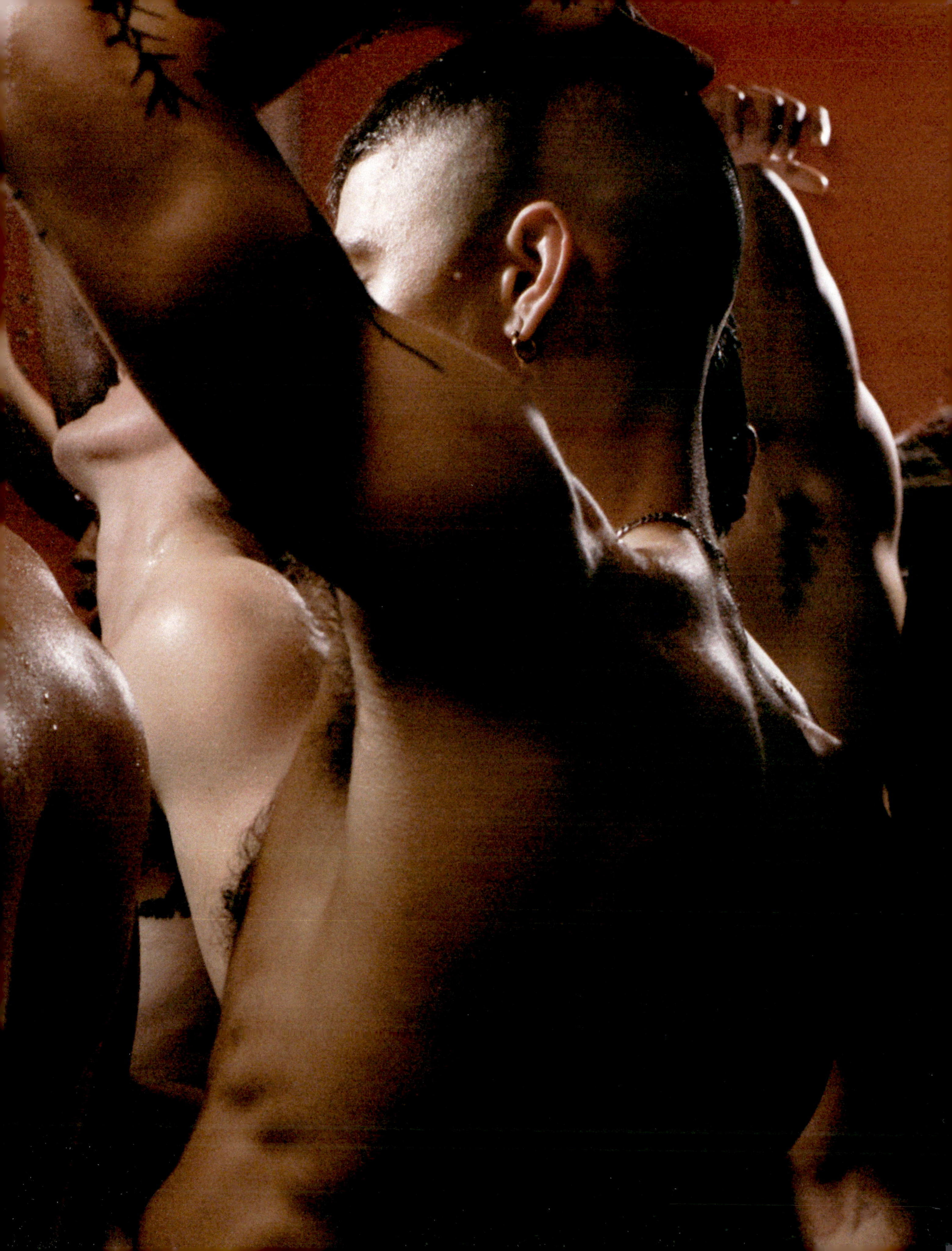

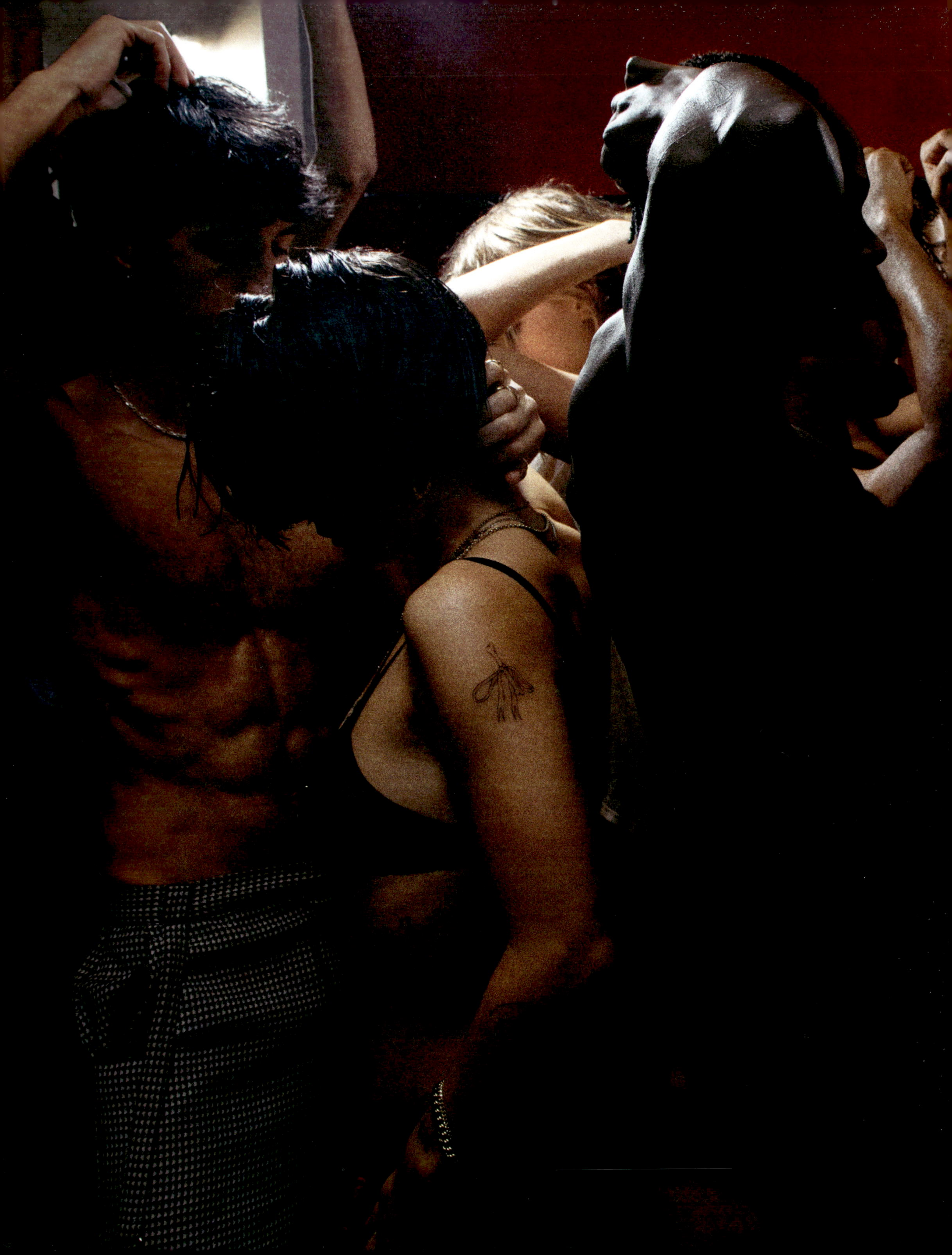

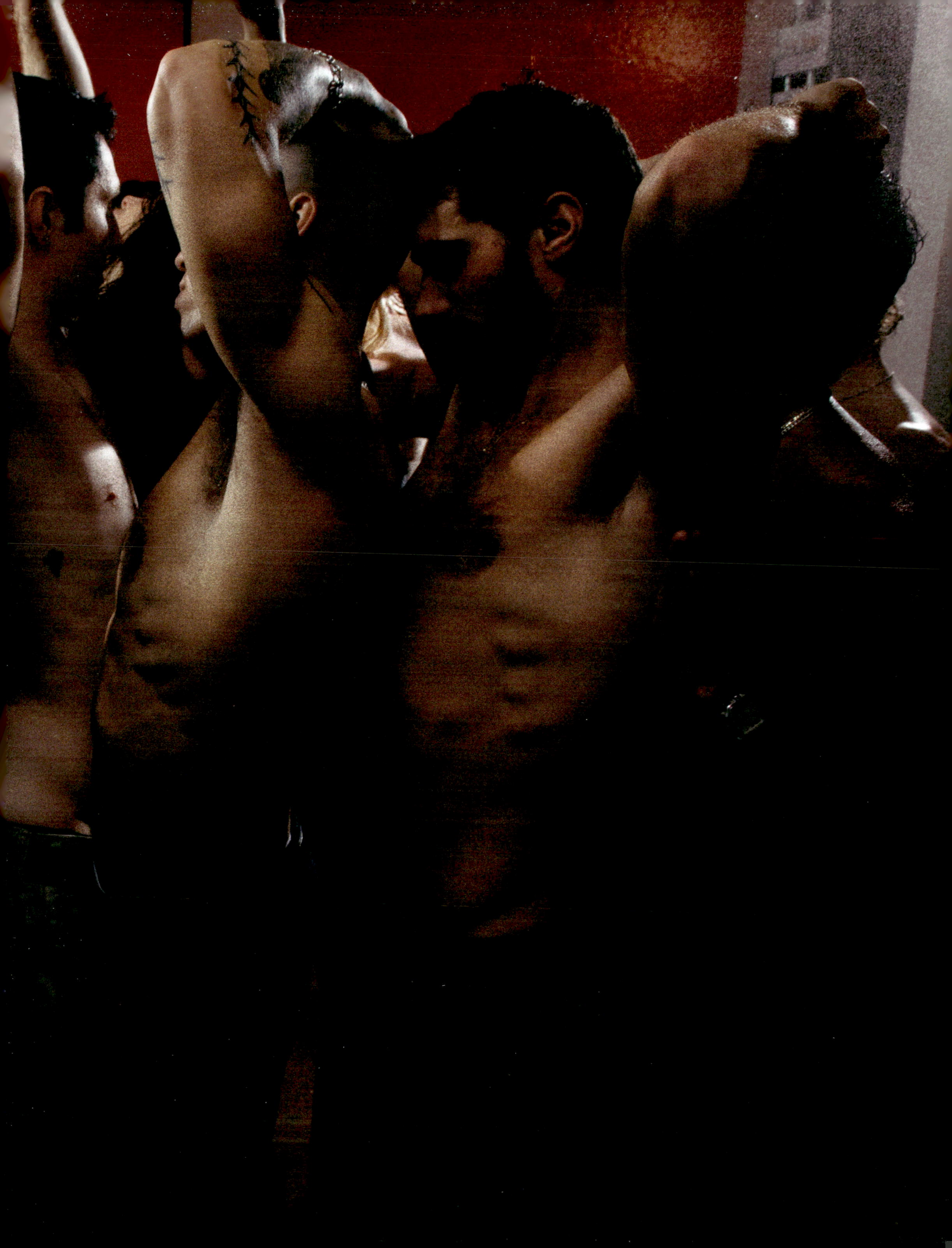

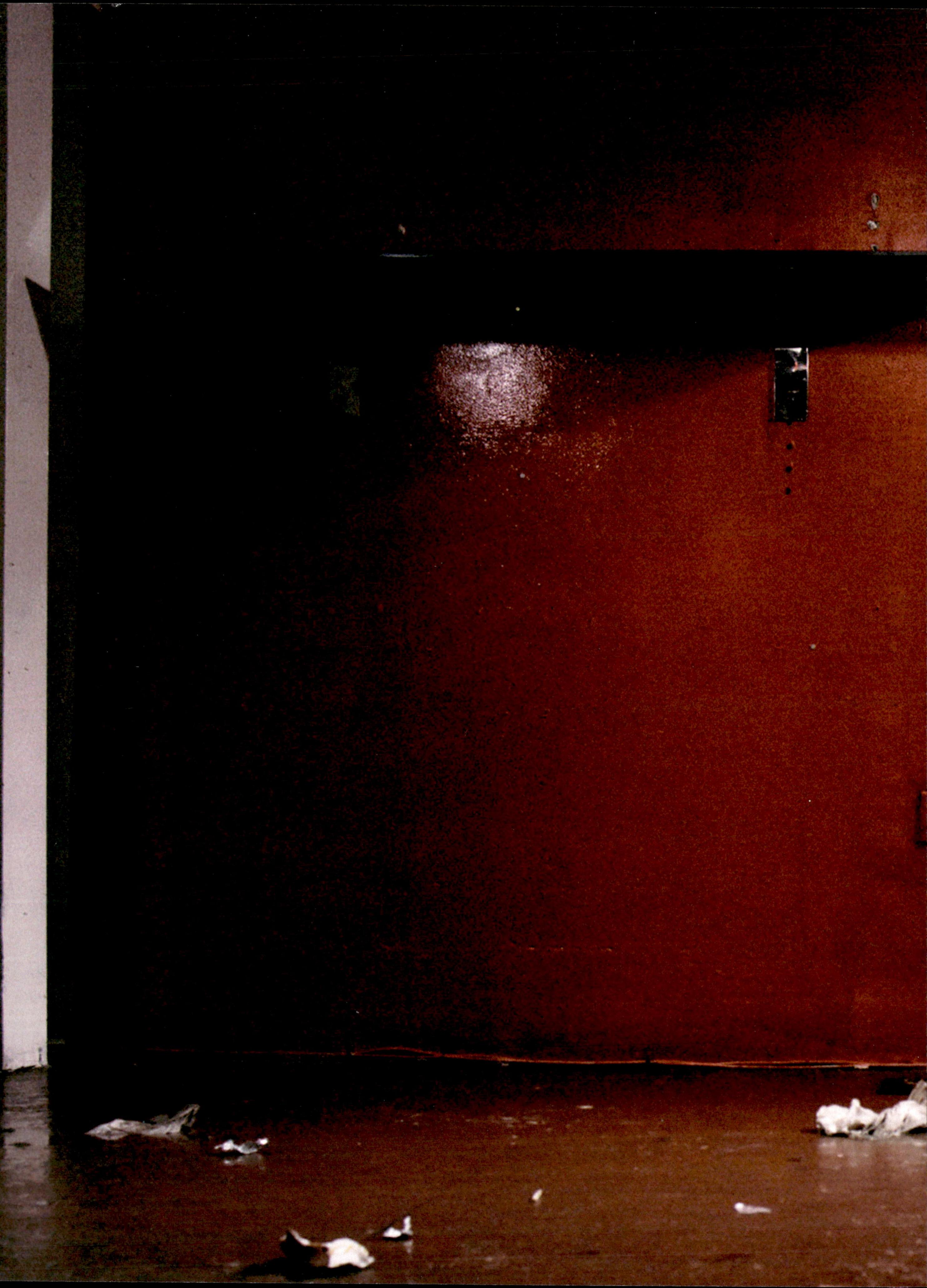

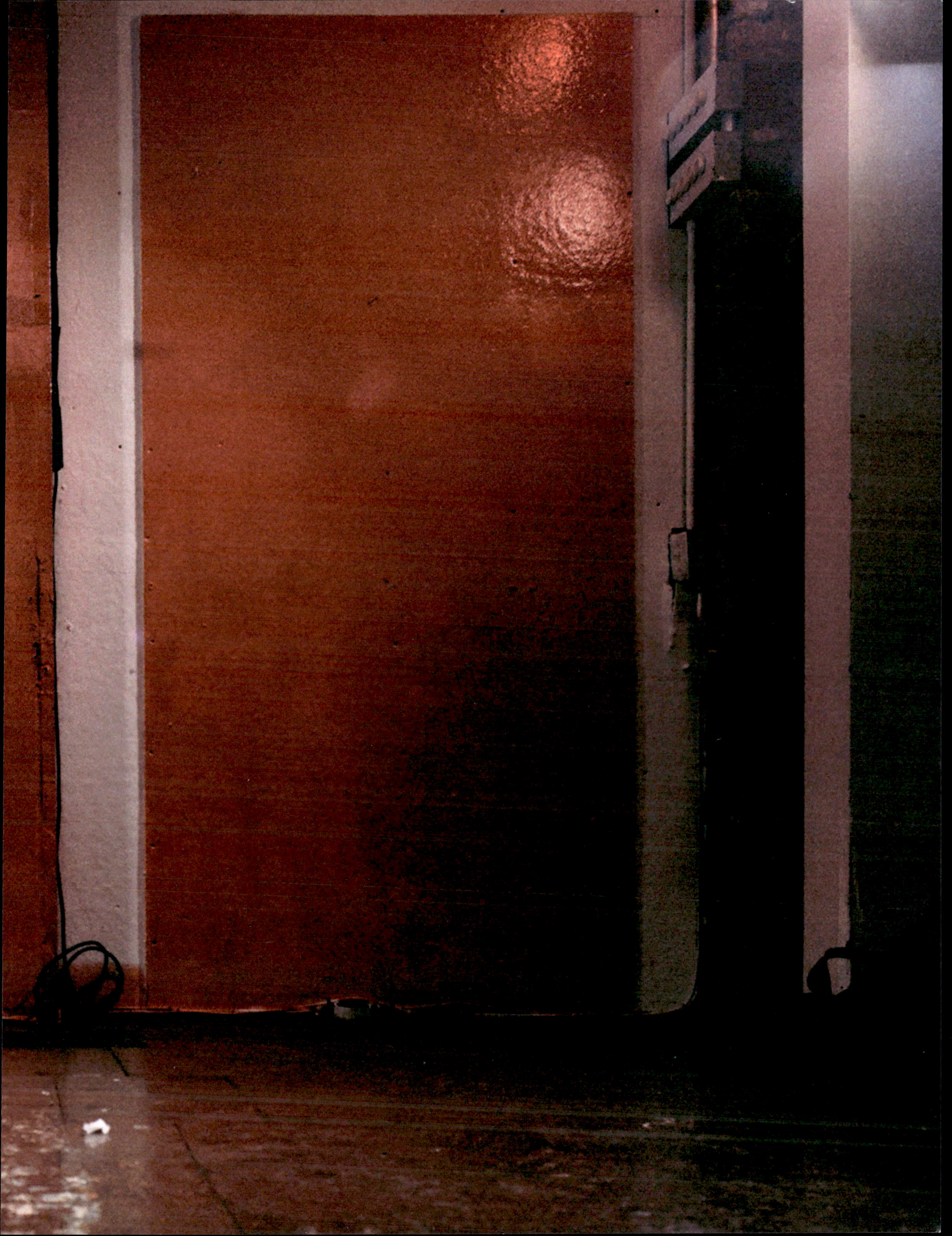

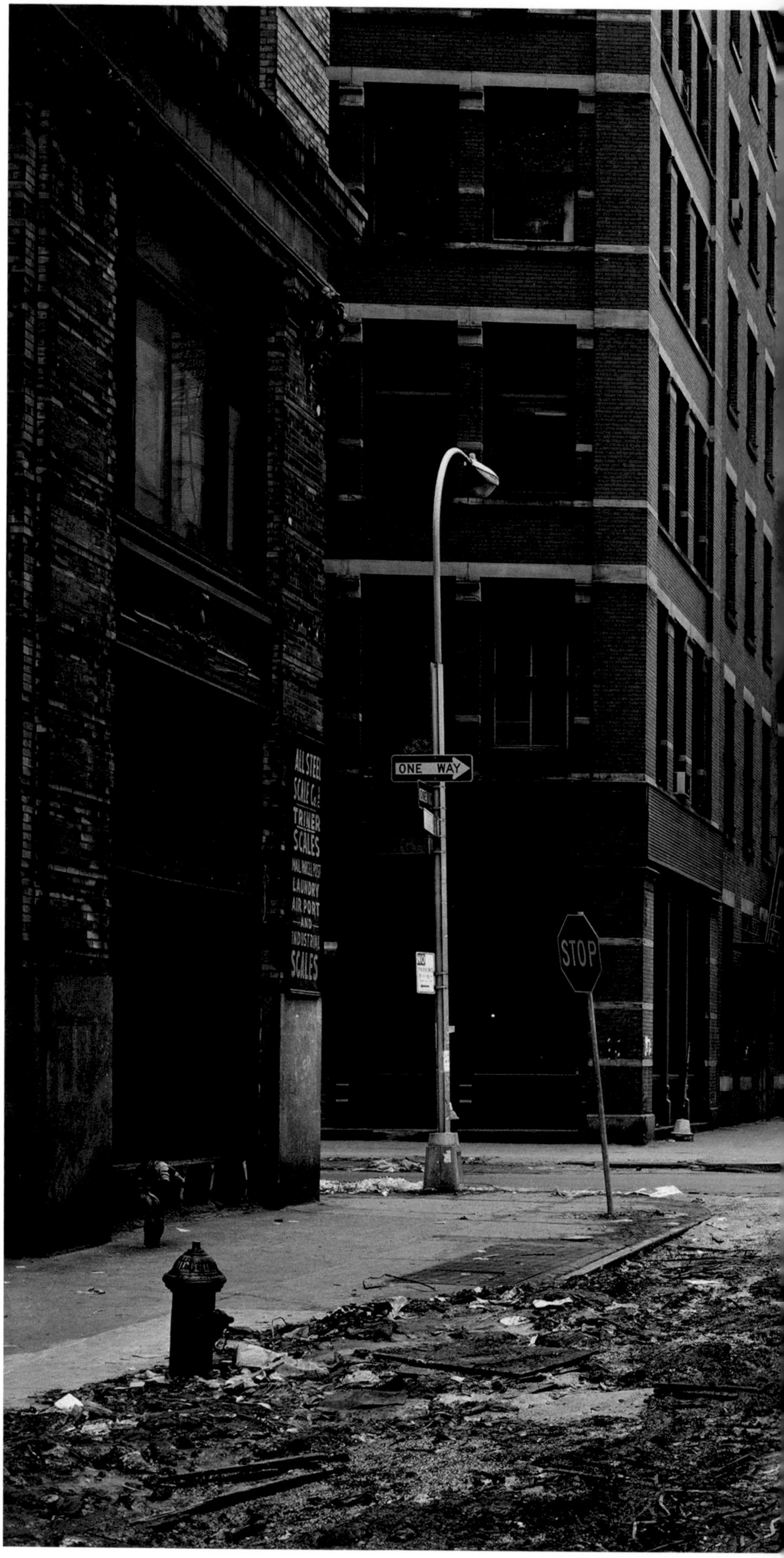

THOMAS STRUTH, *CROSBY STREET, SOHO, NEW YORK*, 1978

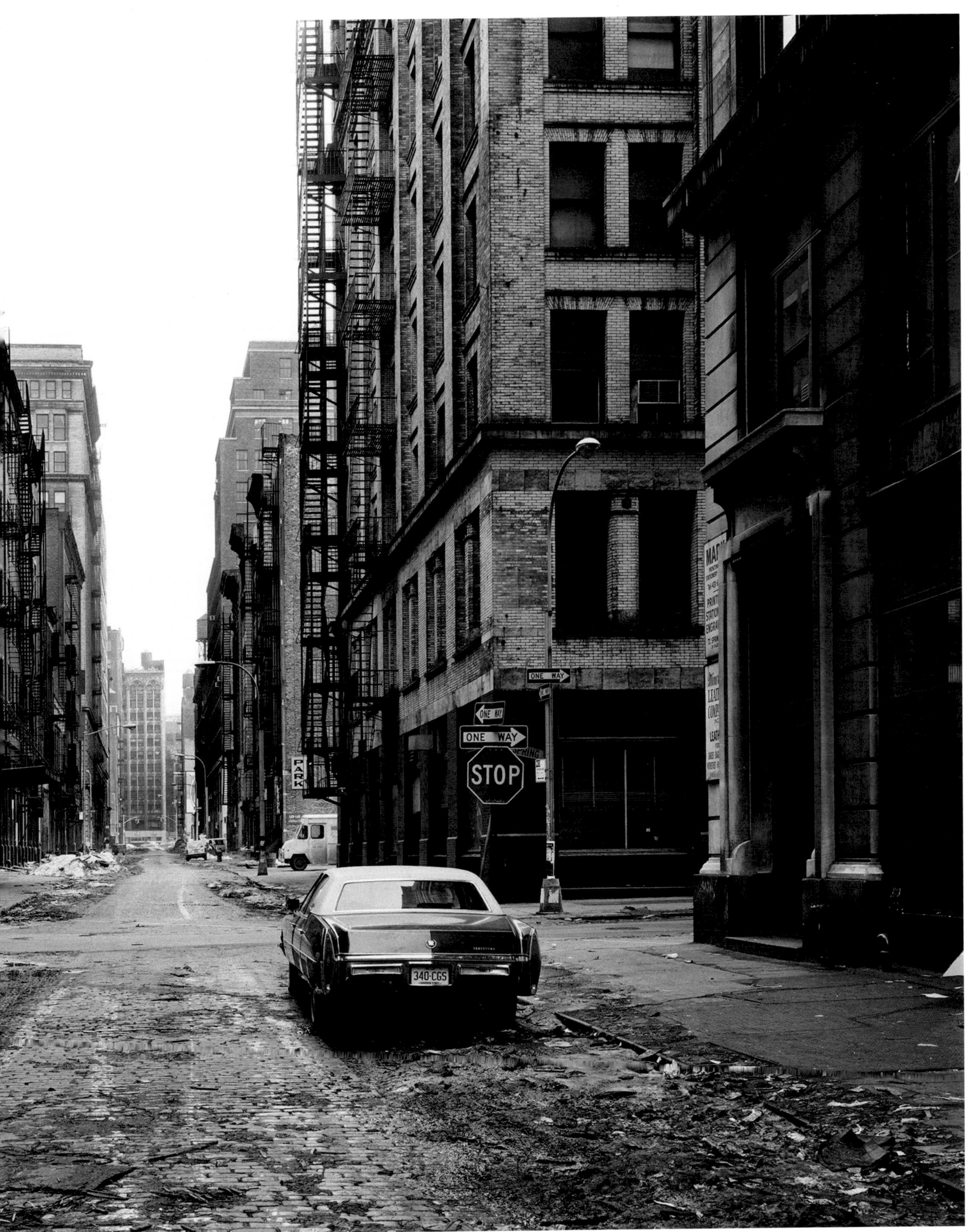

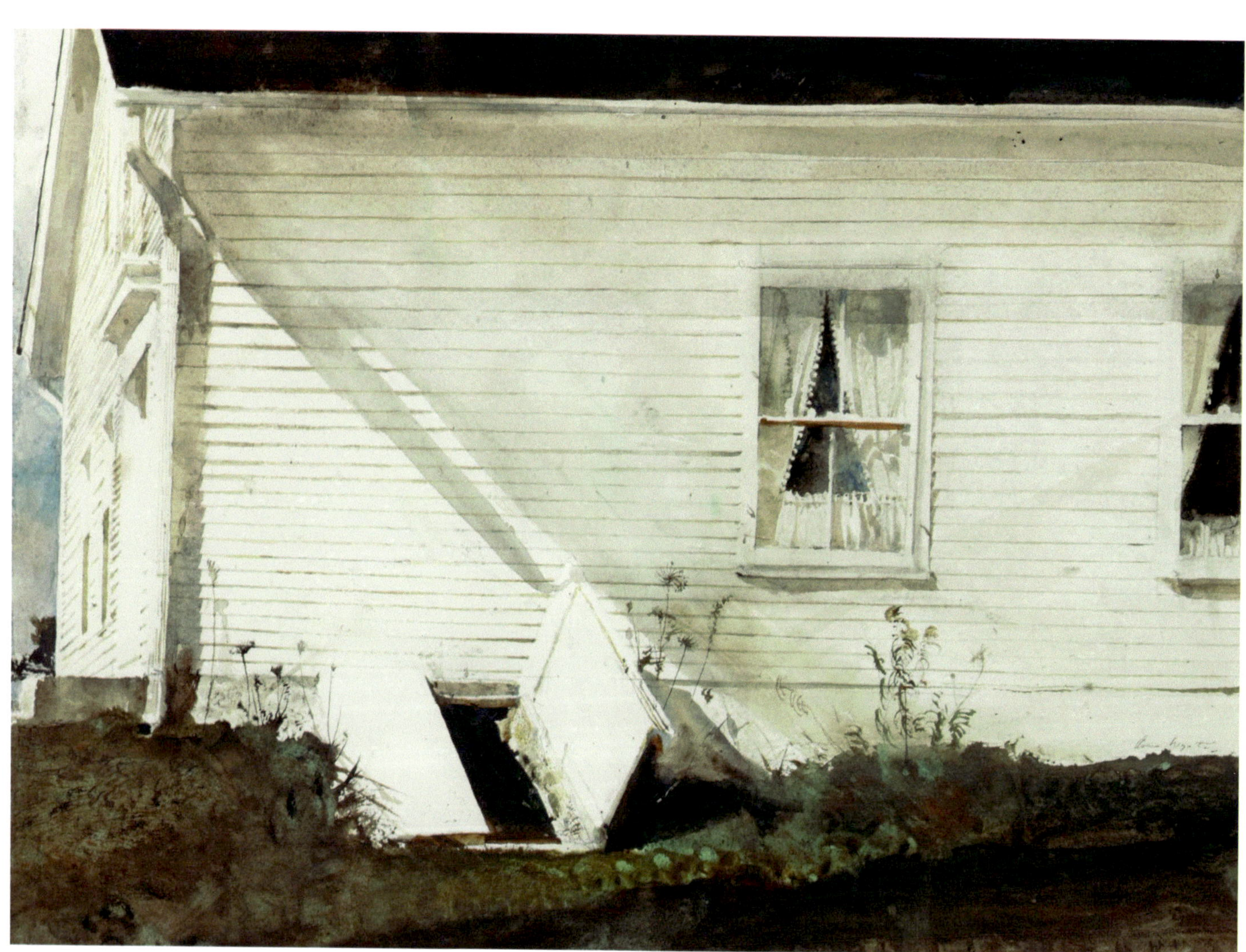

ANDREW WYETH, *ELSIE'S HOUSE*, 1983

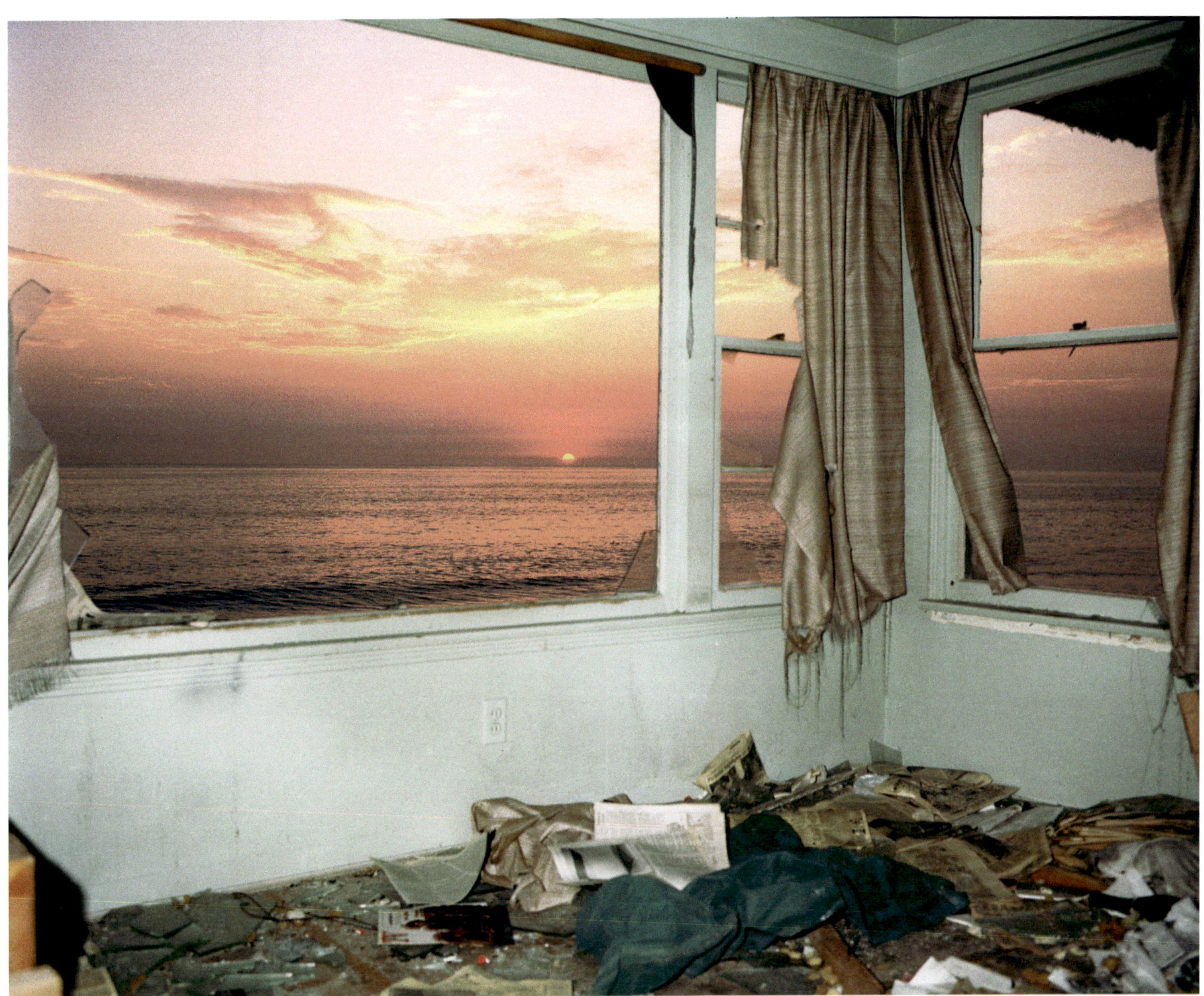

JOHN DIVOLA, *ZUMA #85*, 1977

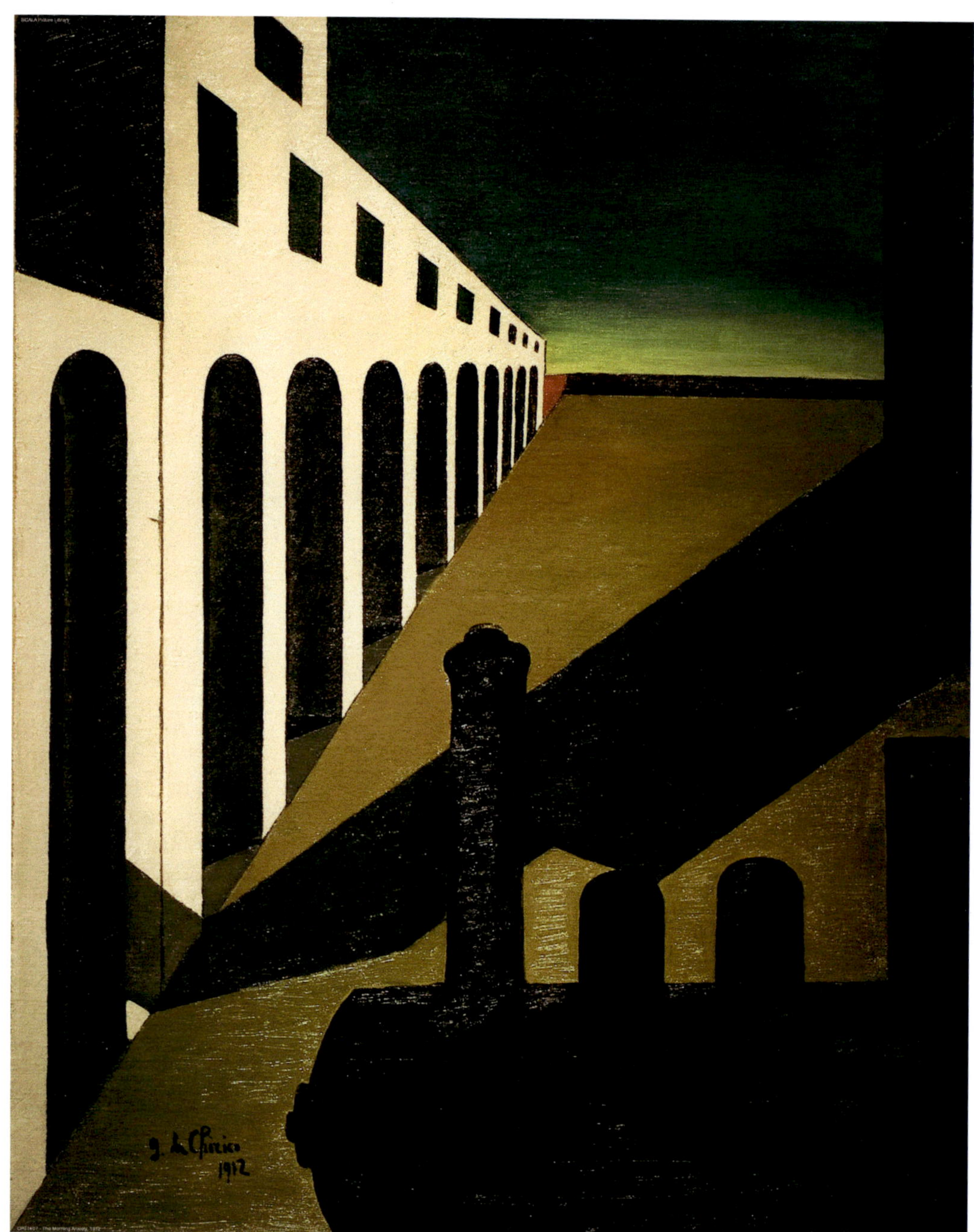

GIORGIO DE CHIRICO, *THE MORNING ANXIETY*, 1912

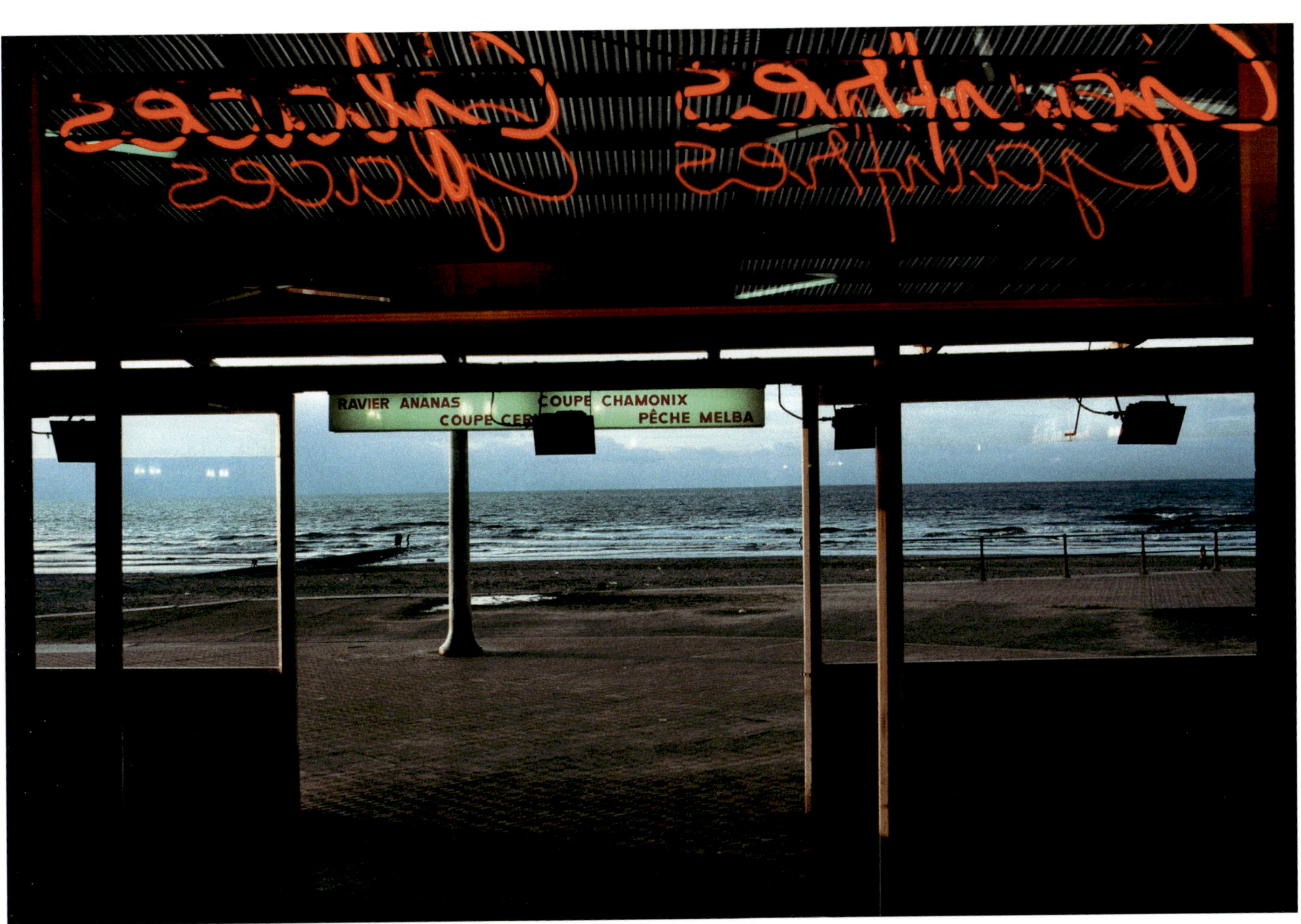

HARRY GRUYAERT, *OSTEND, BELGIUM,* 1988

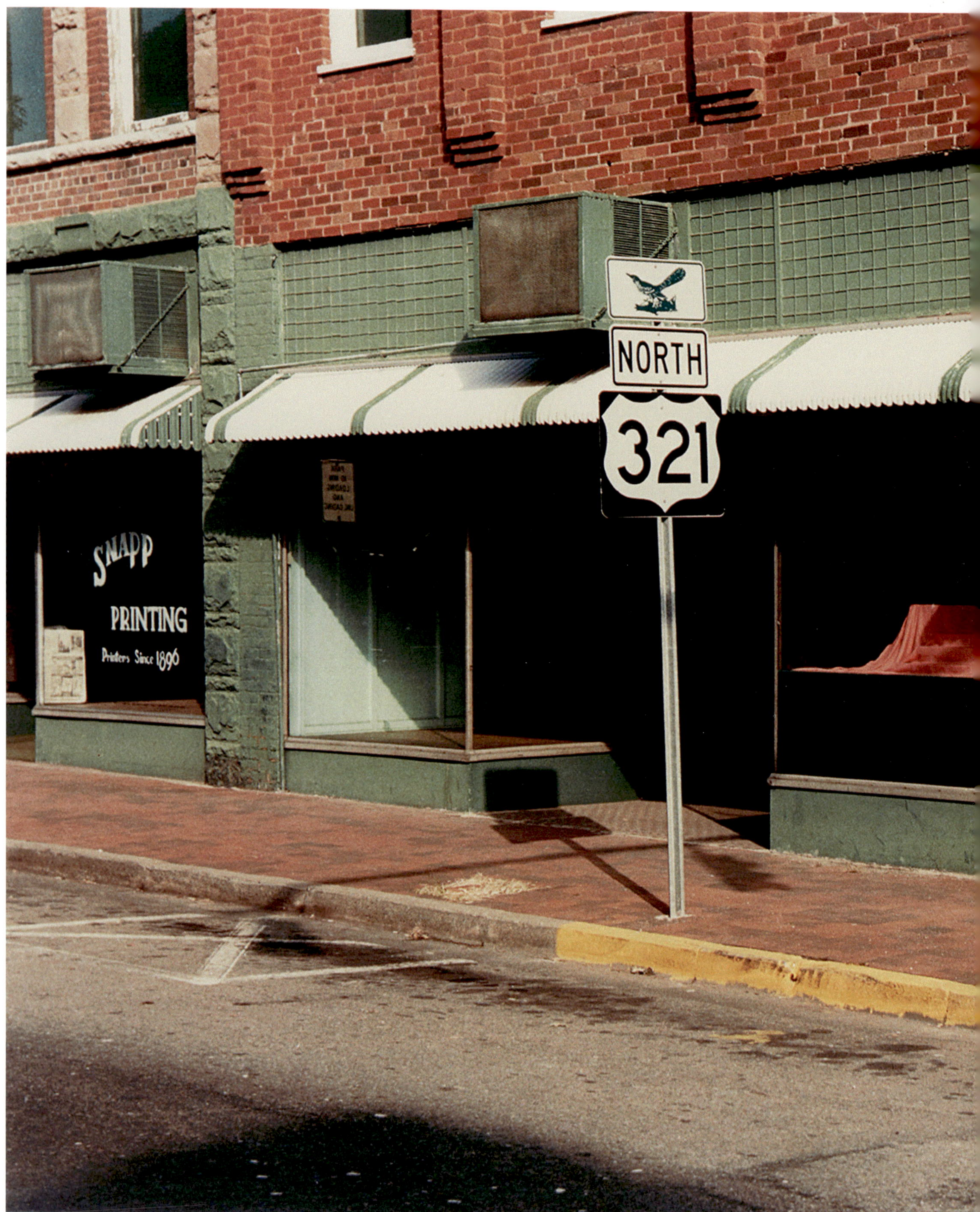

WILLIAM EGGLESTON, *UNTITLED*, C. 1983–1986

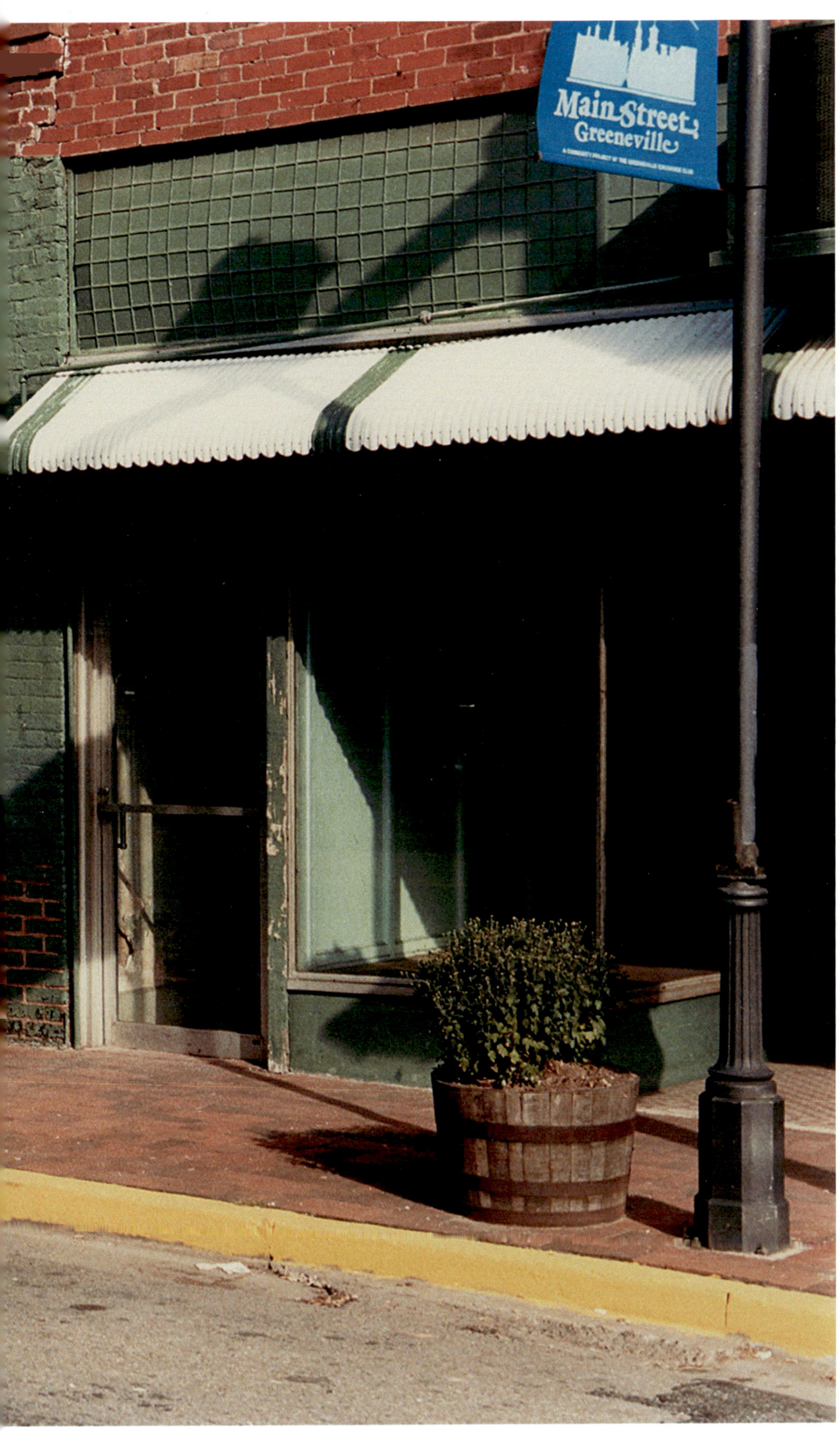

Main Street
Greeneville
A COMMUNITY PROJECT OF THE GREENEVILLE KIWANIS CLUB

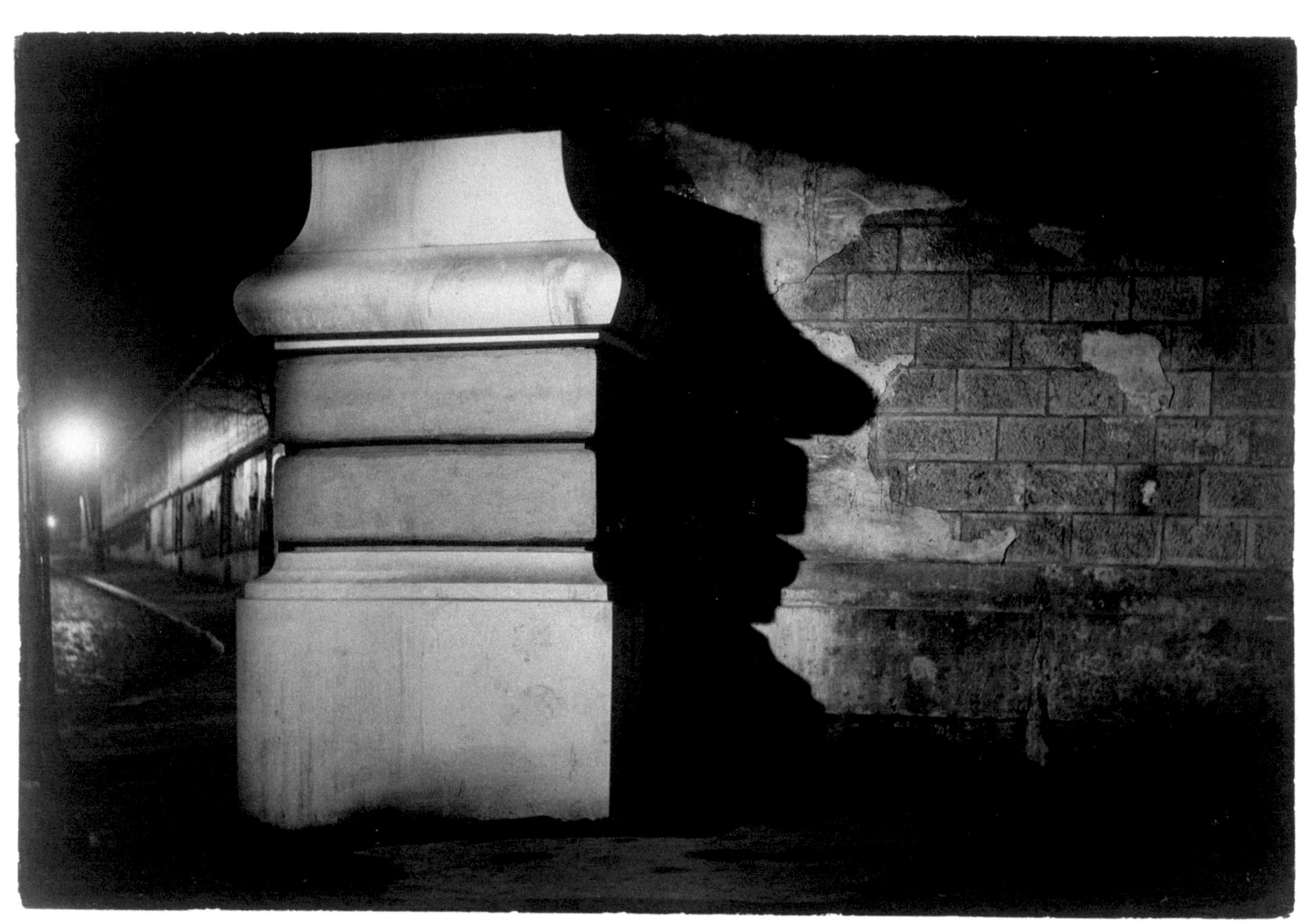

BRASSAÏ, *PILIER DE MÉTRO*, 1934

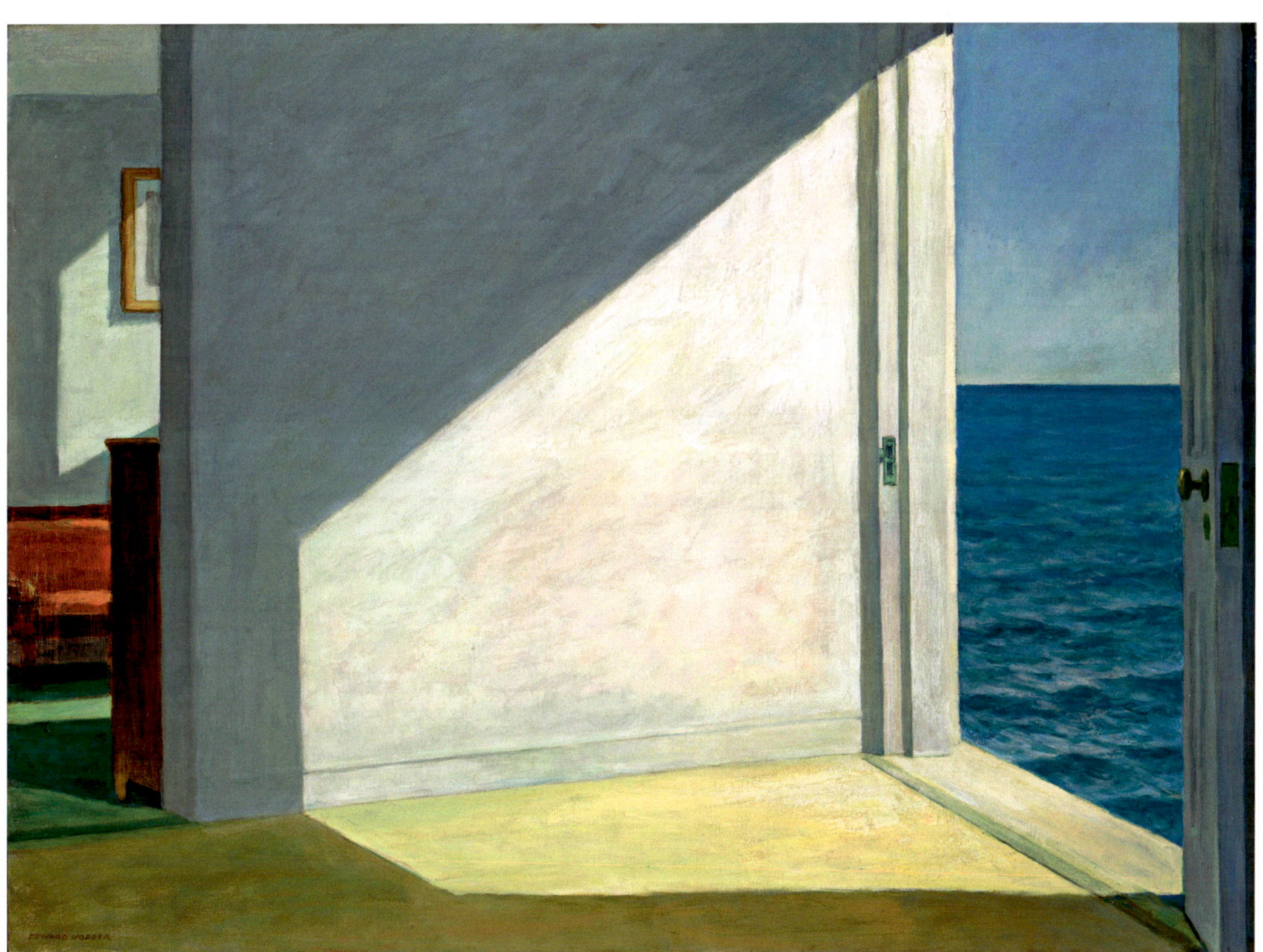

EDWARD HOPPER, *ROOMS BY THE SEA*, 1951

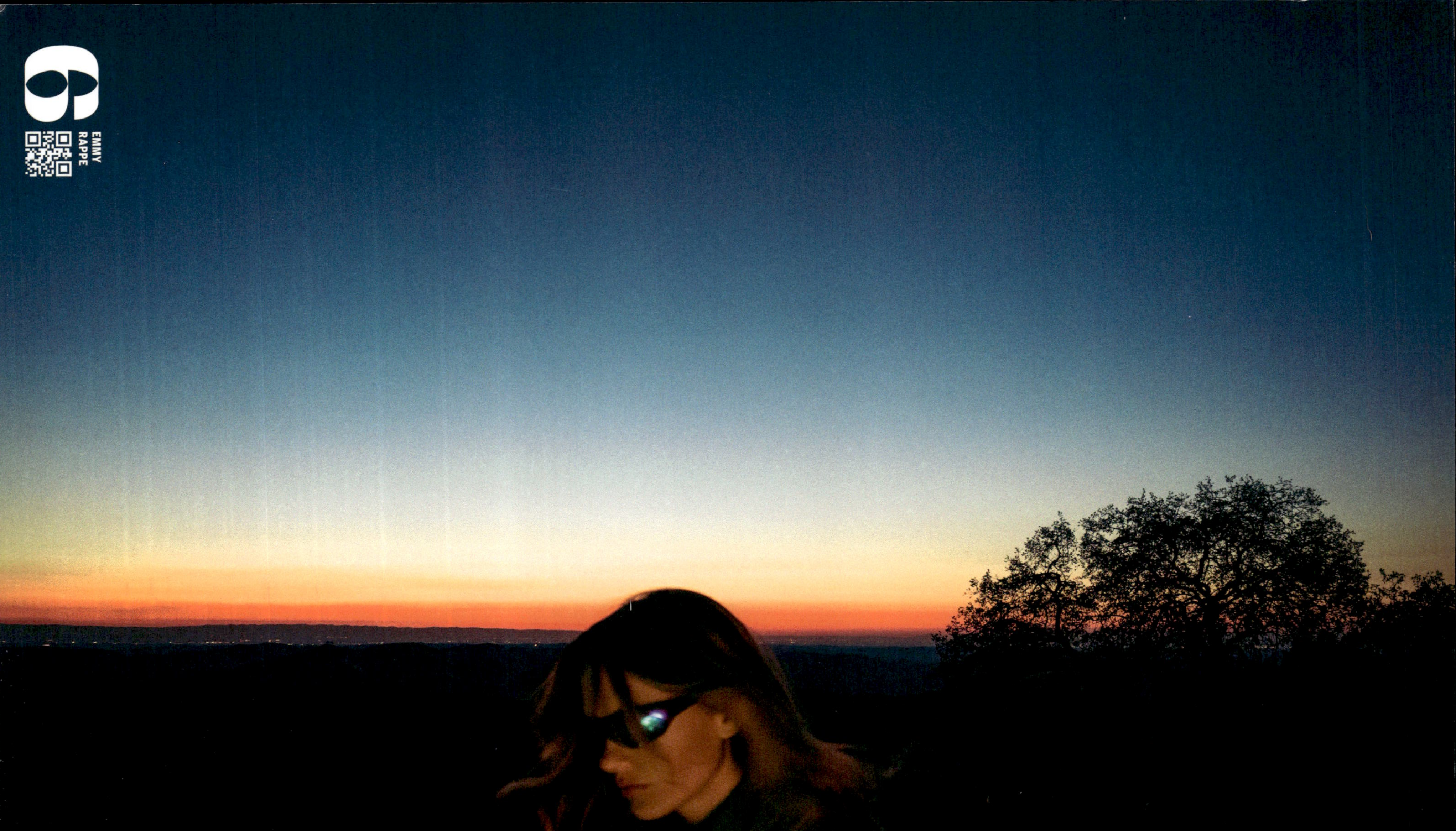

6
EMMY
RAPPE

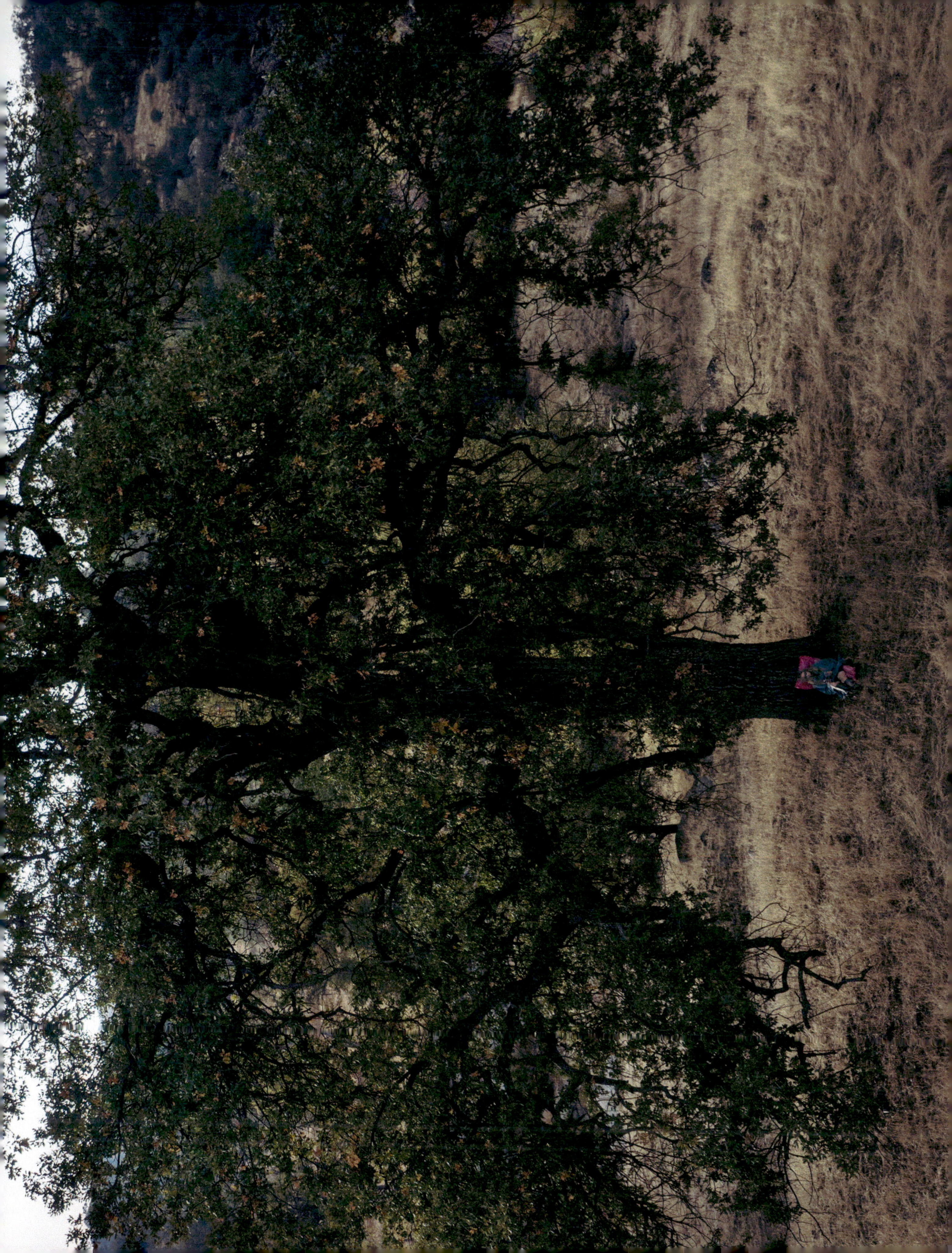

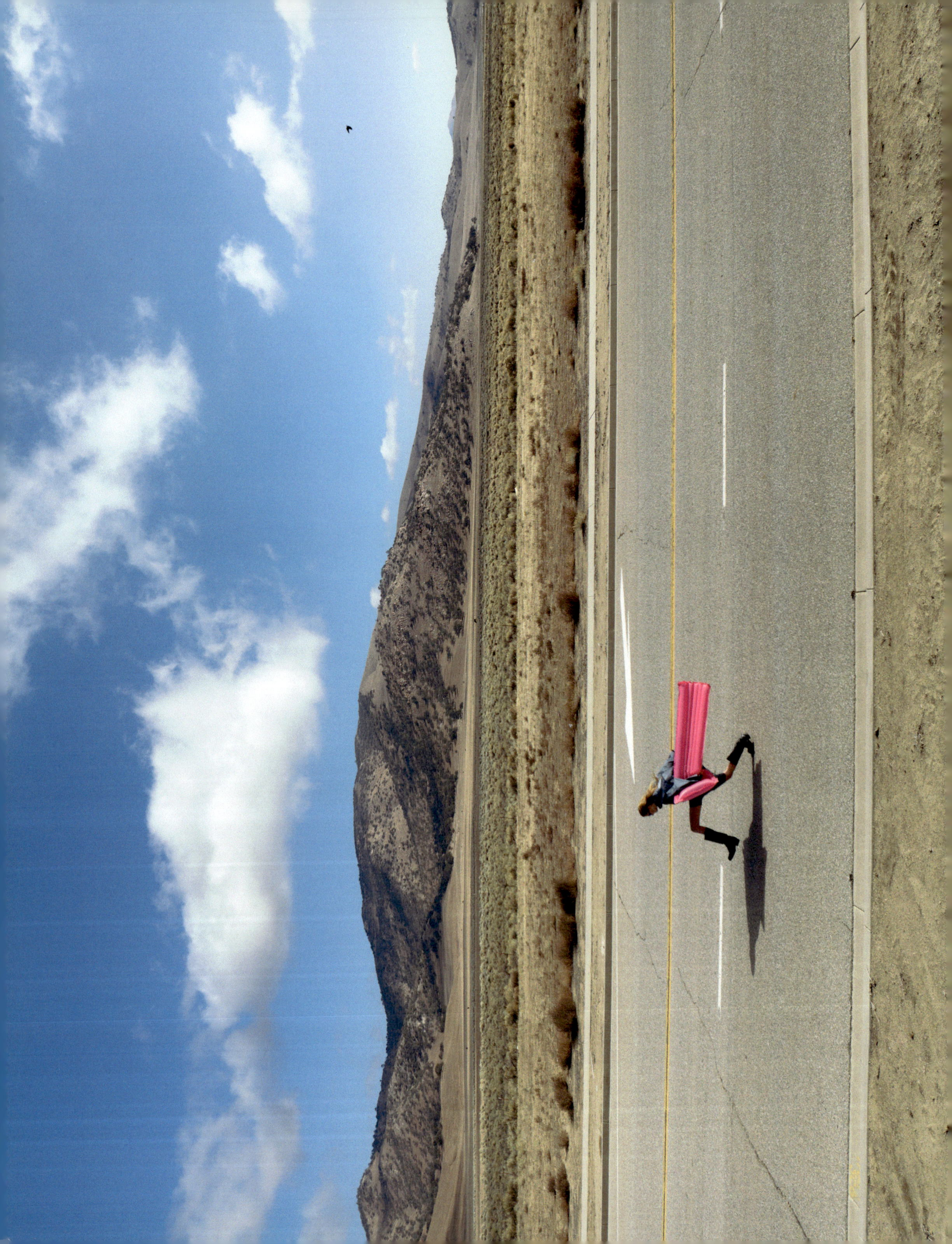

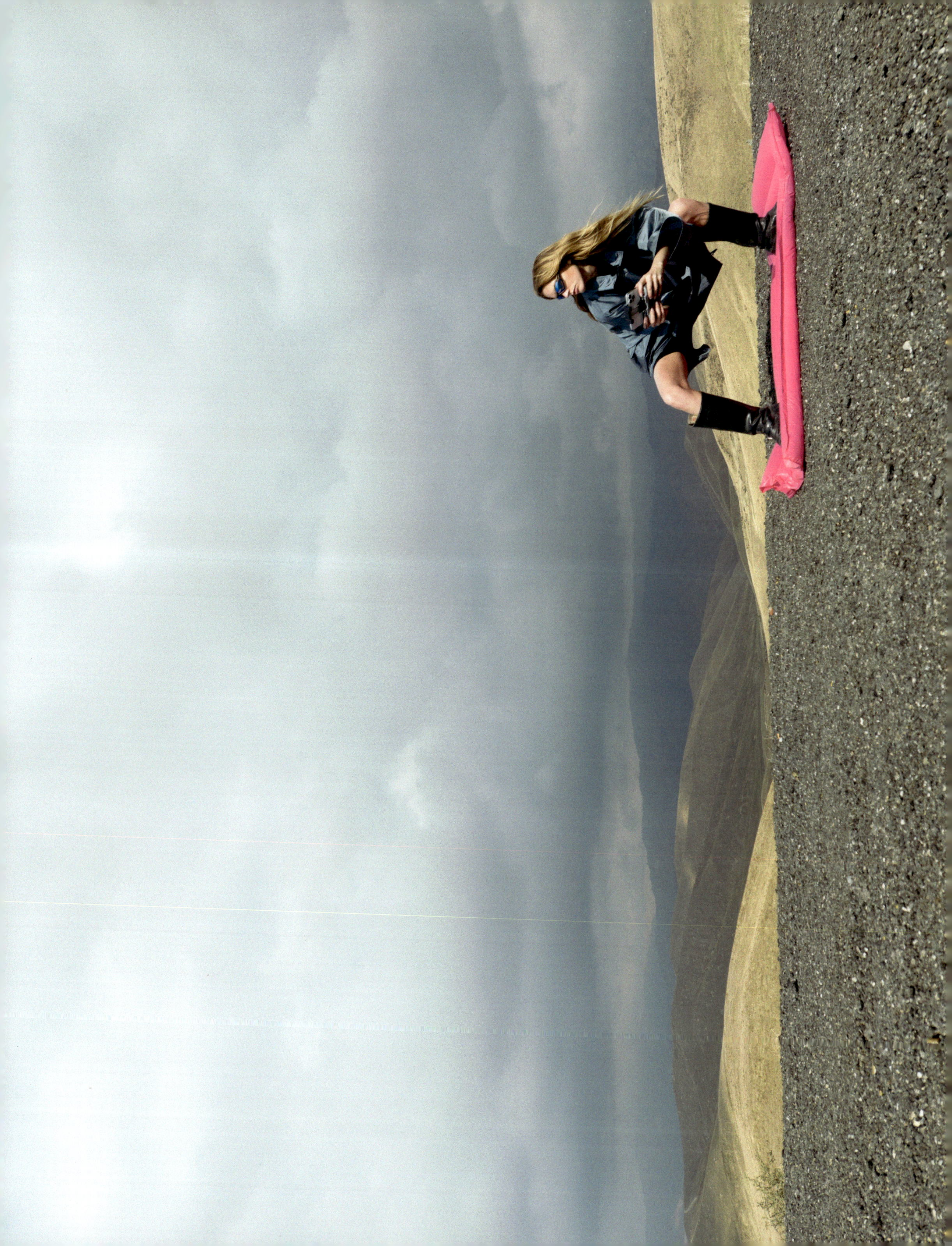

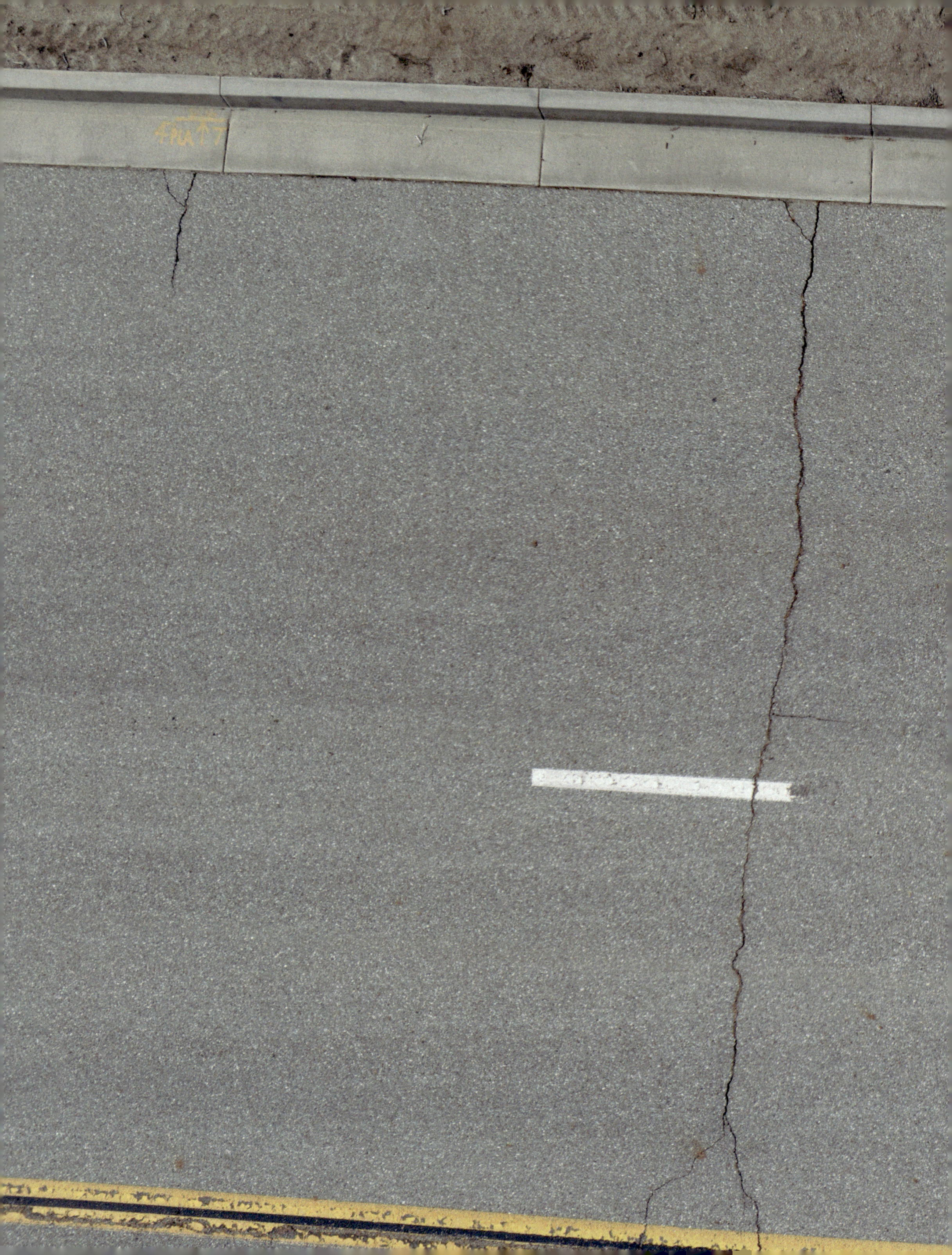

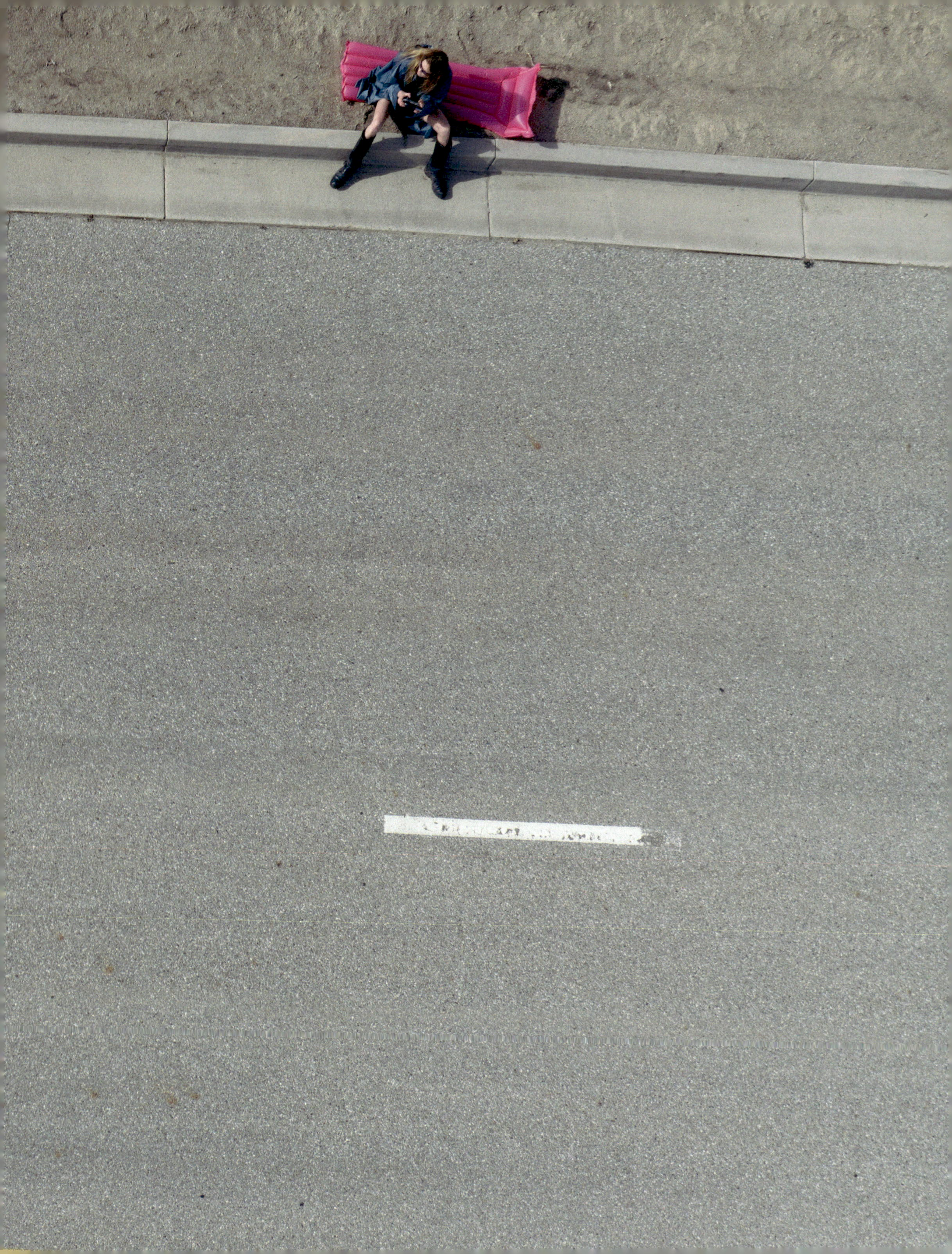

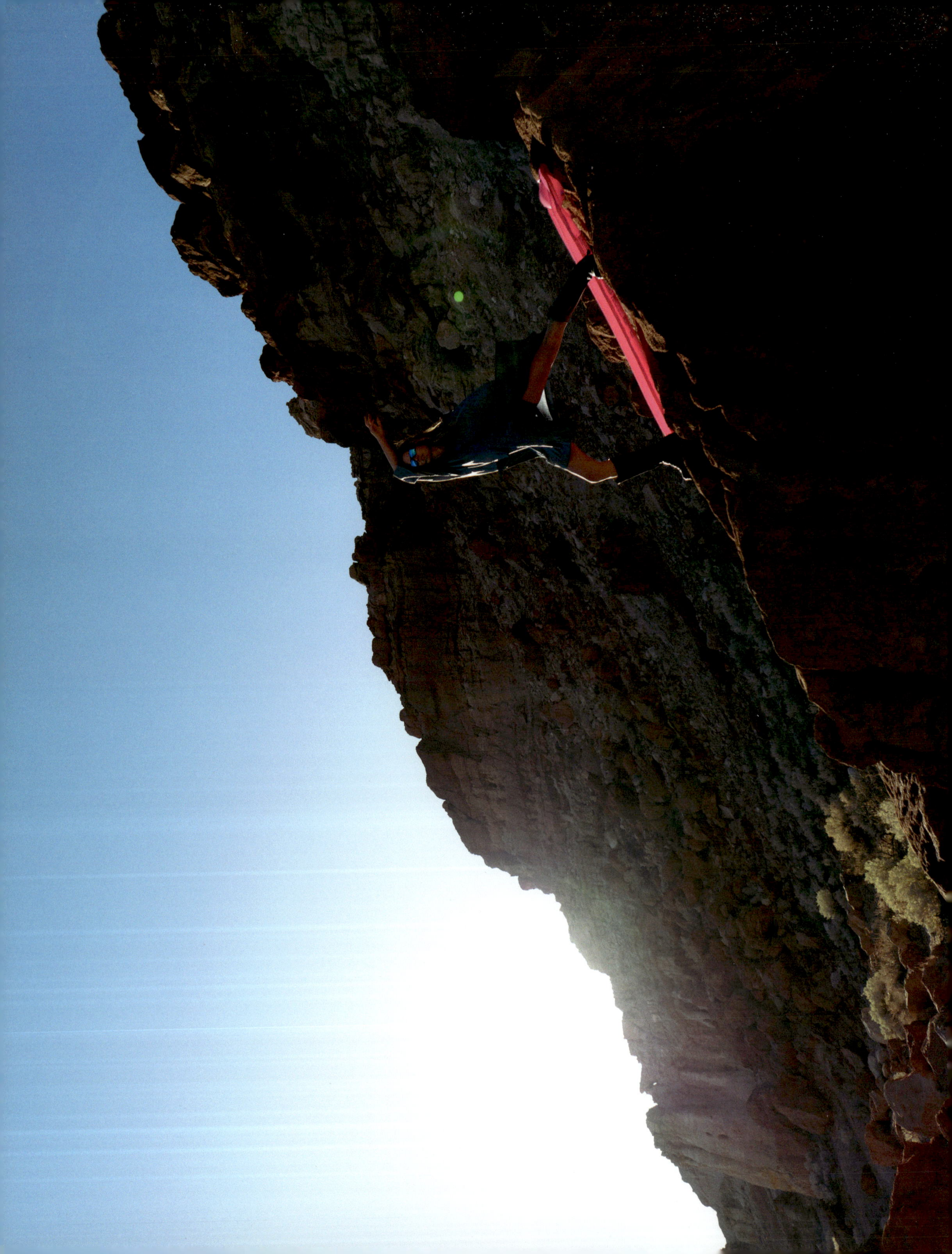

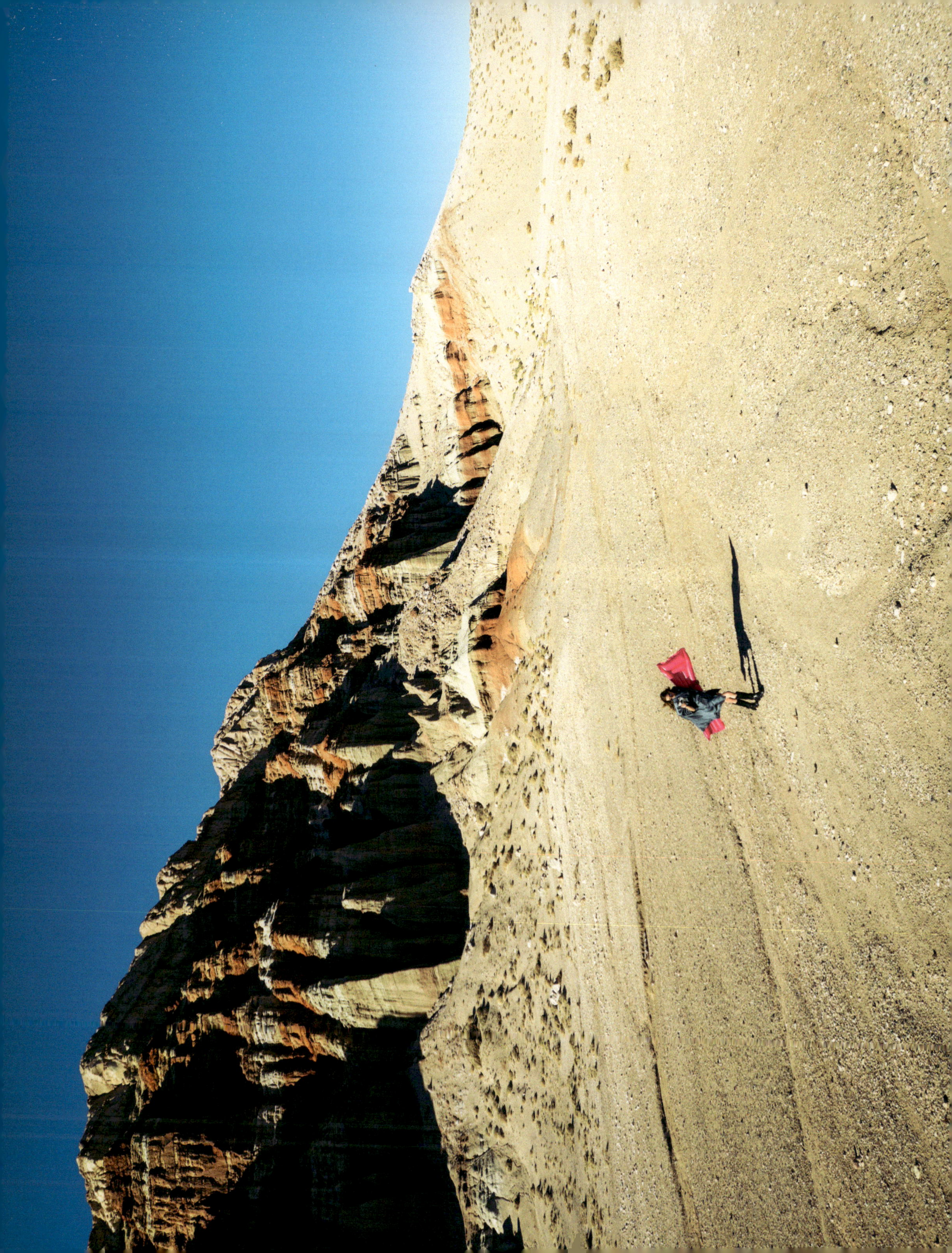

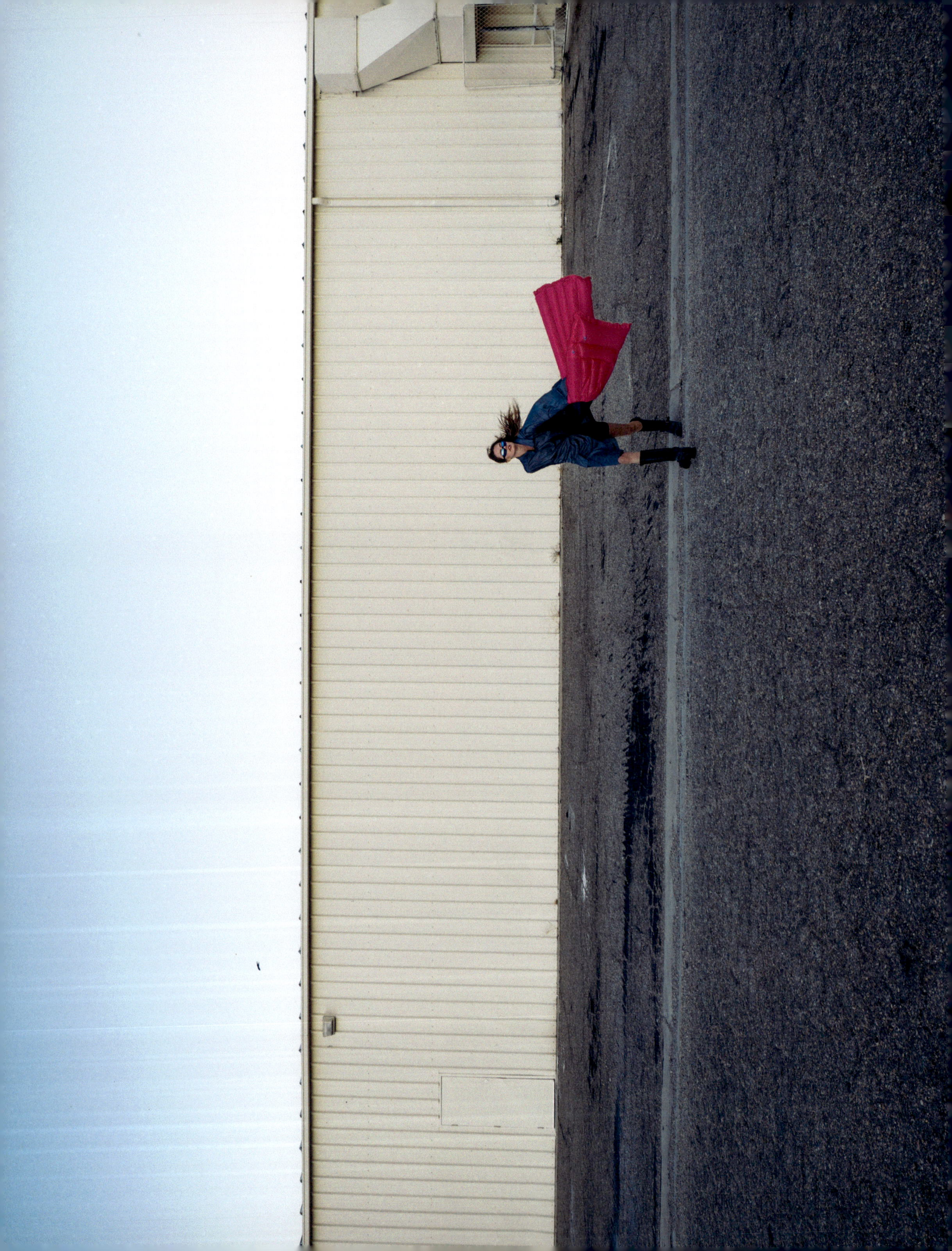

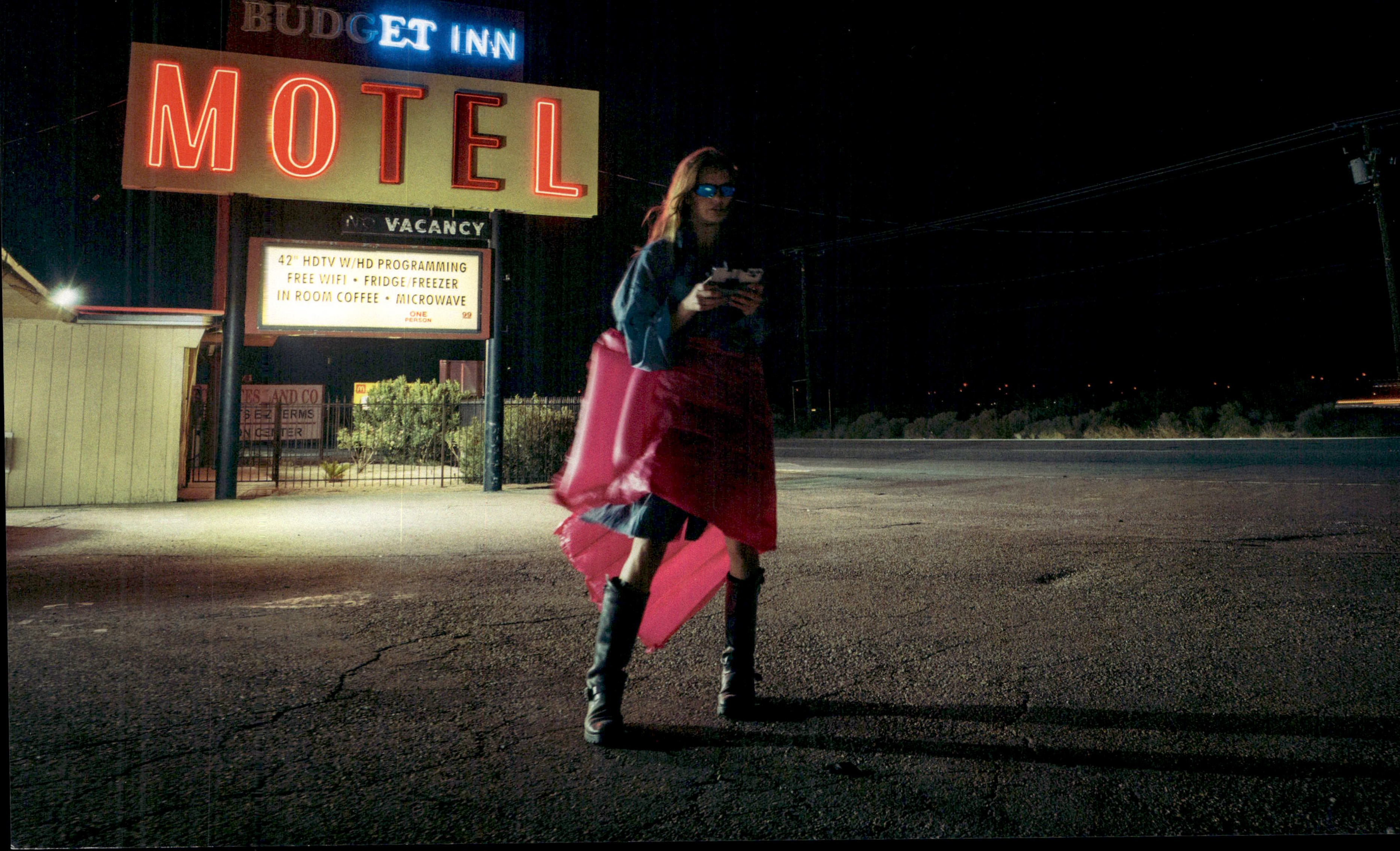
BUDGET INN
MOTEL
NO VACANCY
42" HDTV W/HD PROGRAMMING
FREE WIFI • FRIDGE/FREEZER
IN ROOM COFFEE • MICROWAVE
ONE PERSON 99

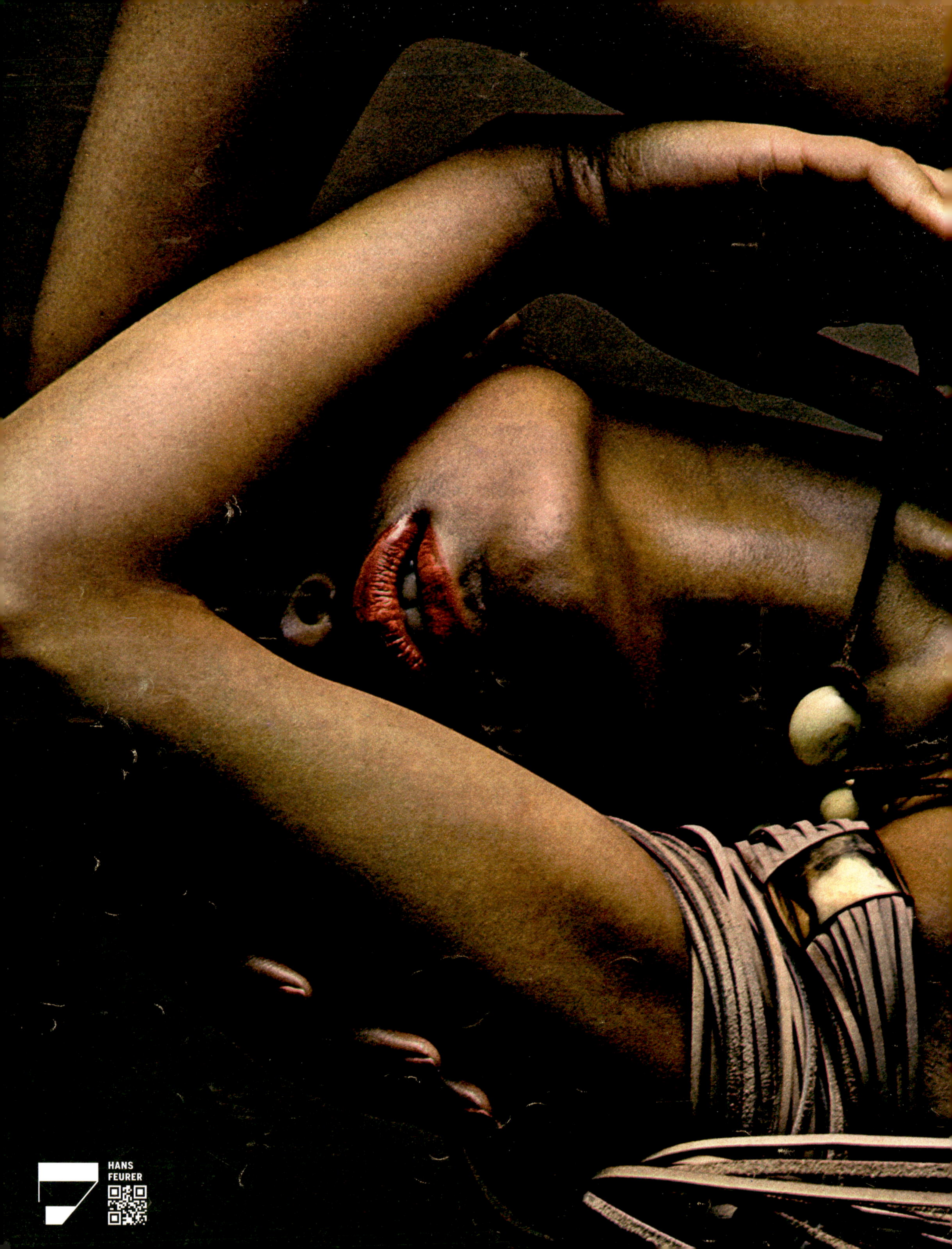
HANS
FEURER

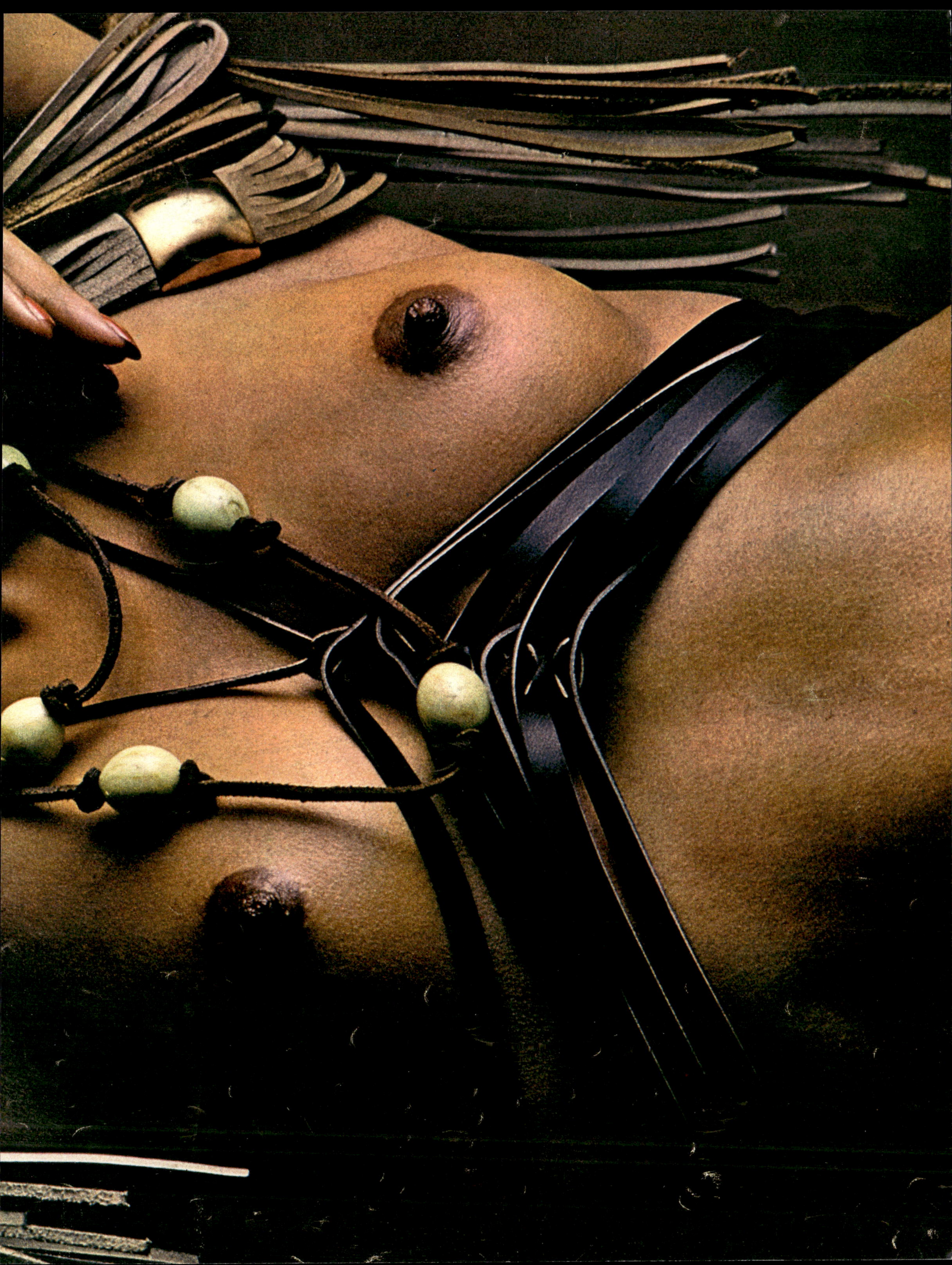

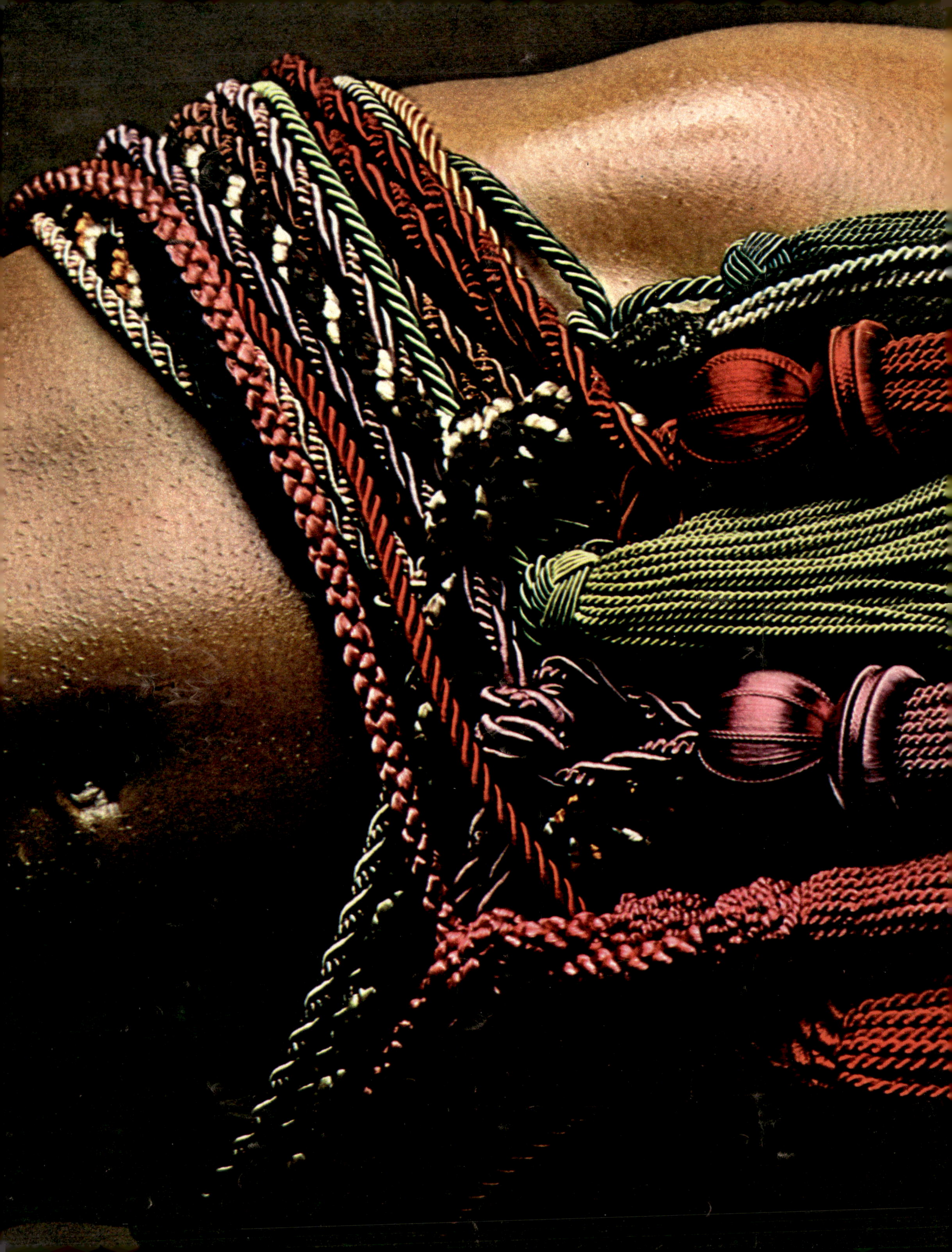

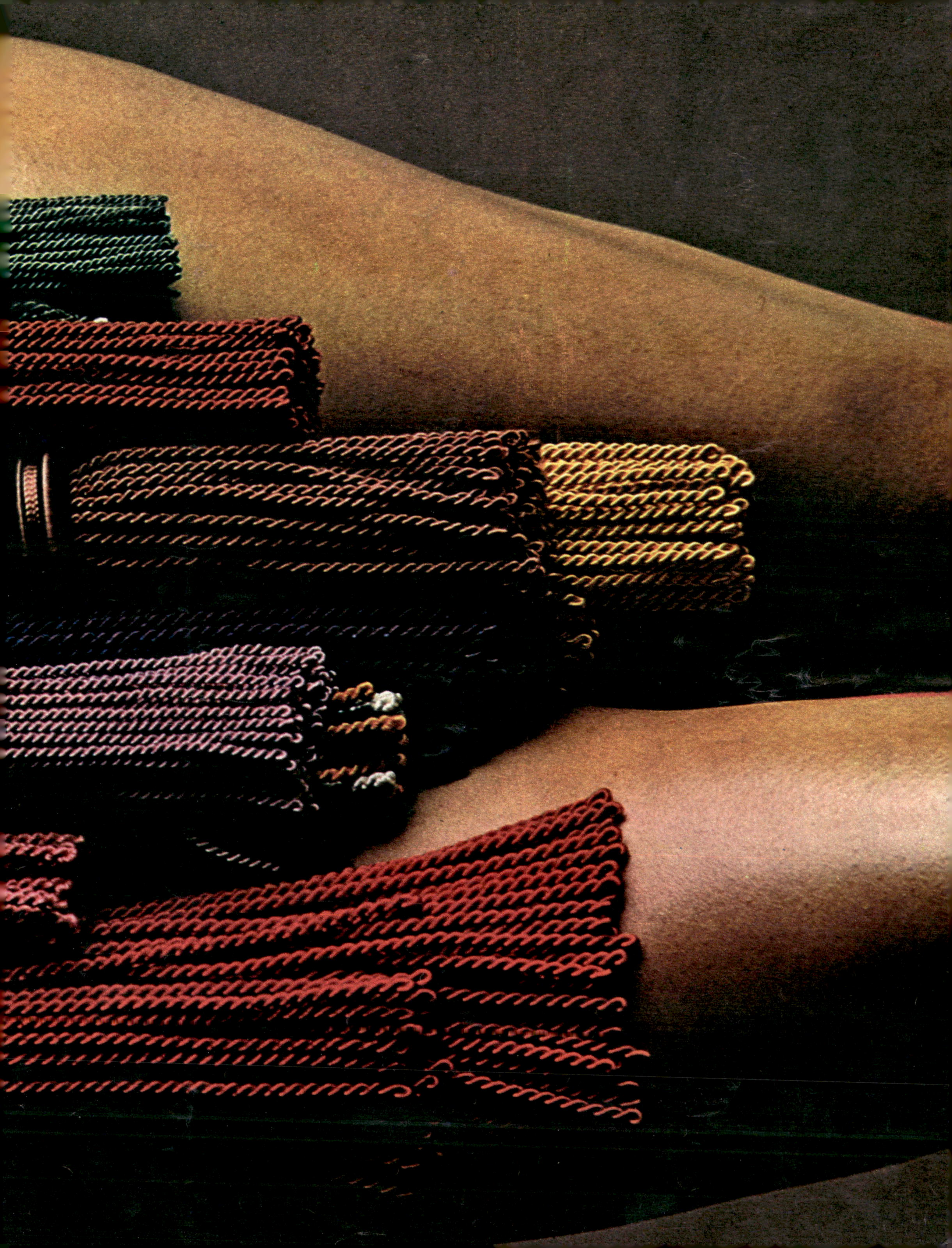

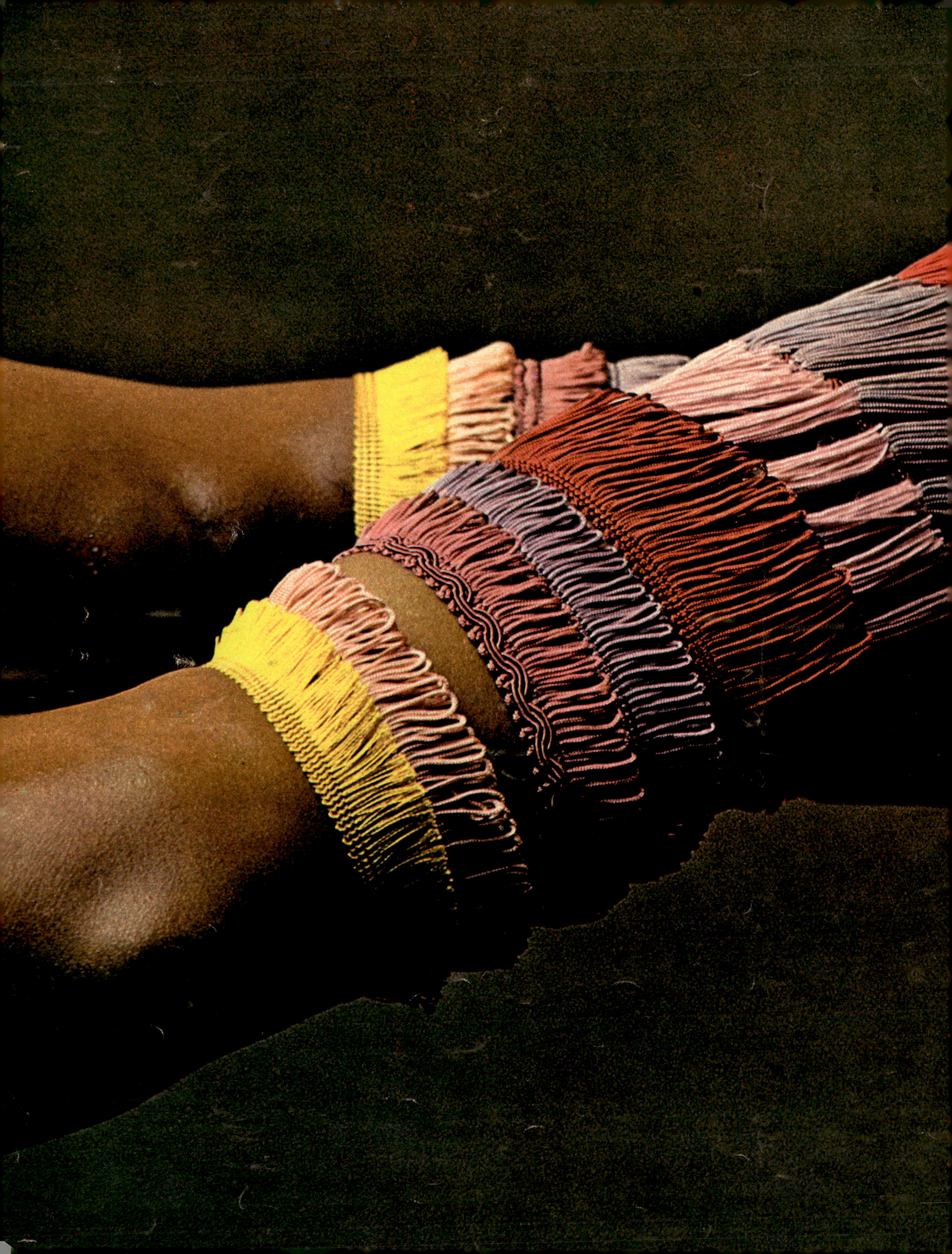

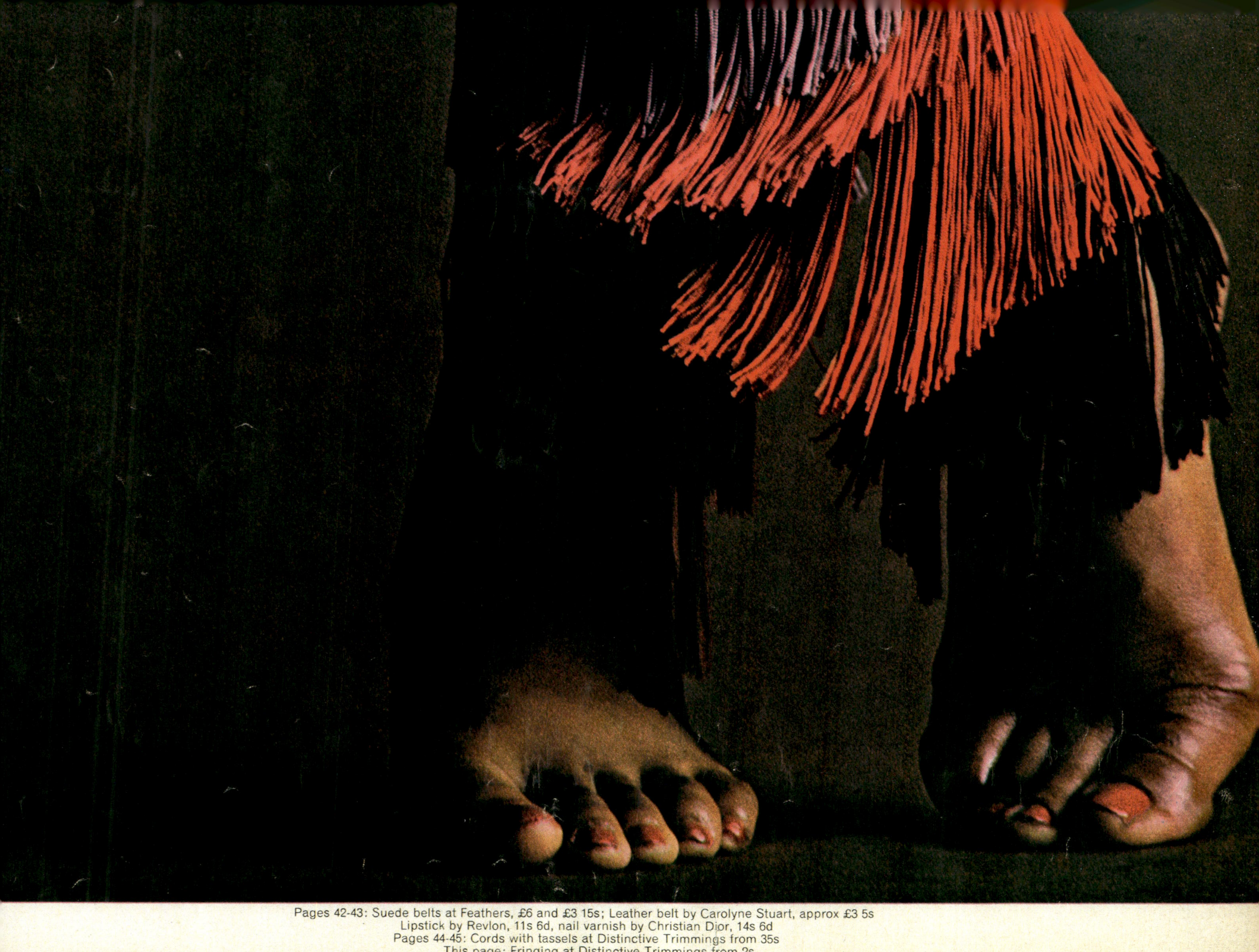

Pages 42-43: Suede belts at Feathers, £6 and £3 15s; Leather belt by Carolyne Stuart, approx £3 5s
Lipstick by Revlon, 11s 6d, nail varnish by Christian Dior, 14s 6d
Pages 44-45: Cords with tassels at Distinctive Trimmings from 35s
This page: Fringing at Distinctive Trimmings from 2s

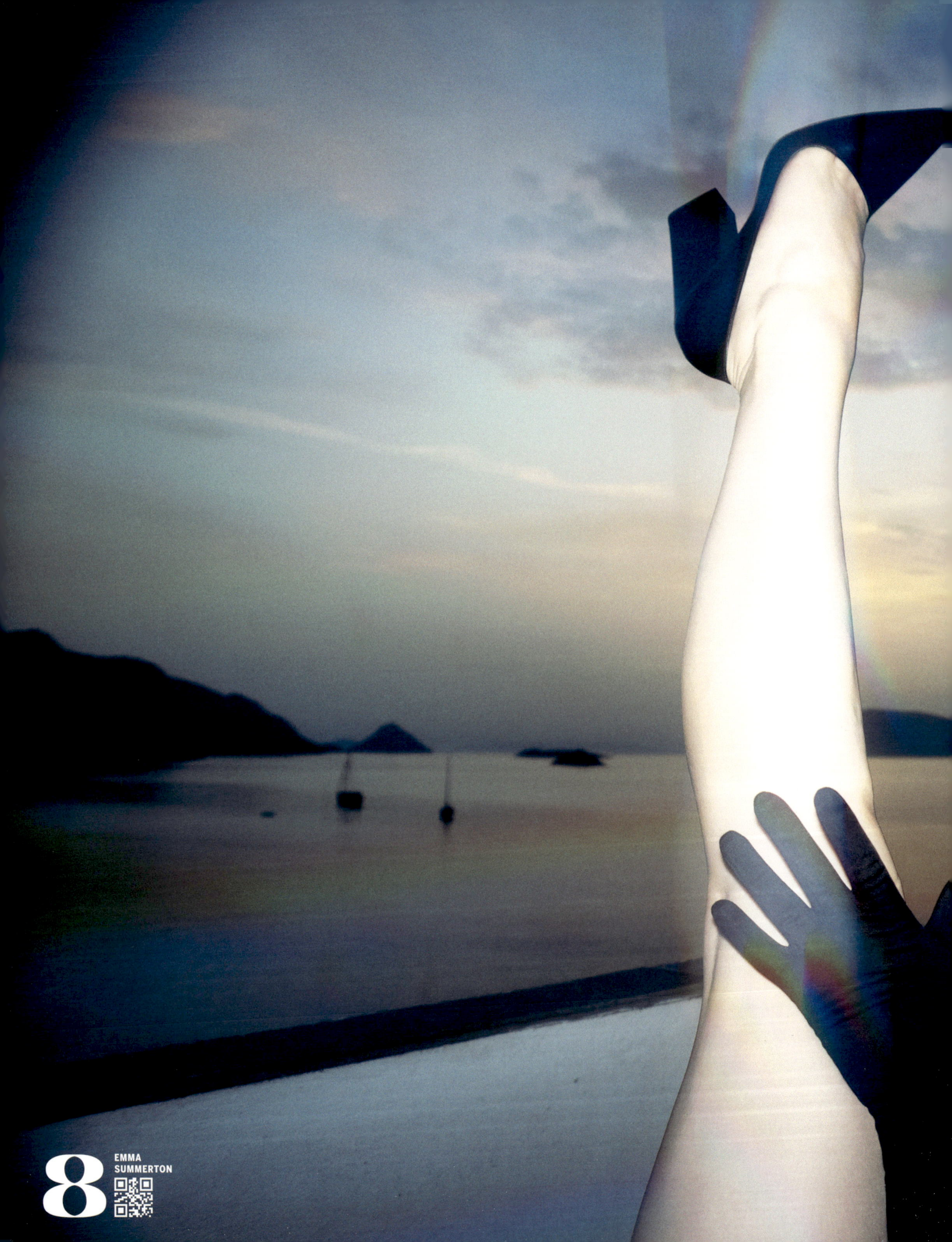
8
EMMA
SUMMERTON

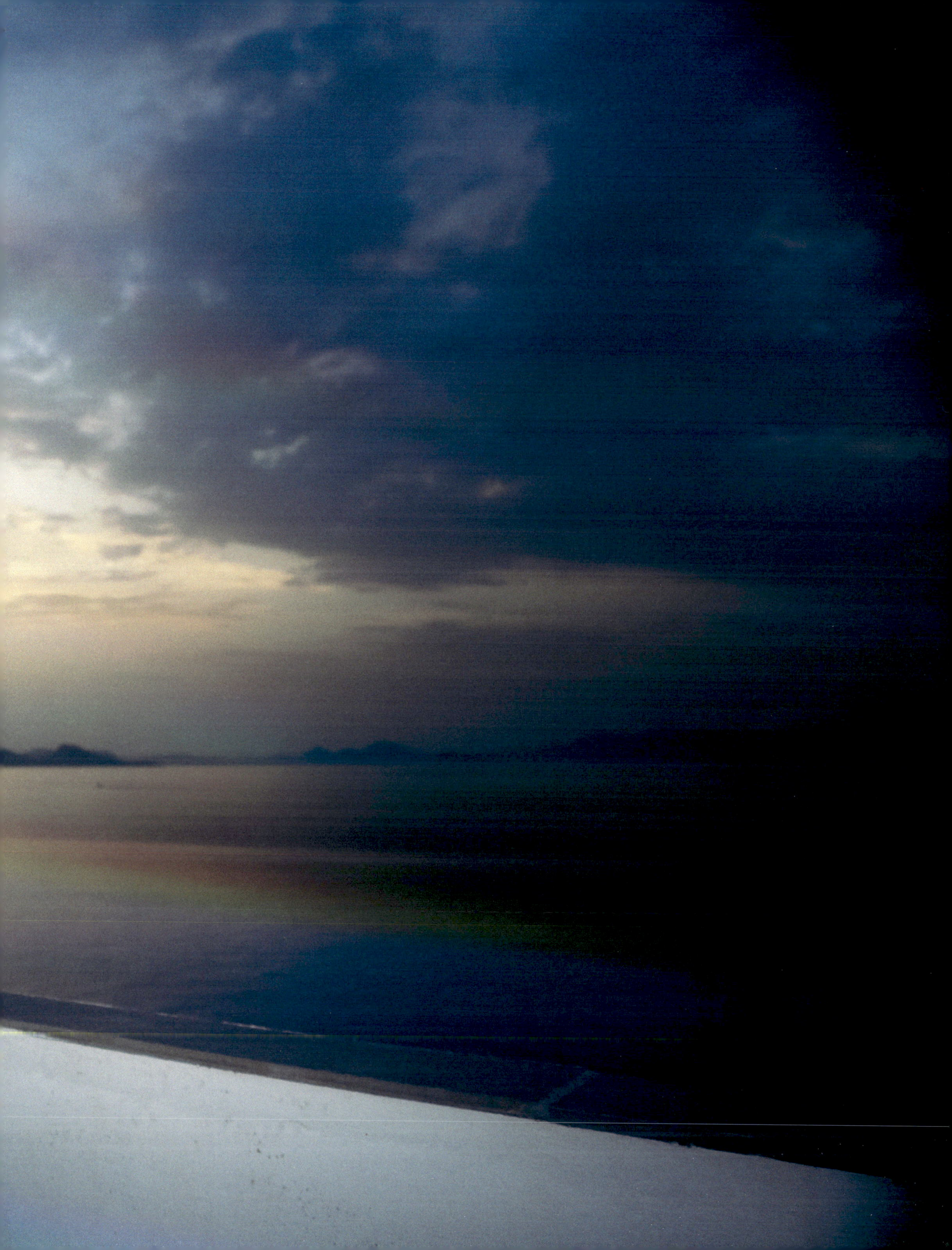

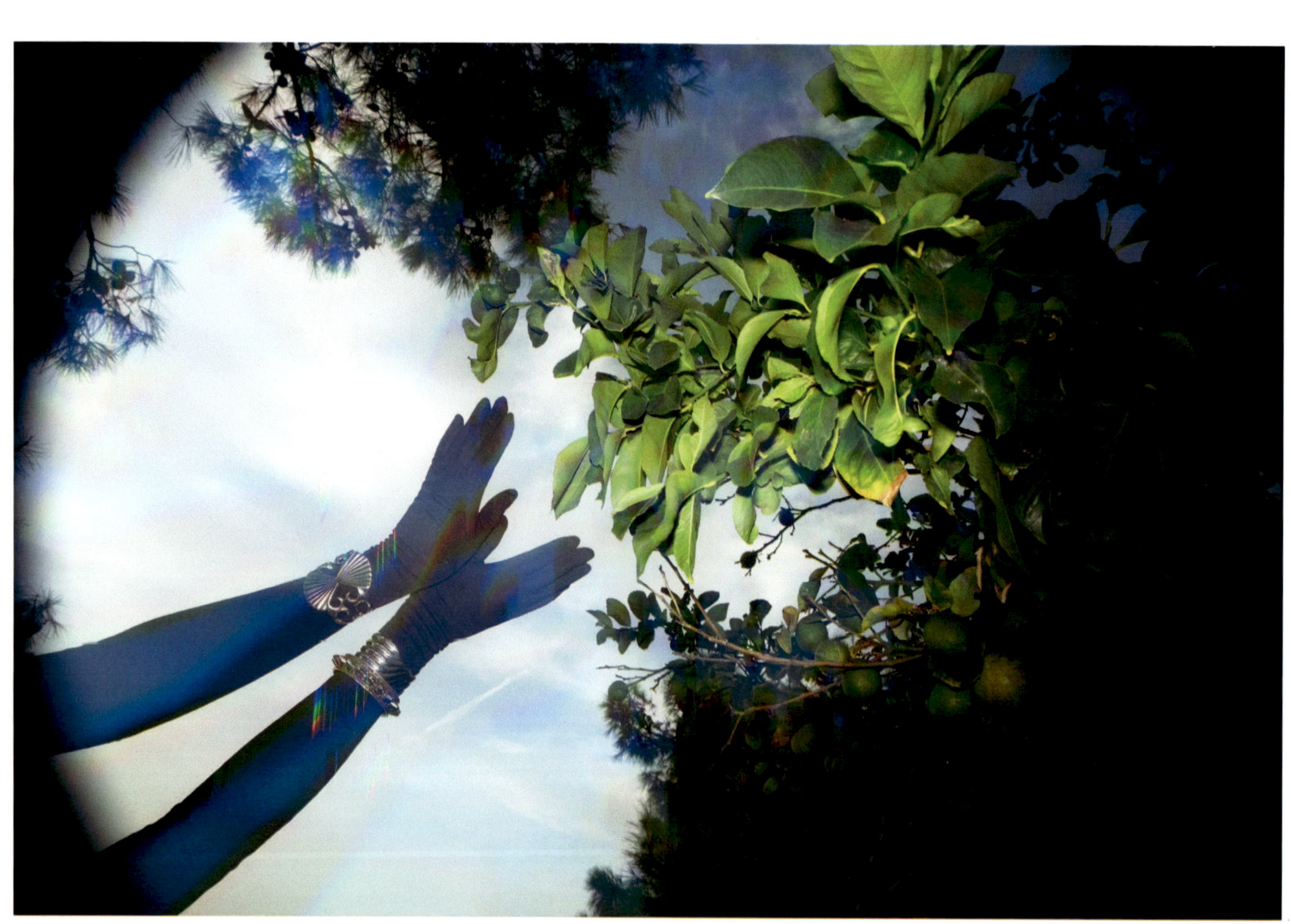

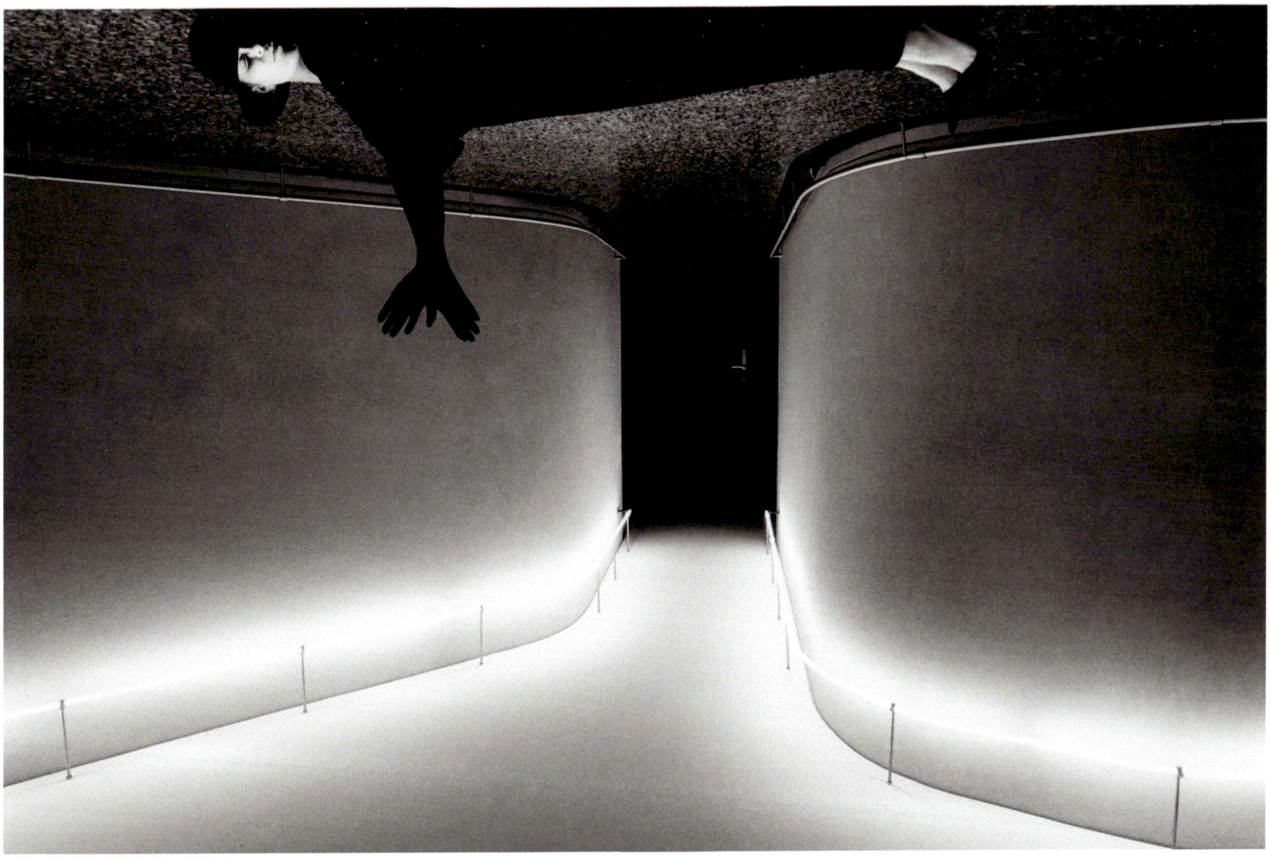

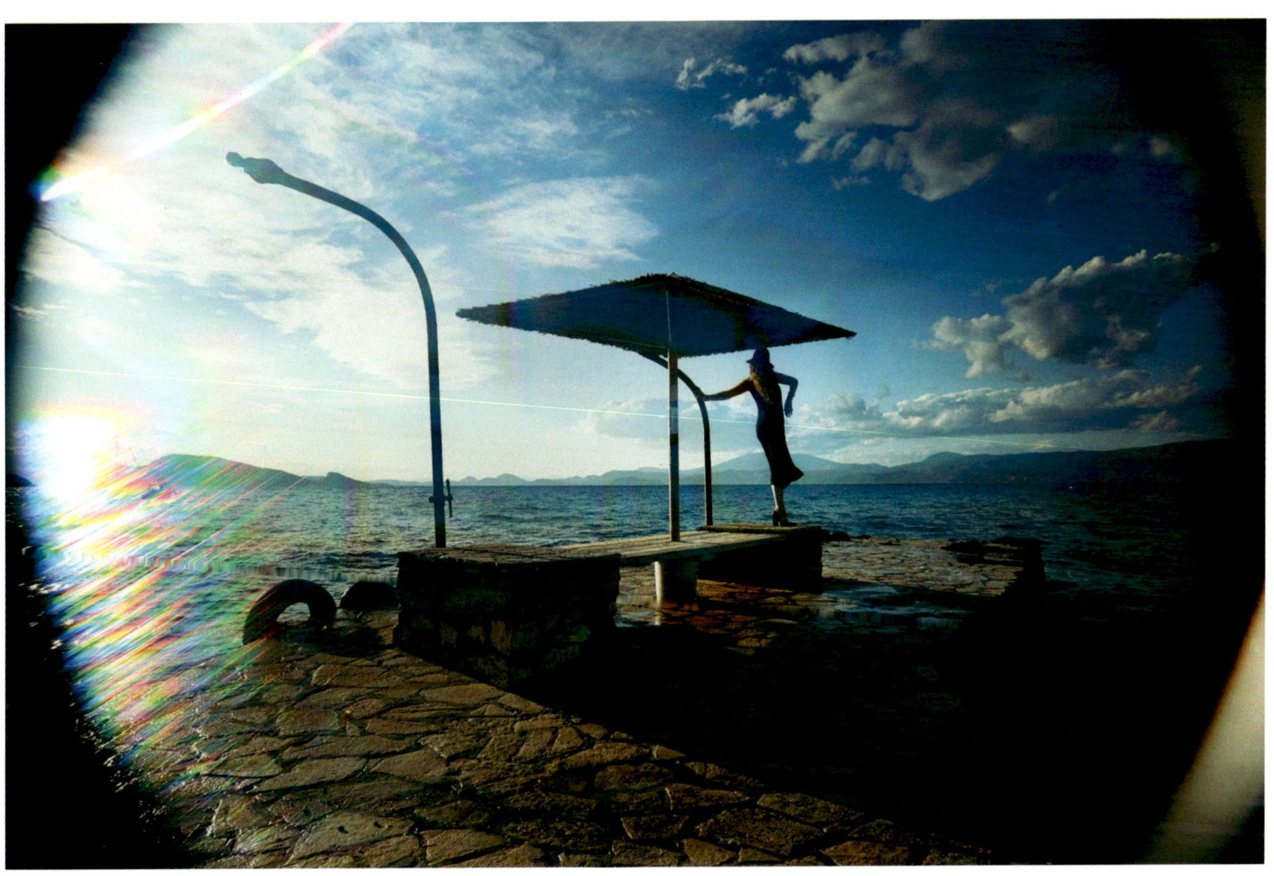

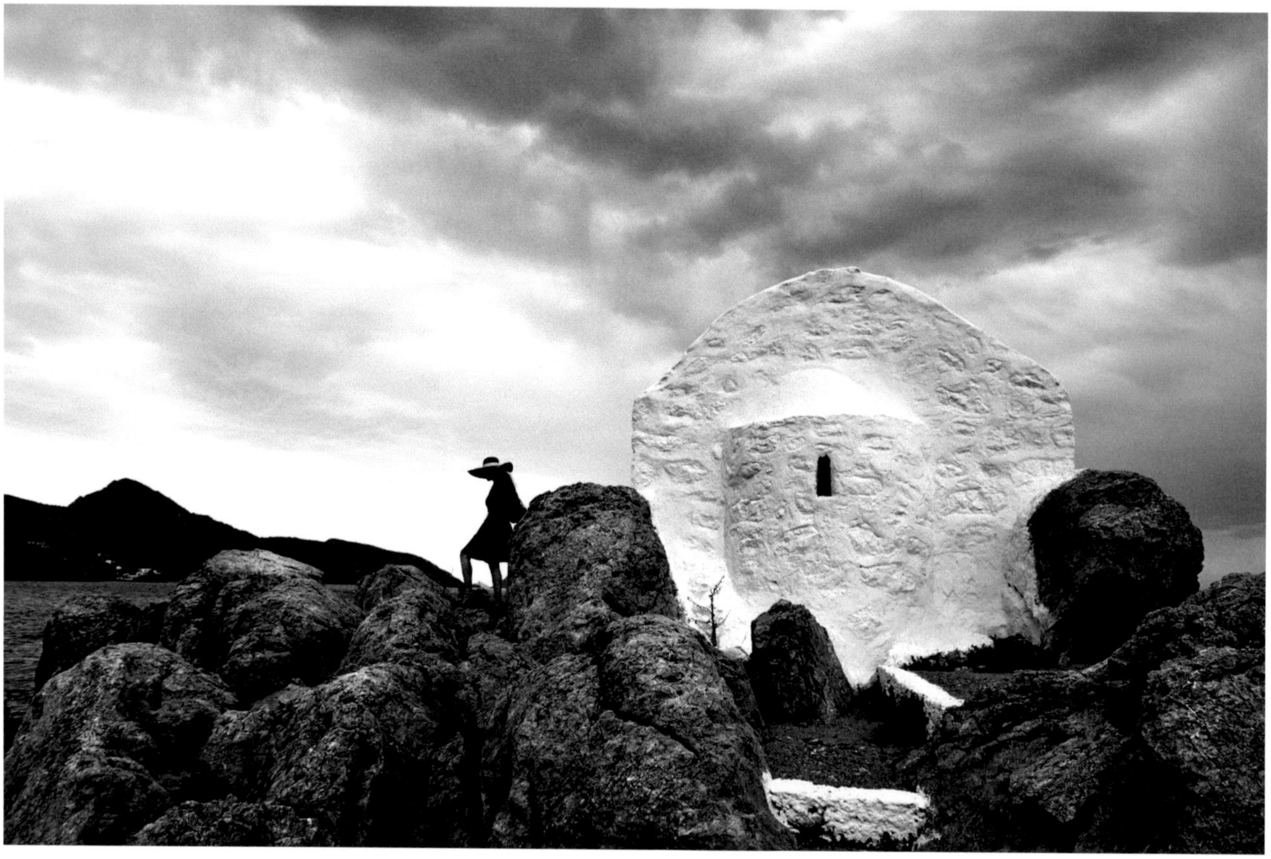

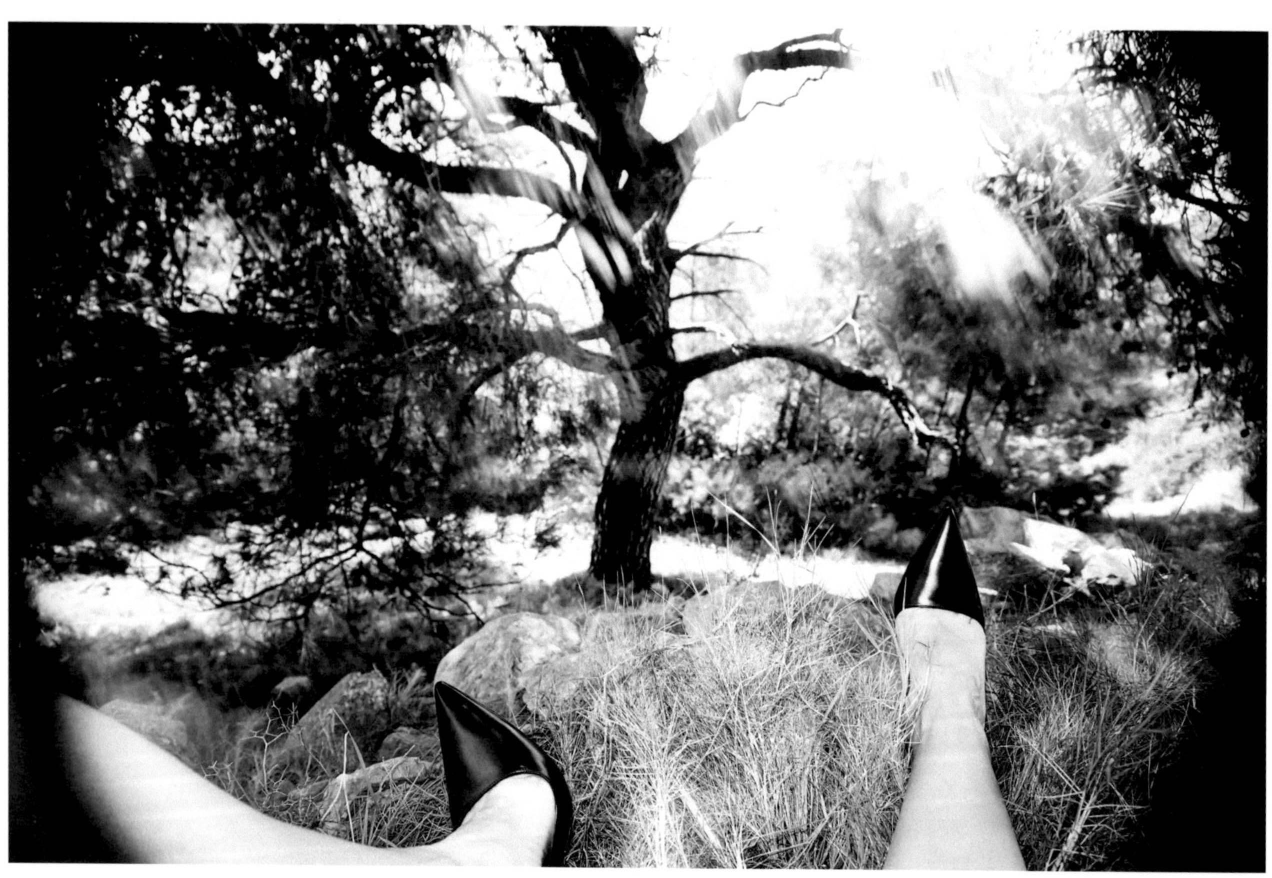

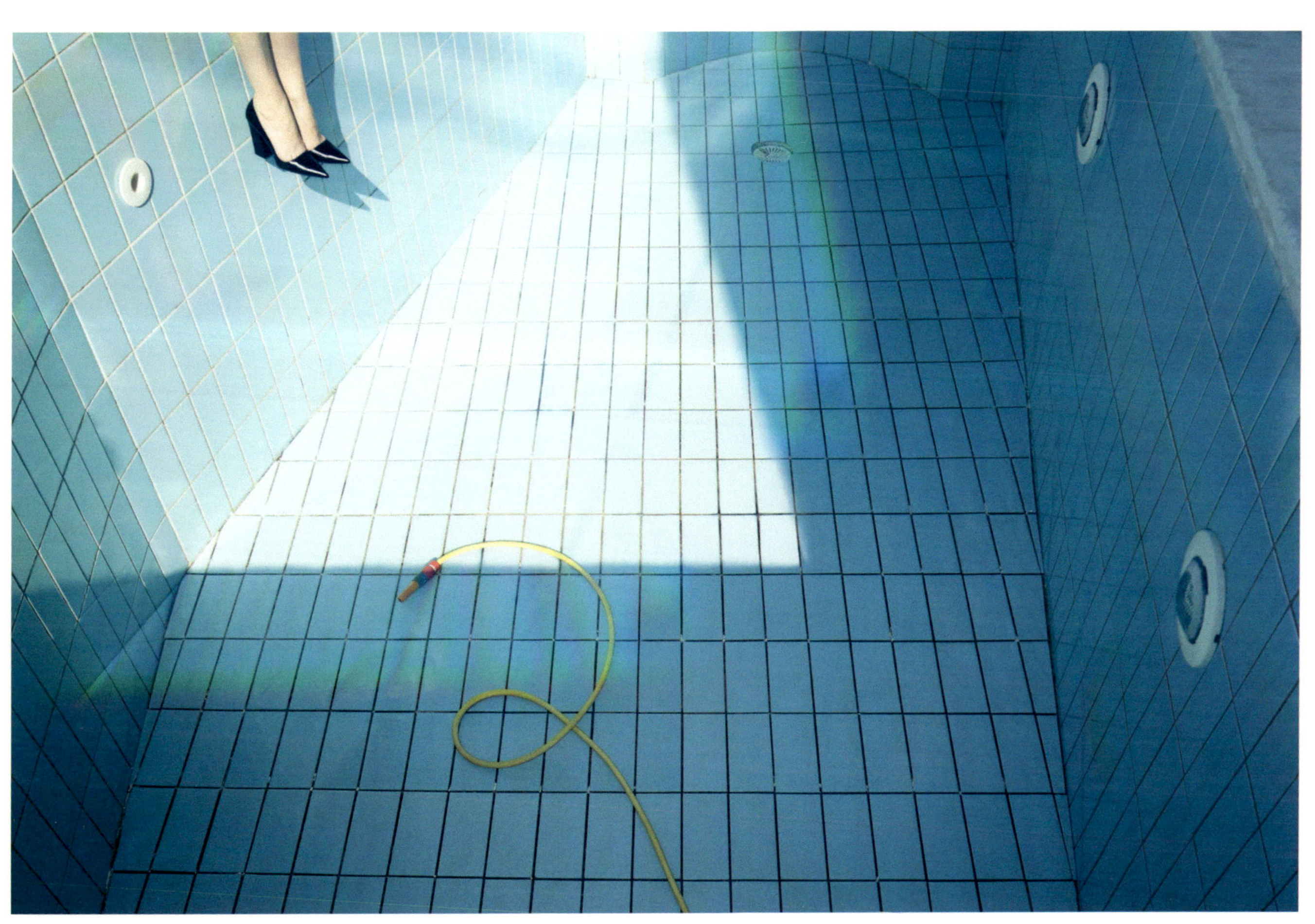

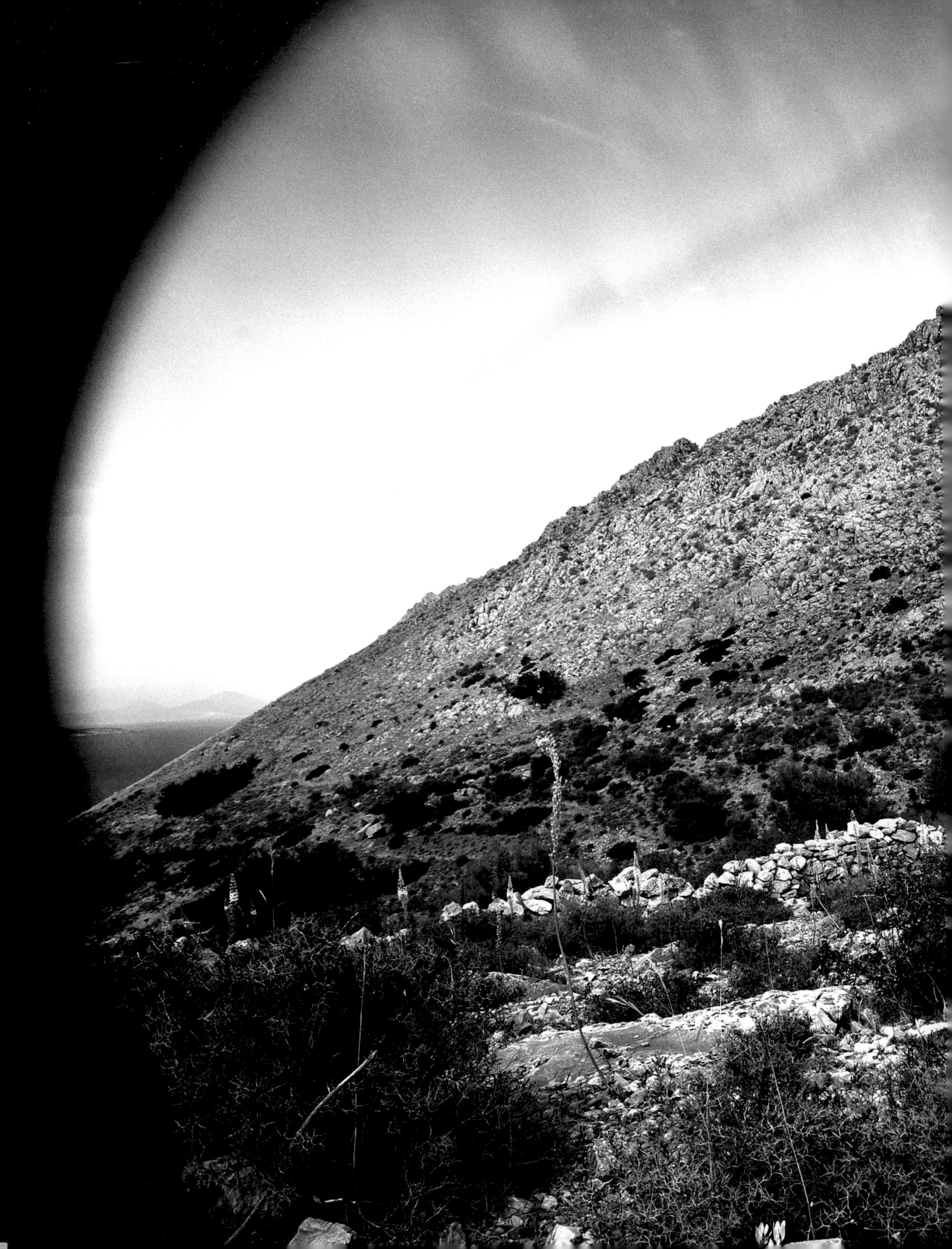

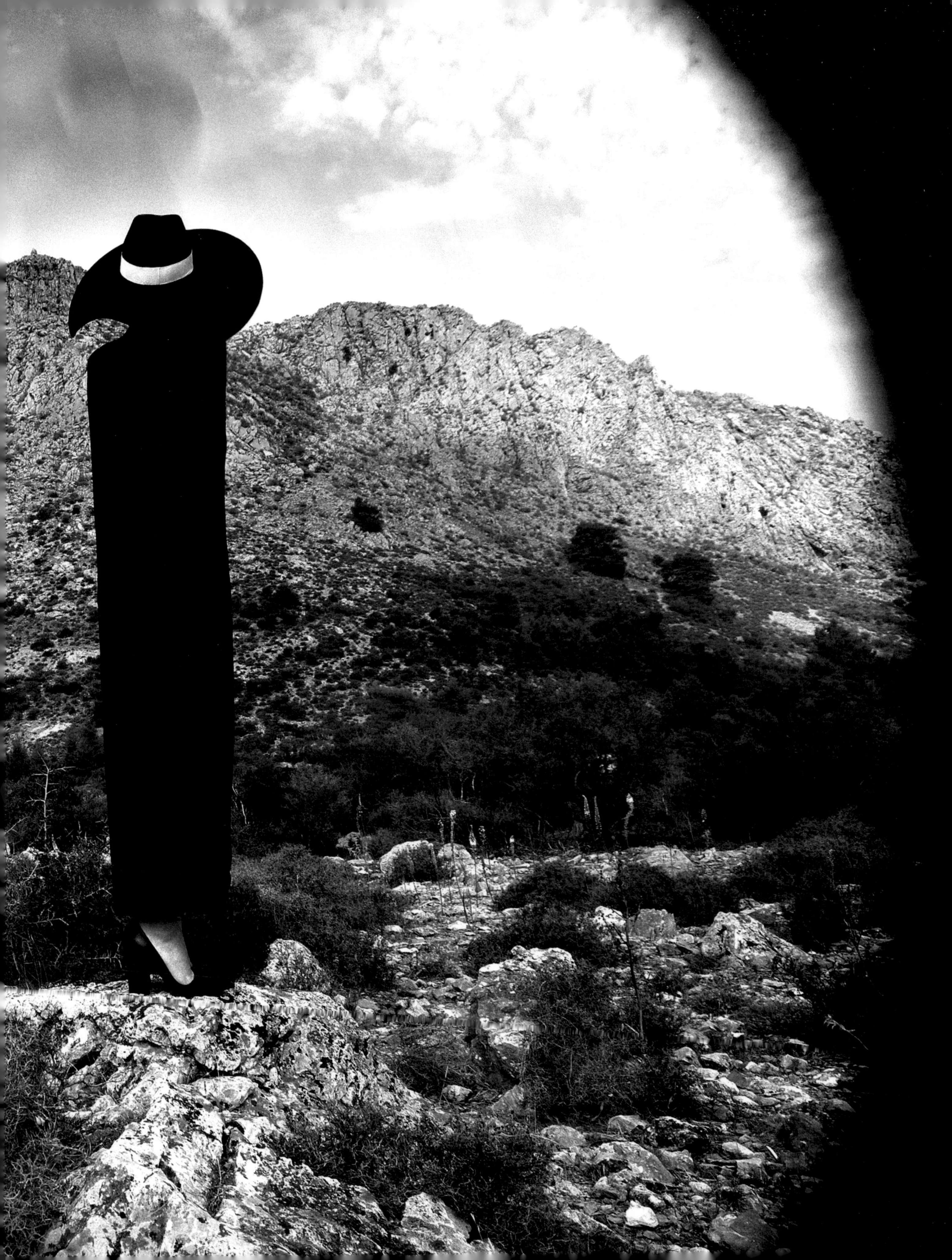

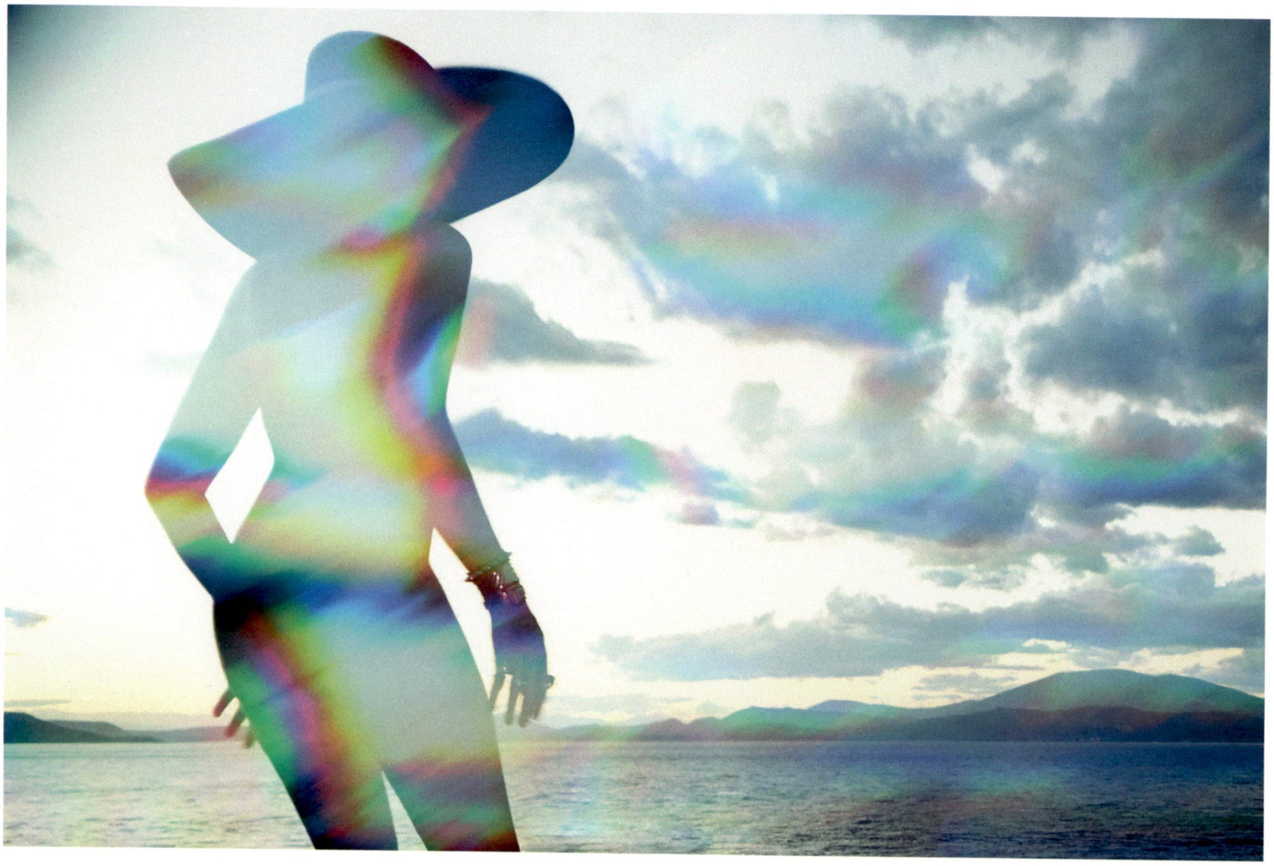

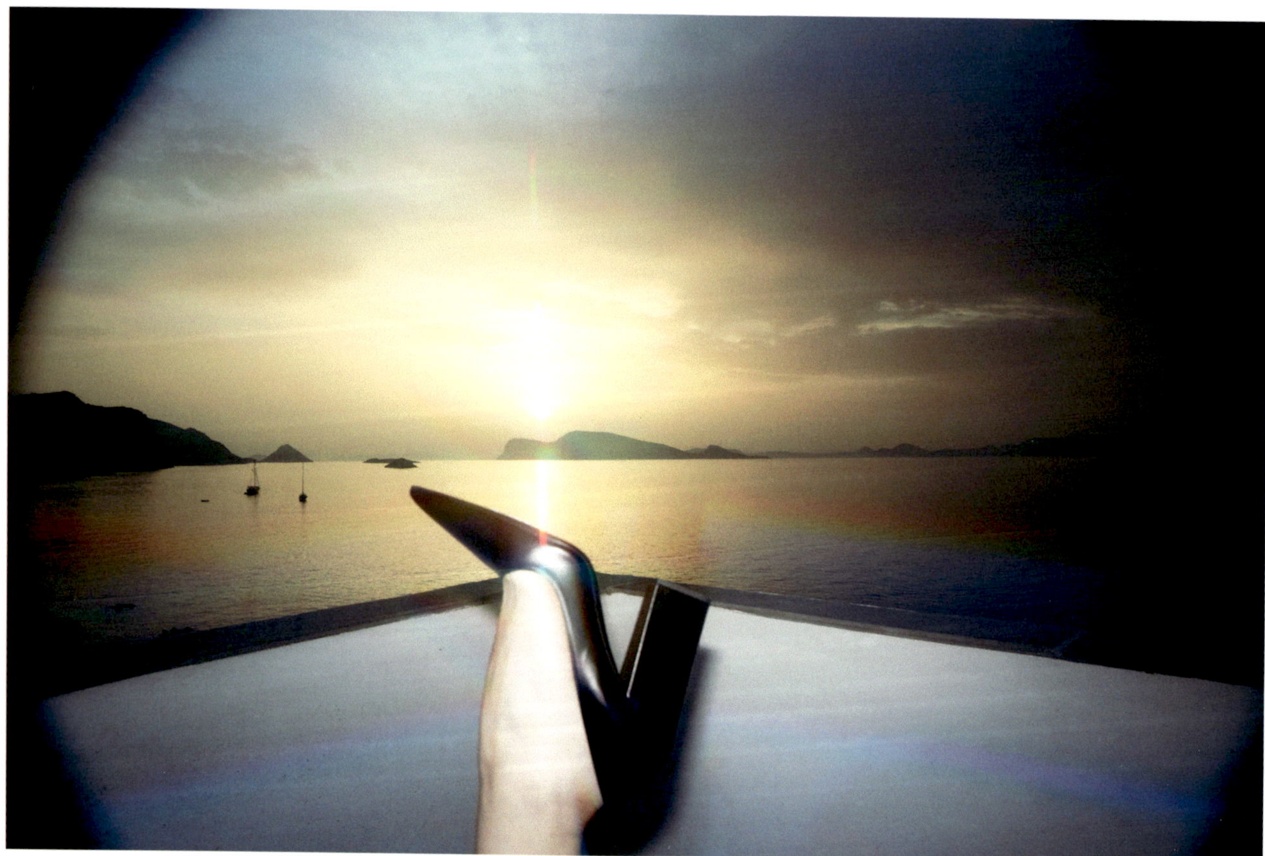

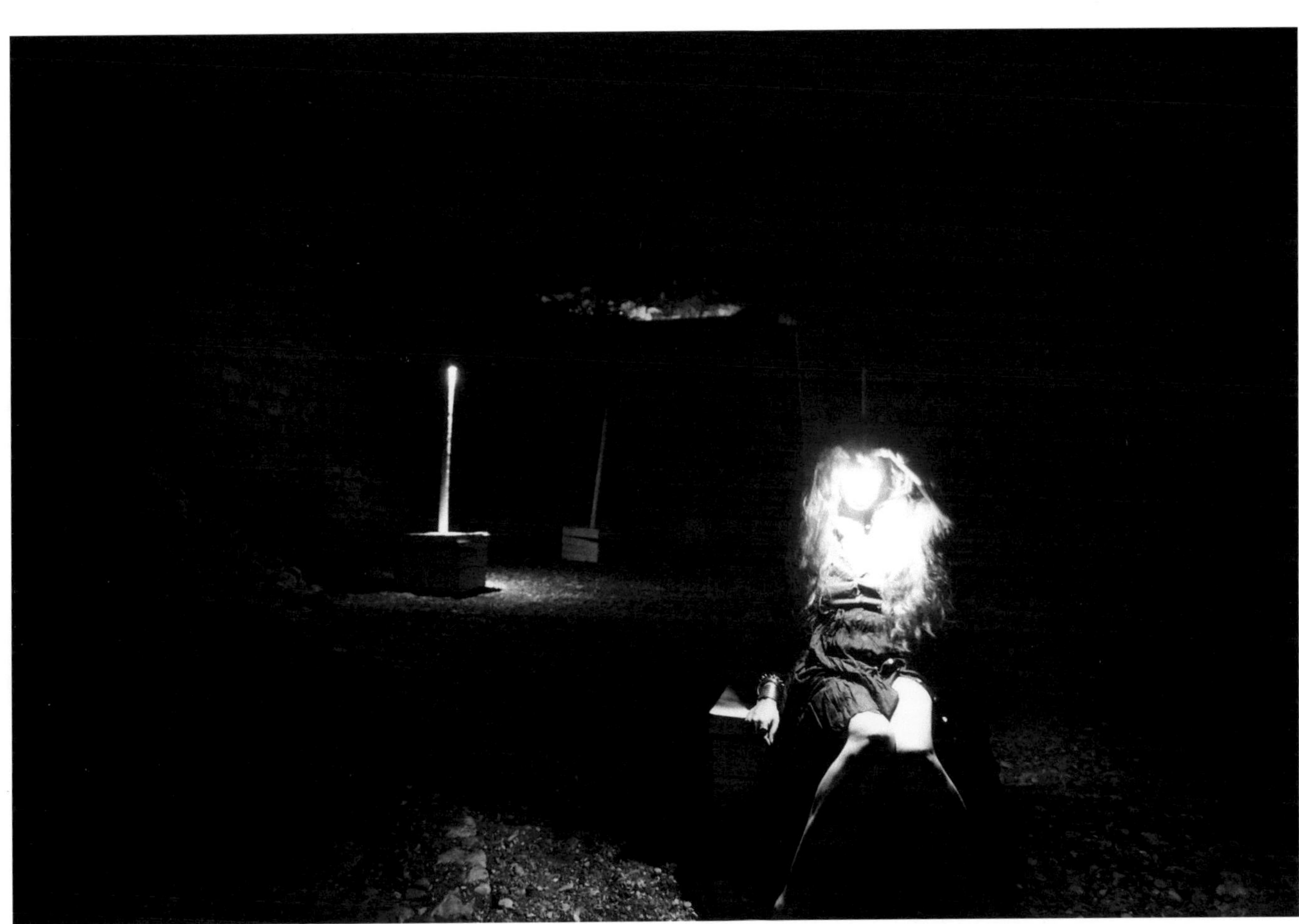

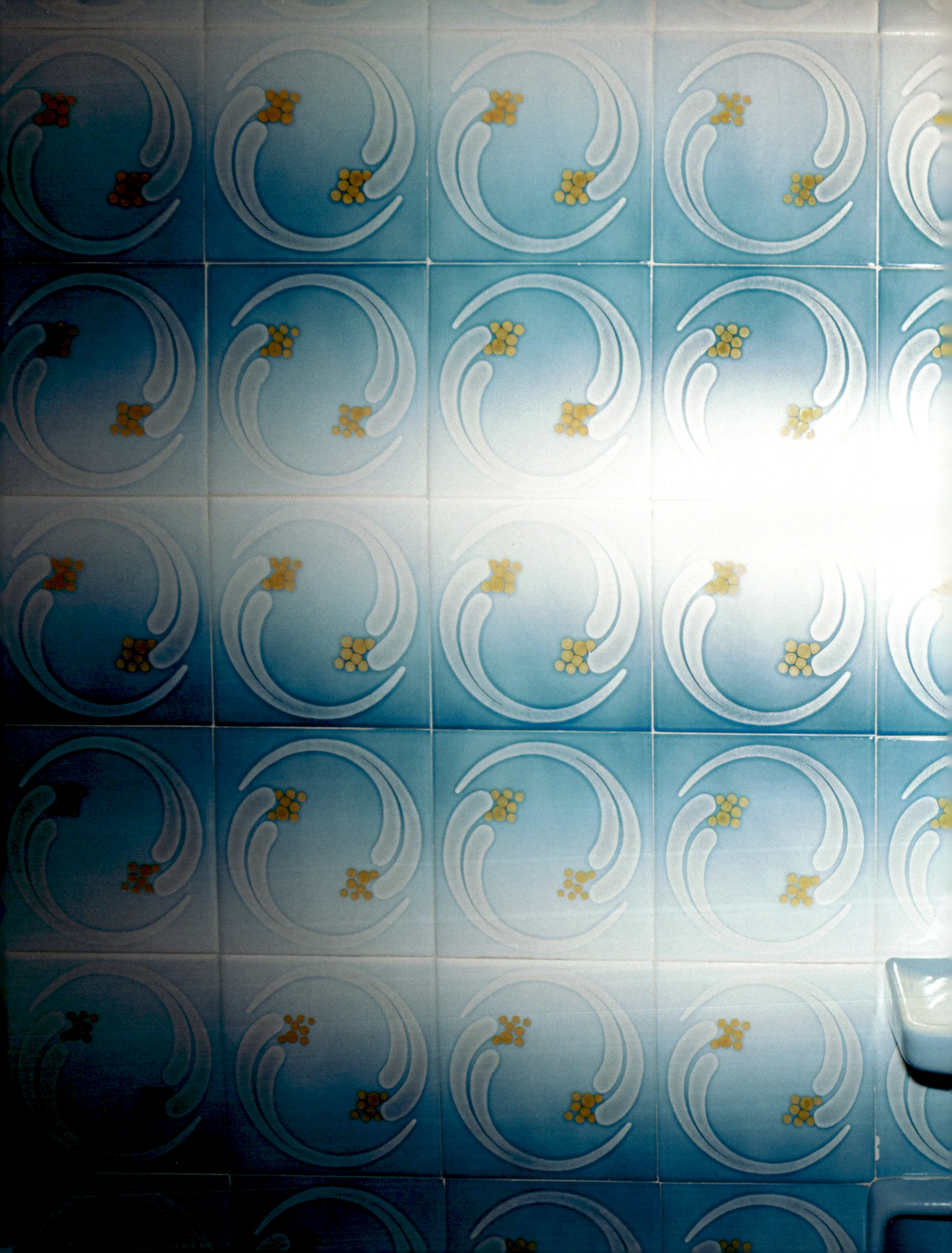

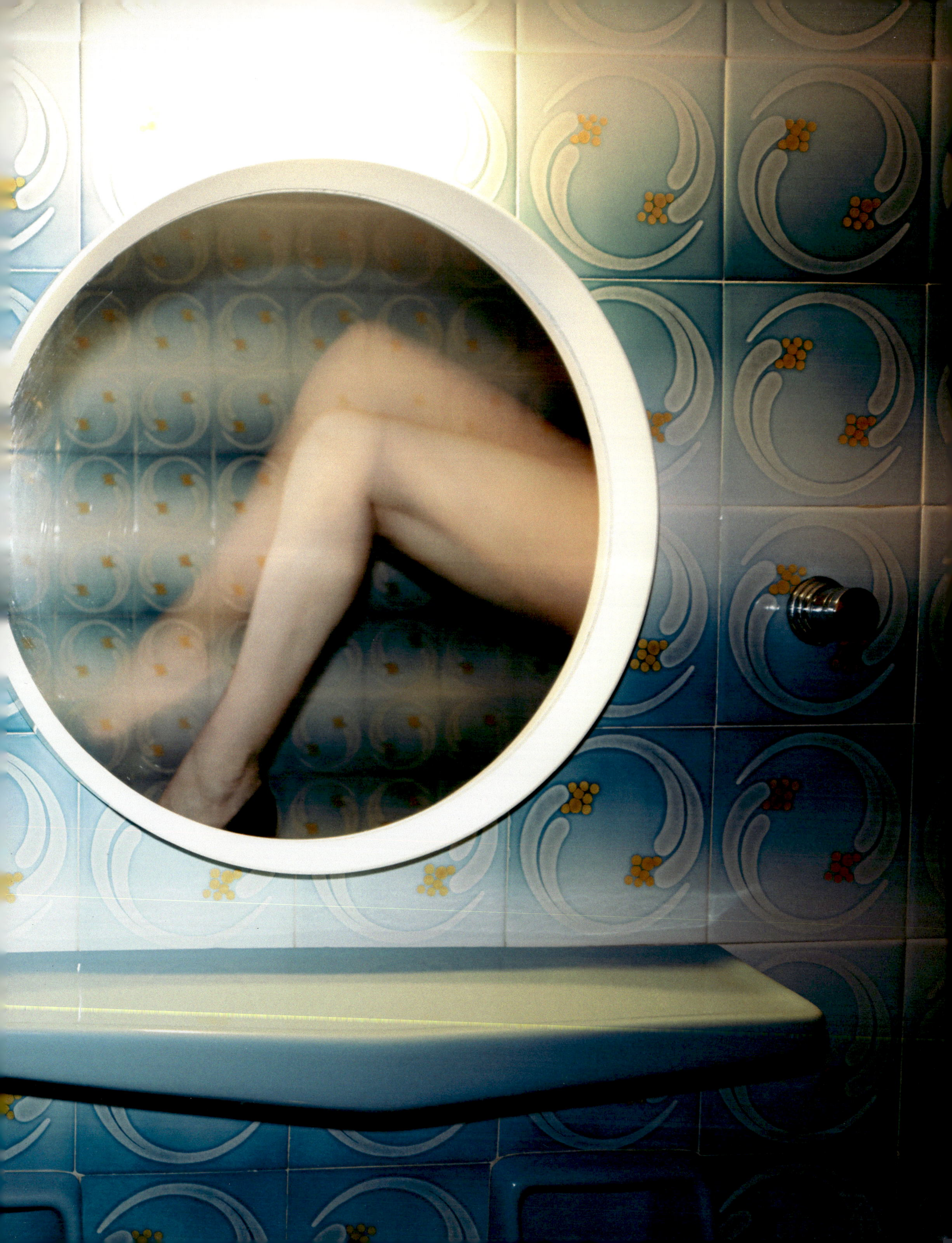

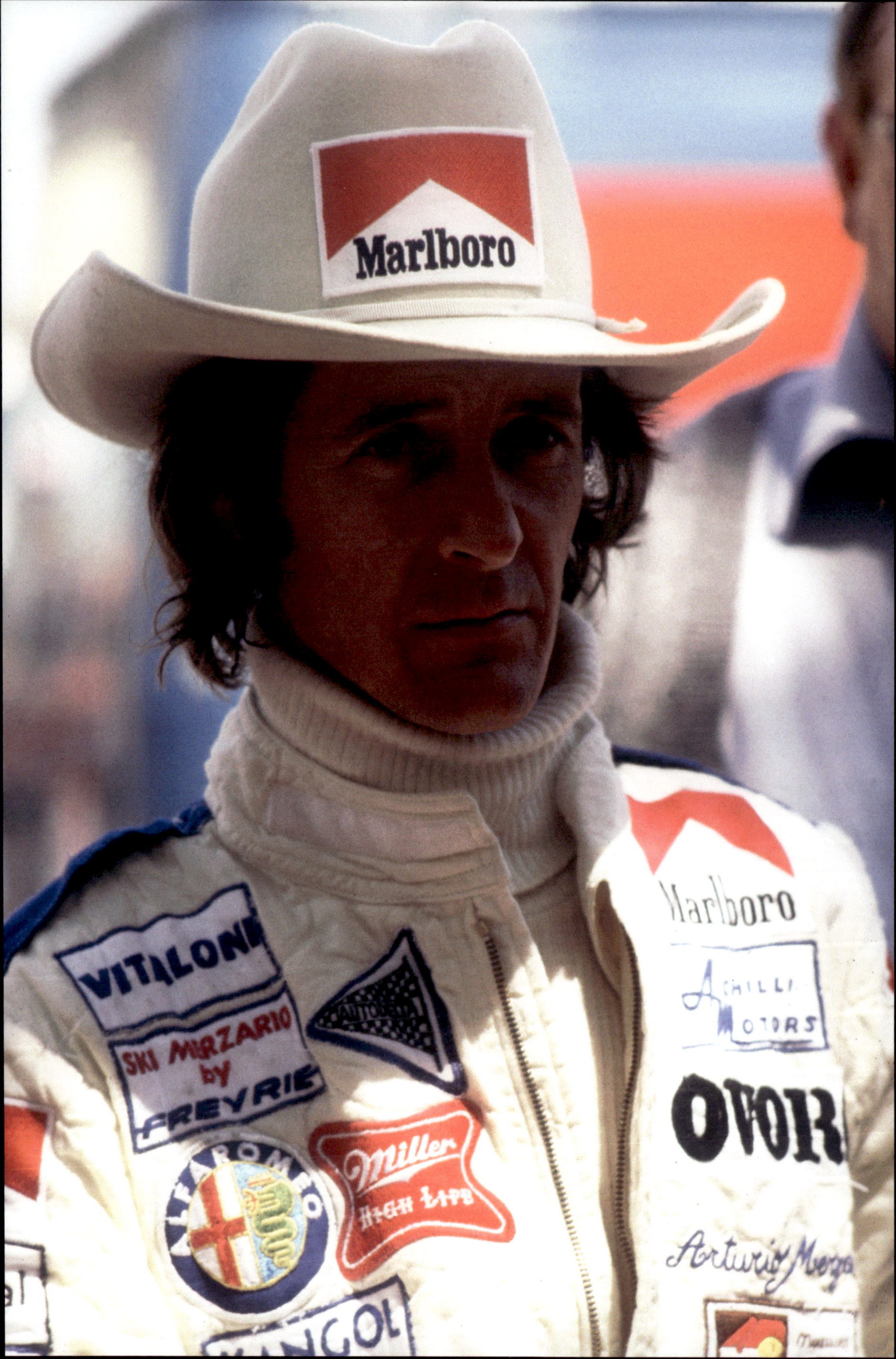

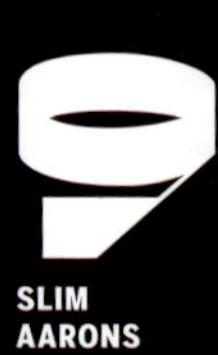
SLIM
AARONS

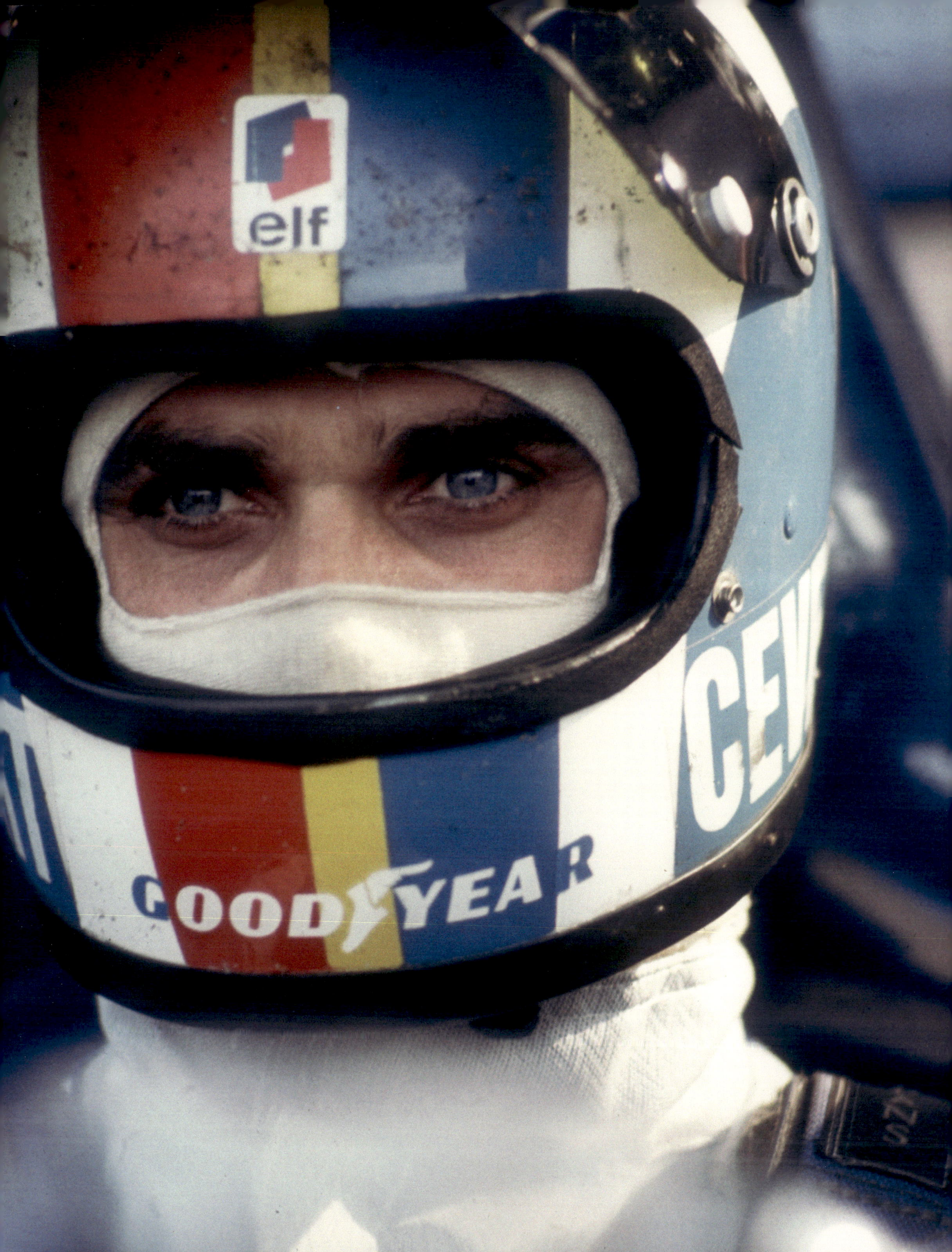
elf
GOODYEAR
CEV

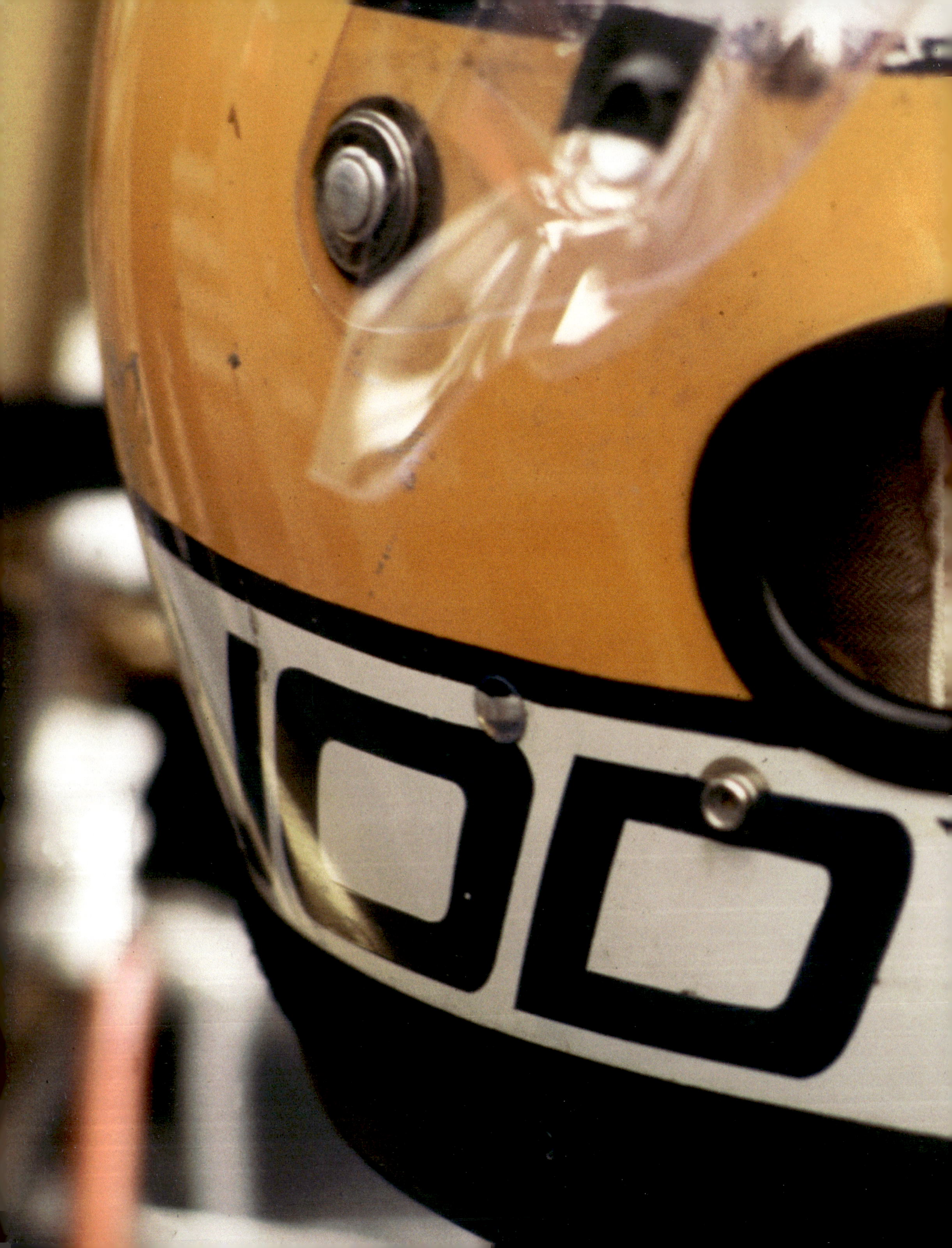

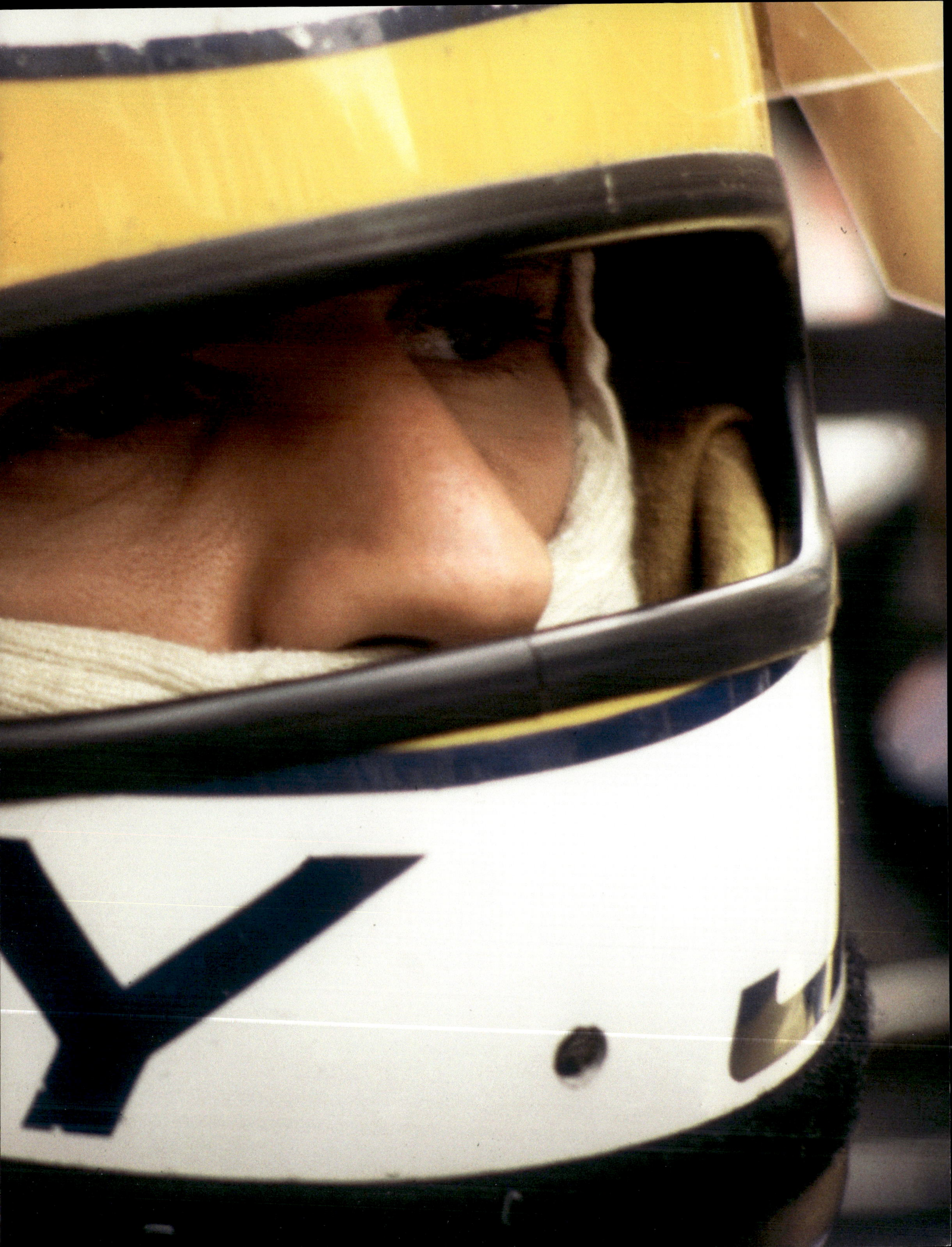

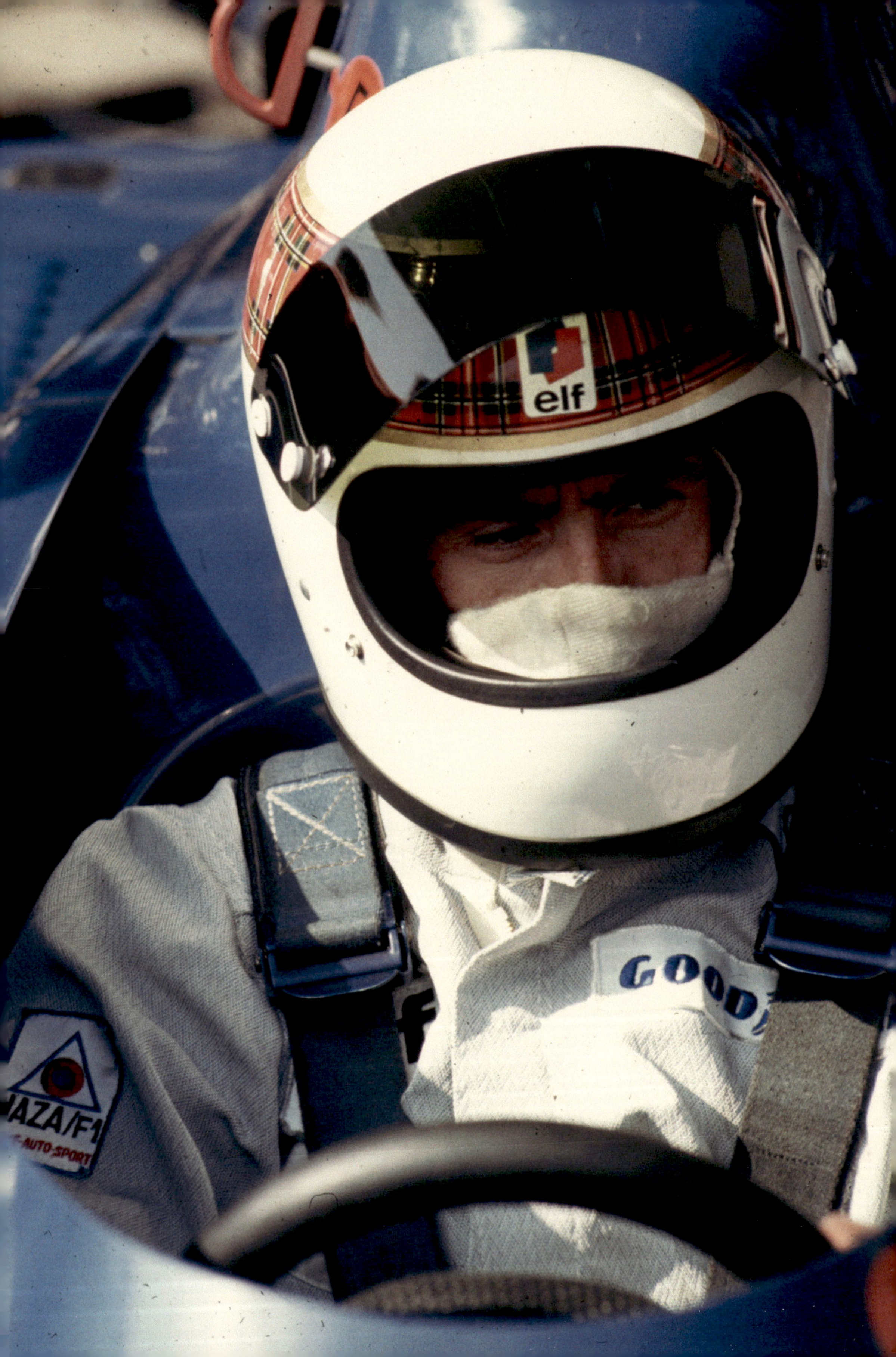
elf
GOOD
AZA/F1
-AUTO-SPORT

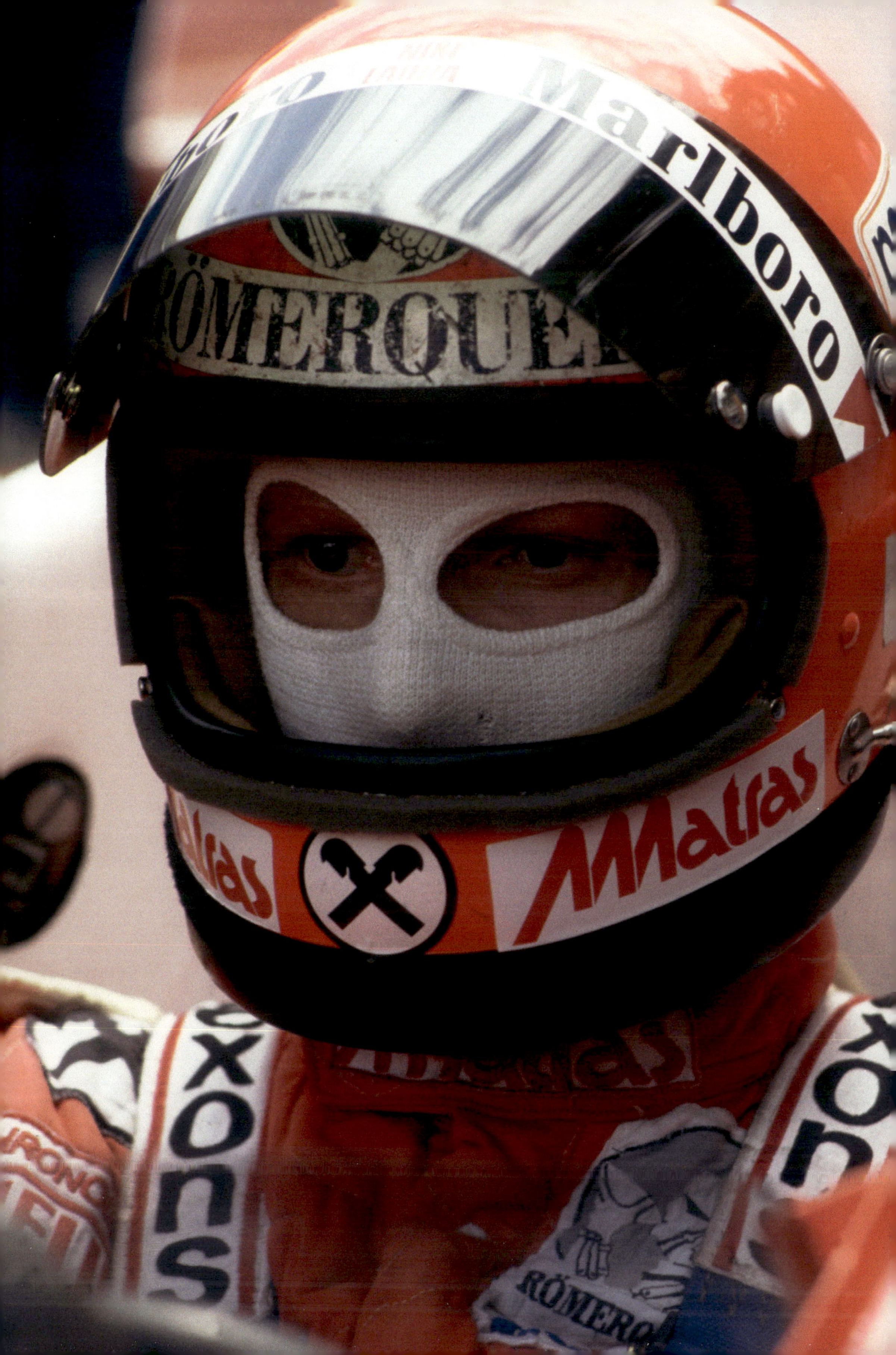
Marlboro
RÖMERQUELLE
Matras
Matras
Matras
RÖMERQ

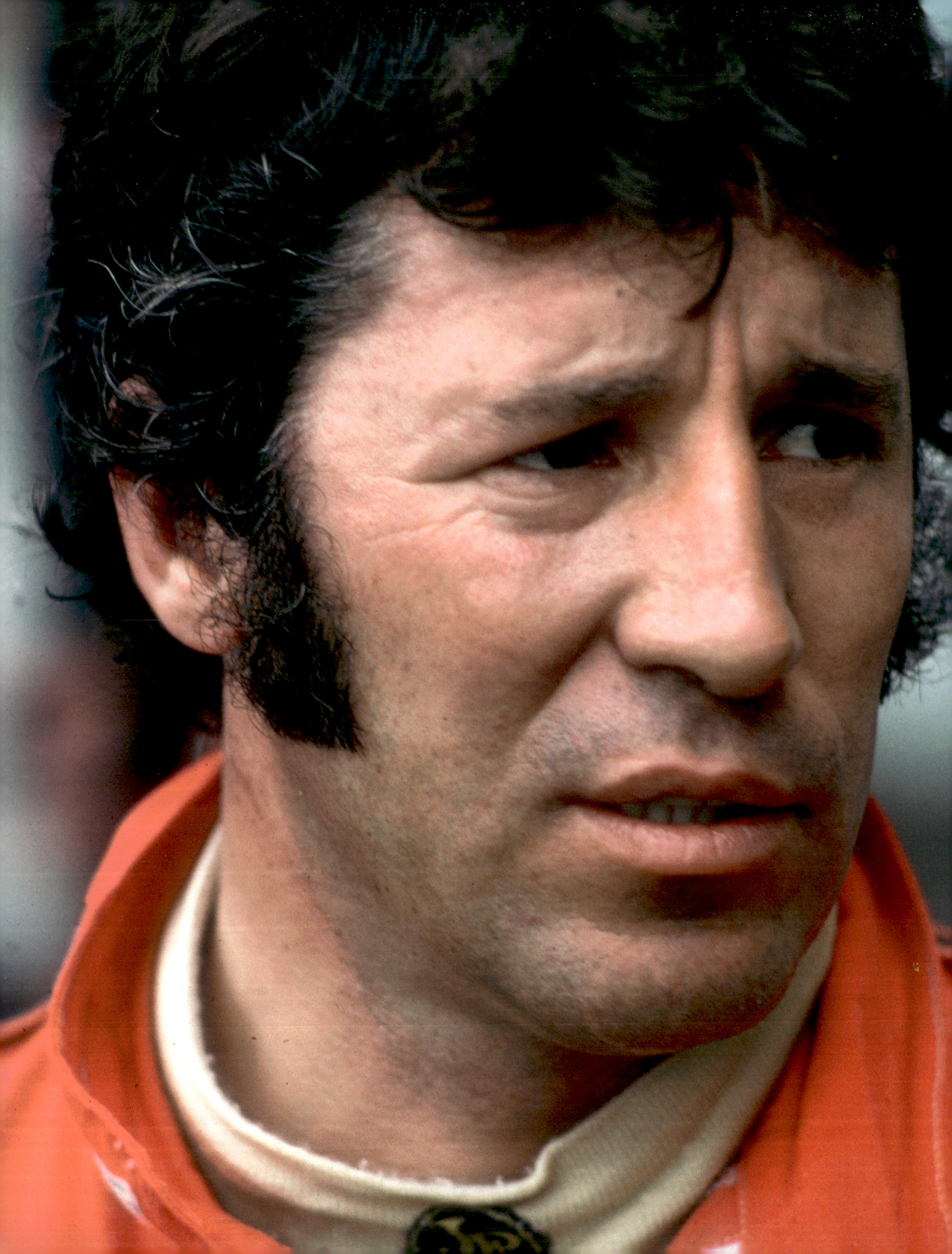

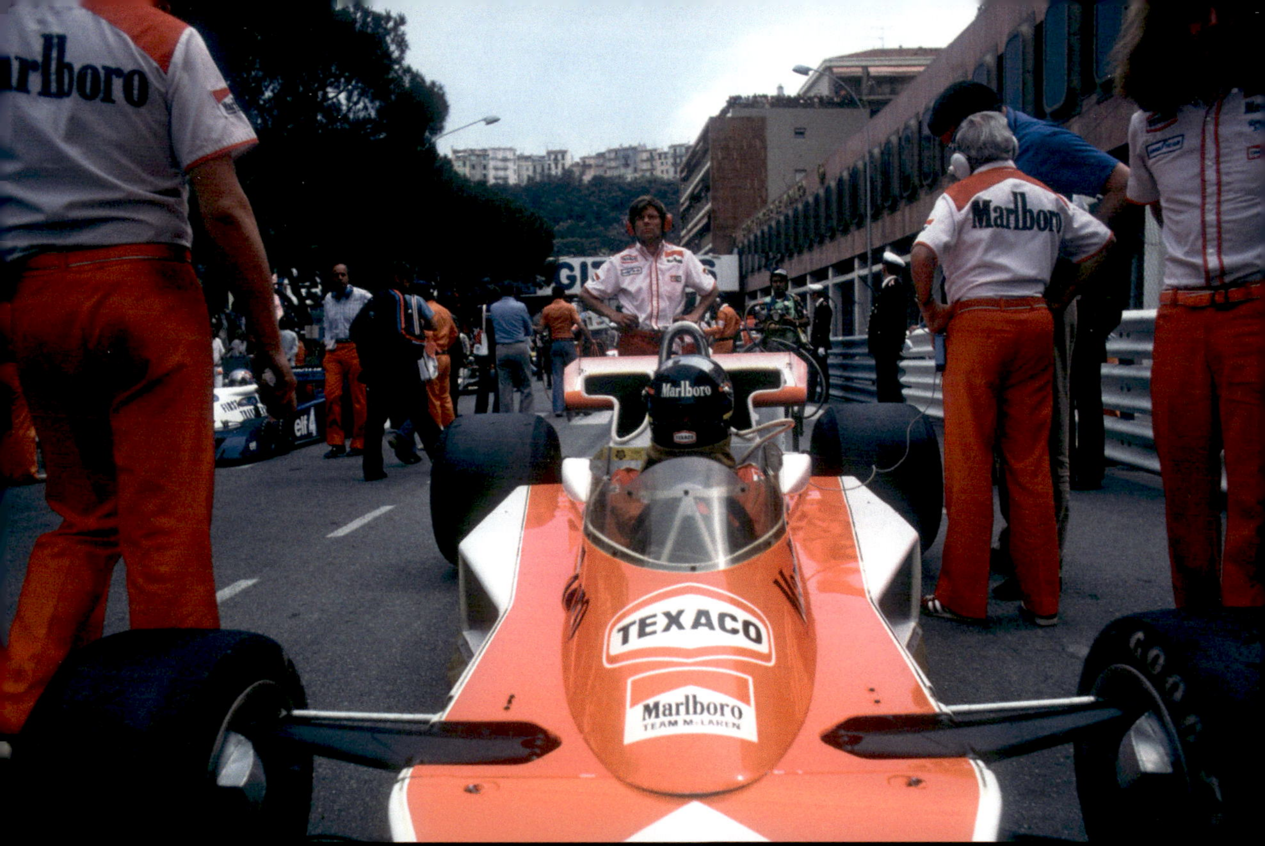

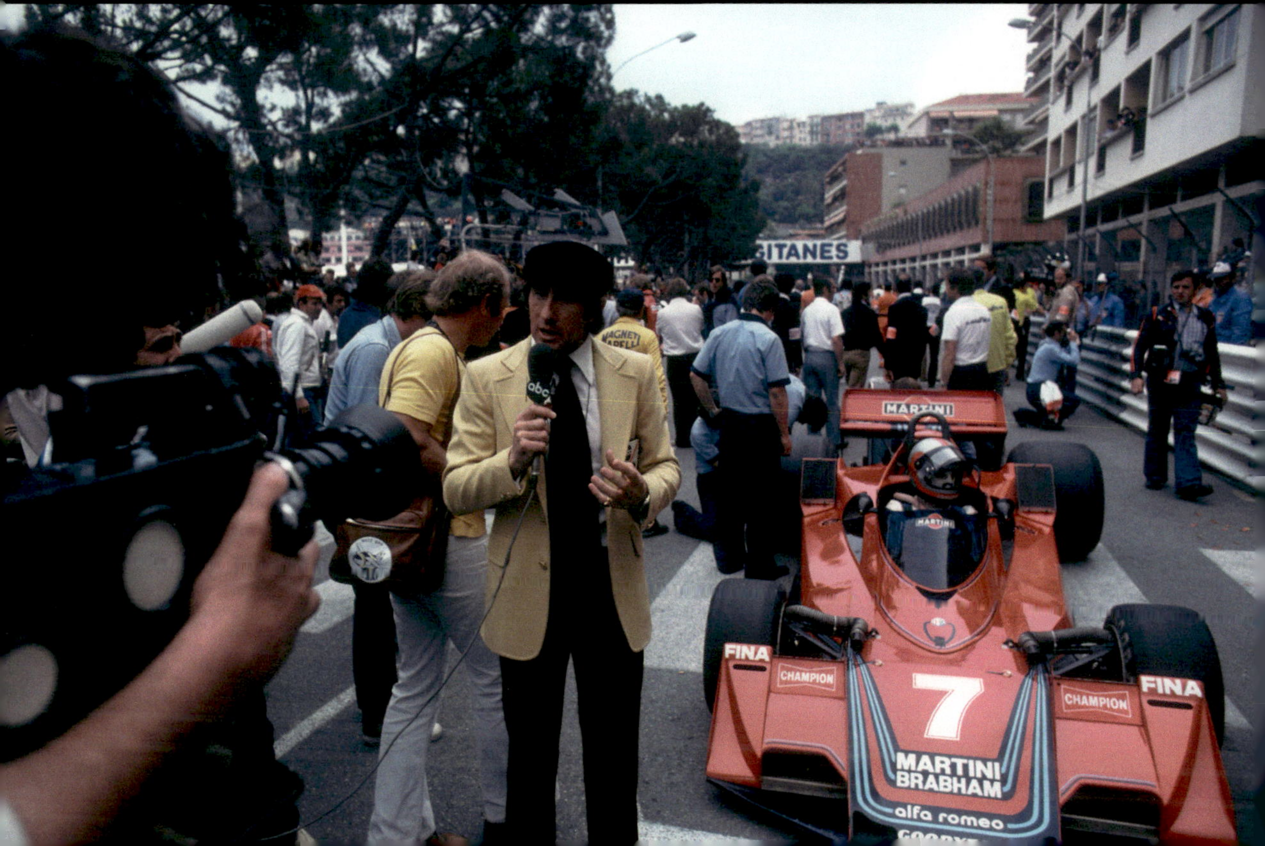

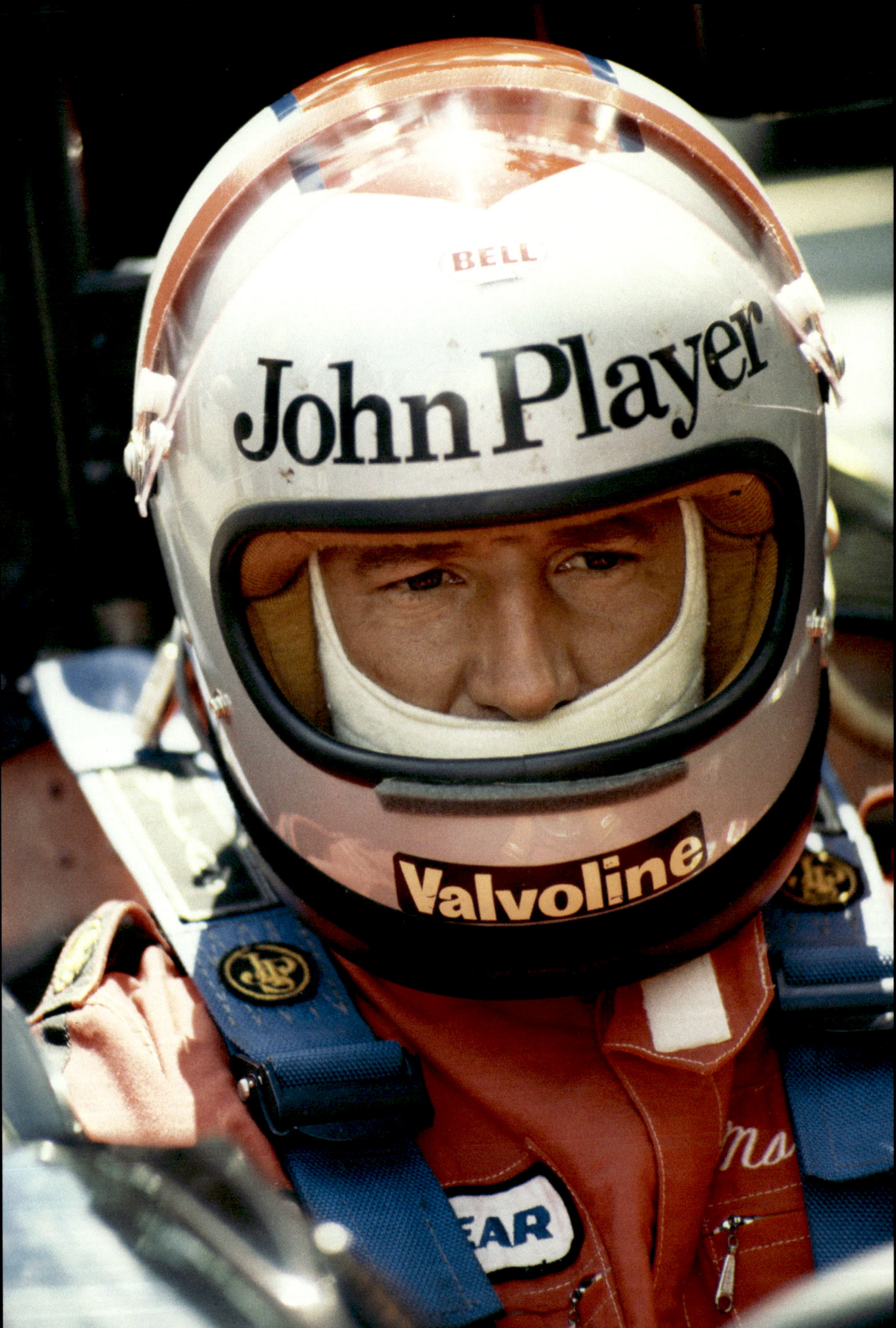

BELL
John Player
Valvoline
GEAR

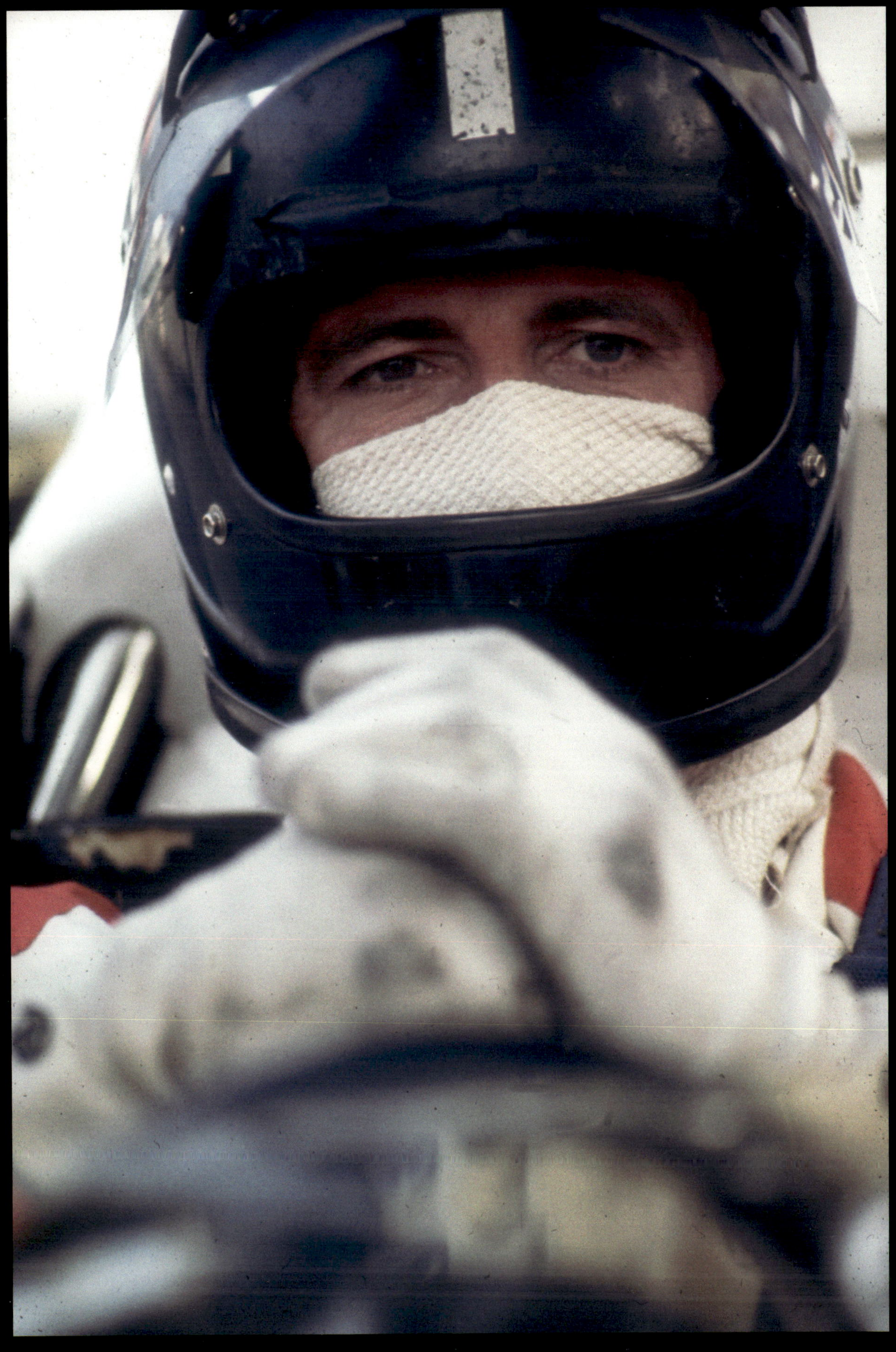

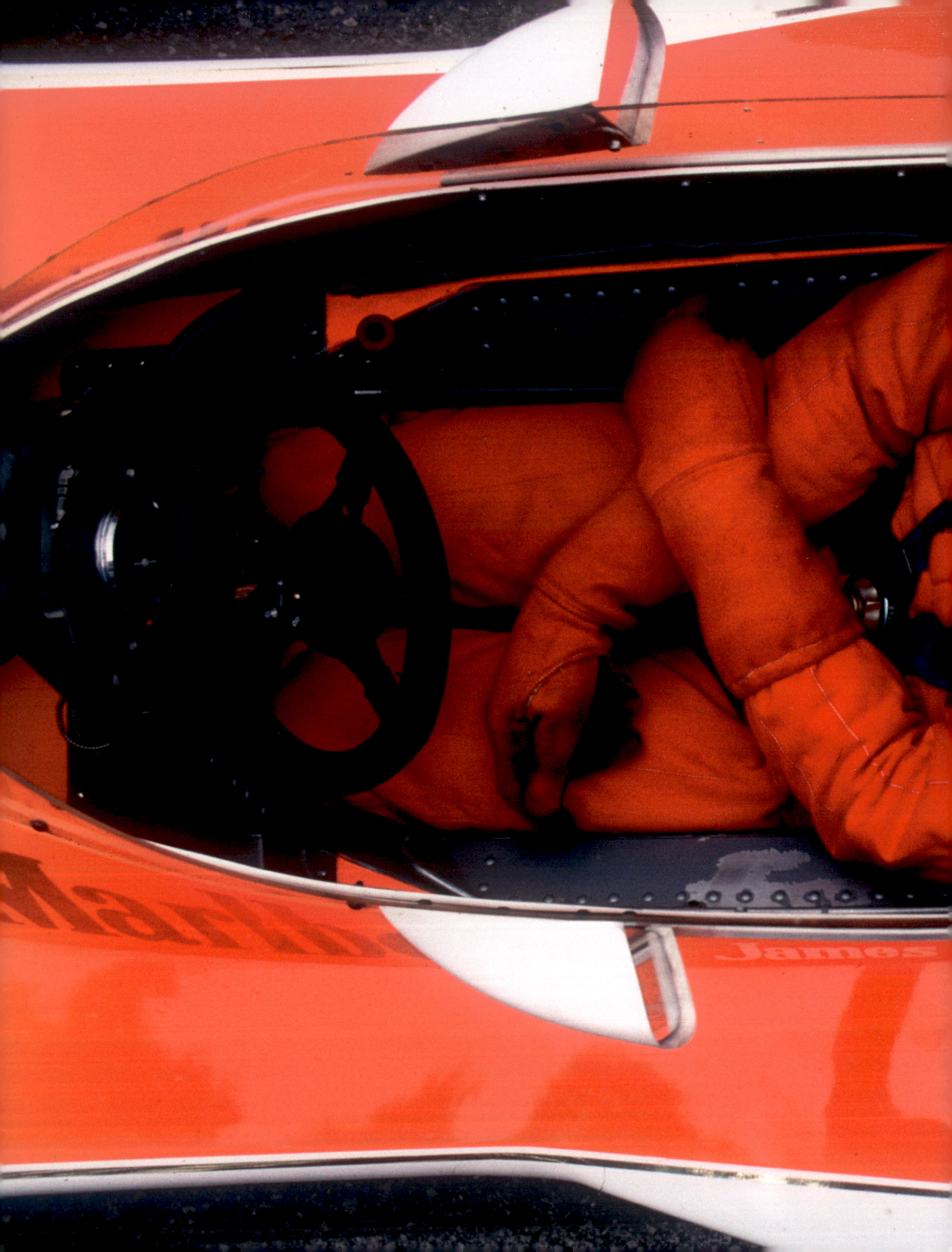
Marlboro
James

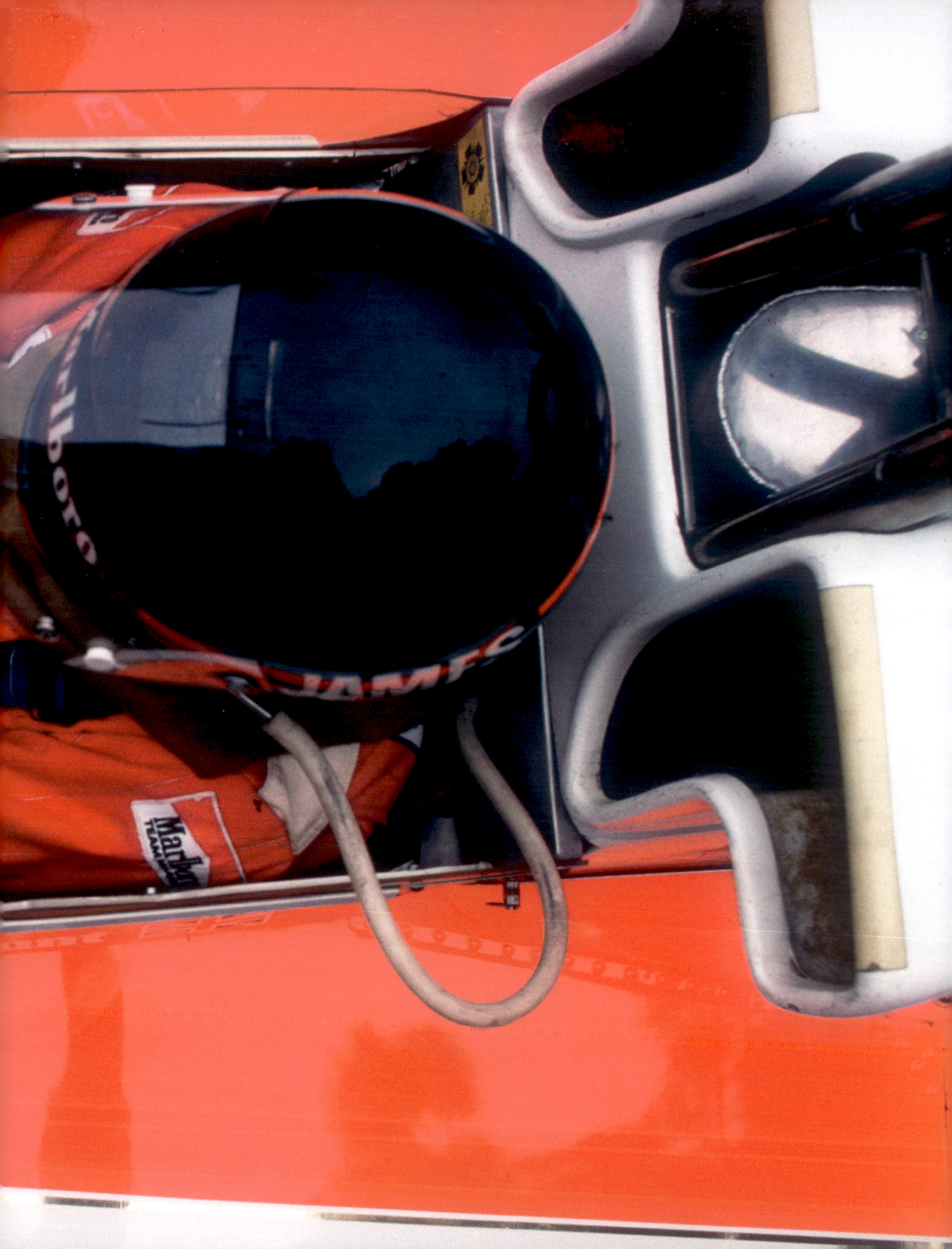

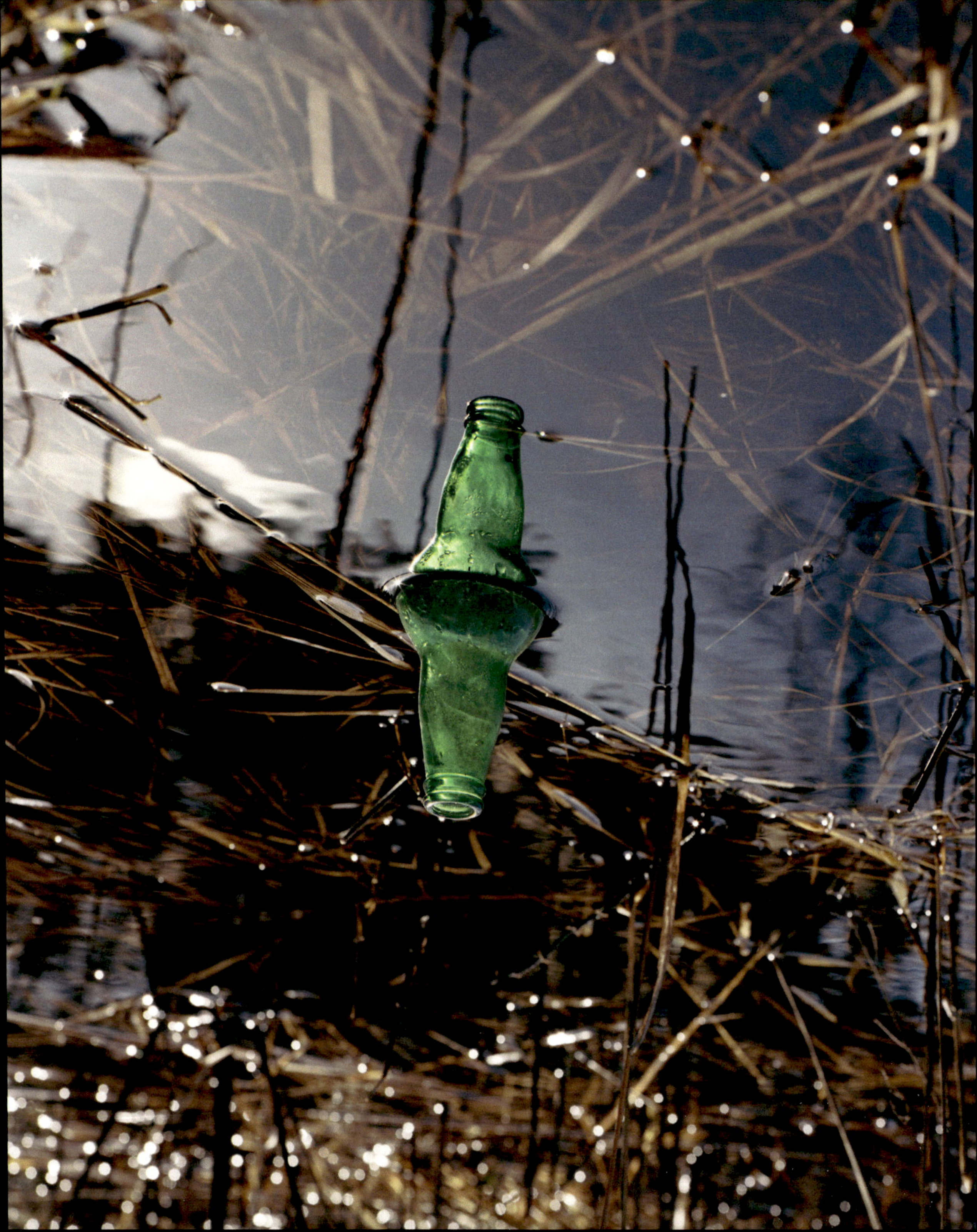

KUBA
RYNIEWICZ

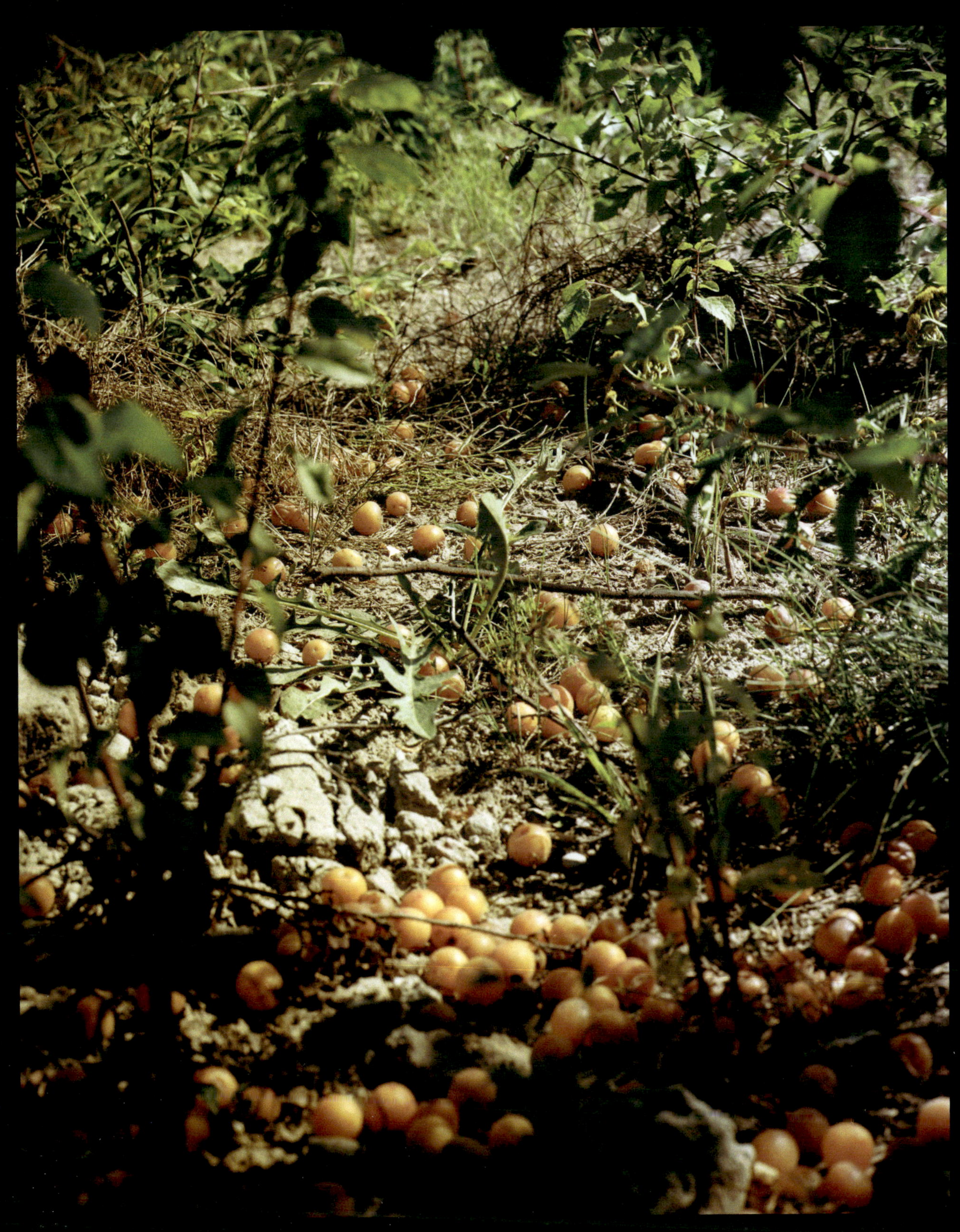

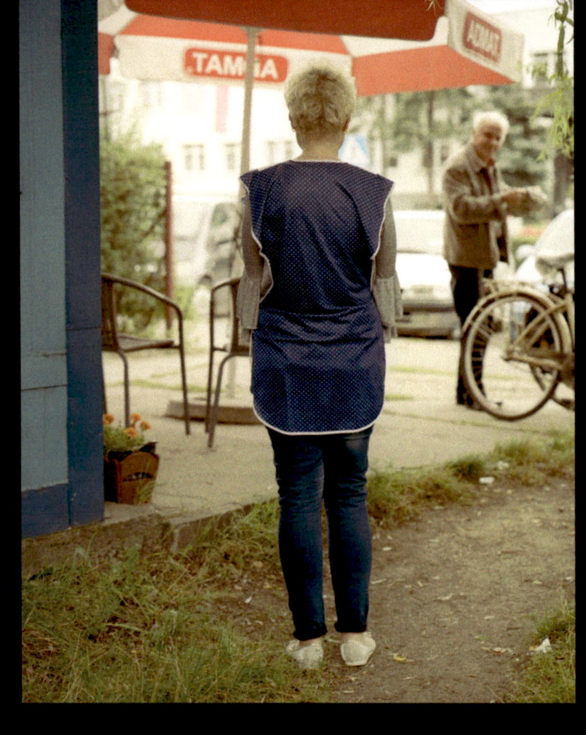
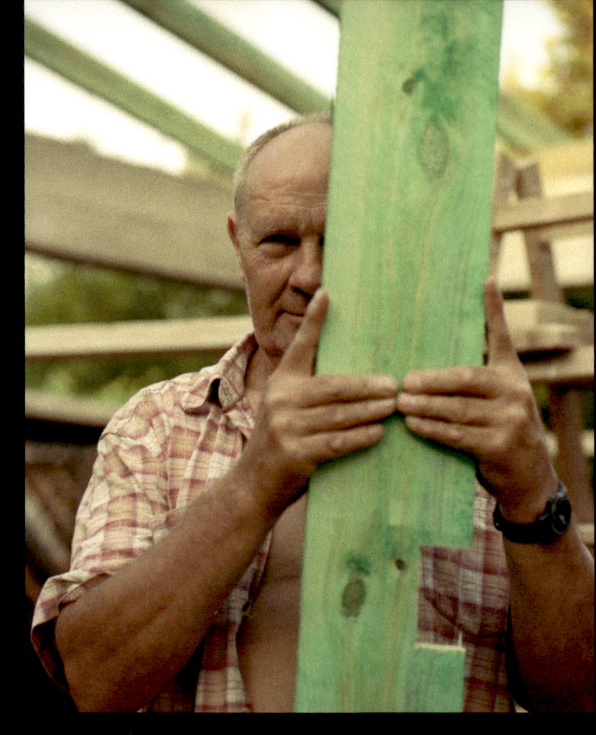
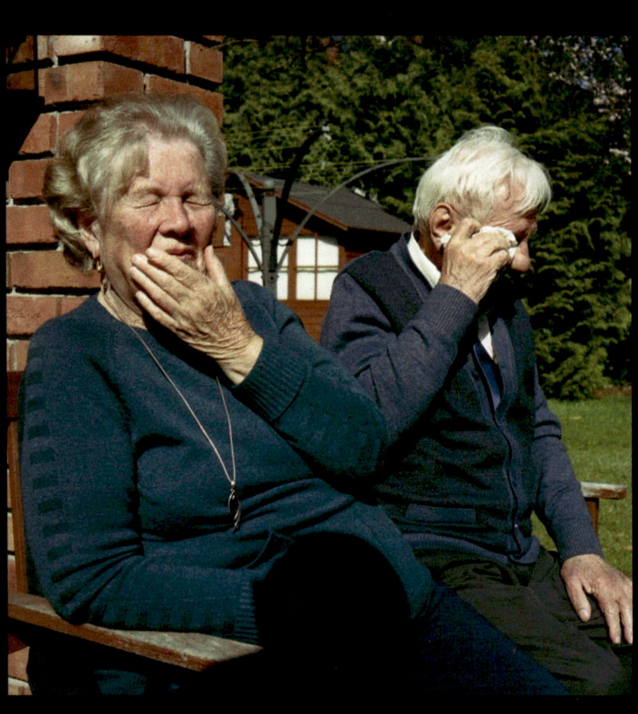
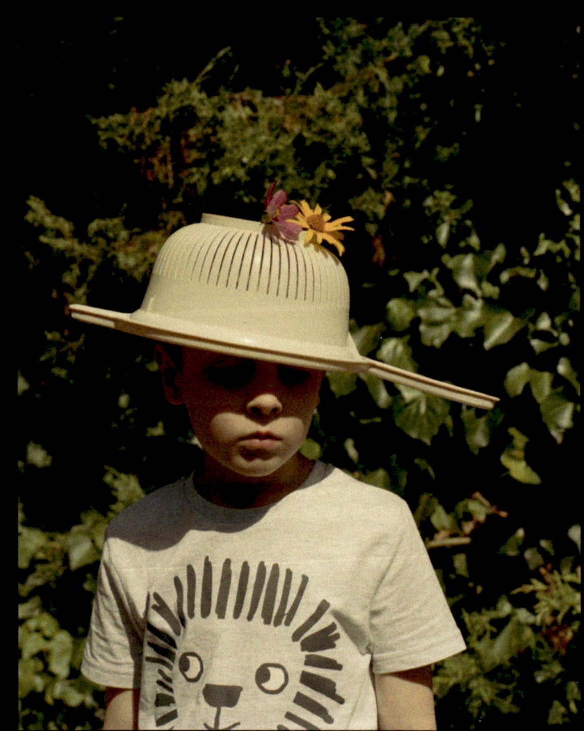

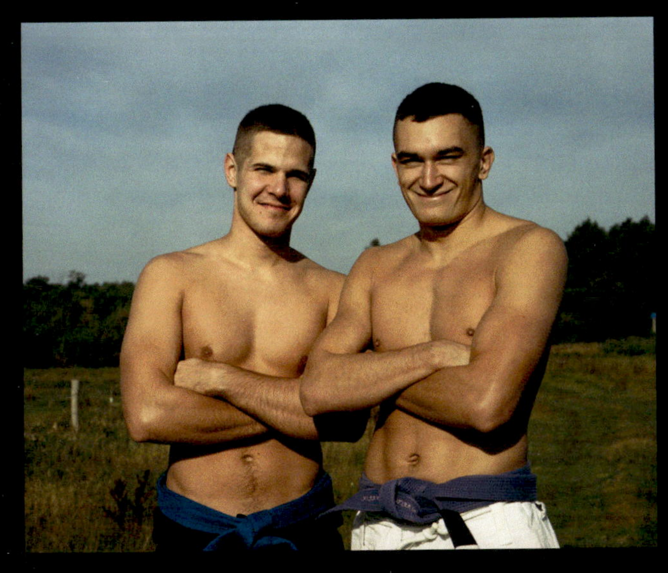

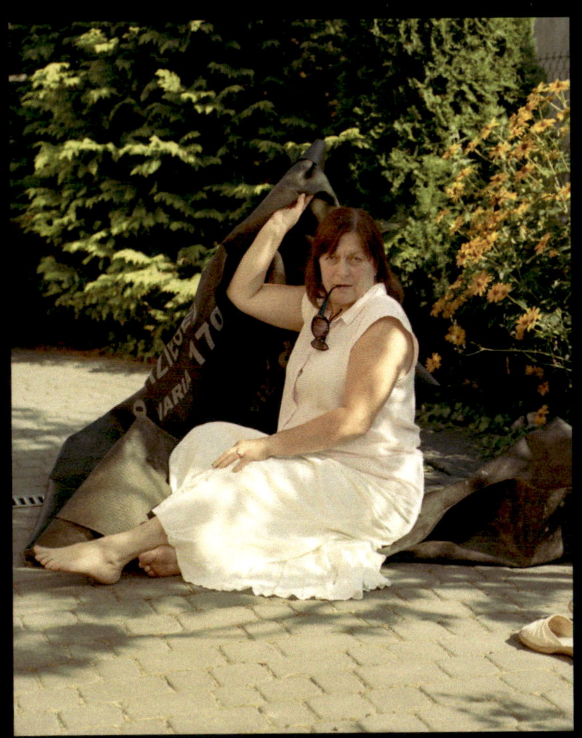

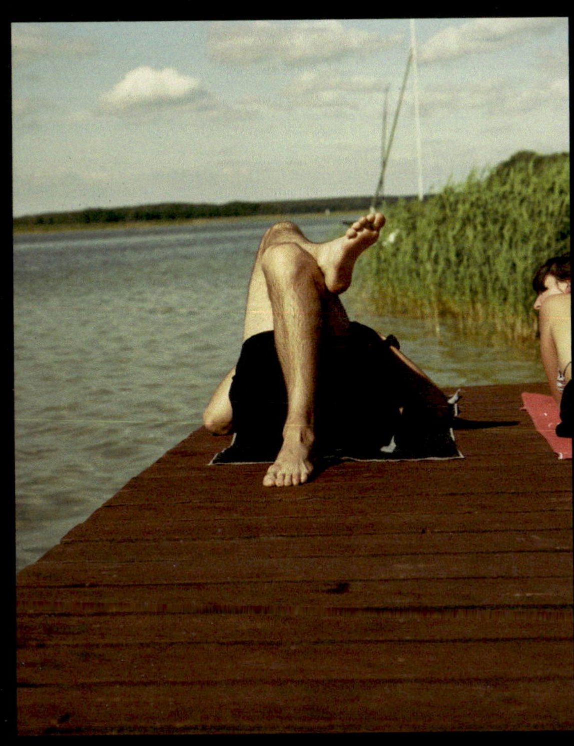

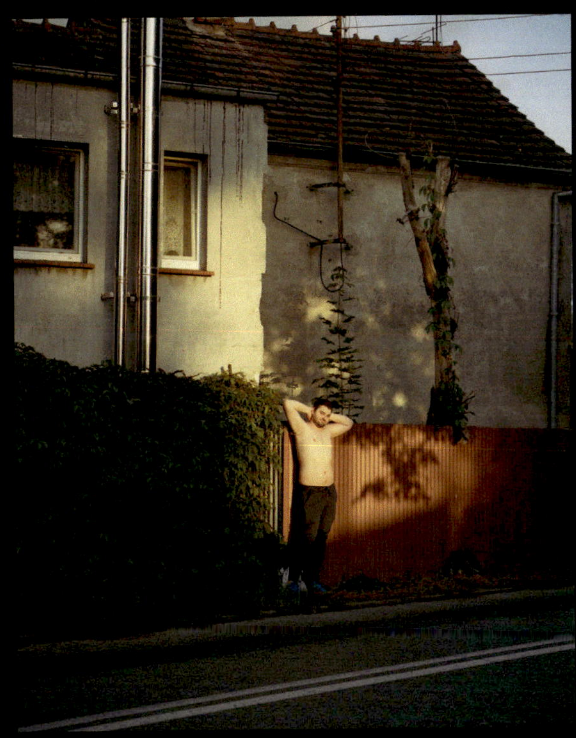

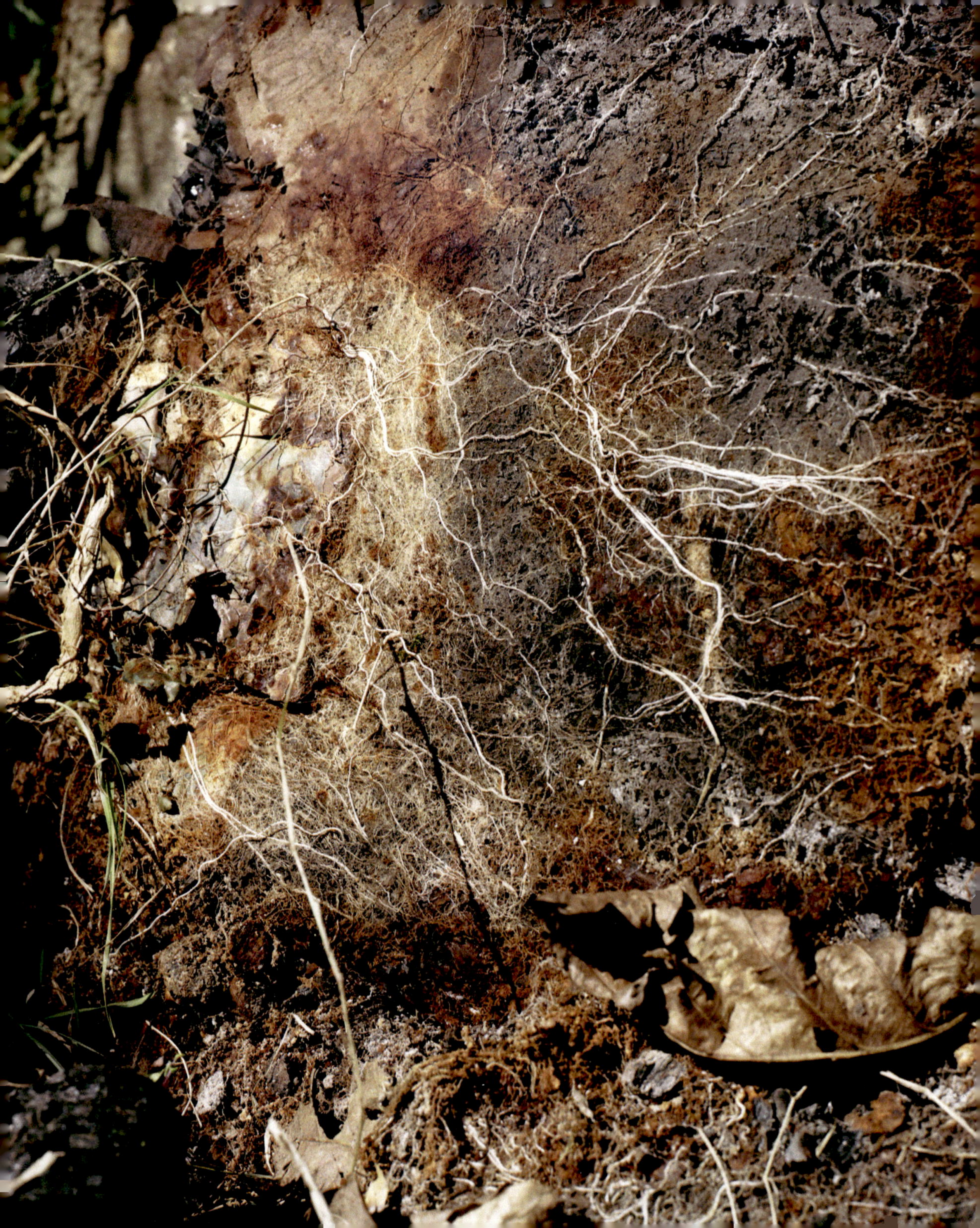

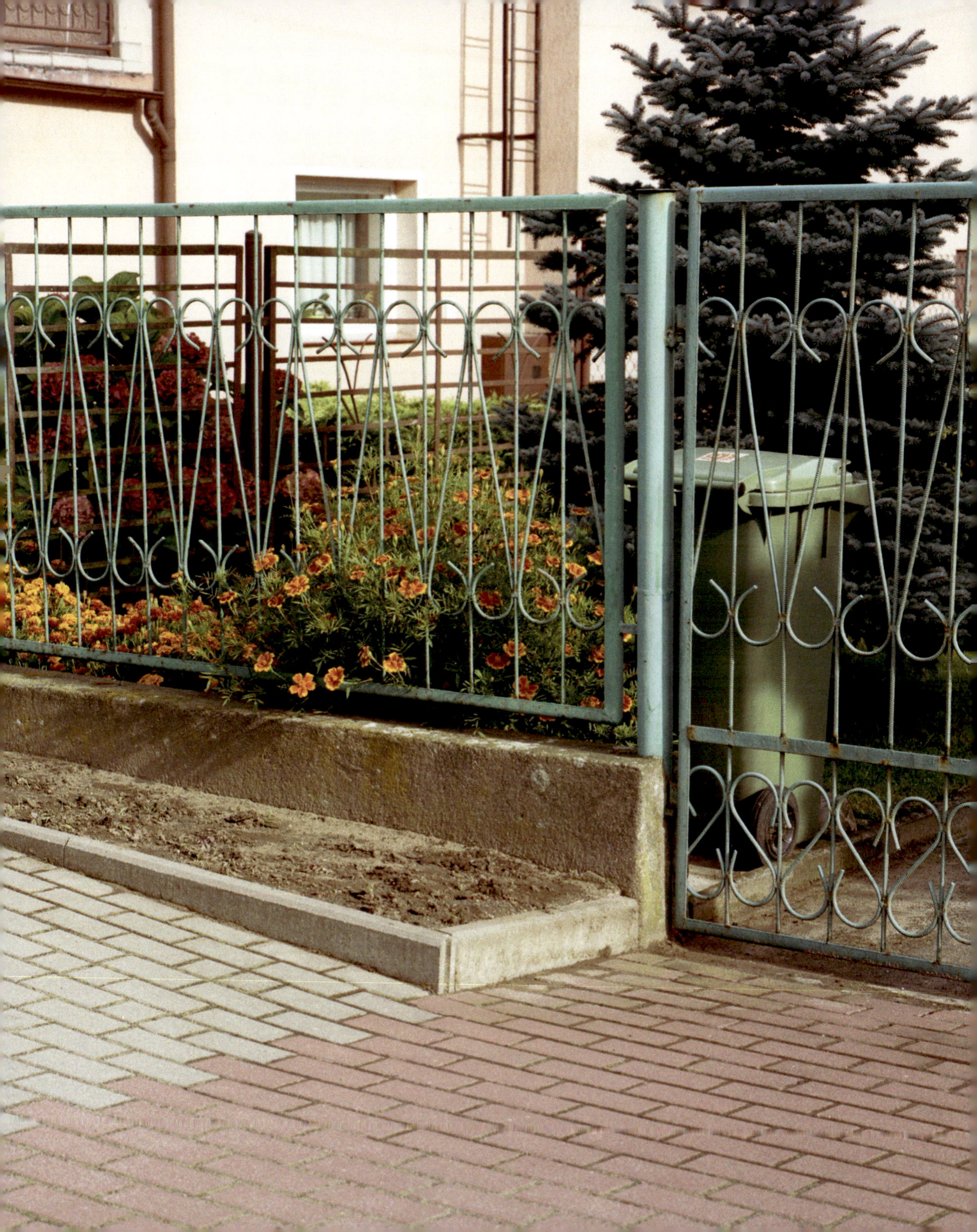

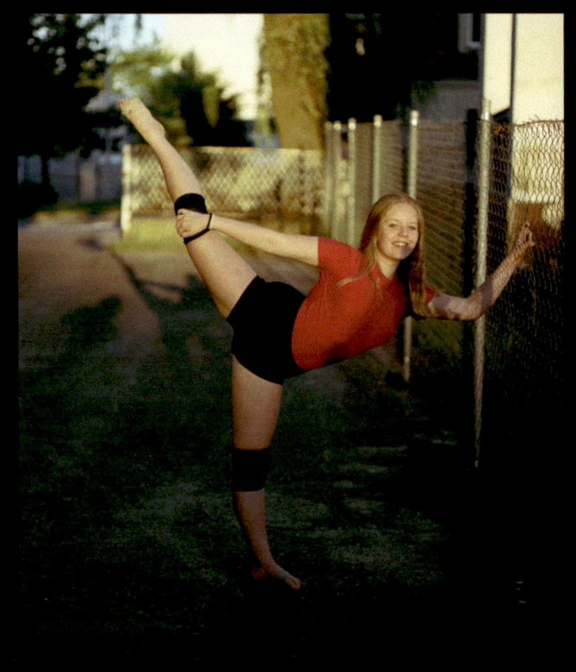
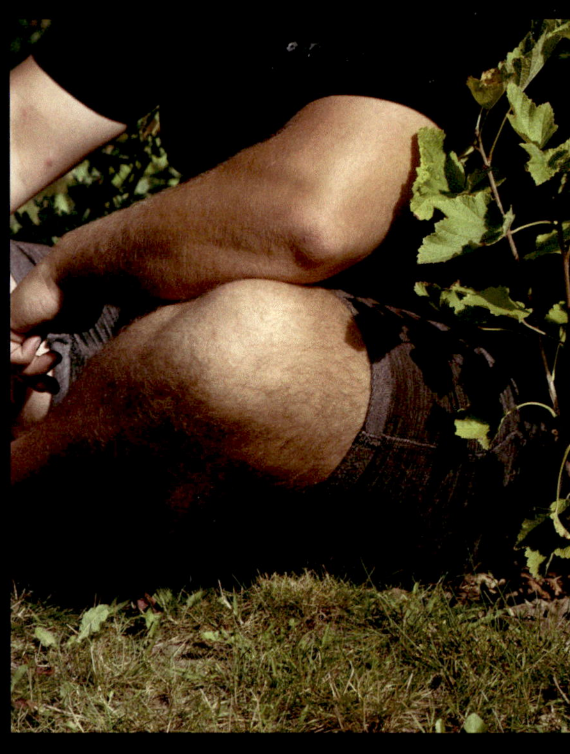
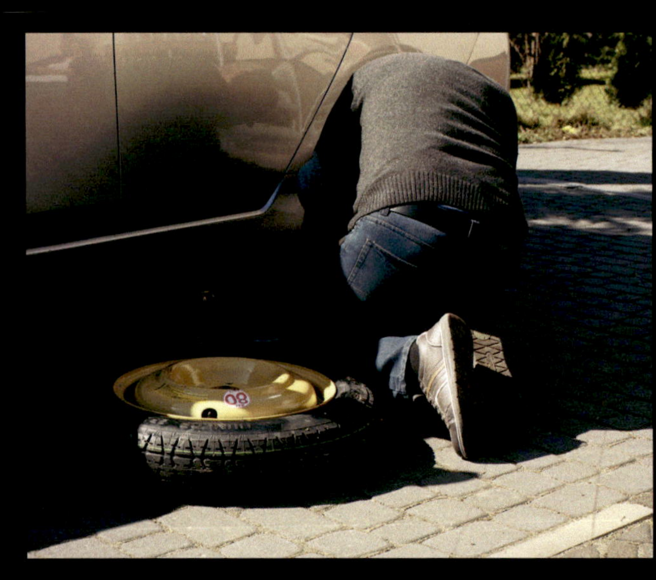
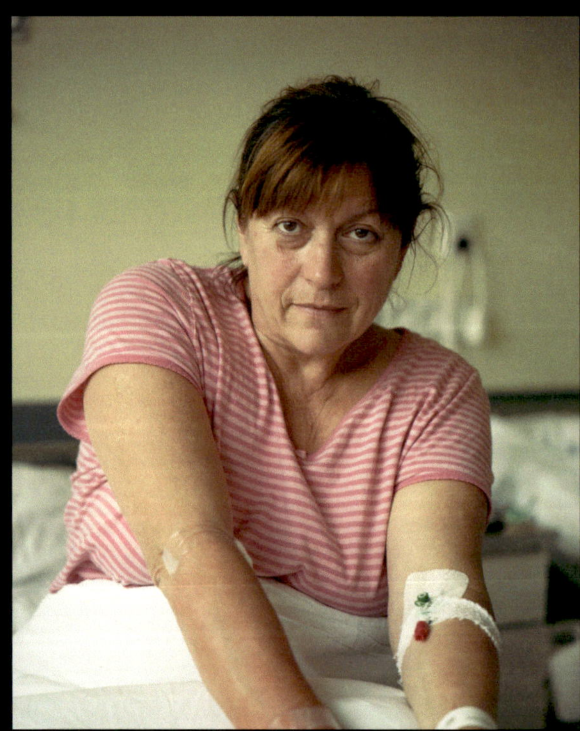

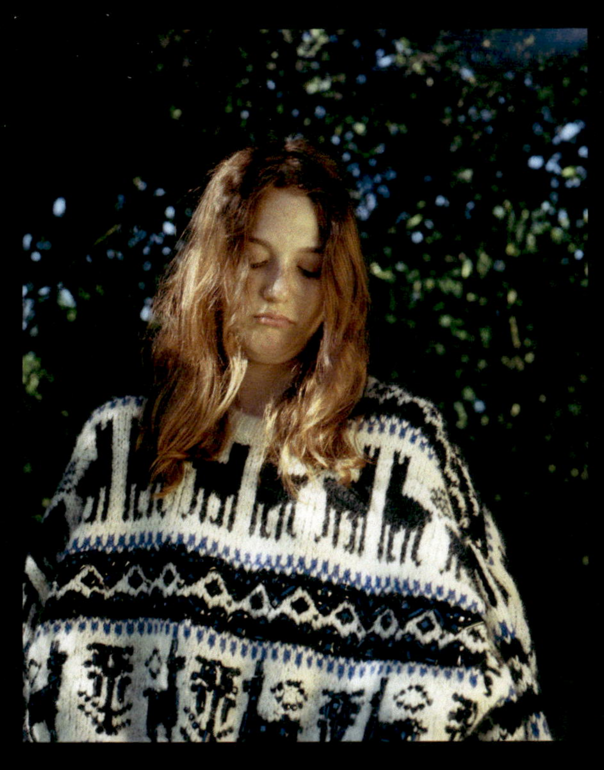
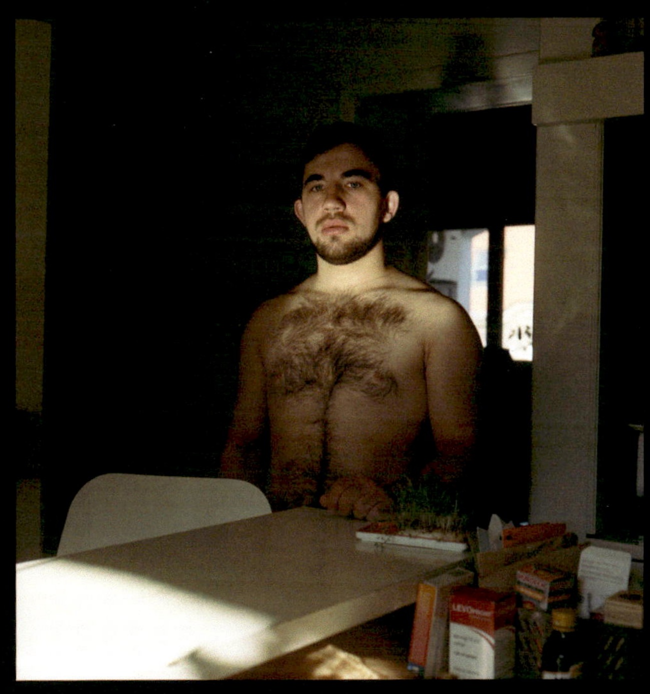
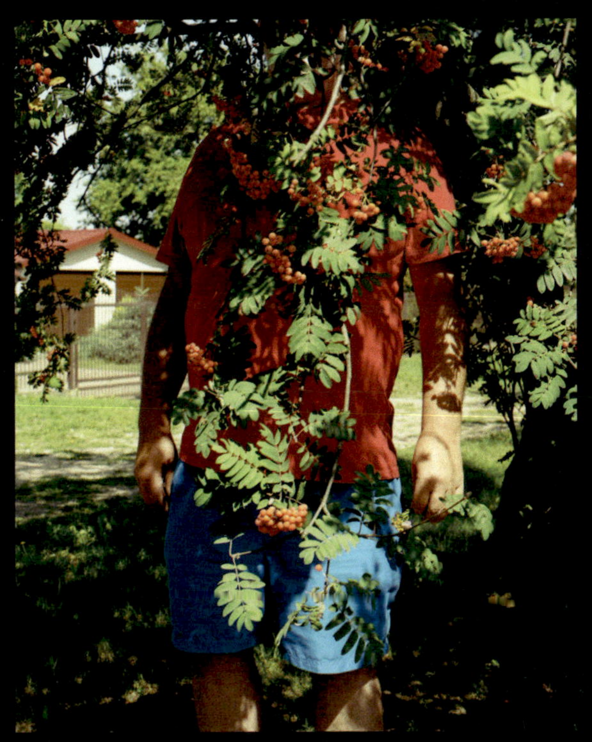
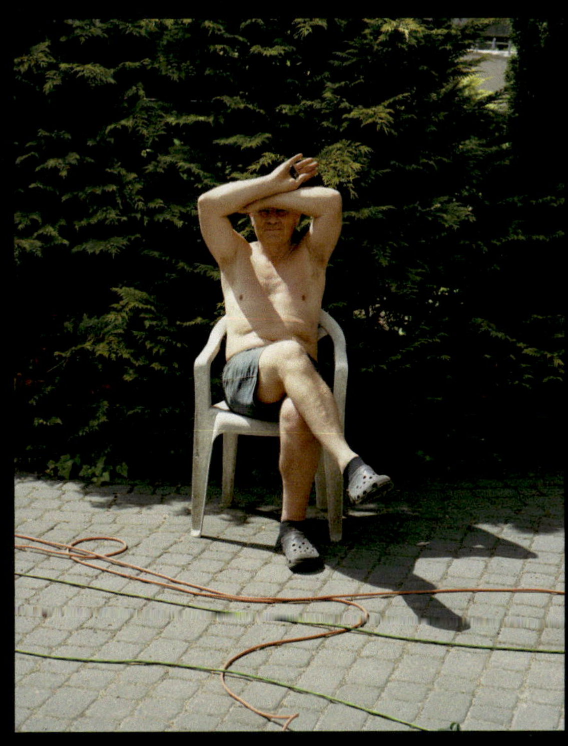

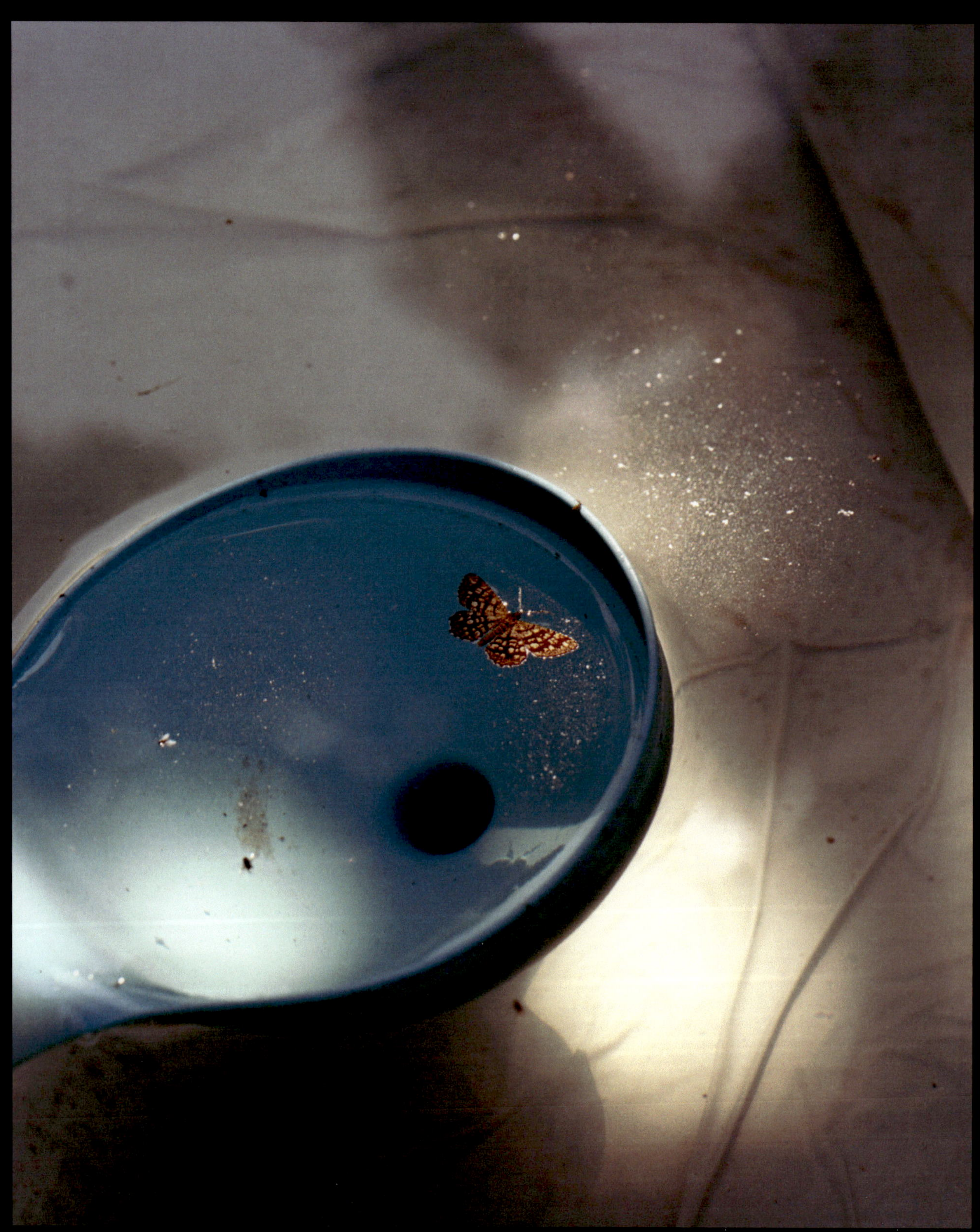

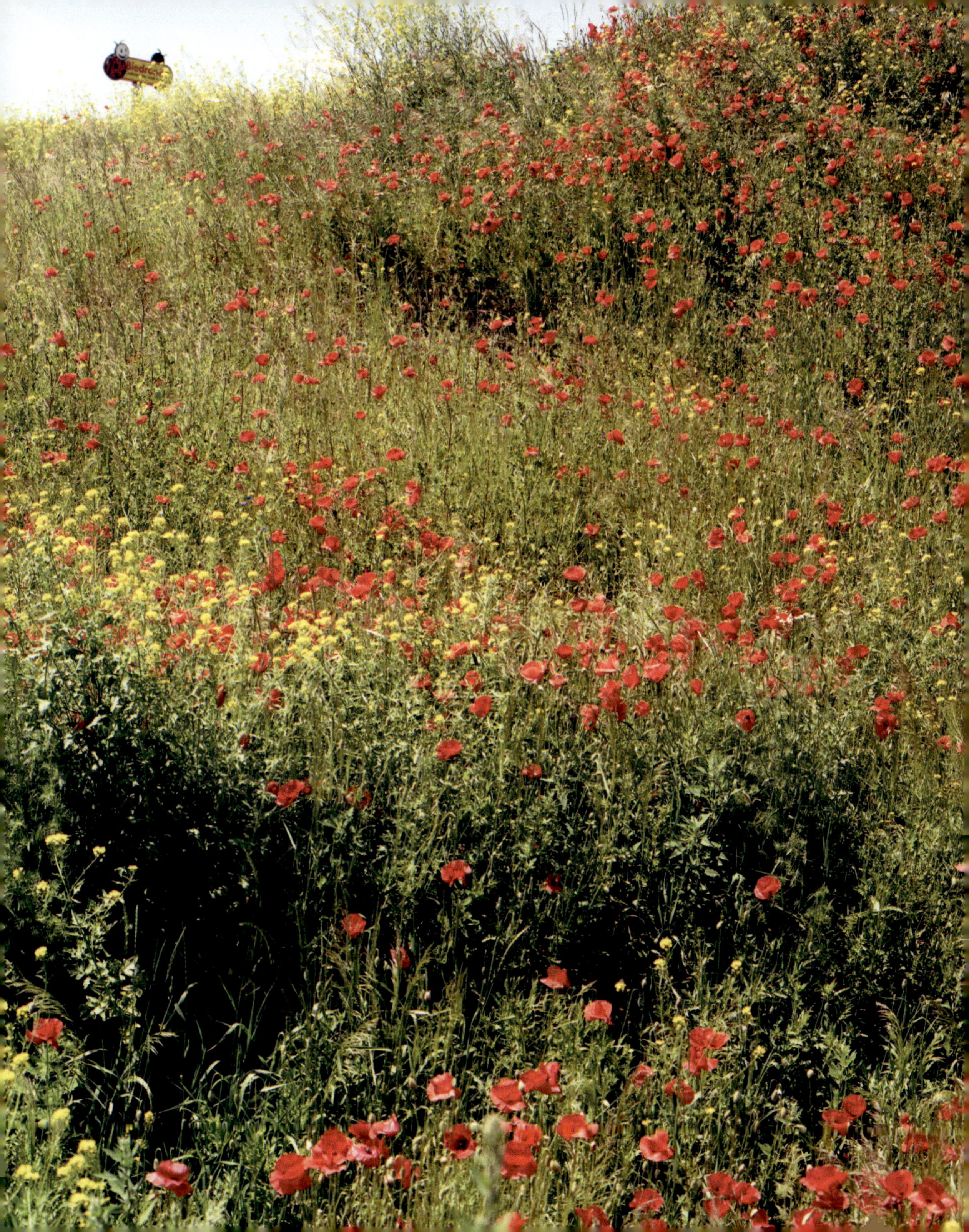

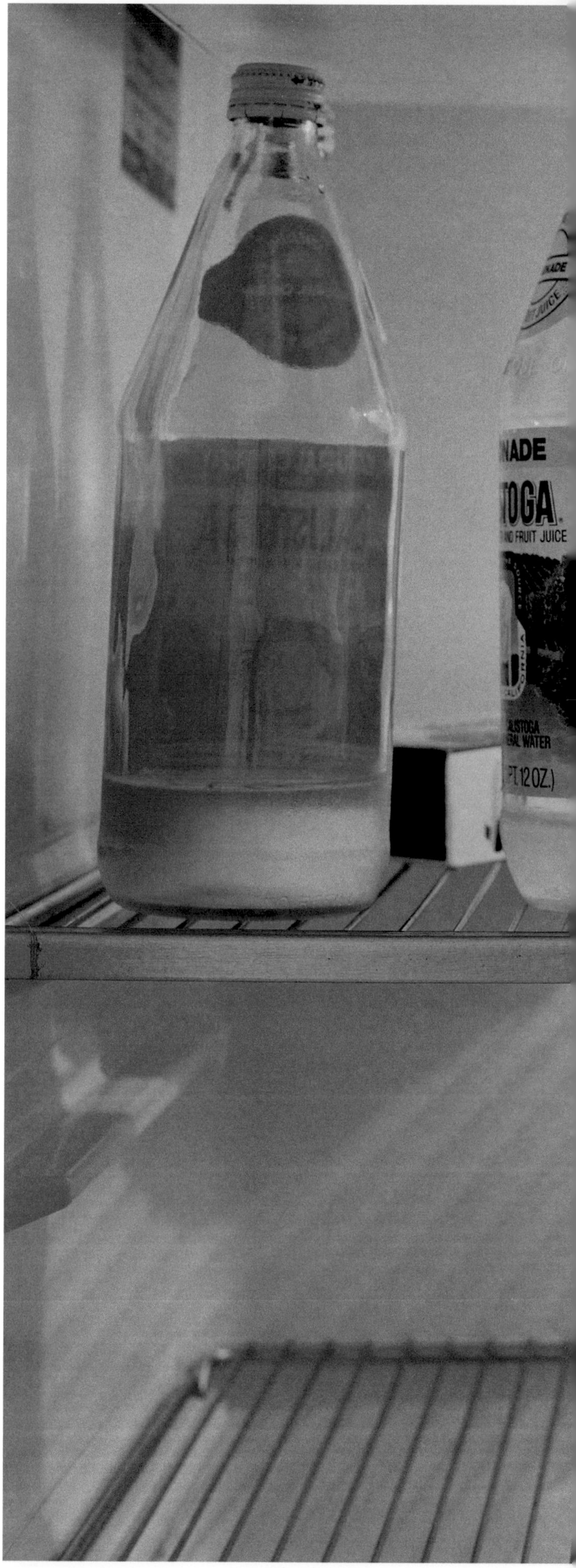

CATHERINE WAGNER, *CHRISTINE T.*, 1991

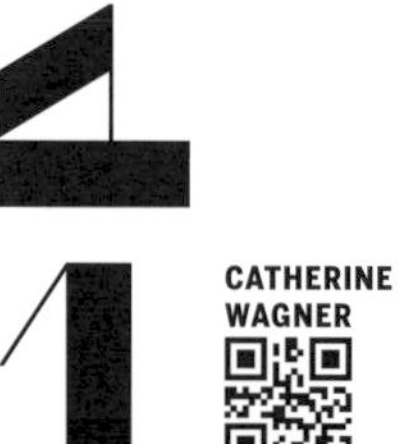

**CATHERINE
WAGNER**

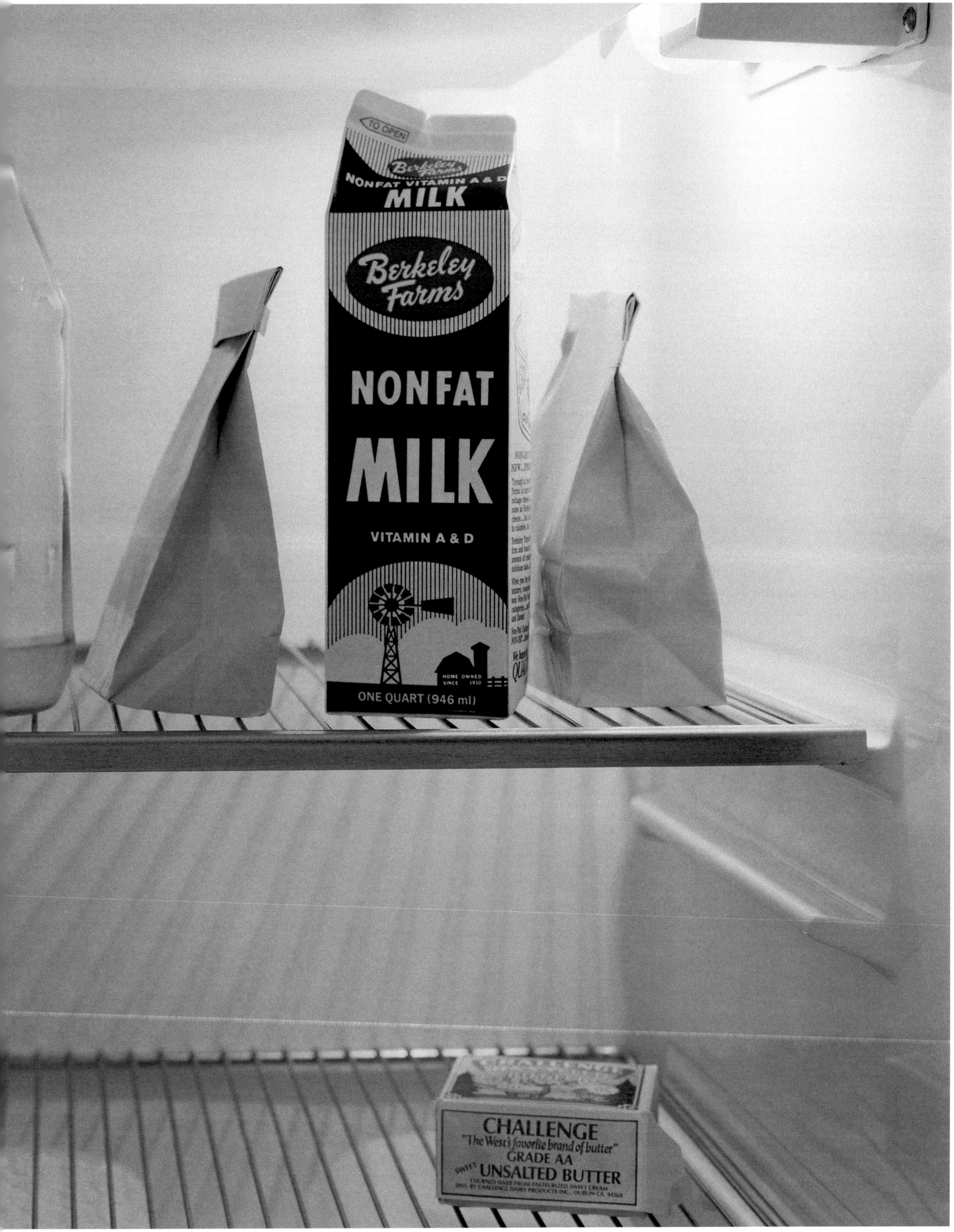

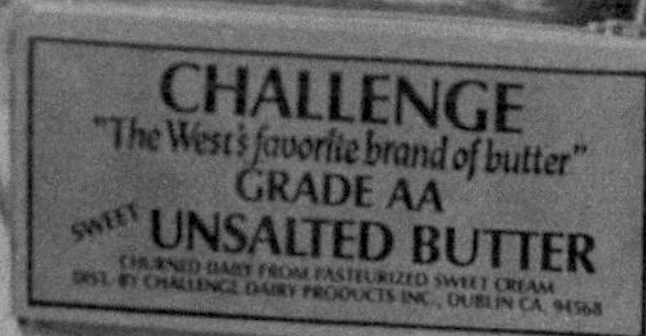

CHALLENGE
"The West's favorite brand of butter"
GRADE AA
SWEET UNSALTED BUTTER
CHURNED DAIRY FROM PASTEURIZED SWEET CREAM
DIST. BY CHALLENGE DAIRY PRODUCTS INC., DUBLIN CA. 94568

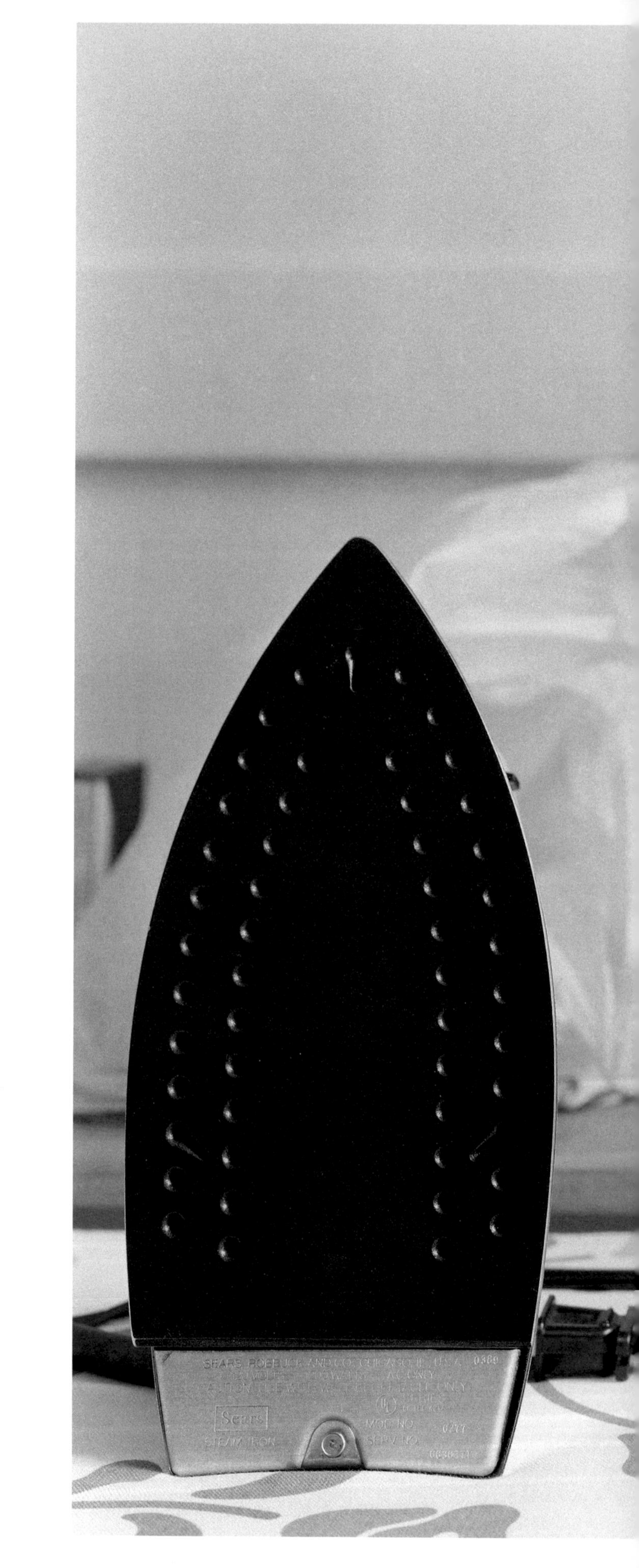

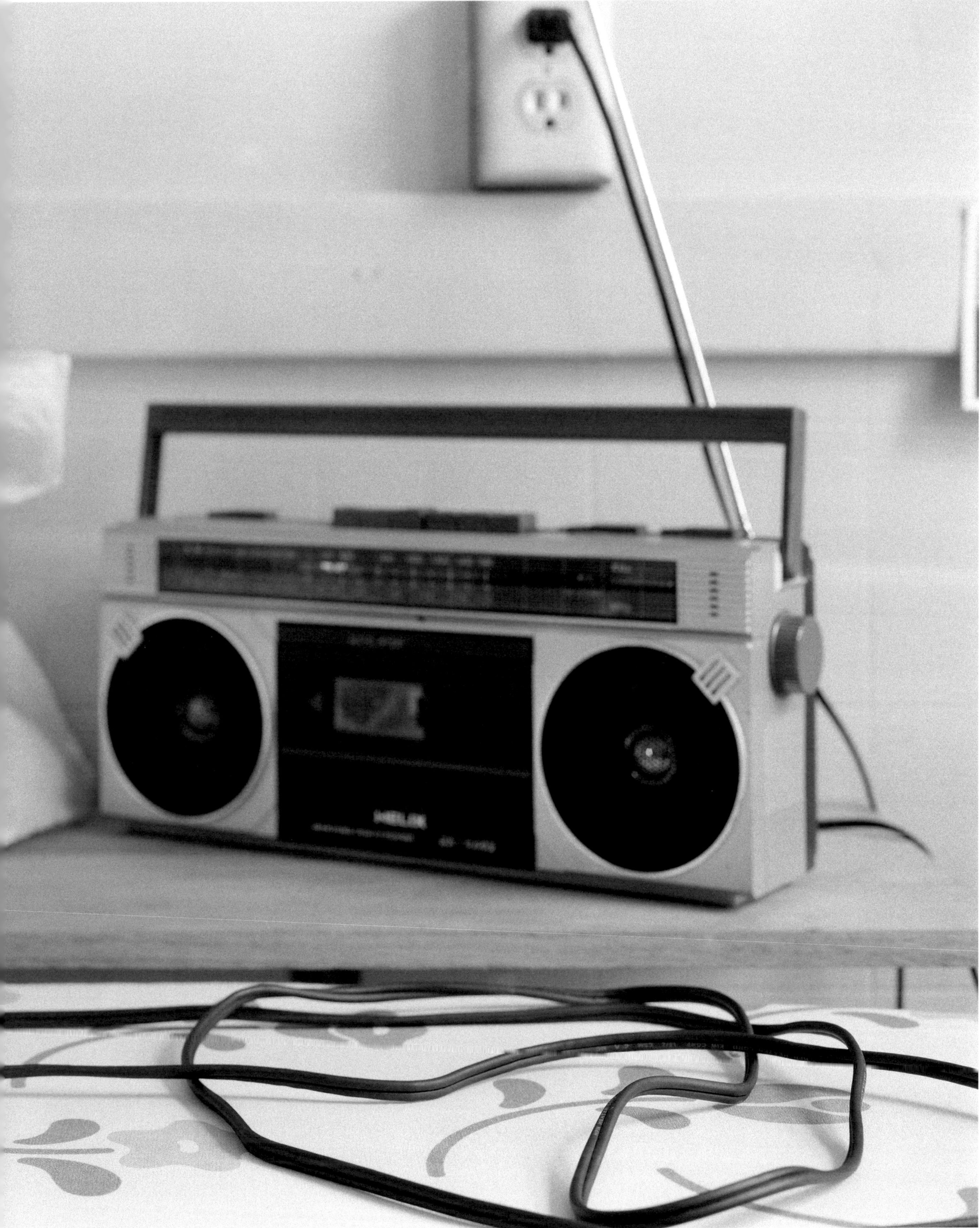

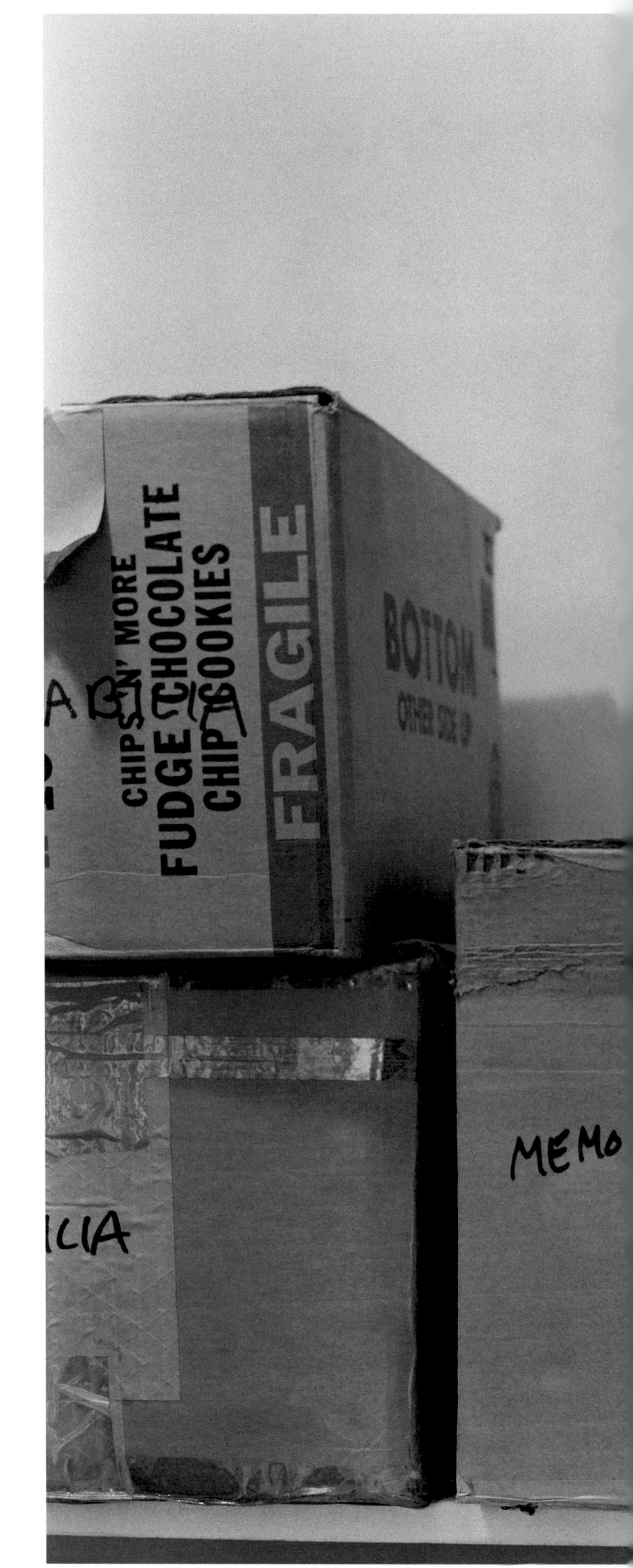

CHIPS N' MORE
FUDGE CHOCOLATE
CHIP COOKIES
FRAGILE
BOTTOM
OTHER SIDE UP
ICIA
MEMO

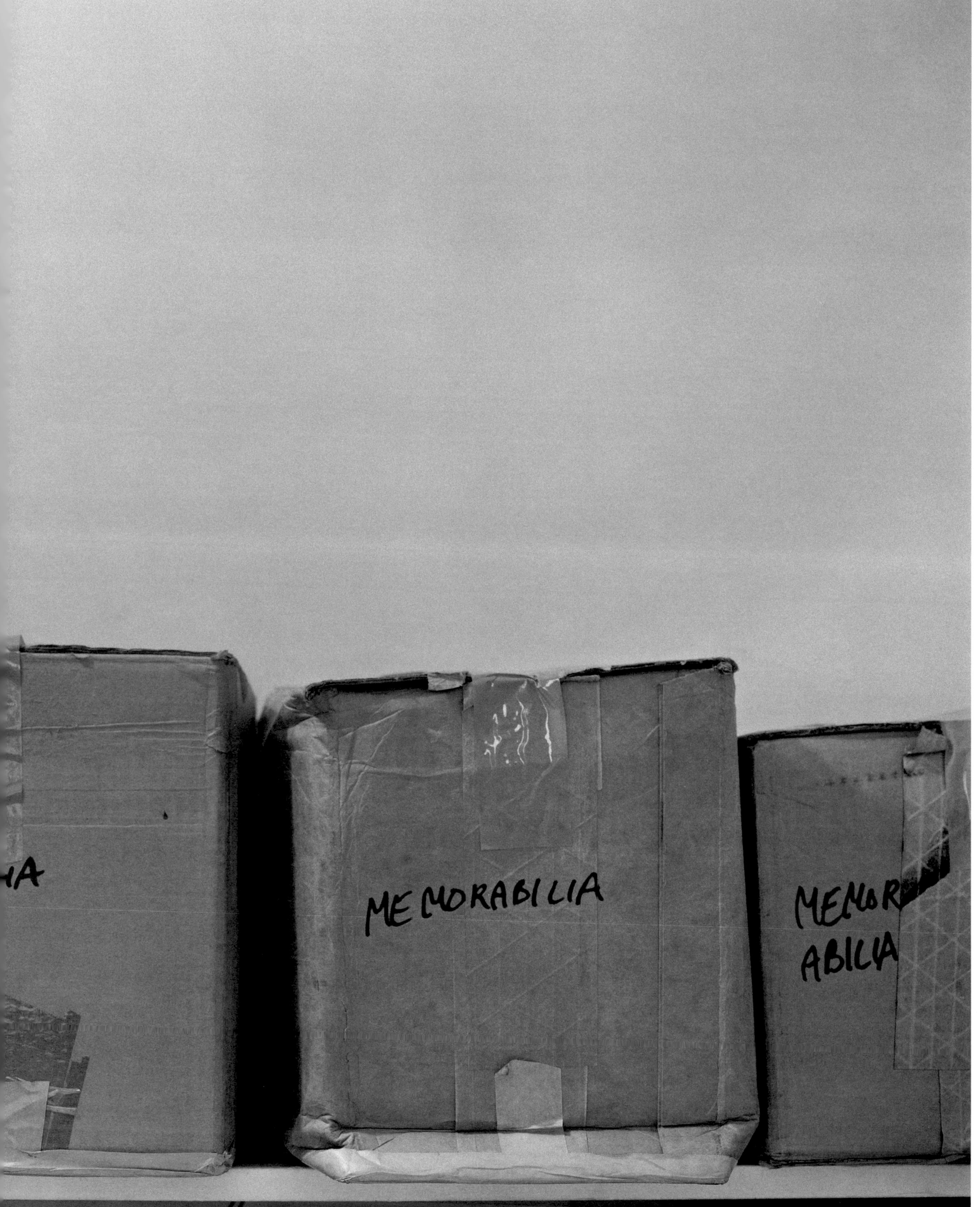
IA
MEMORABILIA
MEMOR
ABILIA

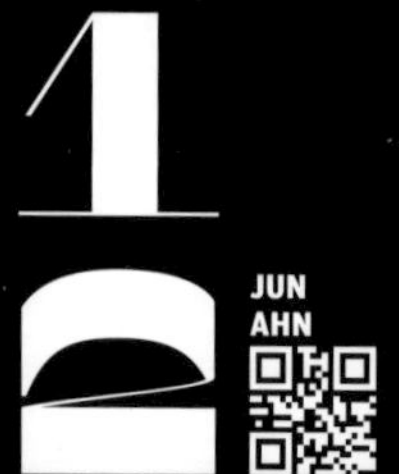
1
JUN
AHN

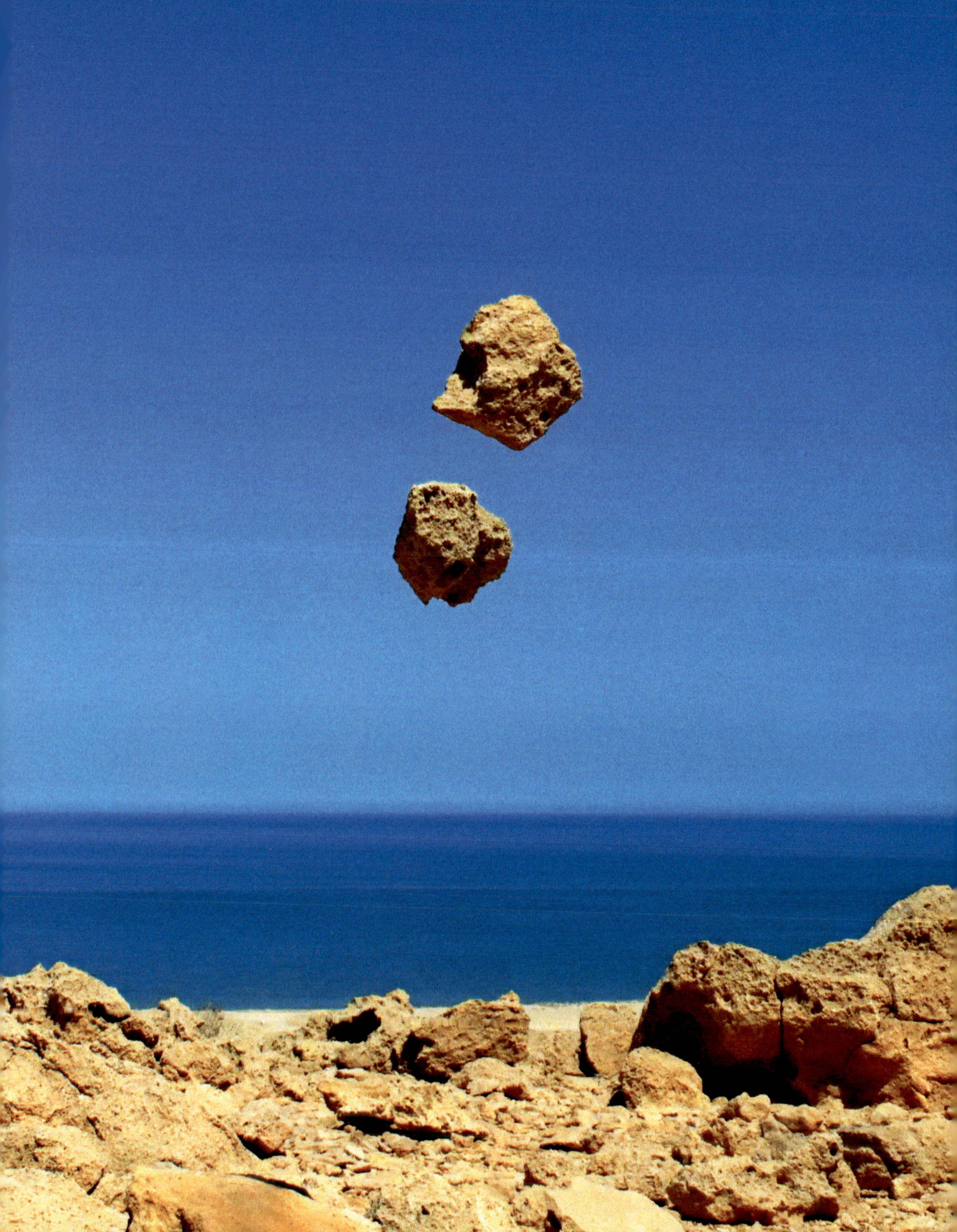

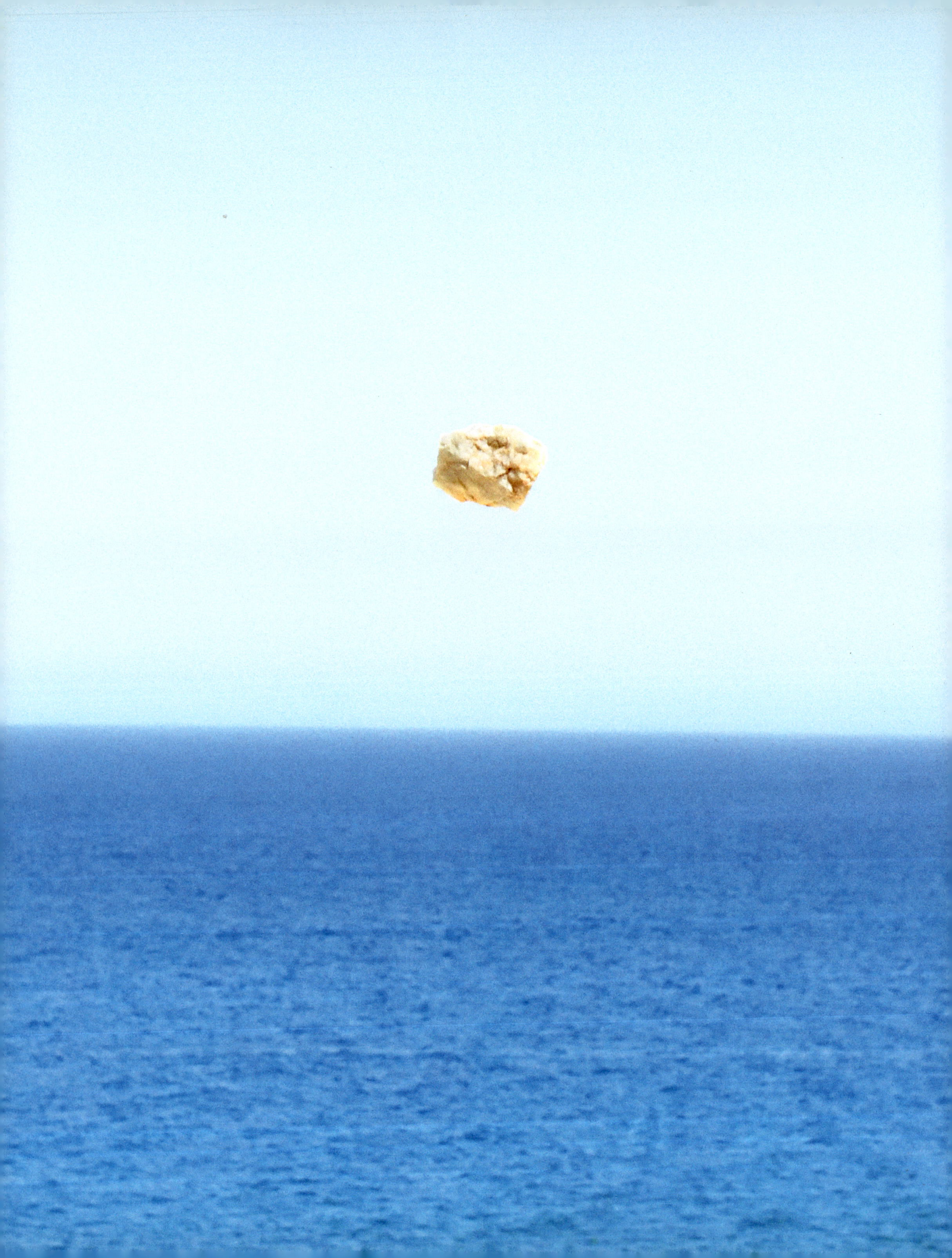

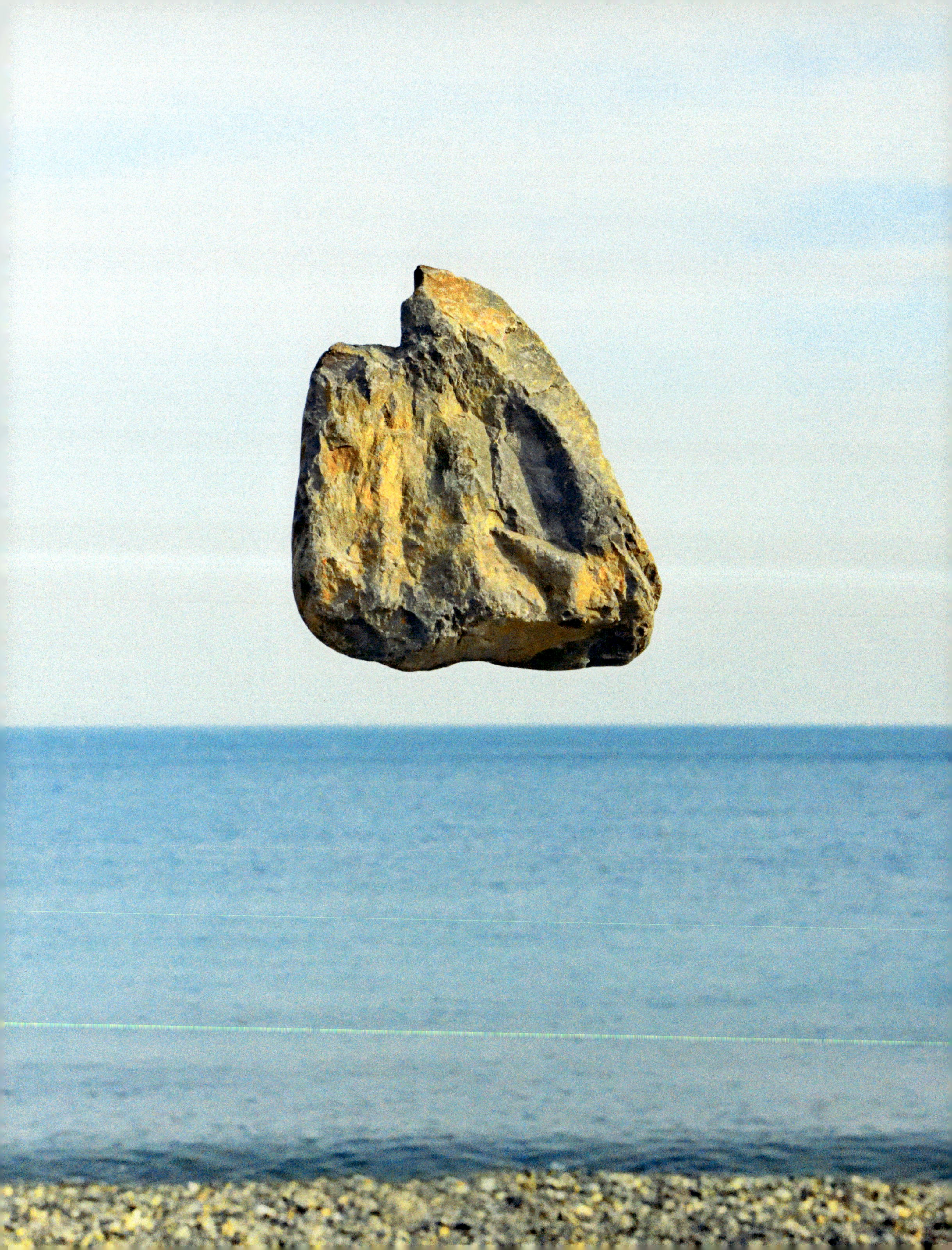

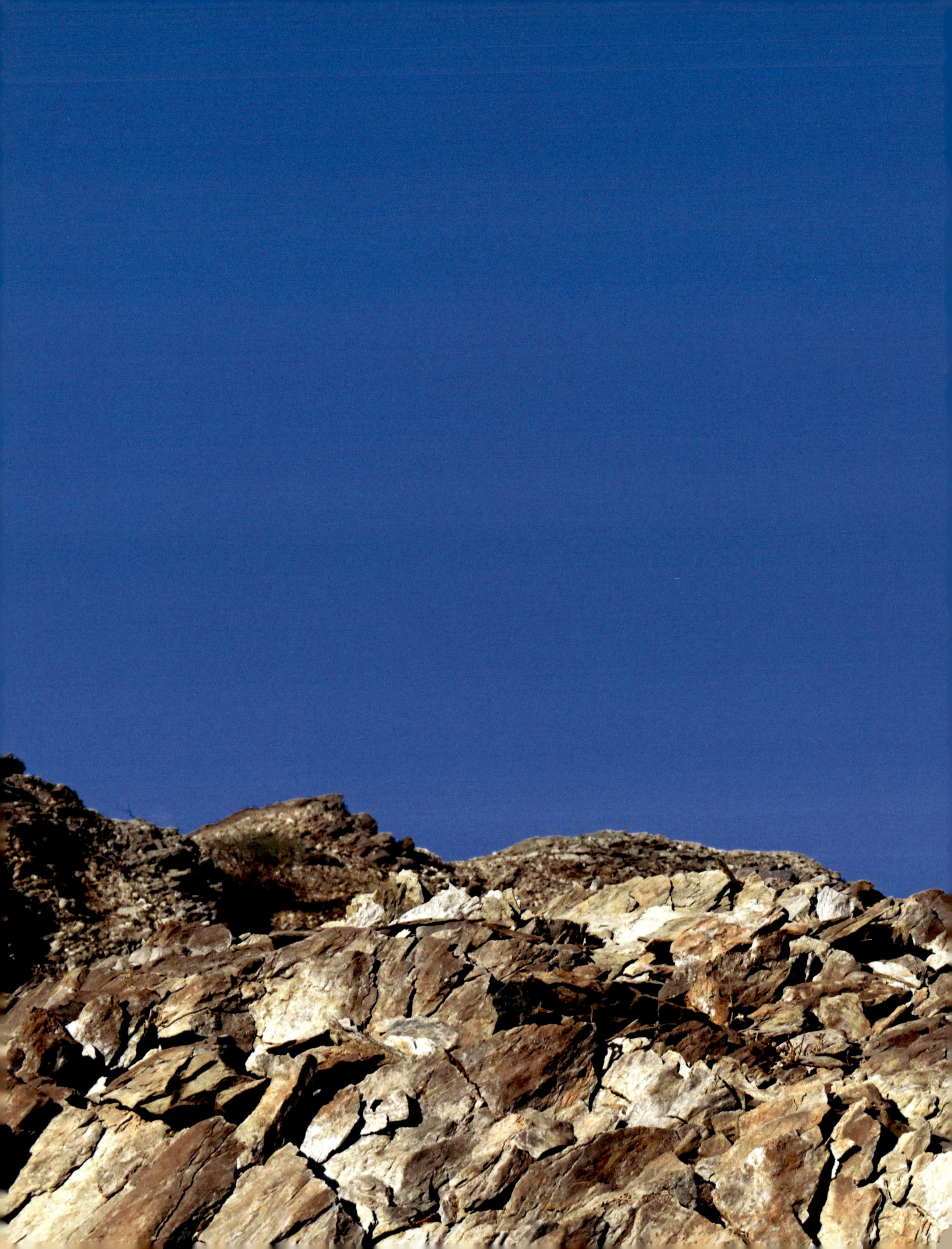

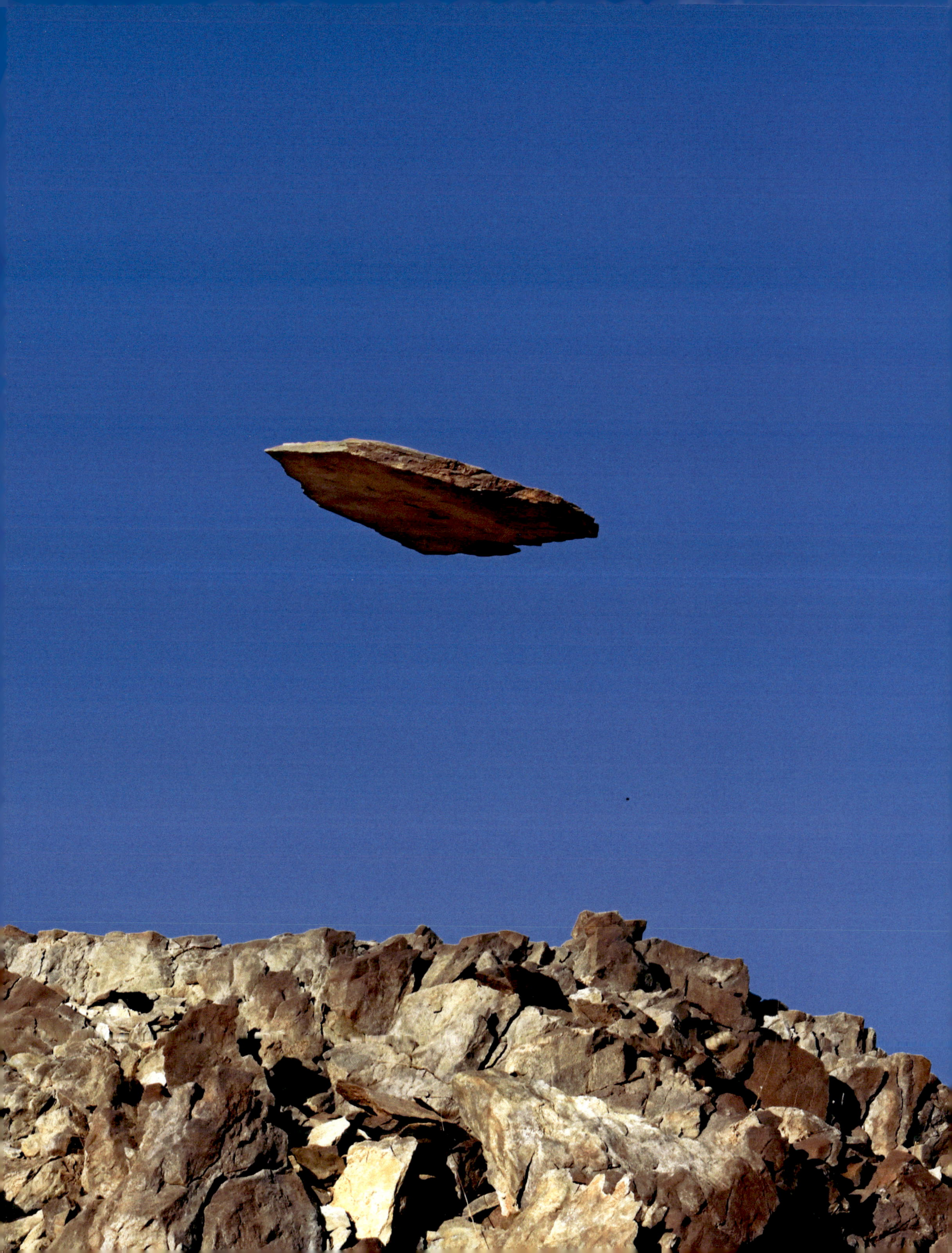

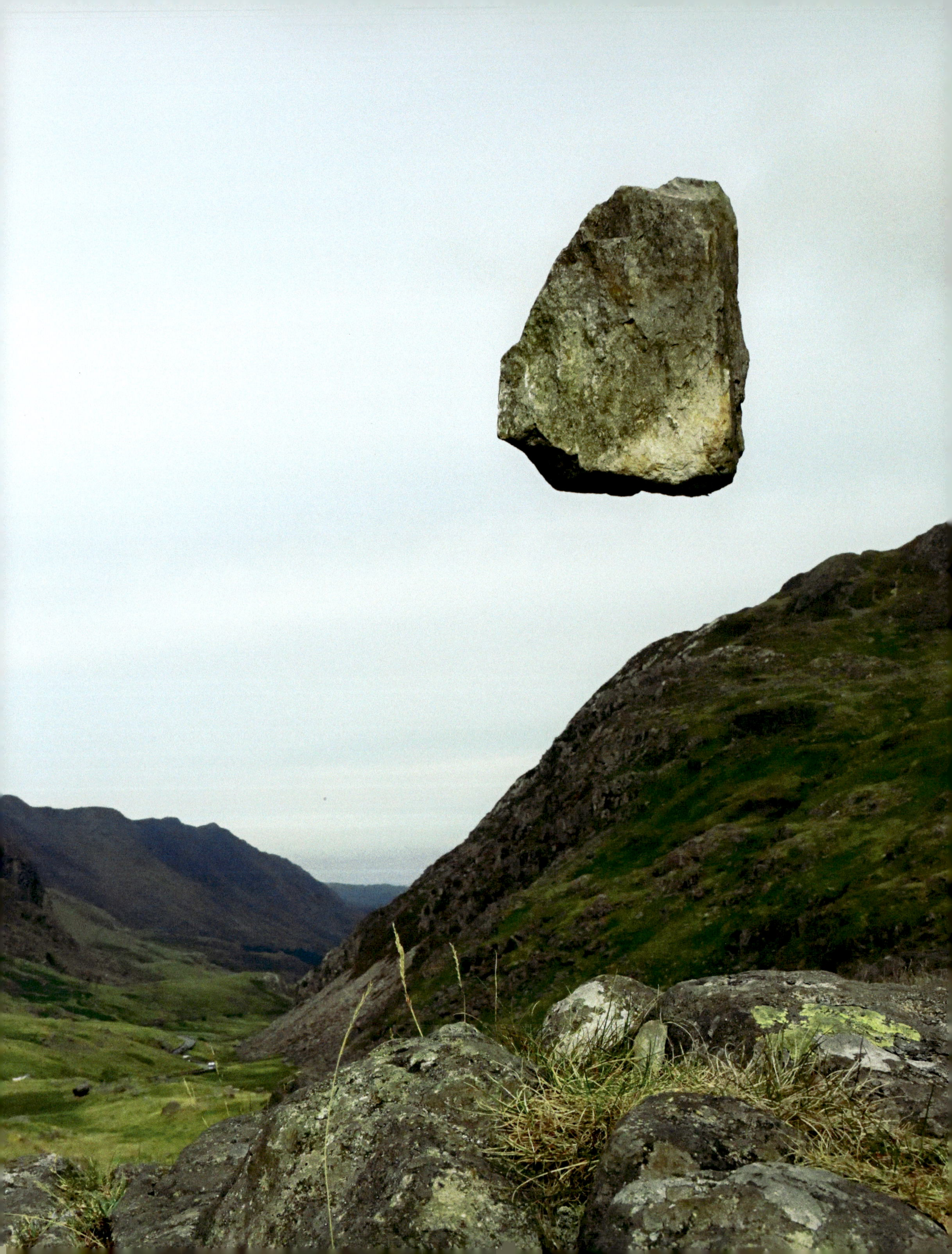

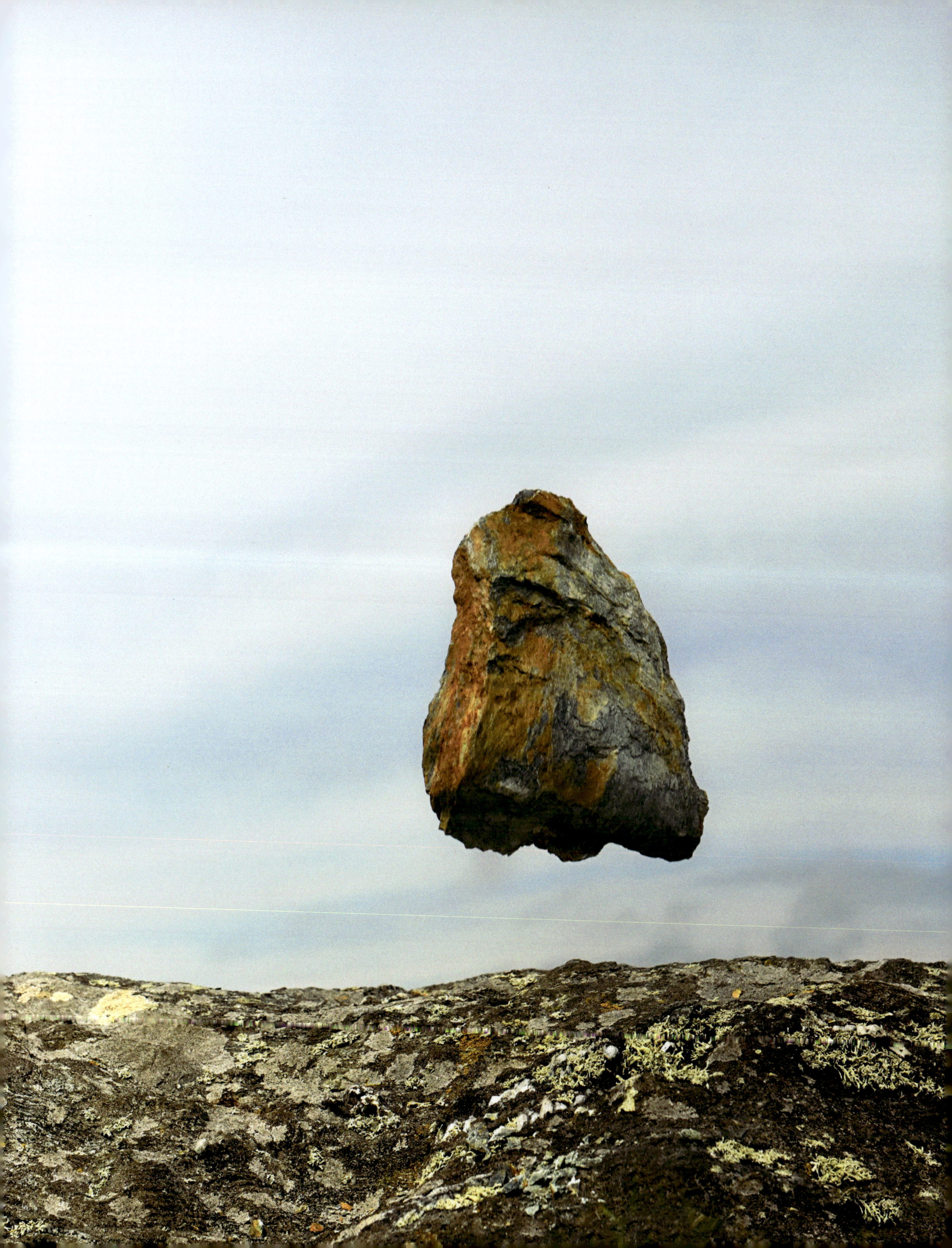

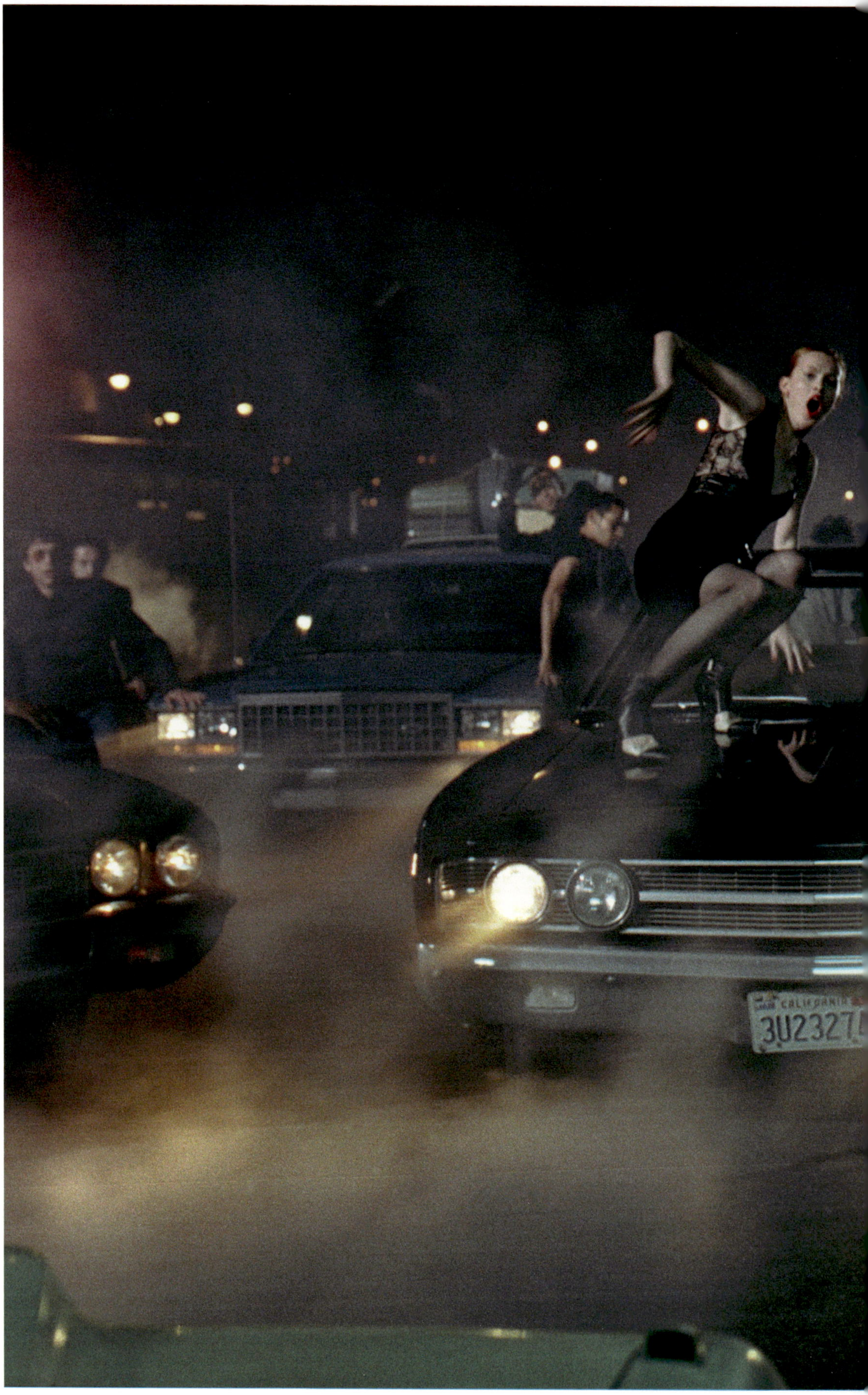

PETER LINDBERGH, *VOGUE ITALIA*, OCTOBER 2000

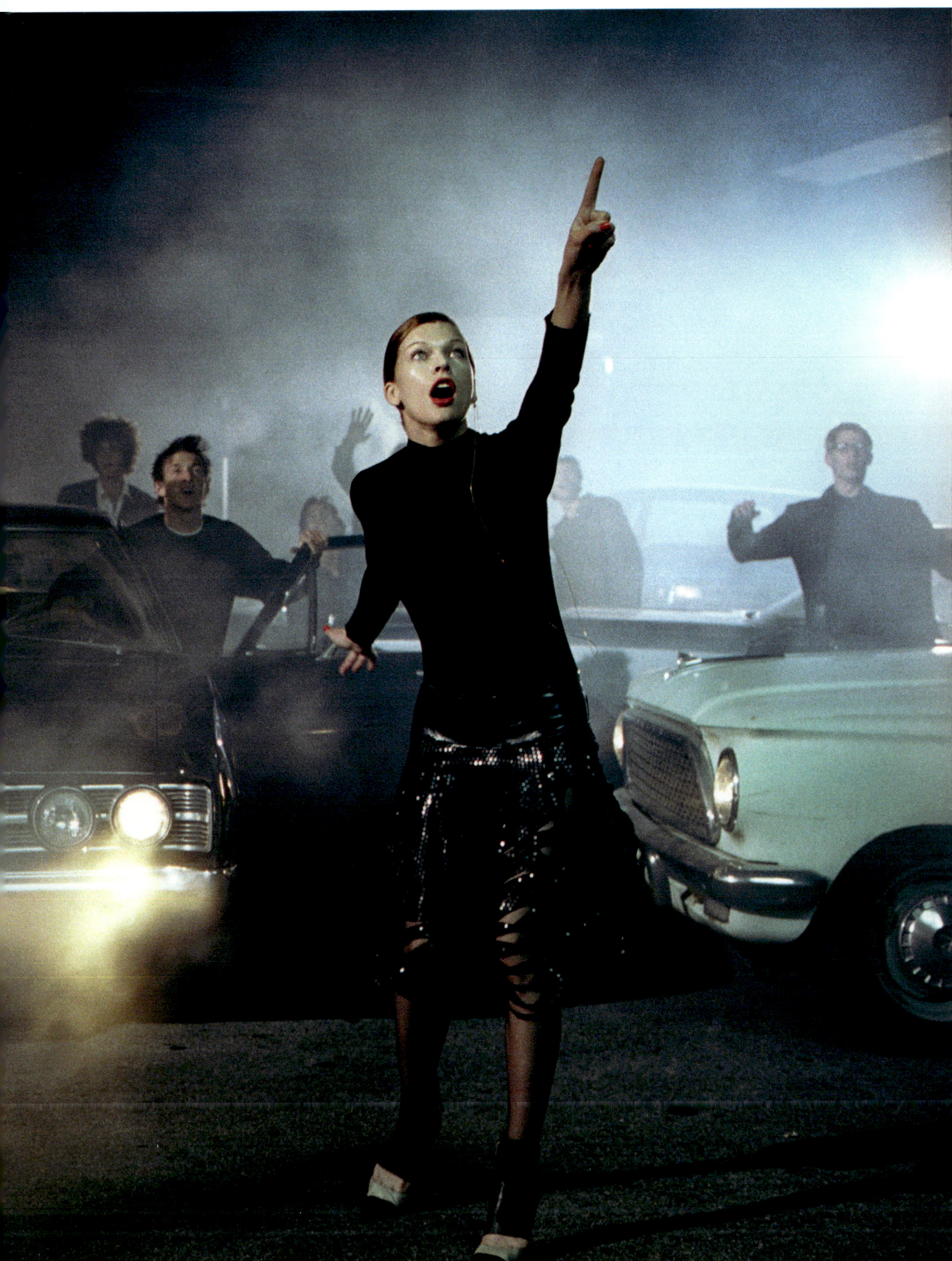

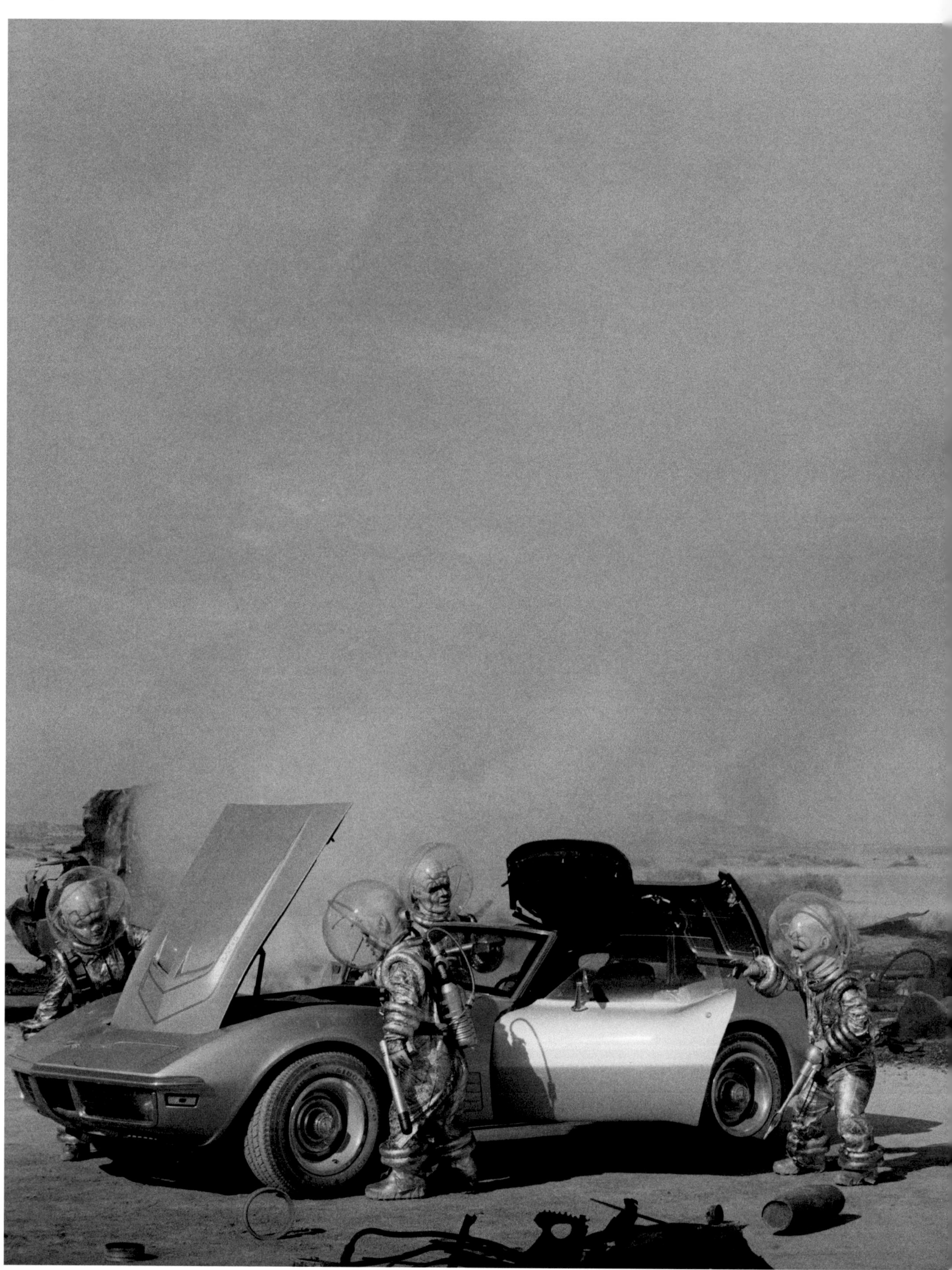

PETER LINDBERGH, *VOGUE ITALIA*, MARCH 2001

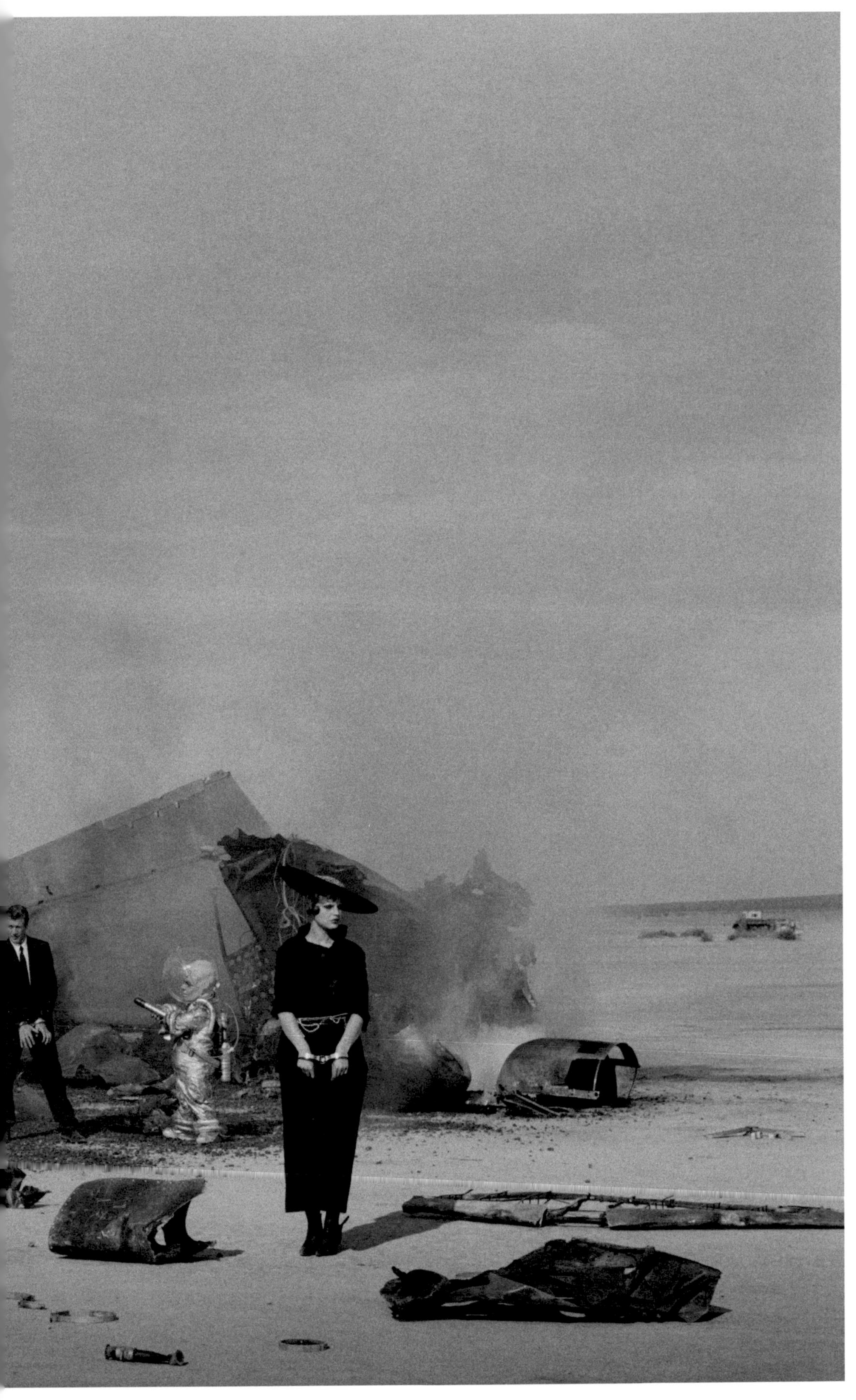

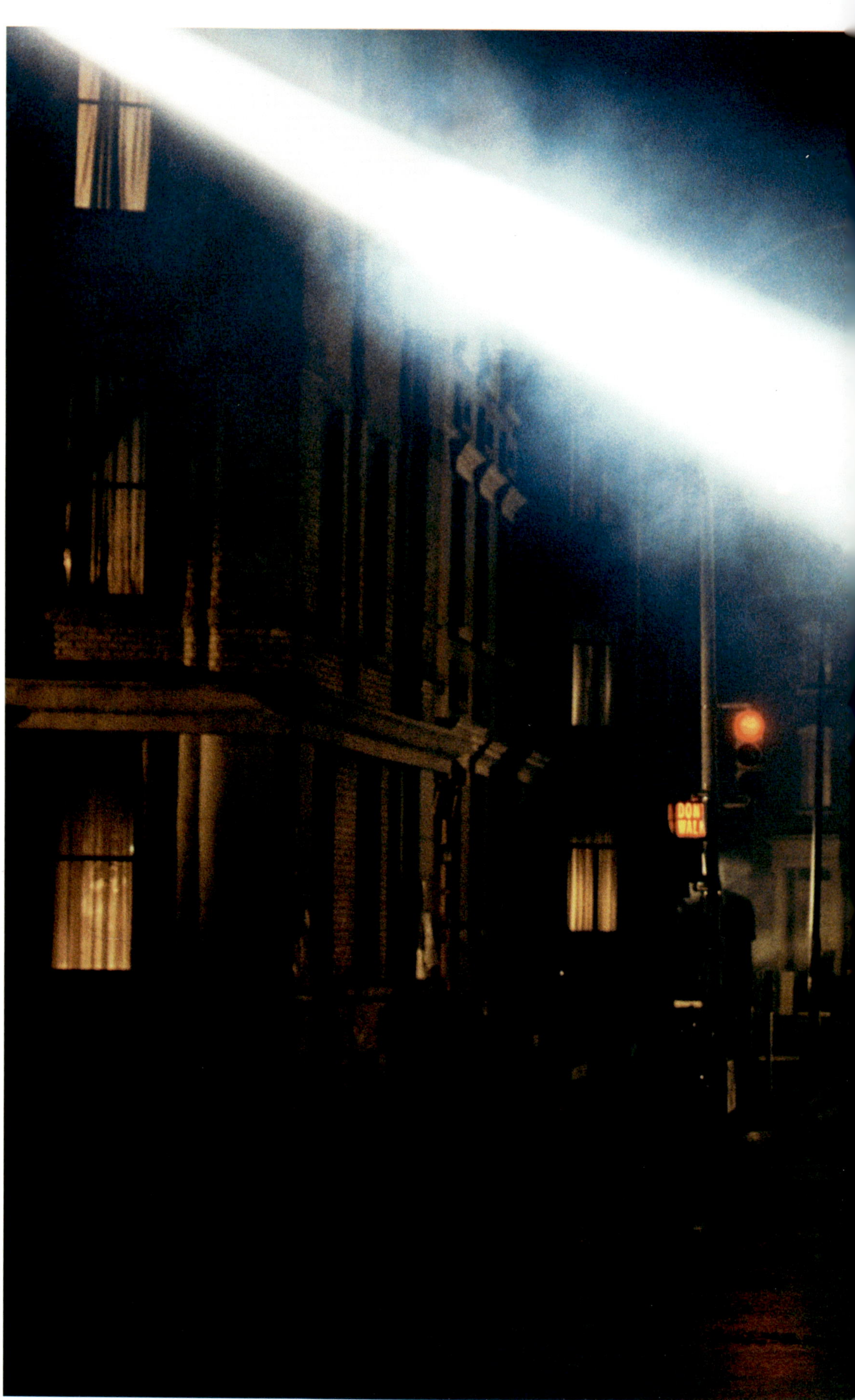

PETER LINDBERGH, *HARPER'S BAZAAR*, SEPTEMBER 2002

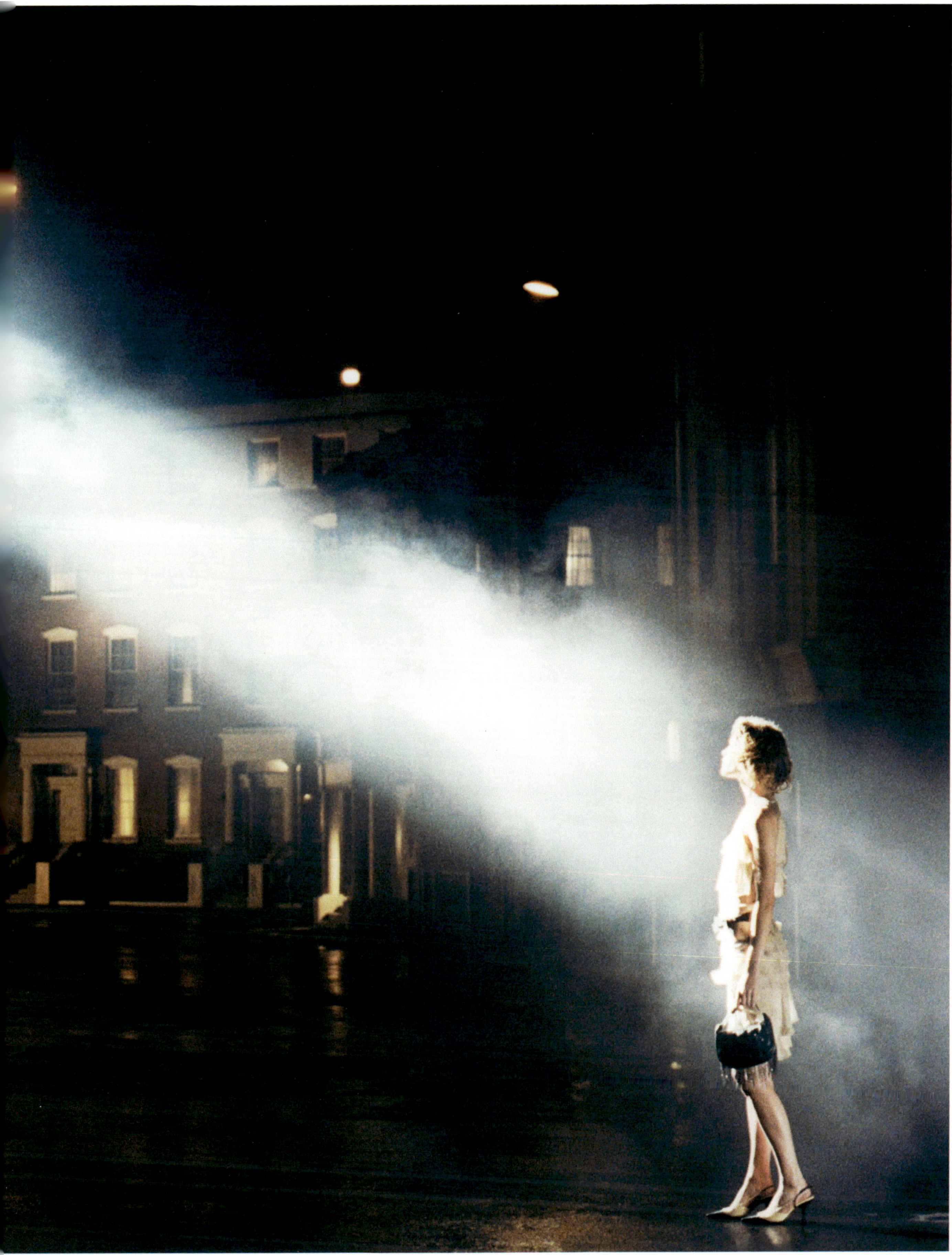

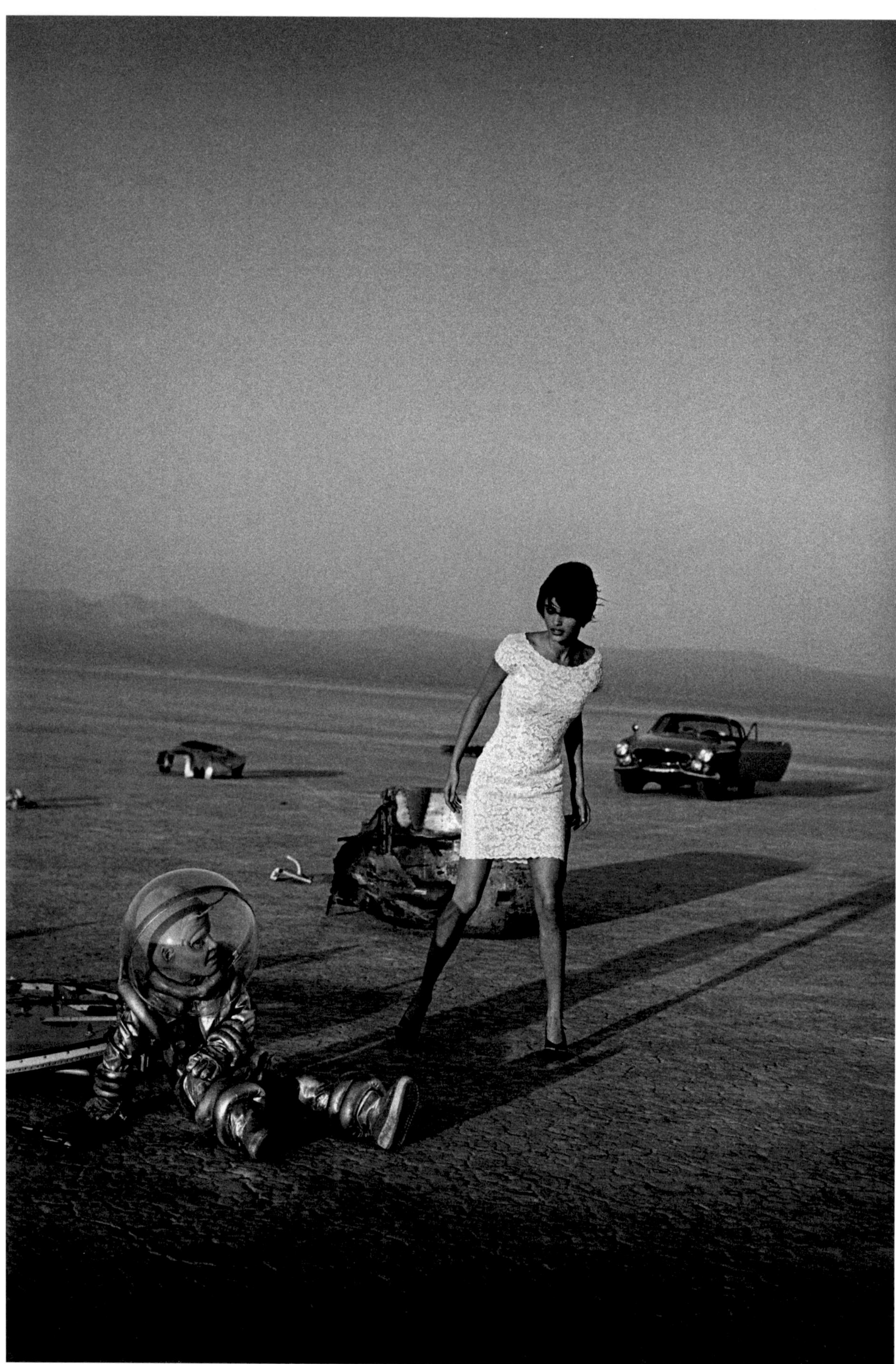

PETER LINDBERGH, *VOGUE ITALIA*, MARCH 1990

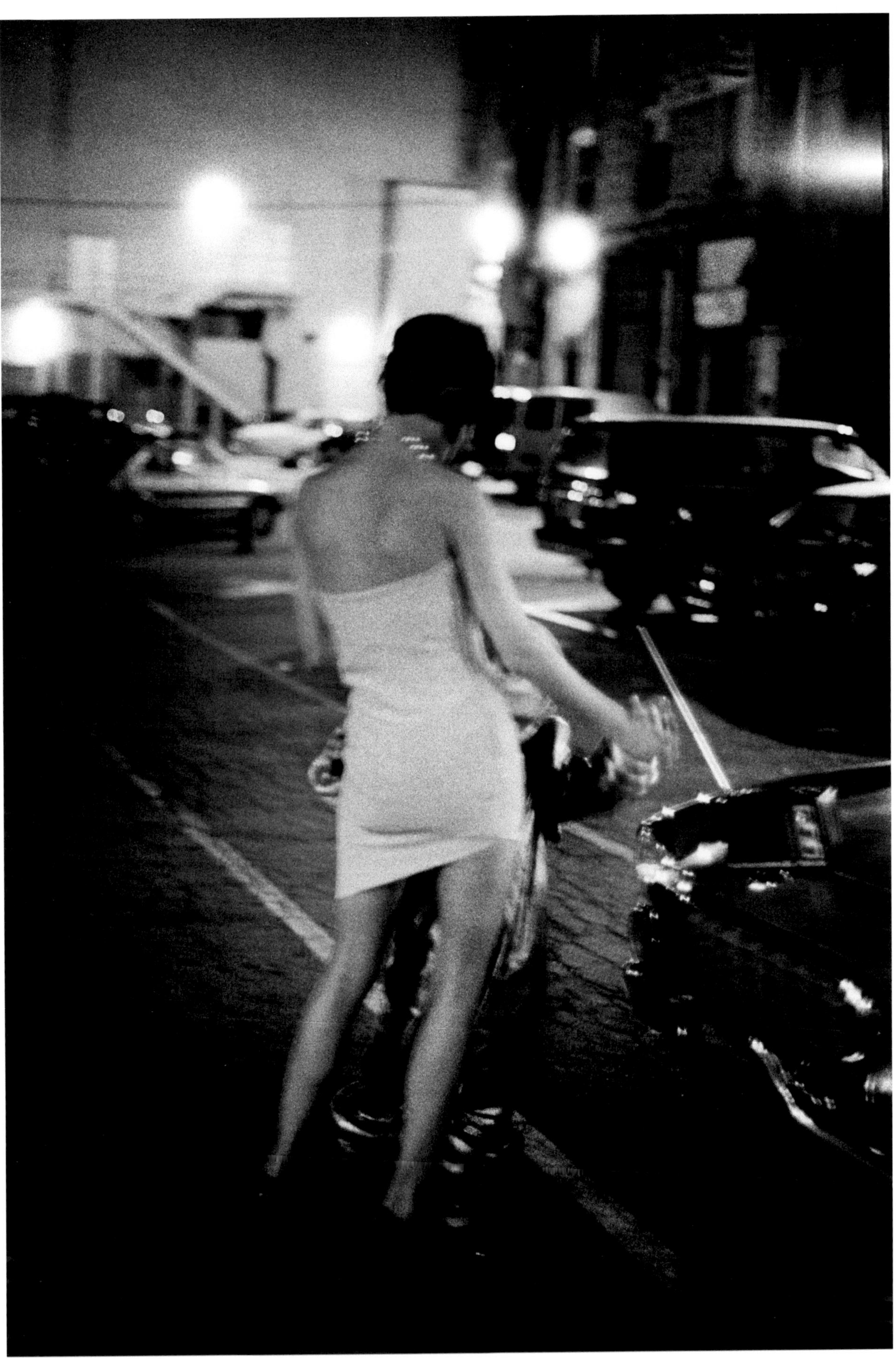

PETER LINDBERGH, *VOGUE ITALIA*, MARCH 1990

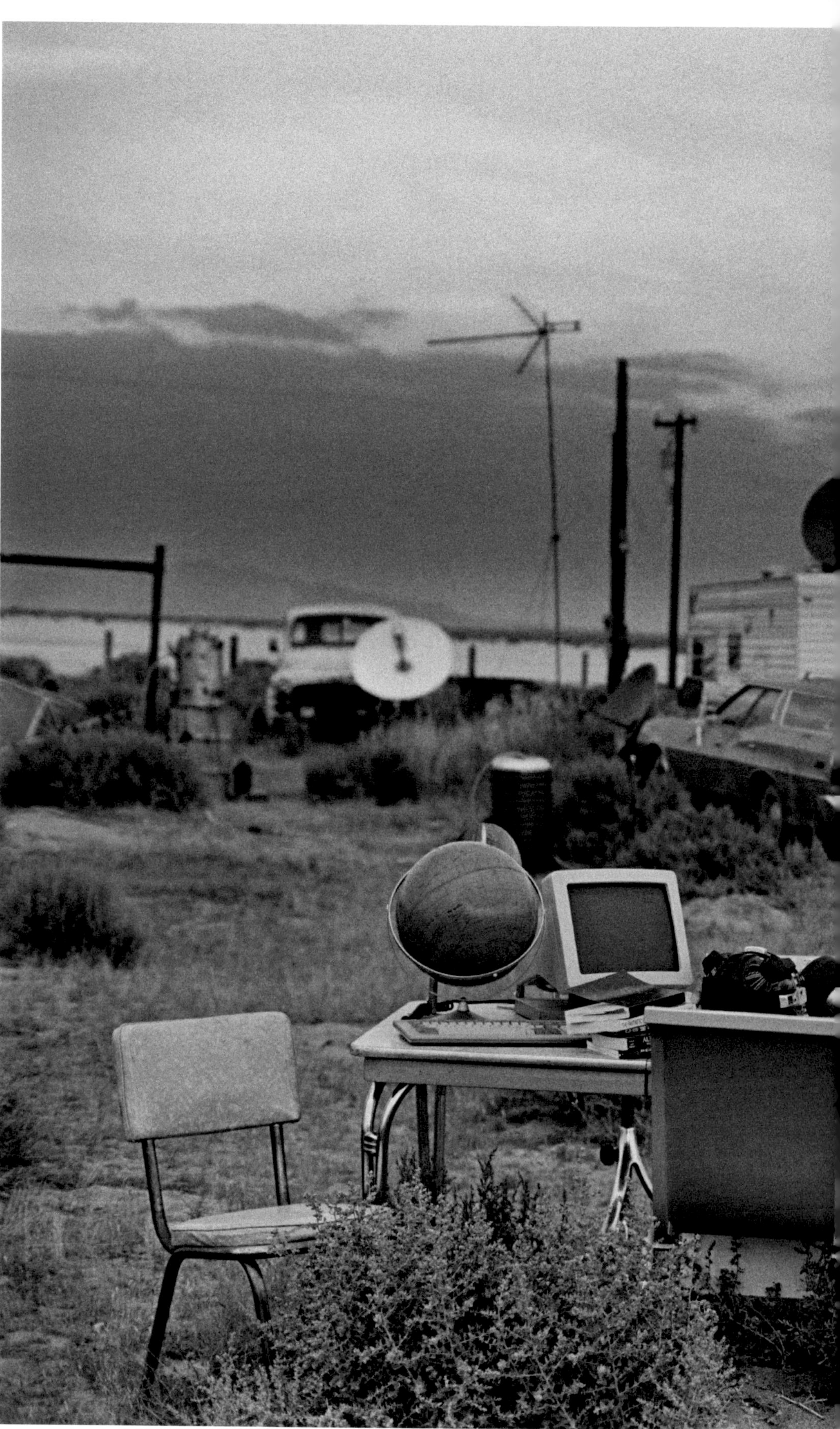

PETER LINDBERGH, *VOGUE ITALIA*, OCTOBER 1998

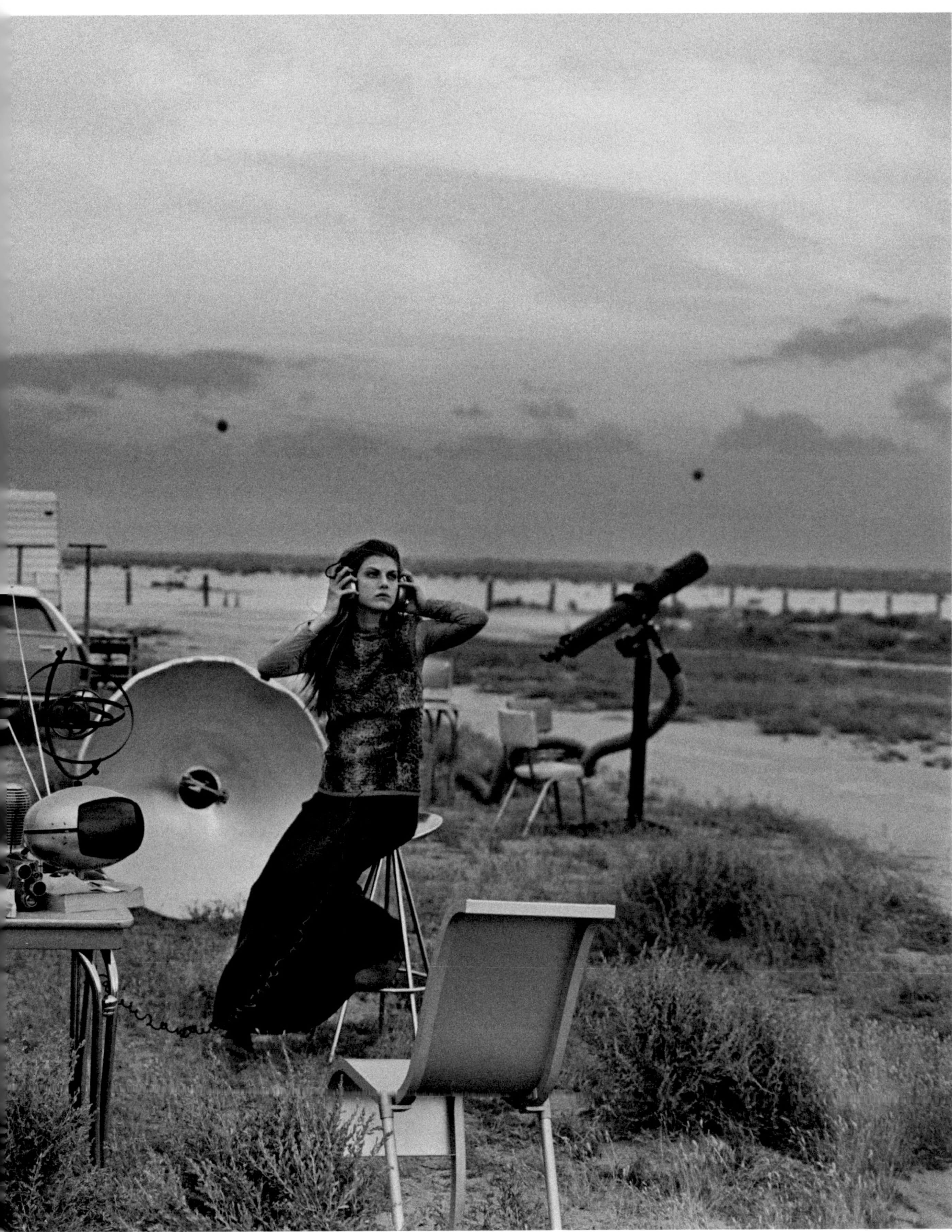

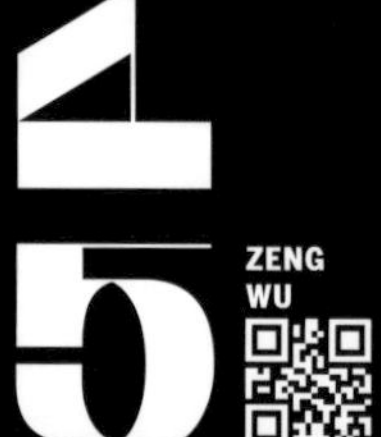
ZENG
WU

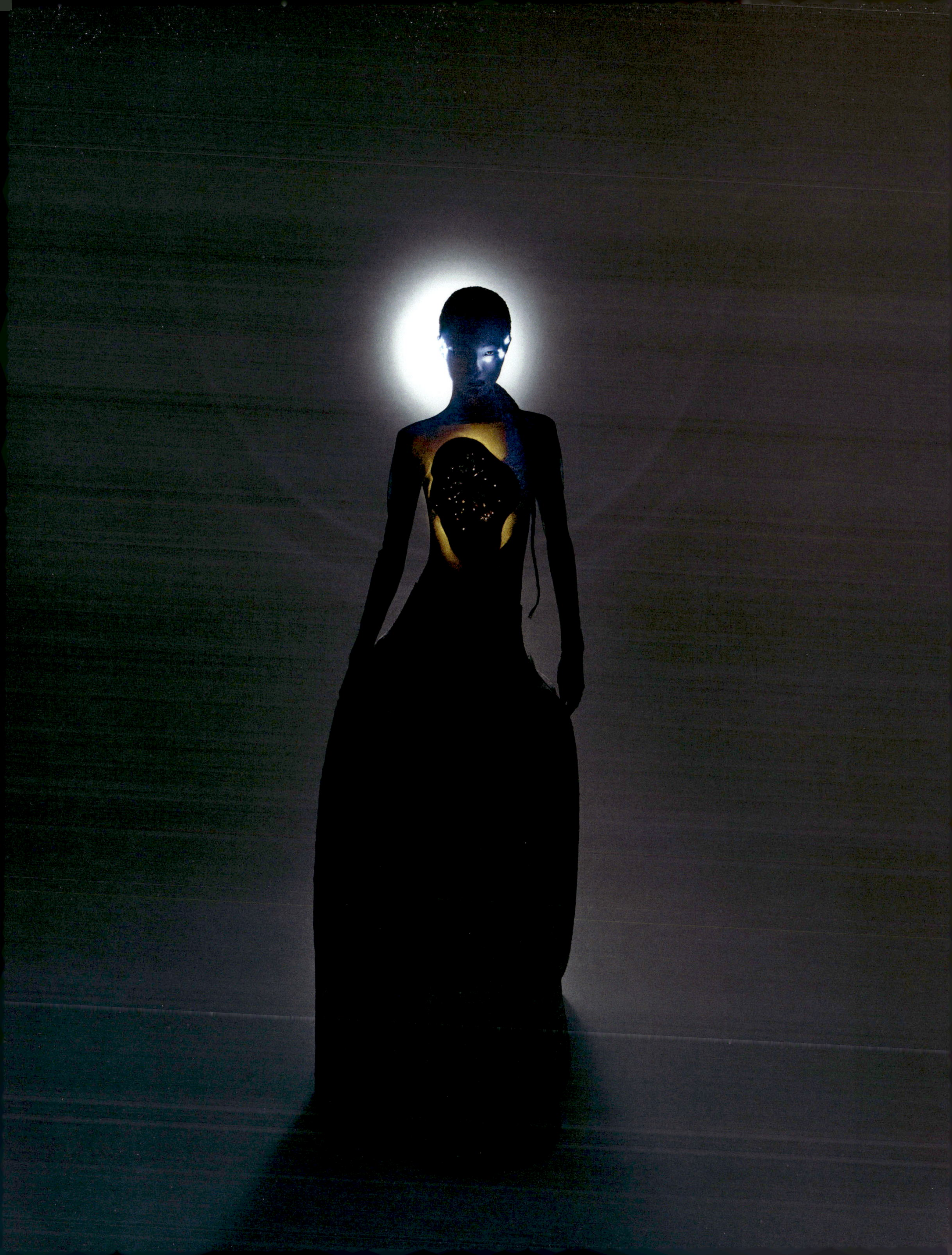

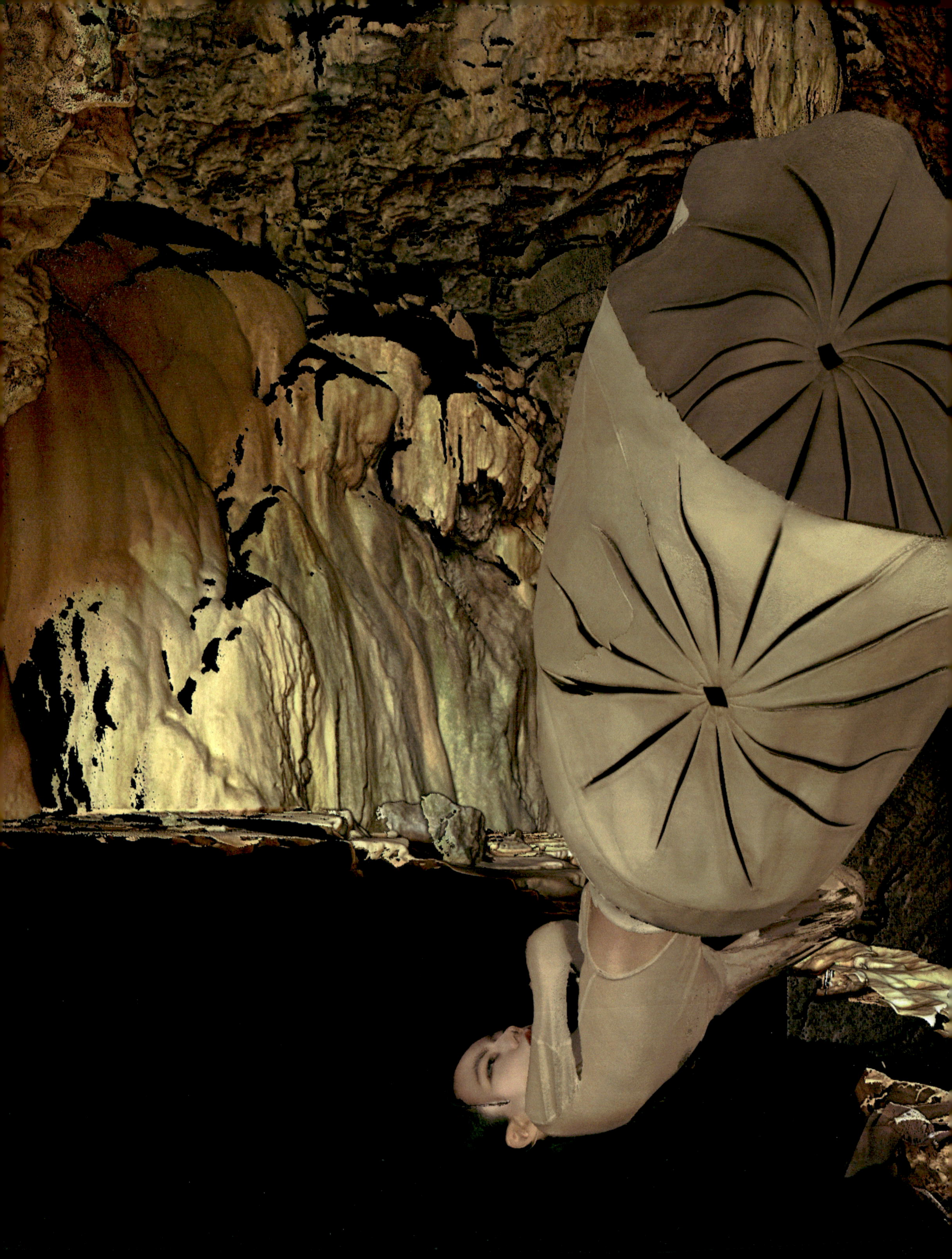

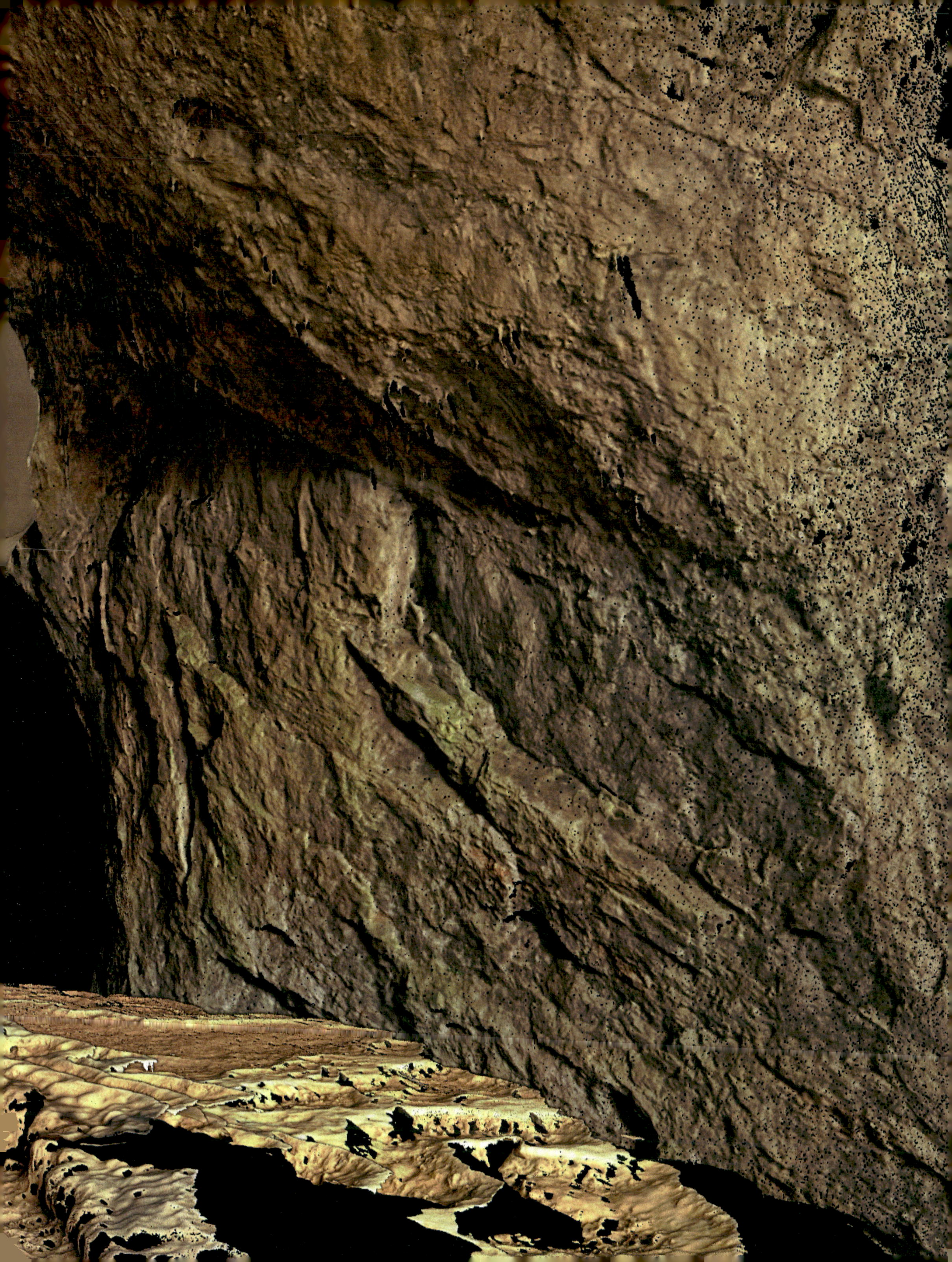

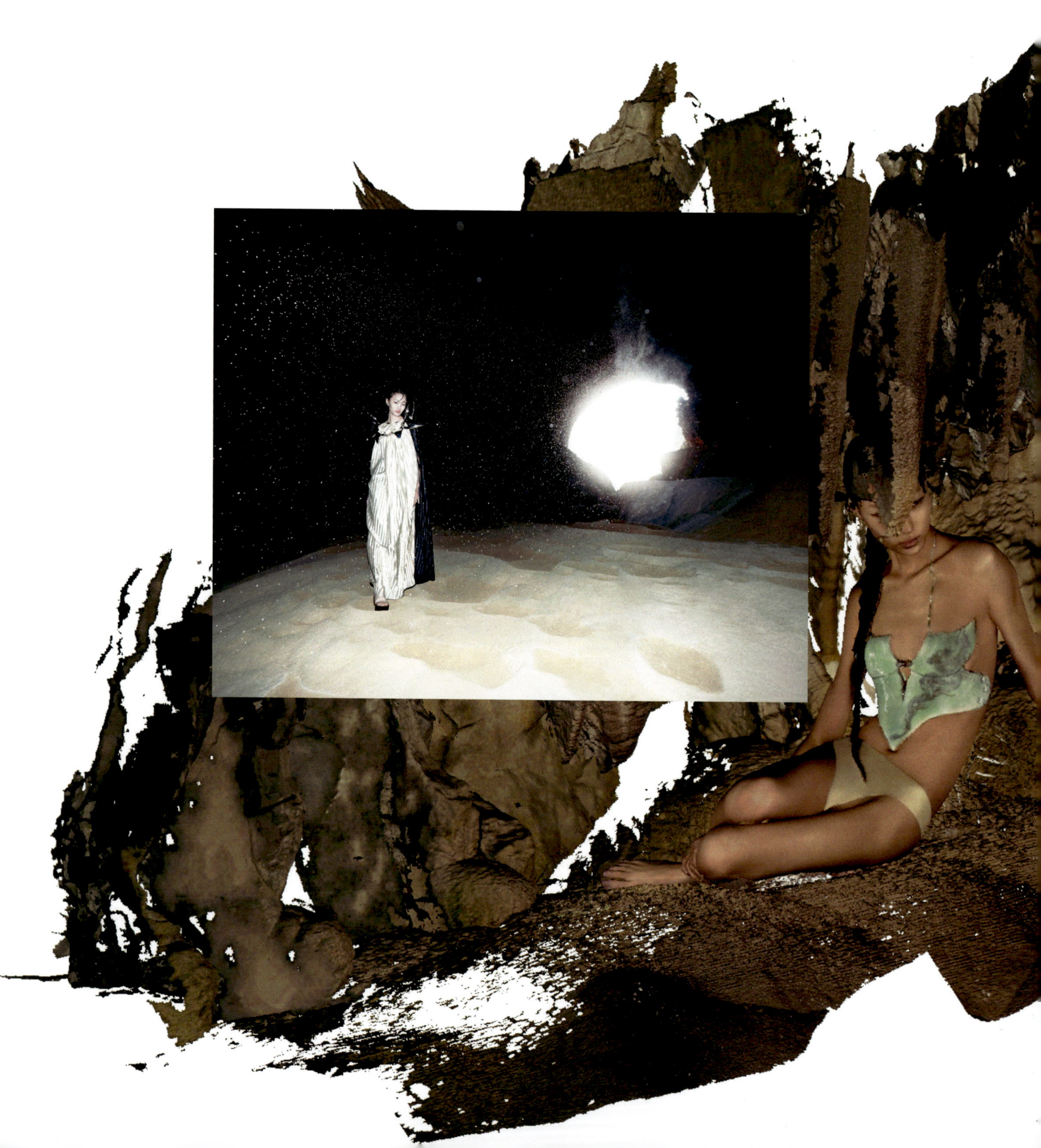

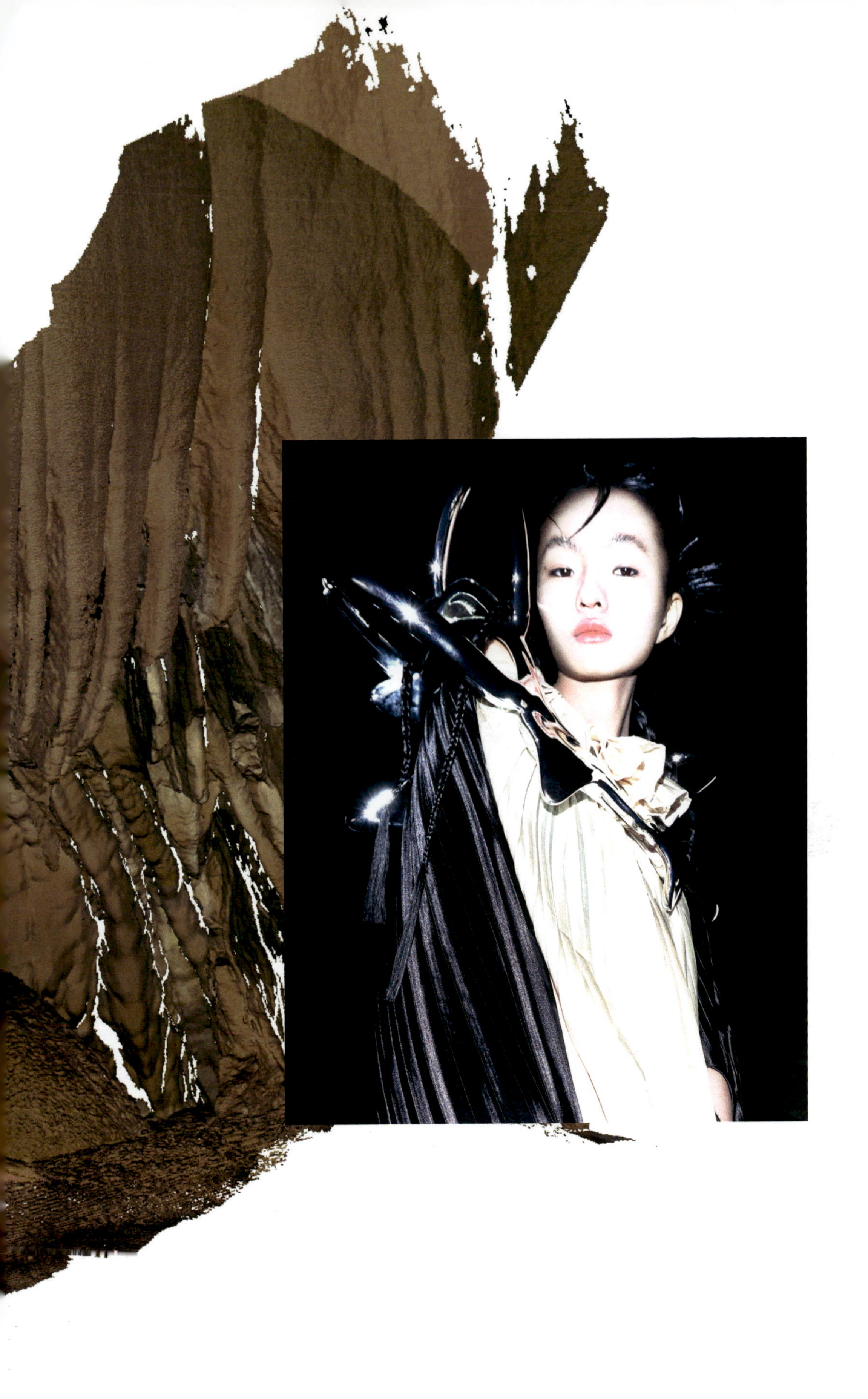

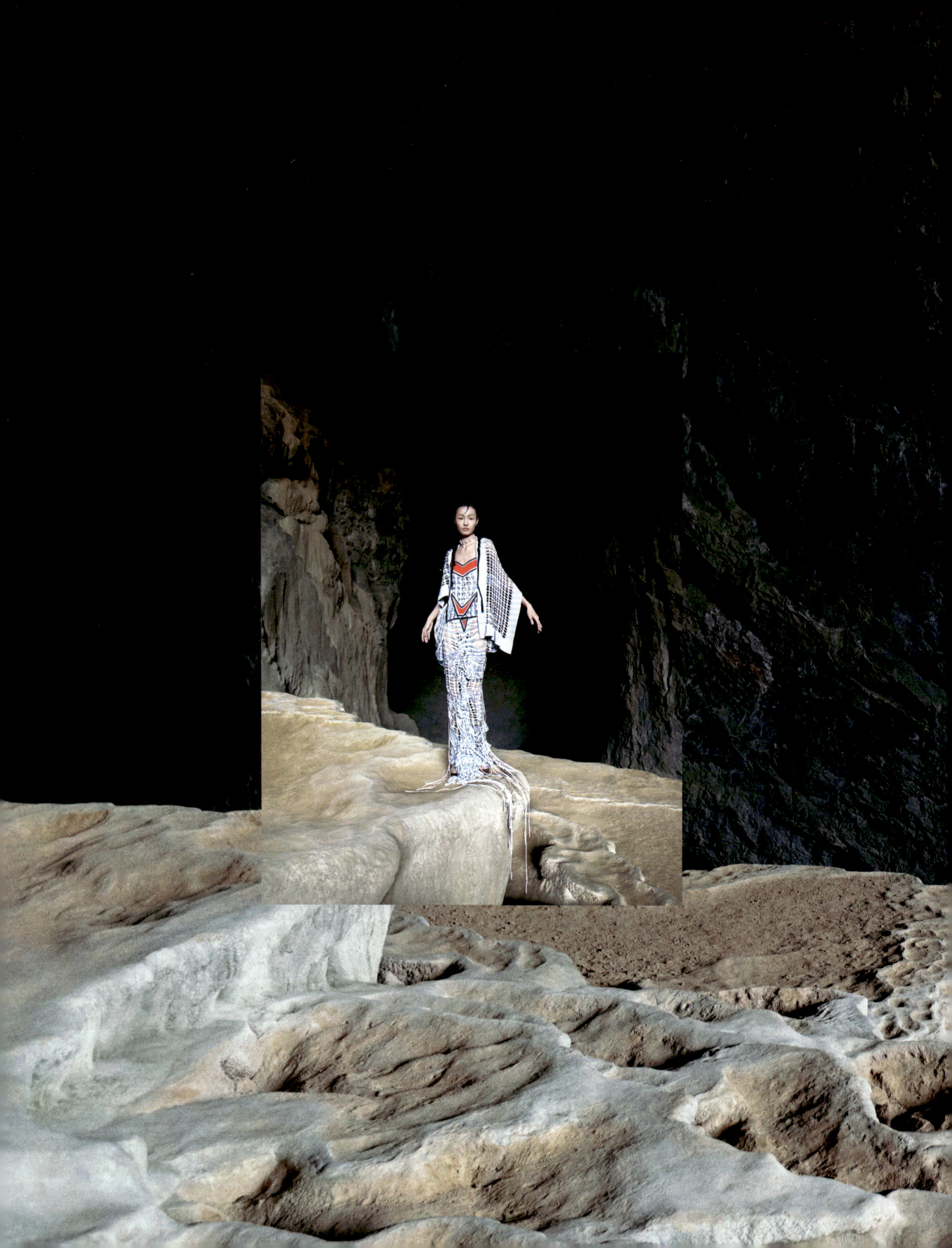

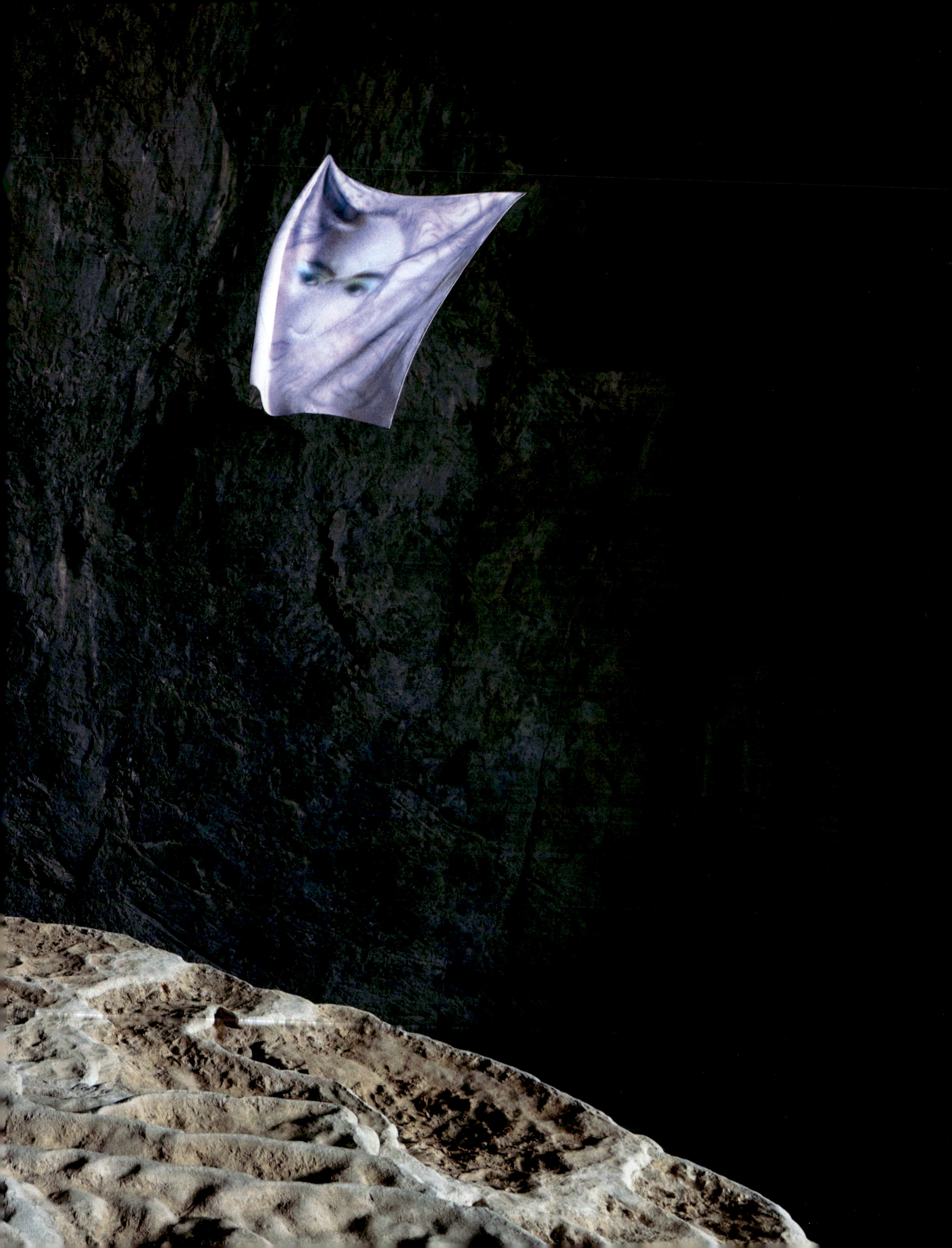

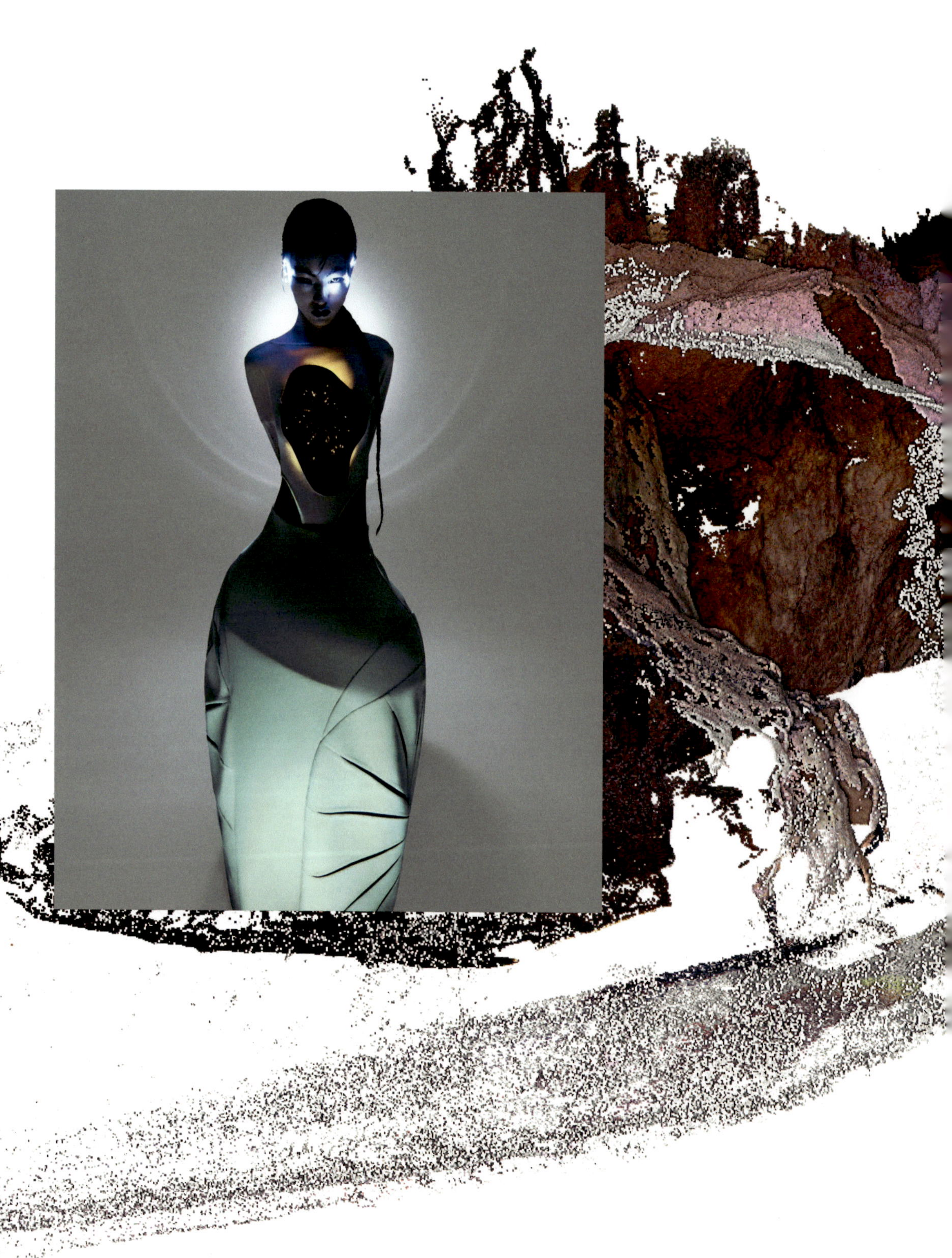

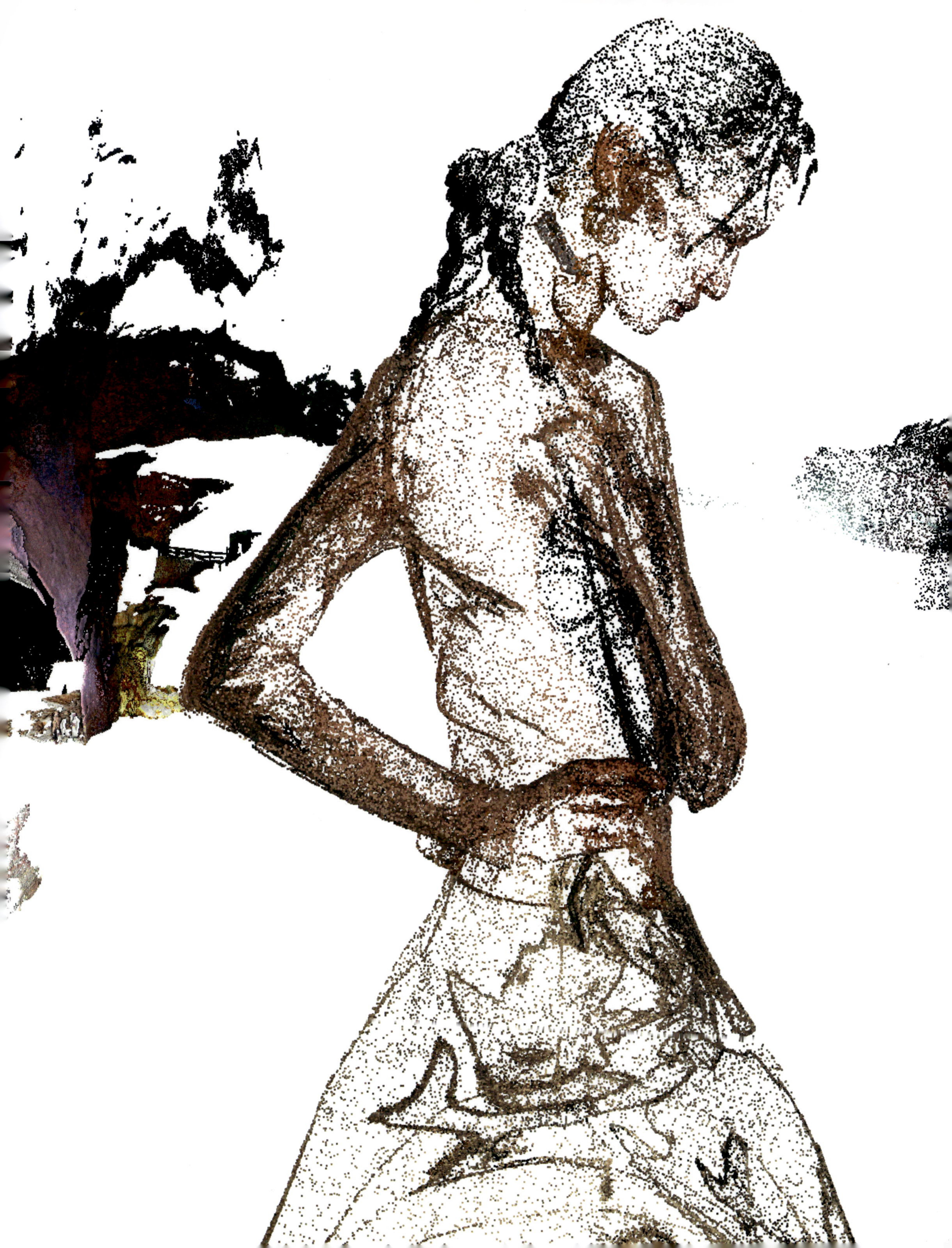

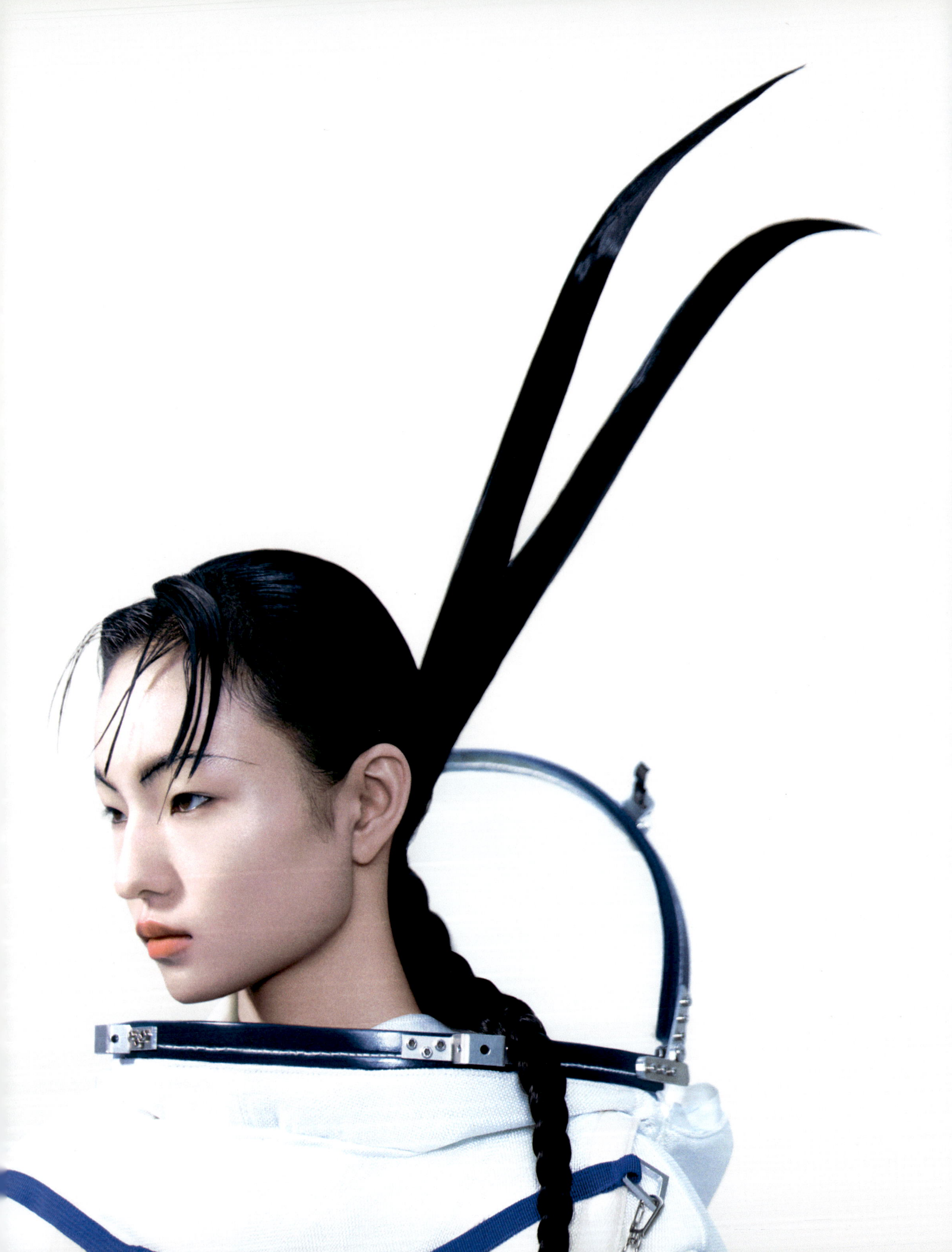

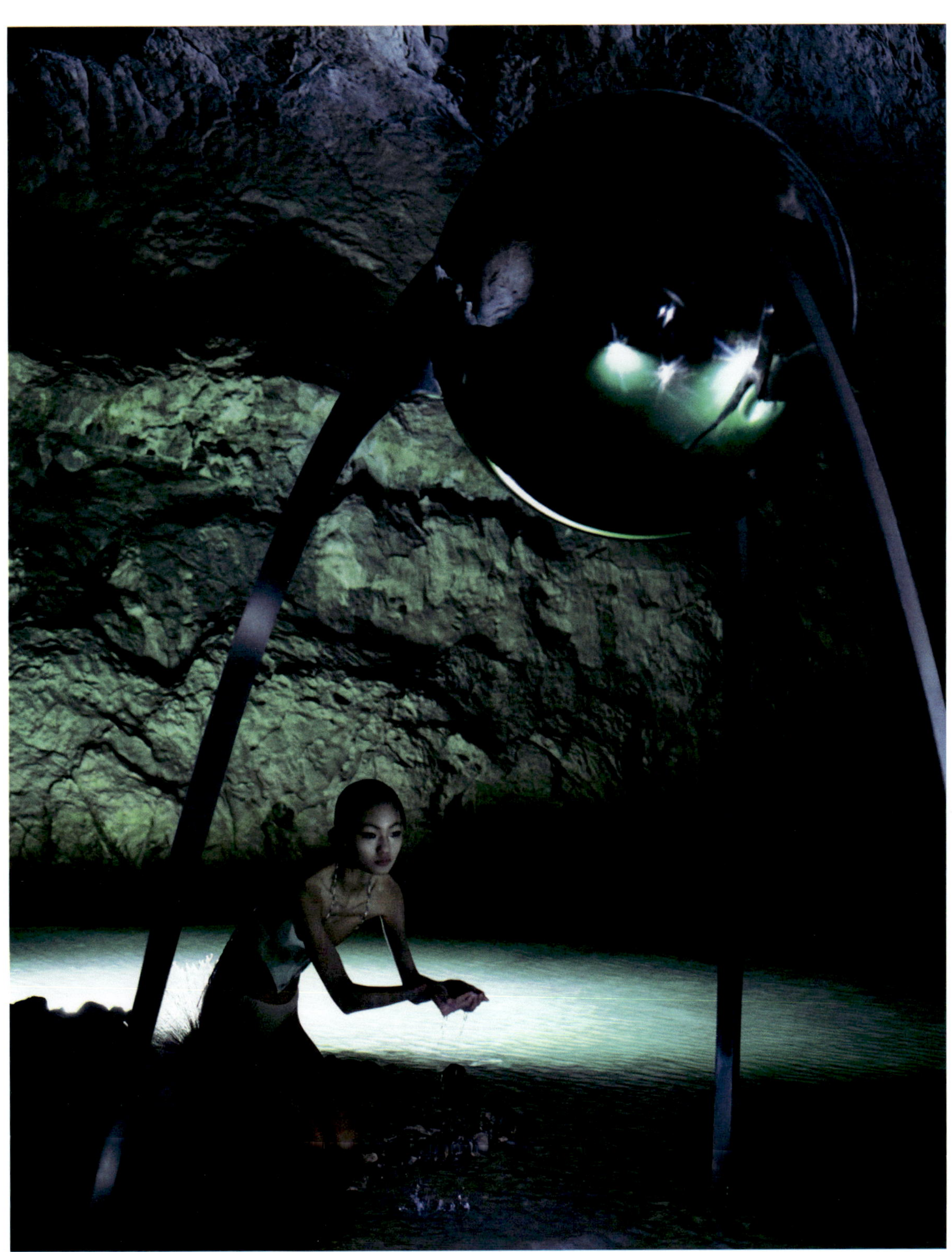

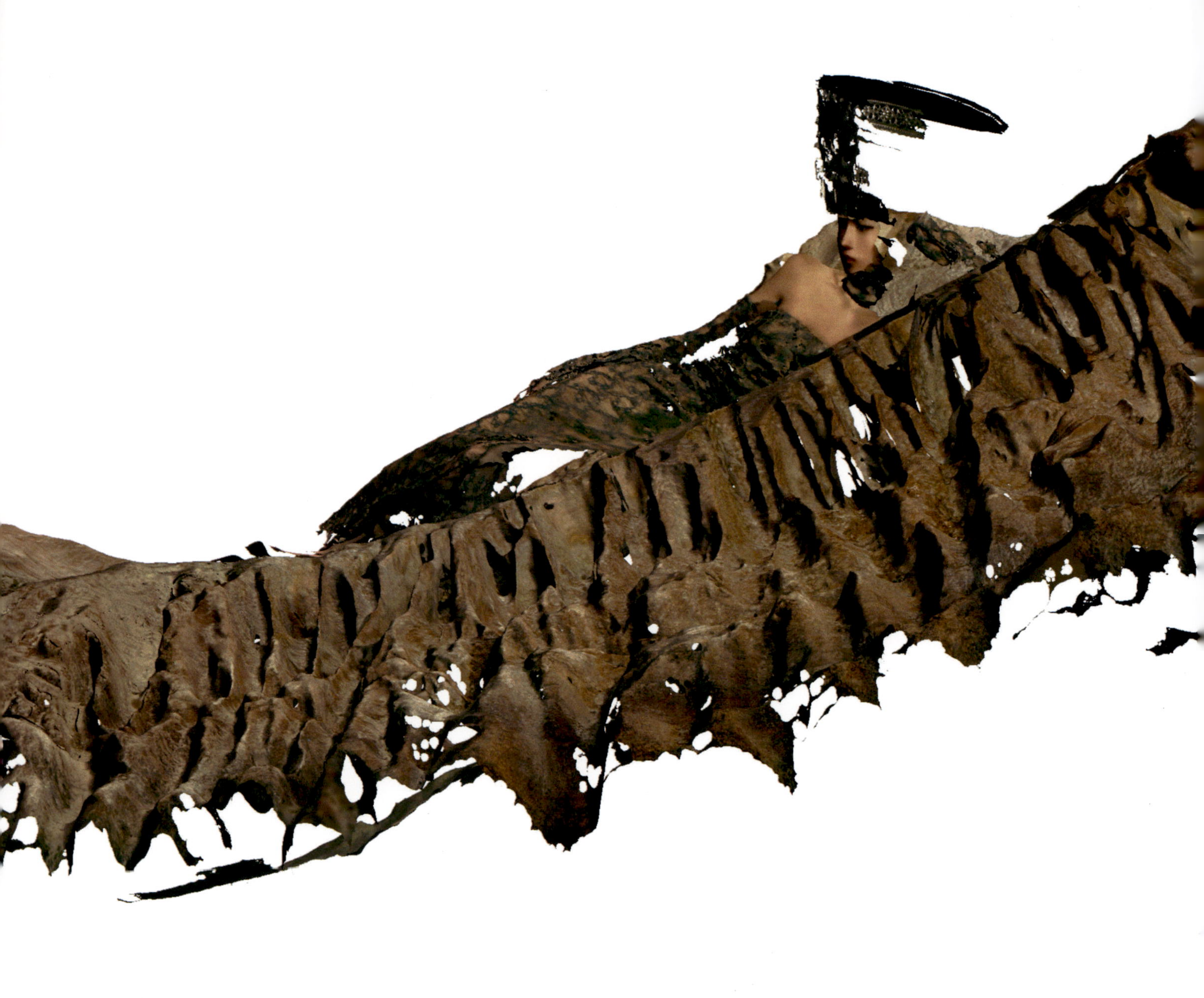

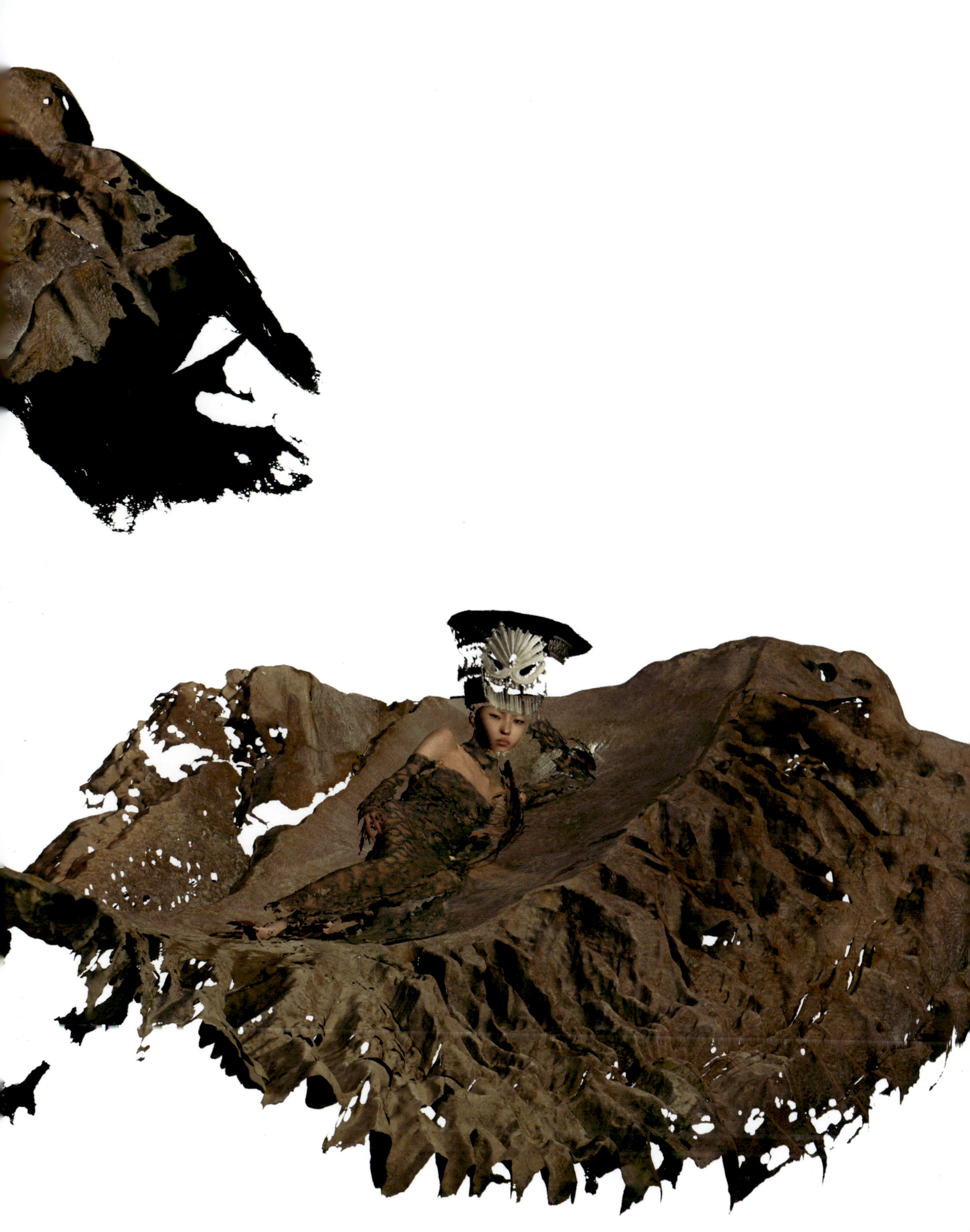

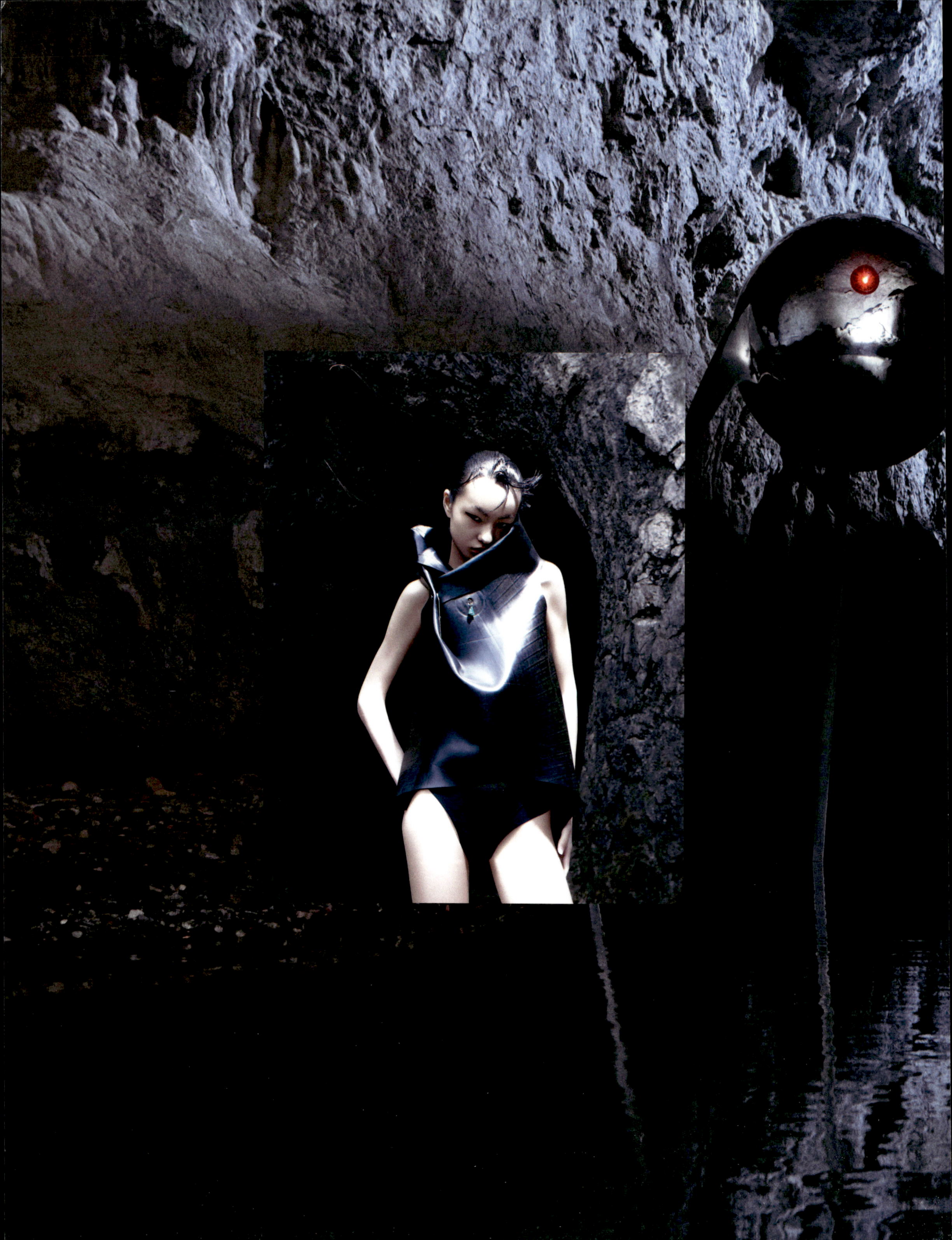

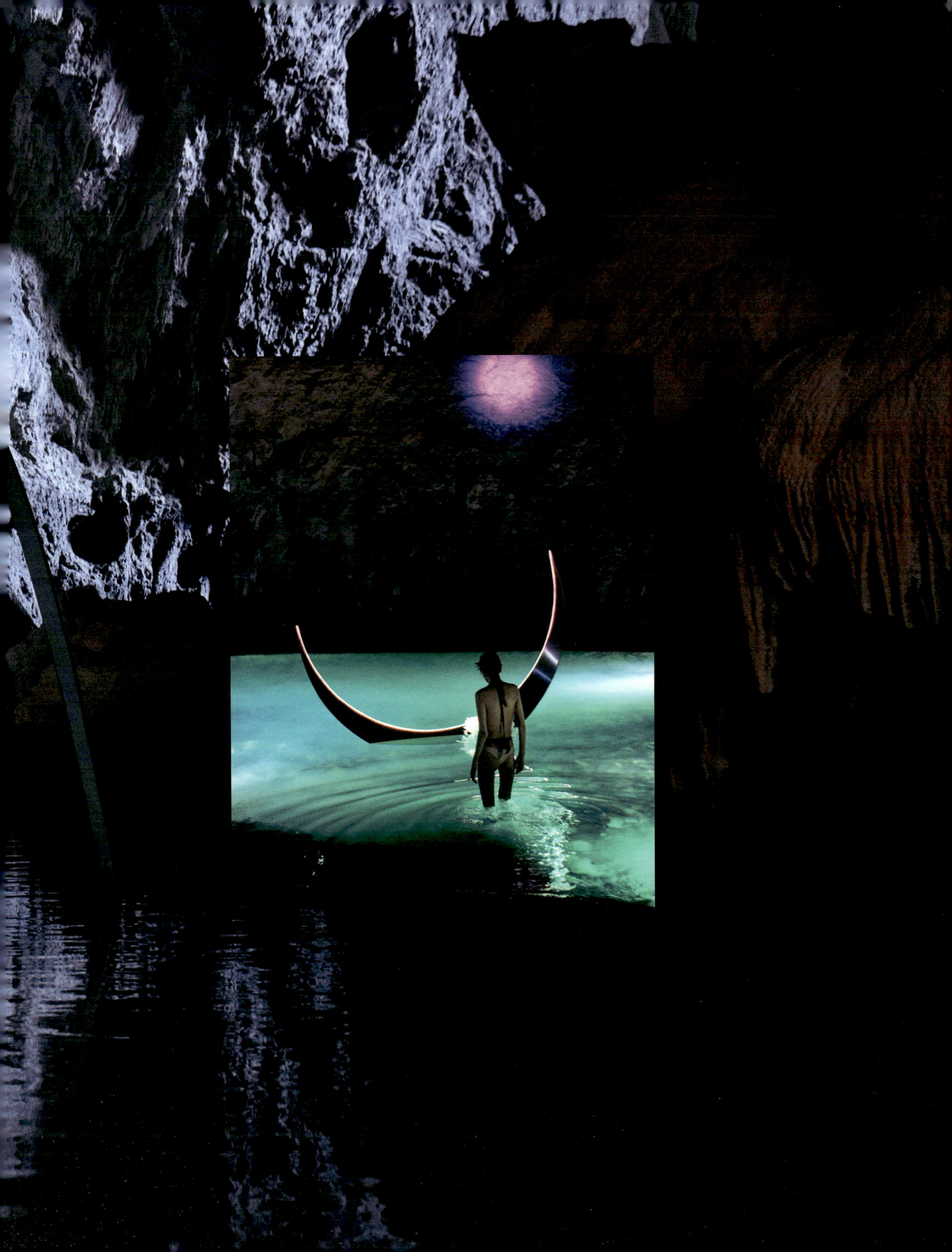

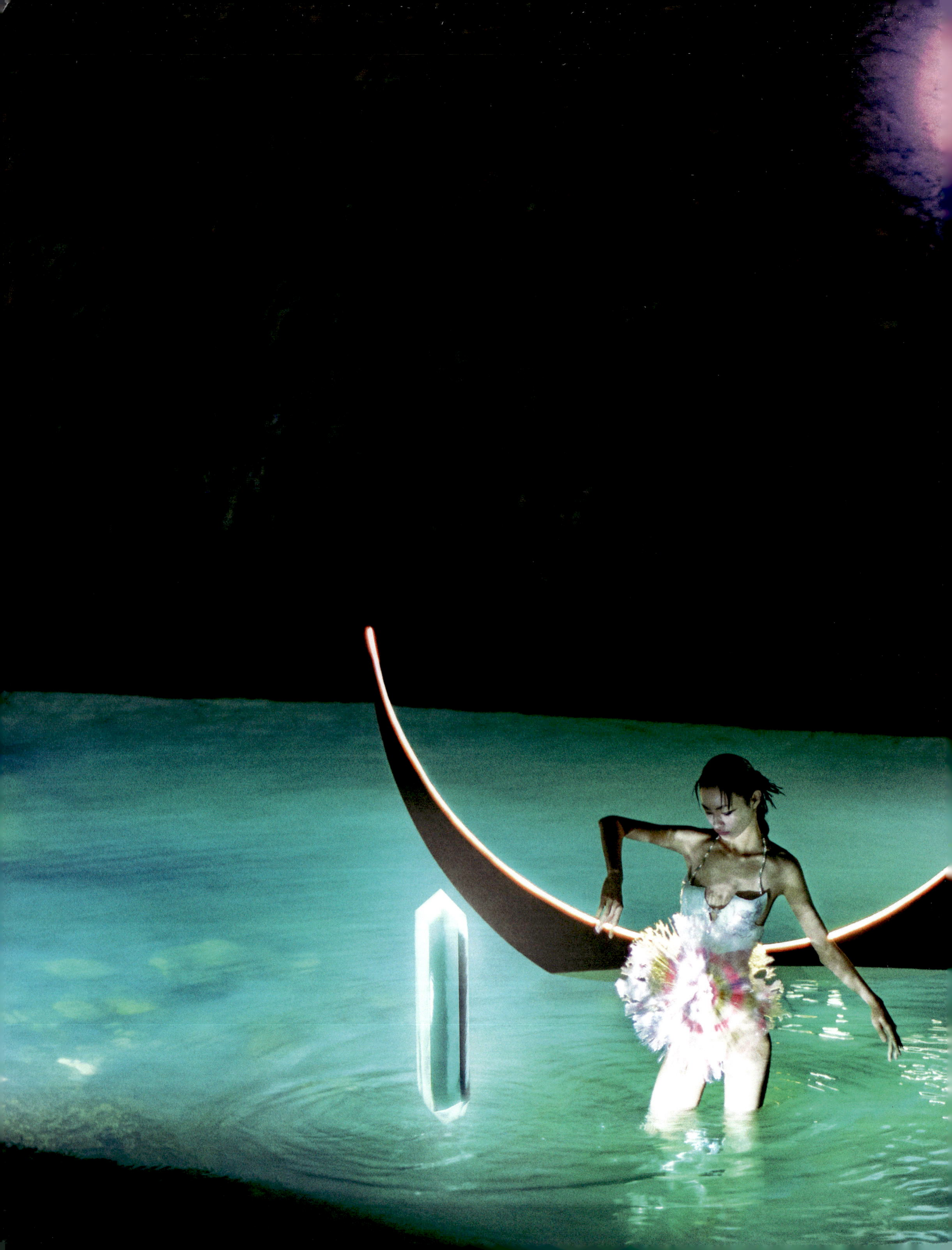

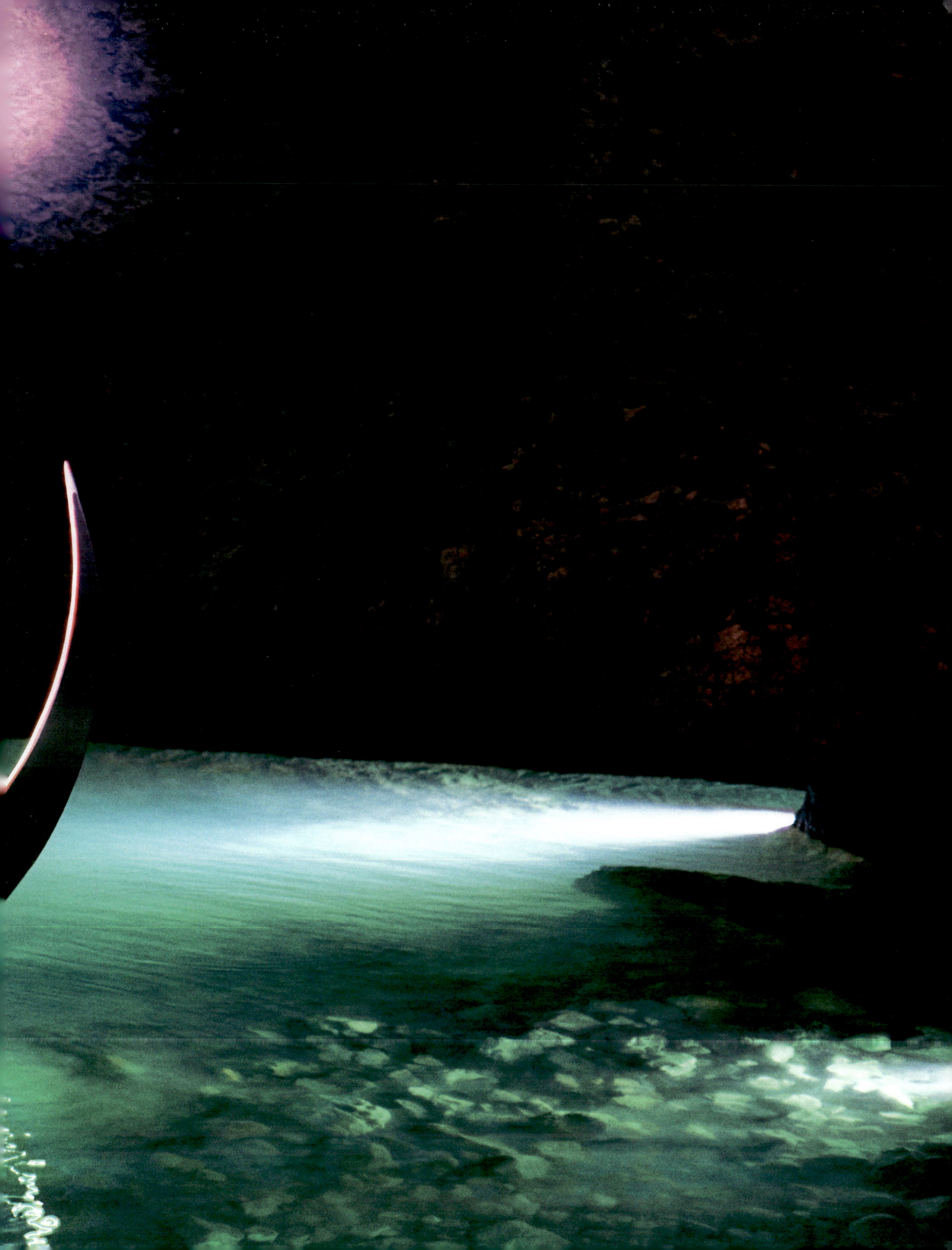

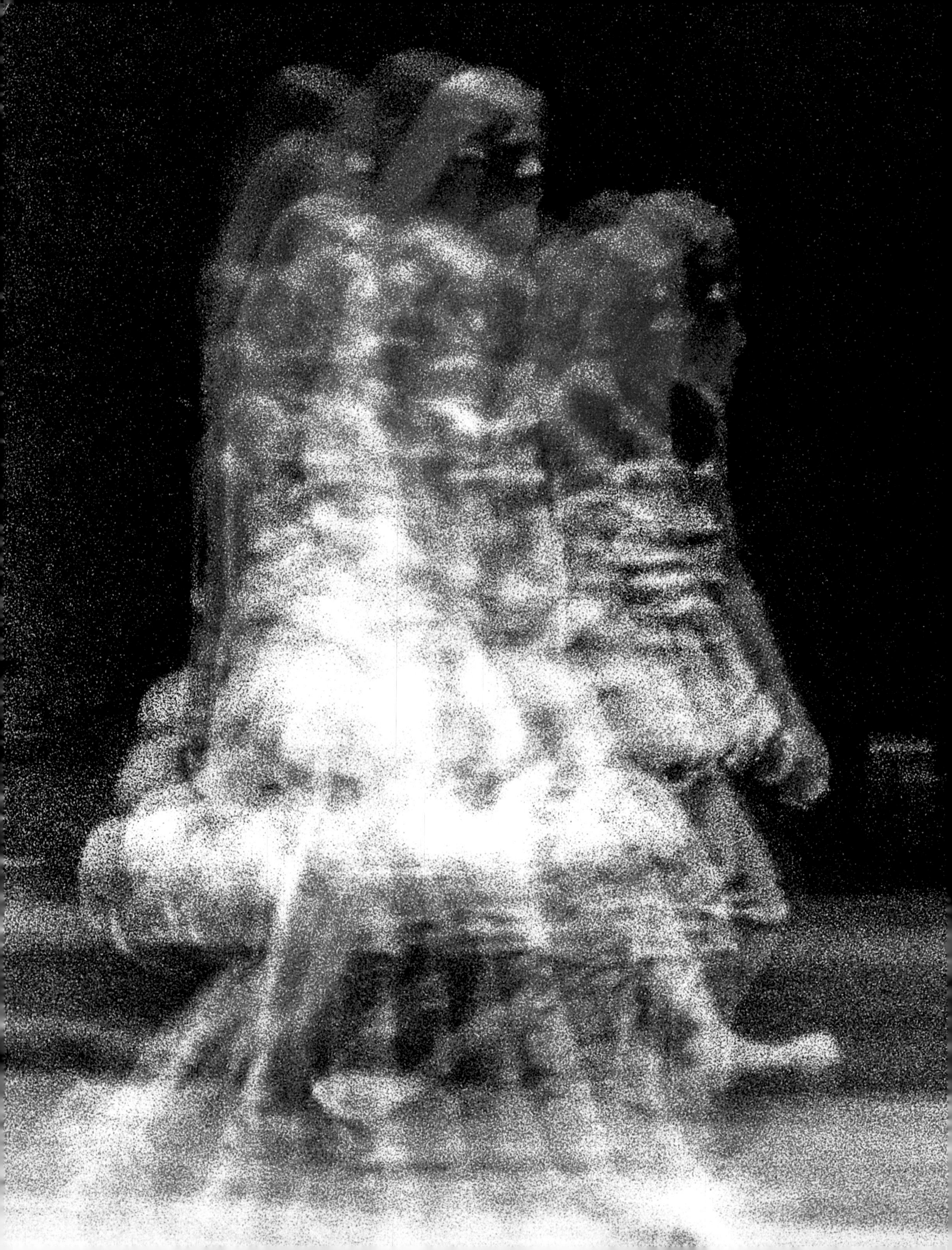

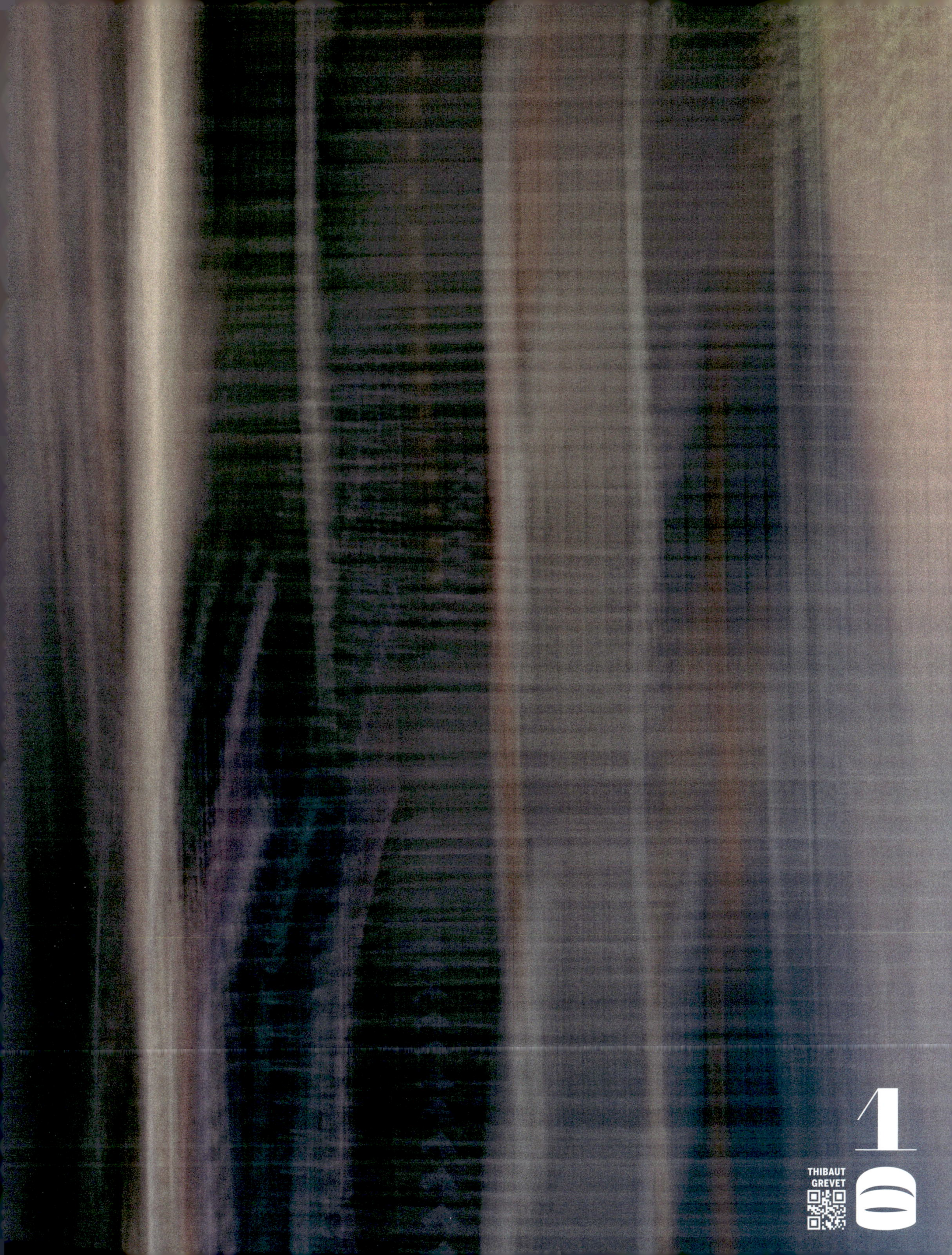

1
THIBAUT
GREVET

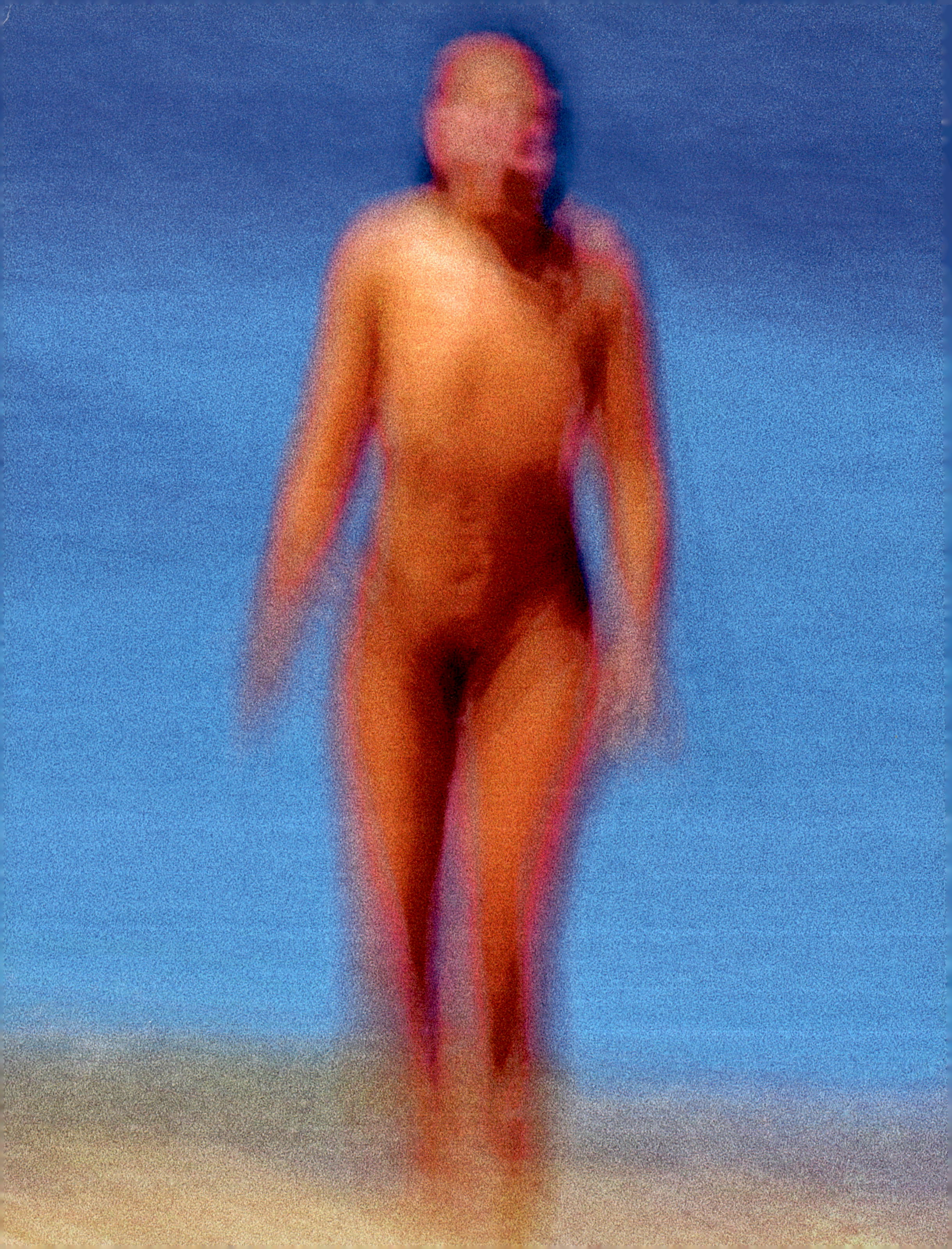

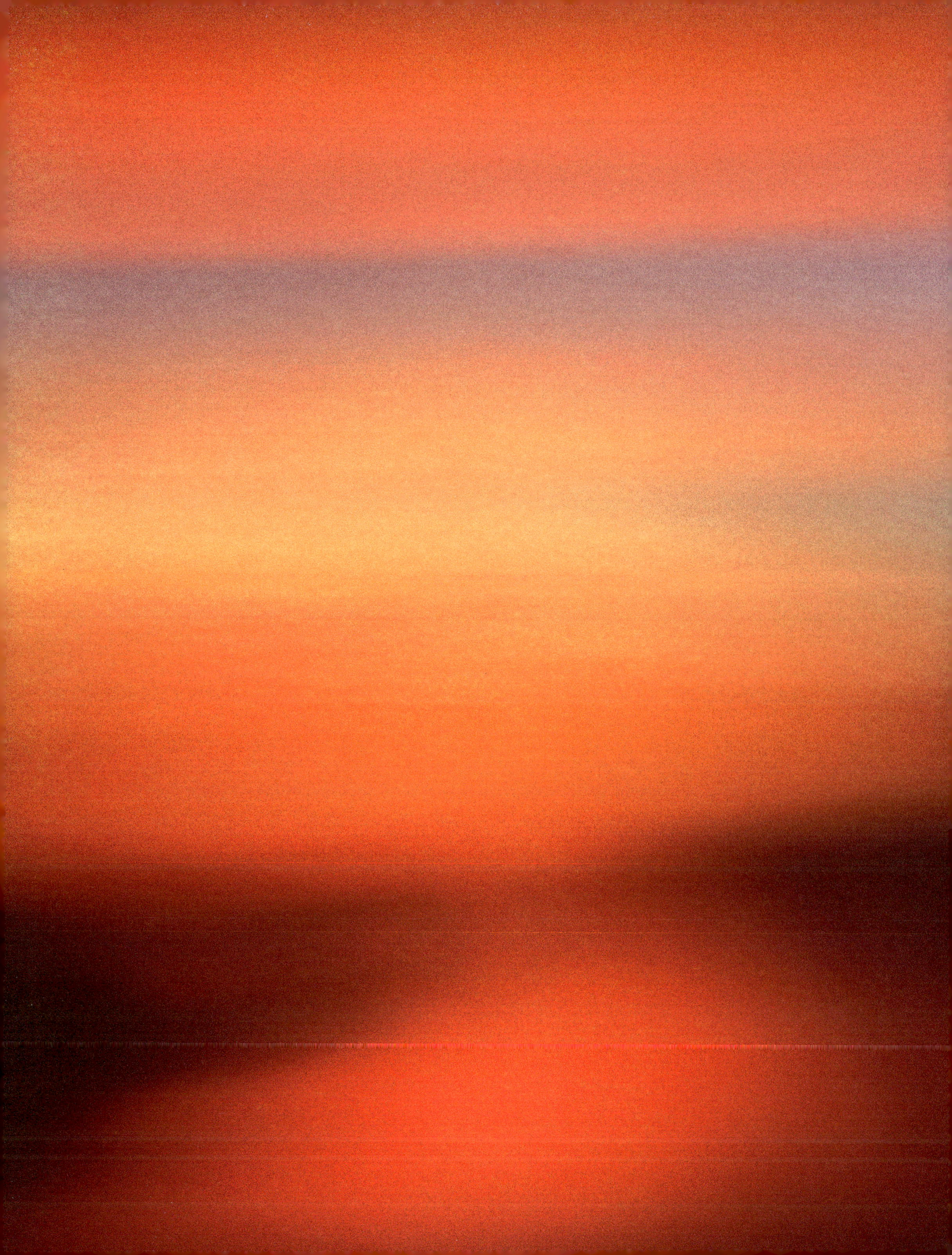

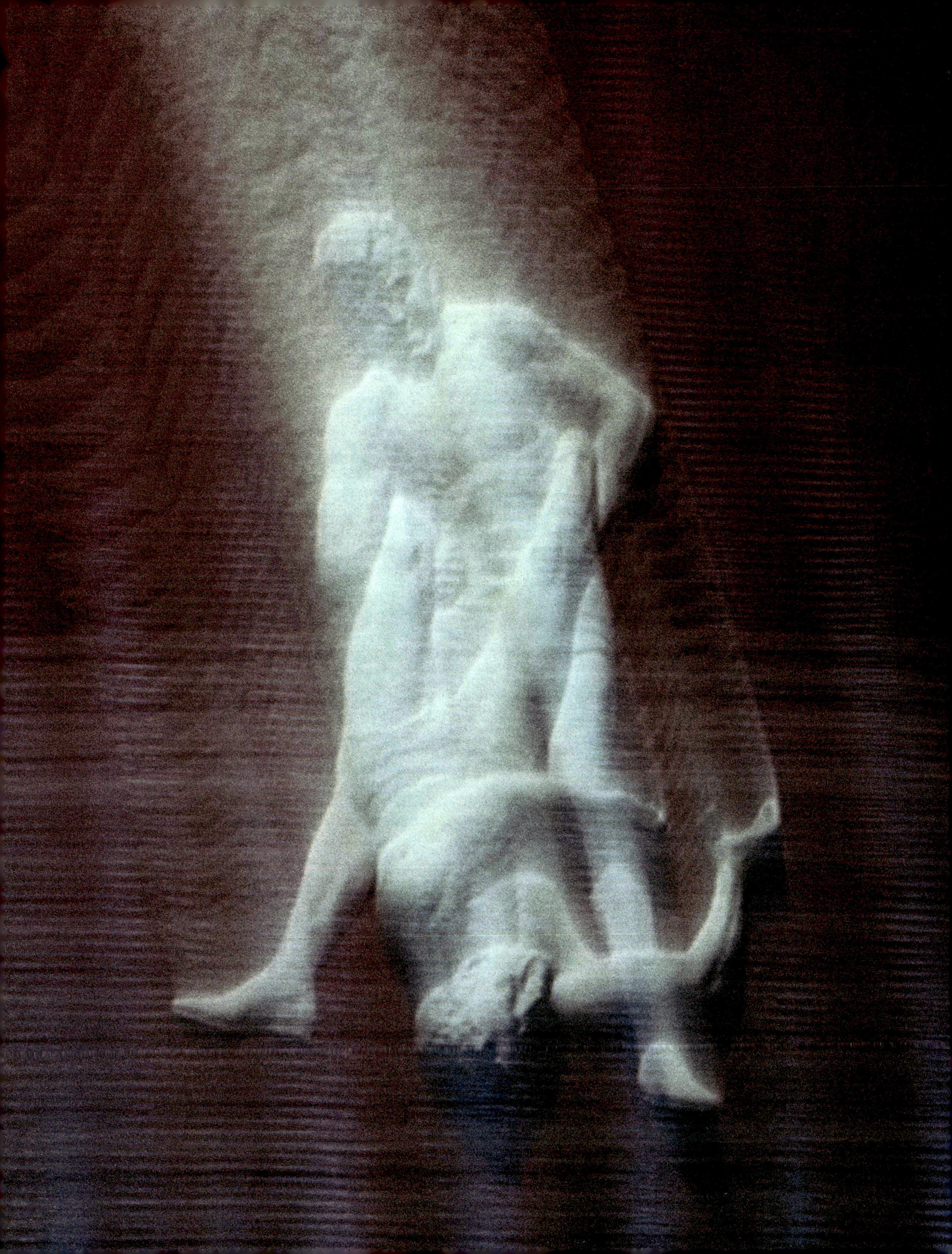

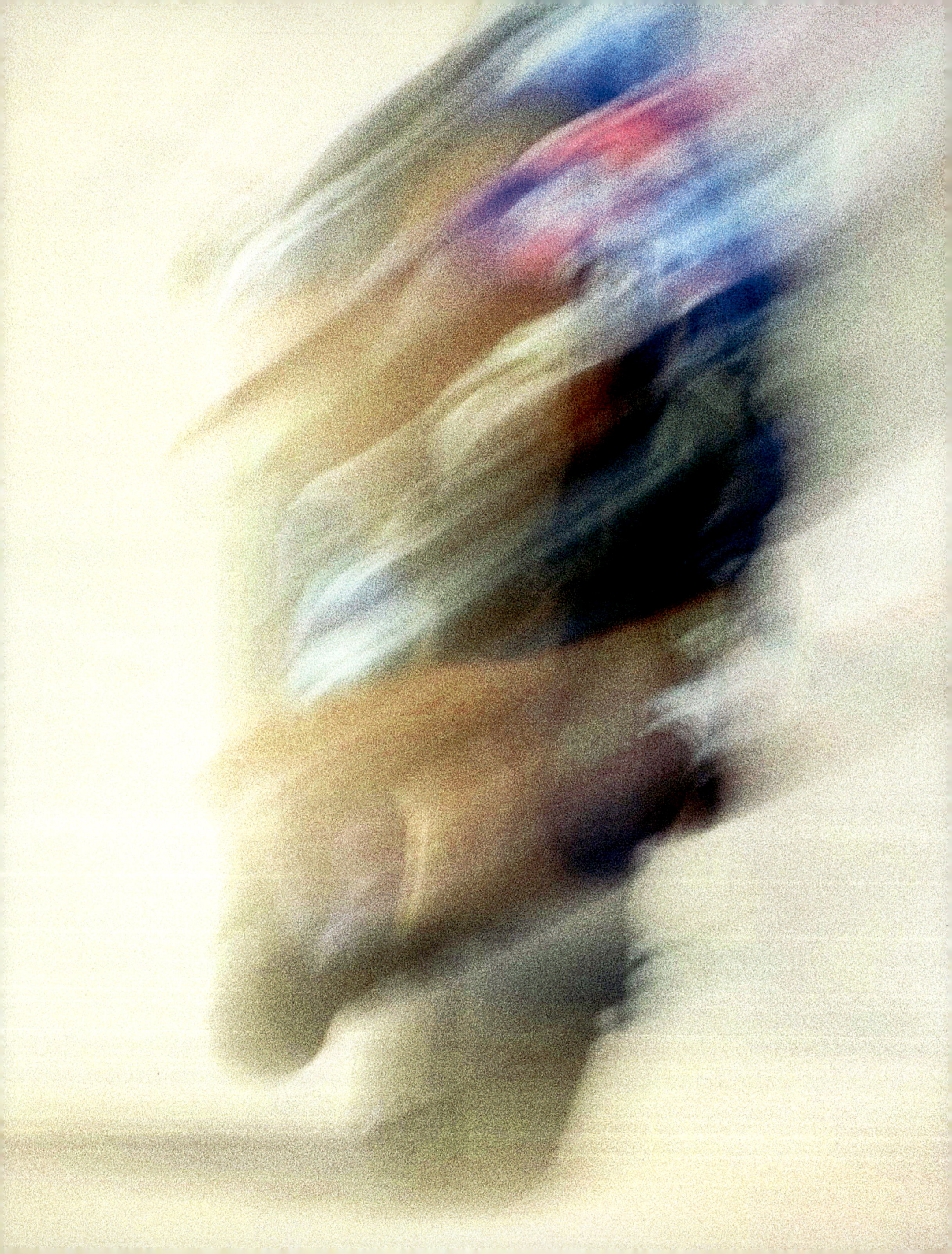

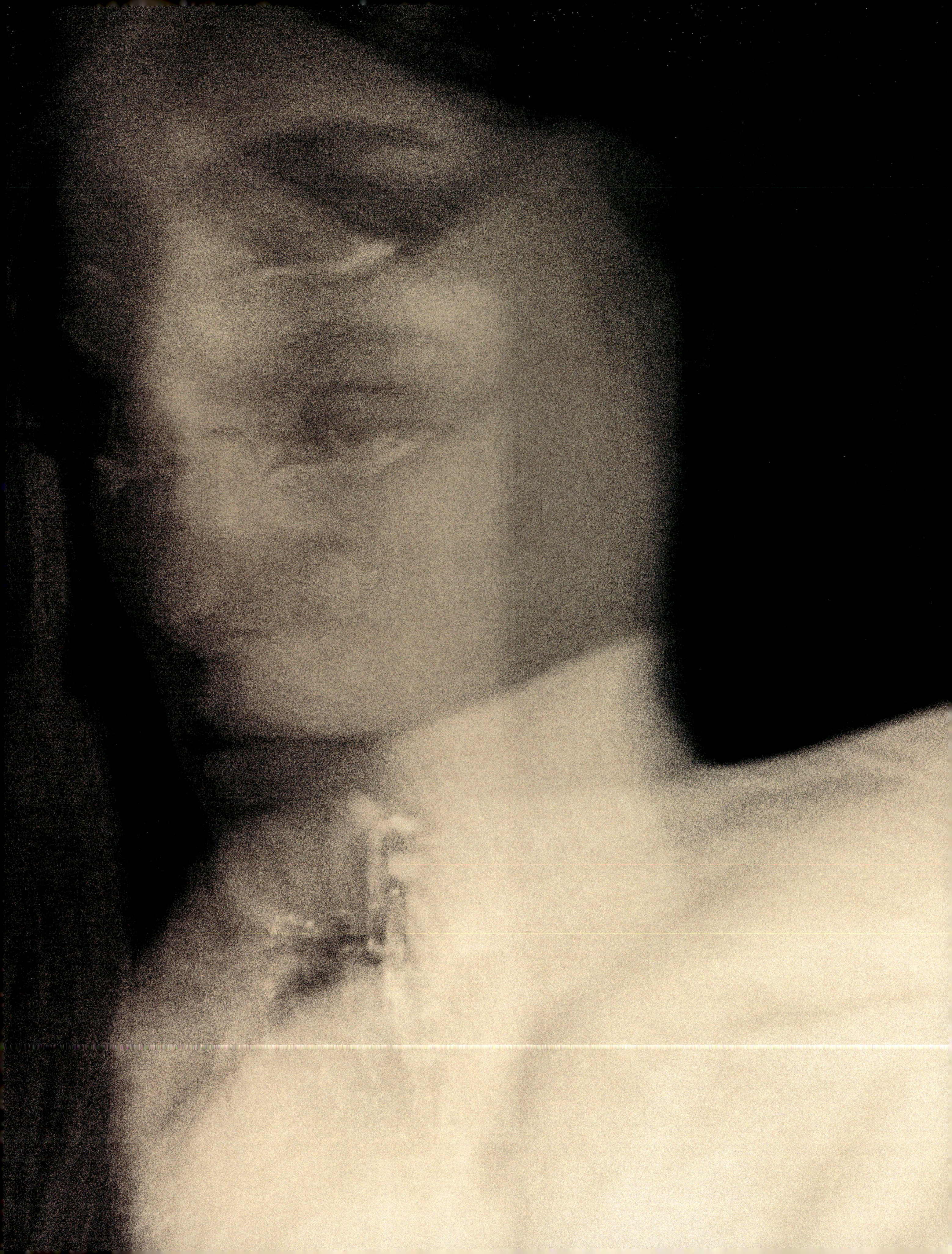

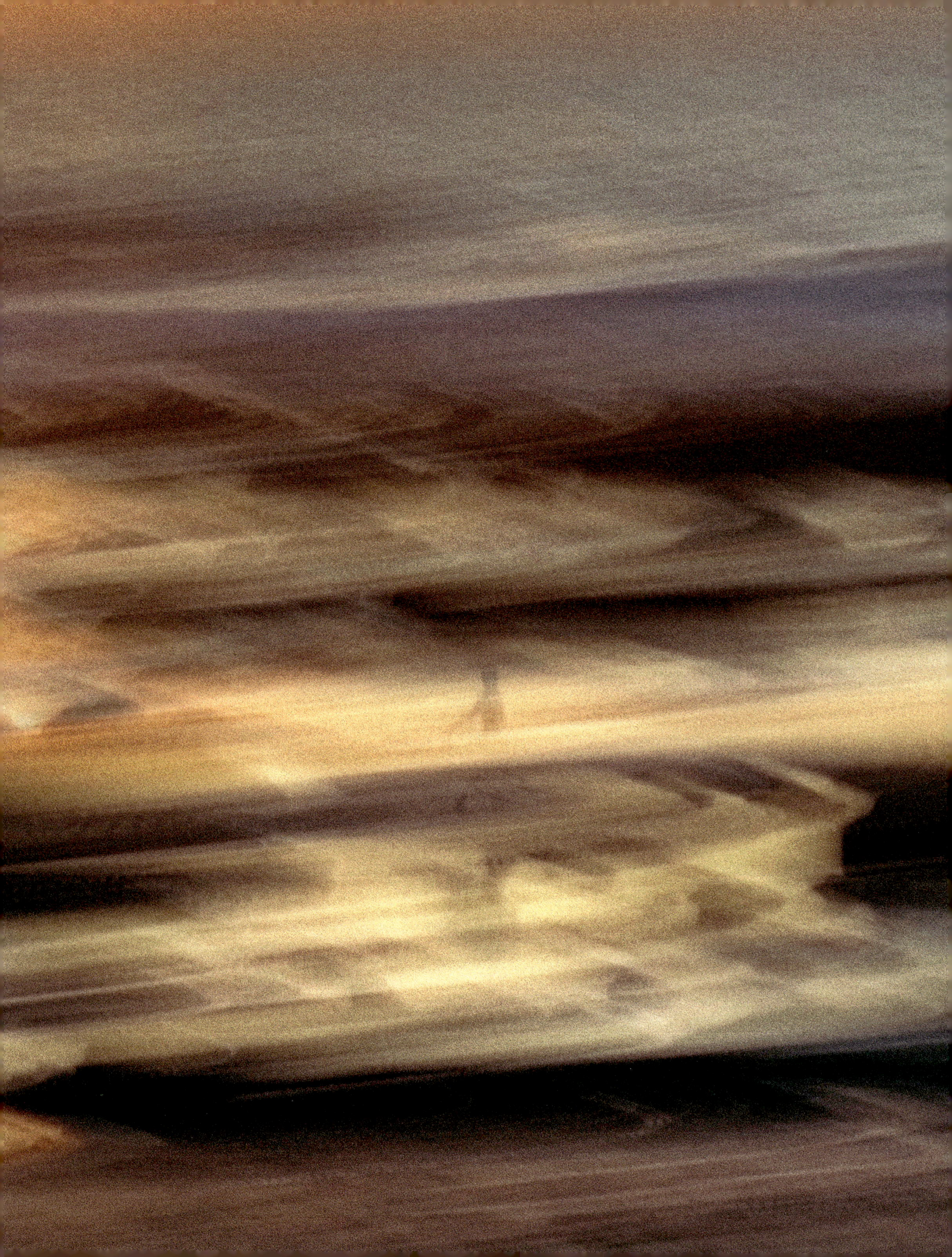

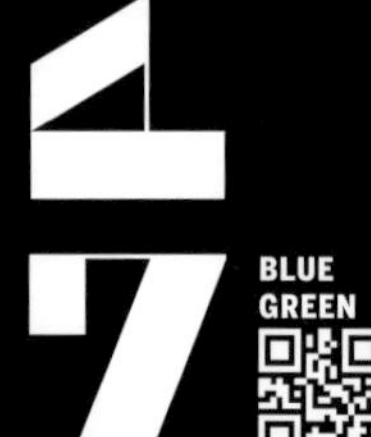
BLUE
GREEN

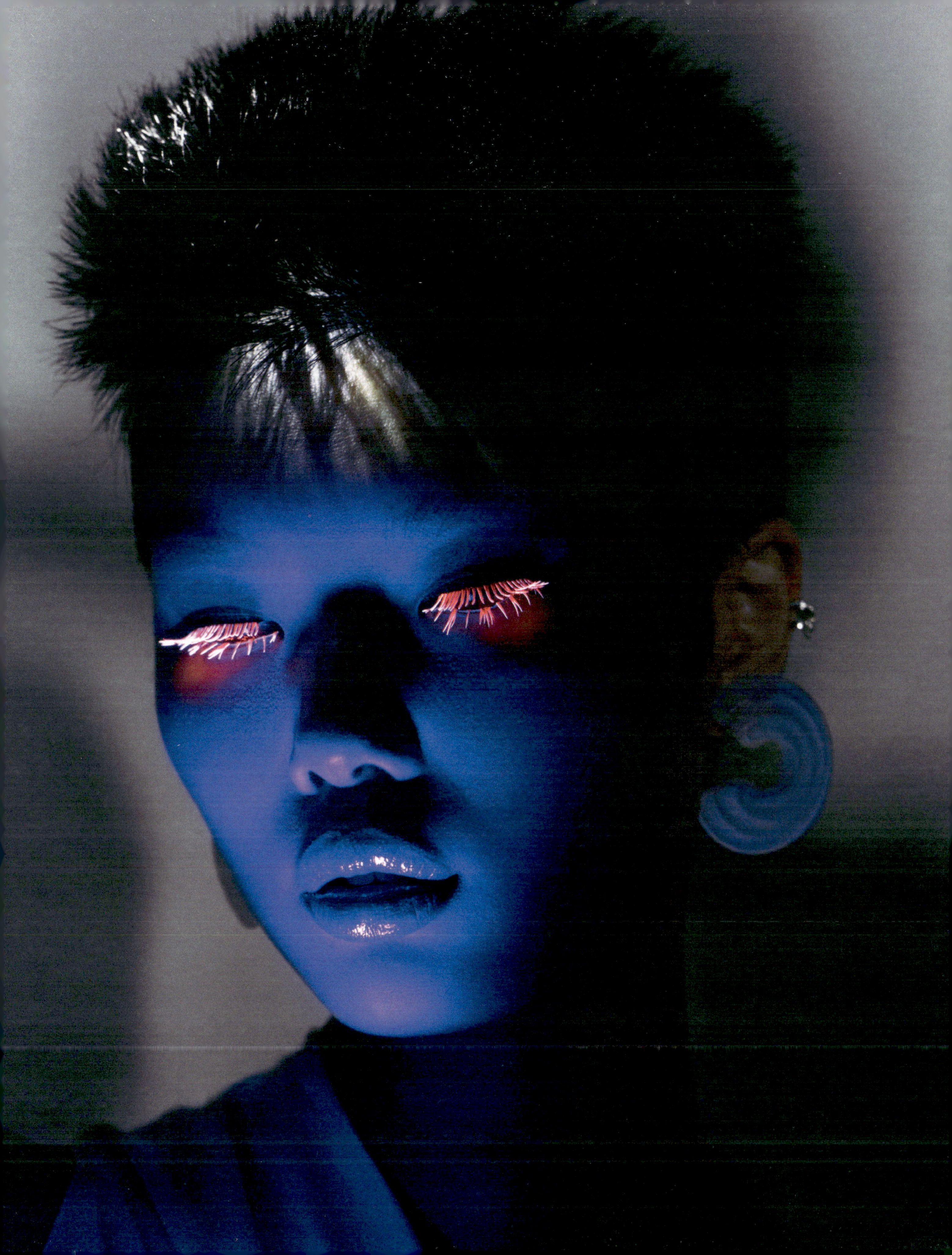

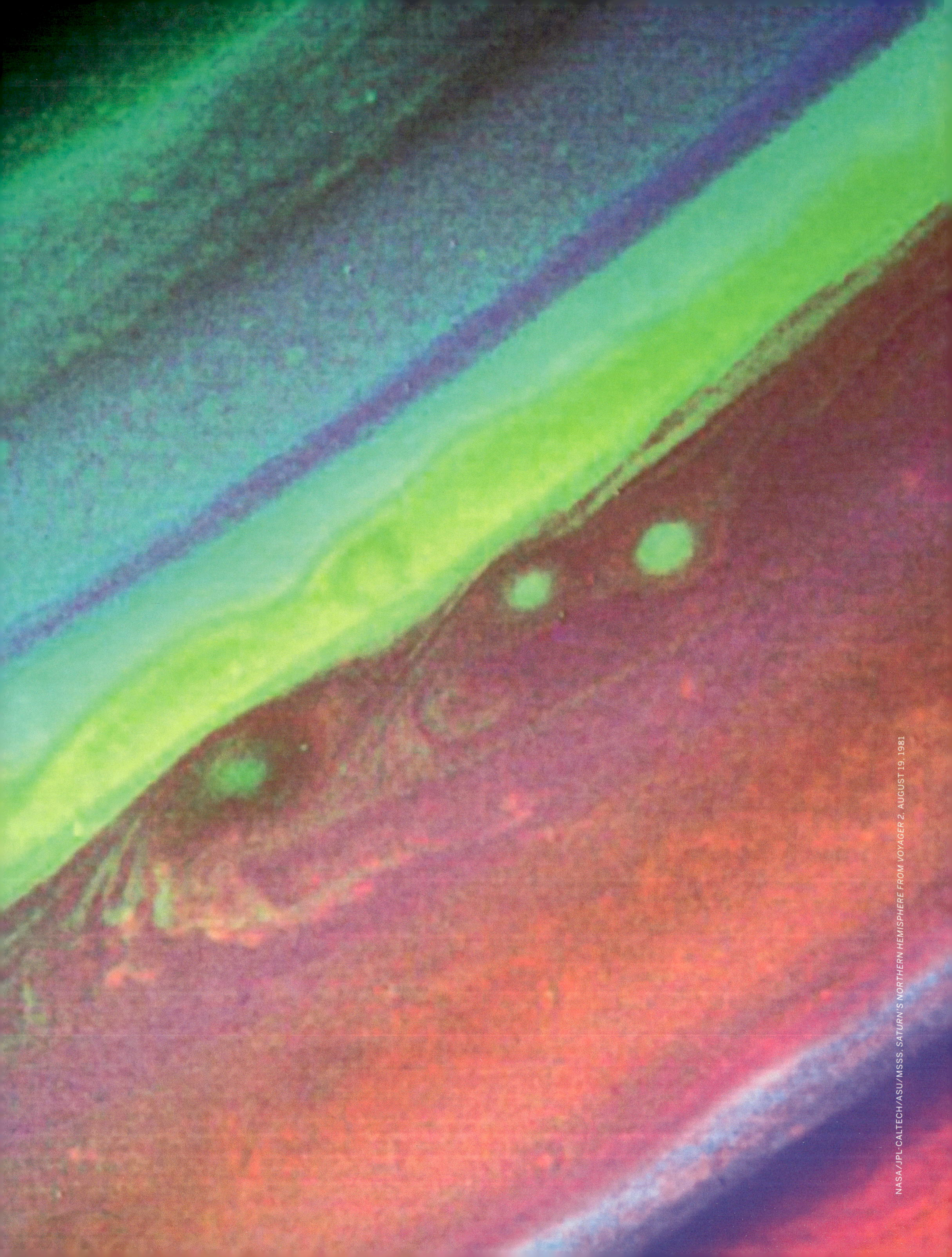

NASA/JPL-CALTECH/ASU/MSSS. SATURN'S NORTHERN HEMISPHERE FROM VOYAGER 2. AUGUST 19, 1981

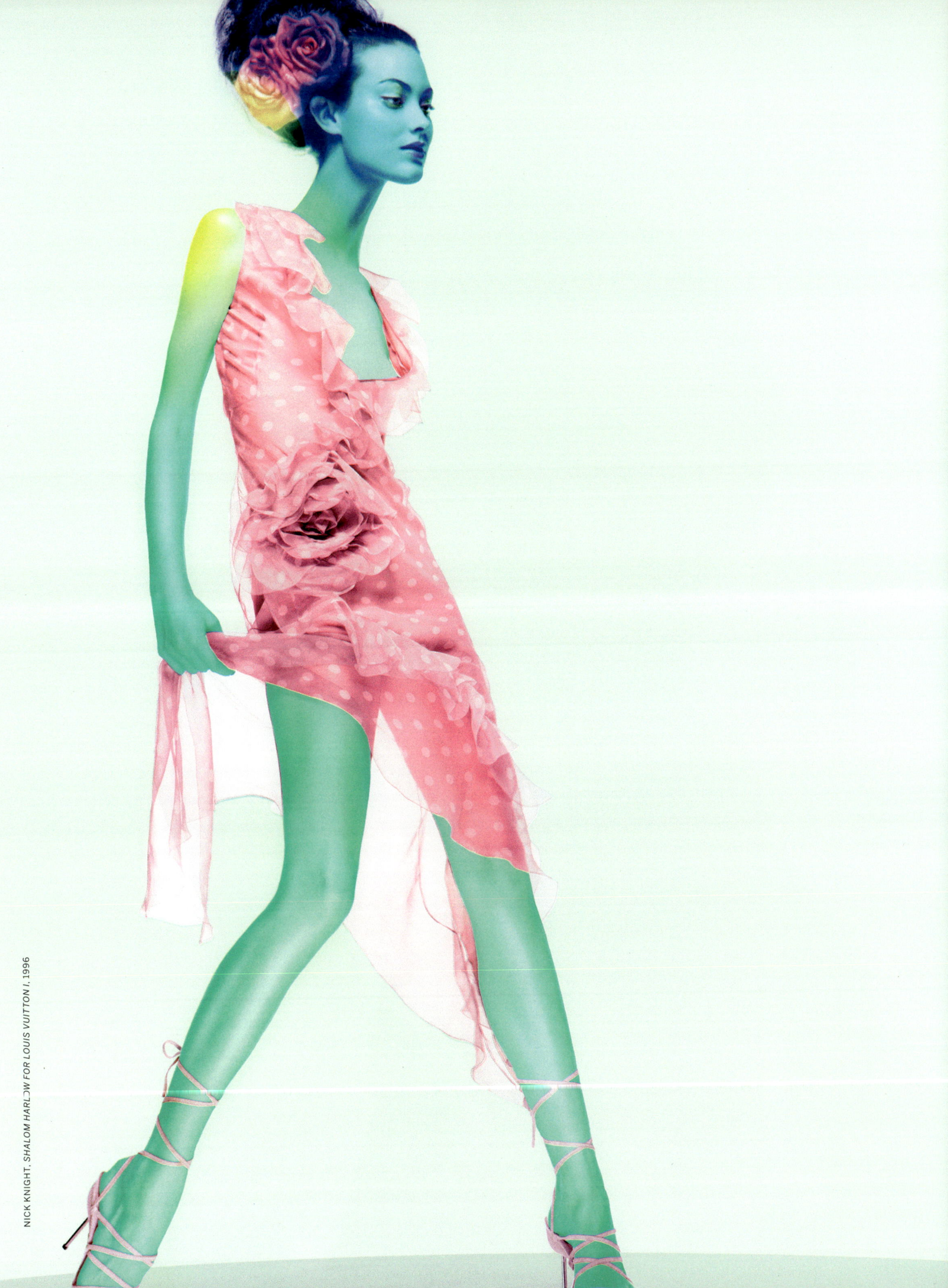

NICK KNIGHT. SHALOM HARLOW FOR LOUIS VUITTON I. 1996

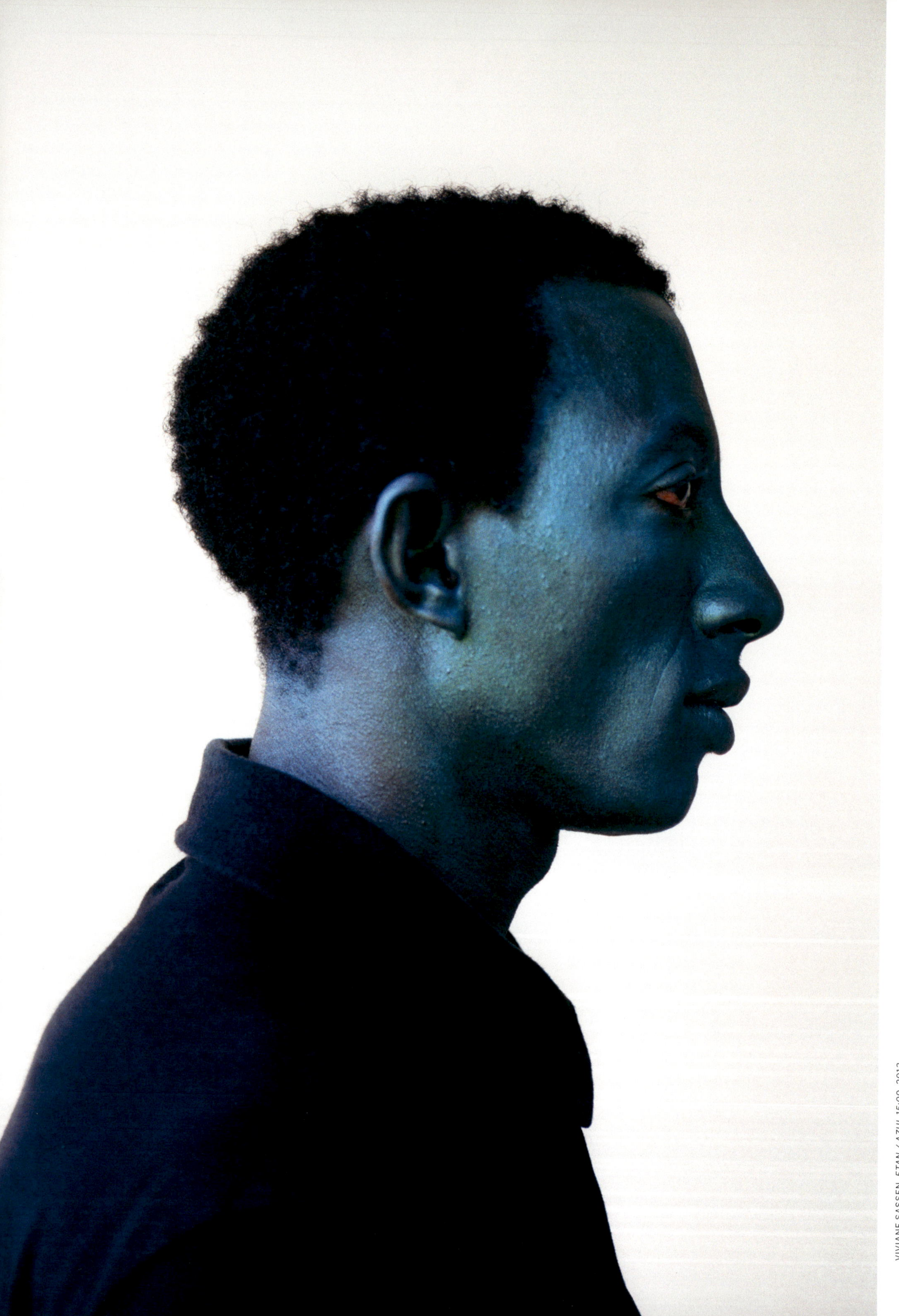

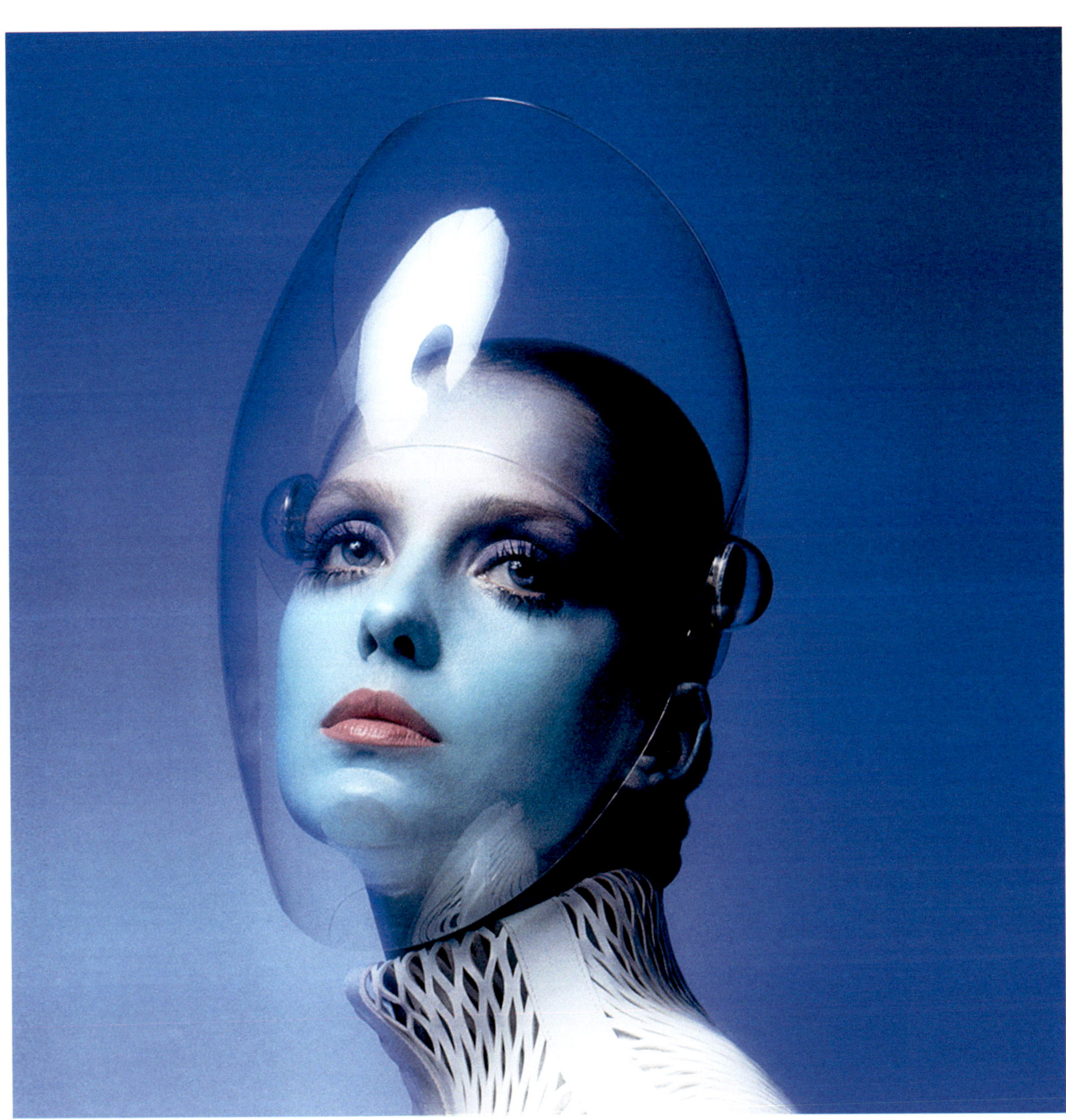

CLIVE ARROWSMITH, *VOGUE* UK, 1970

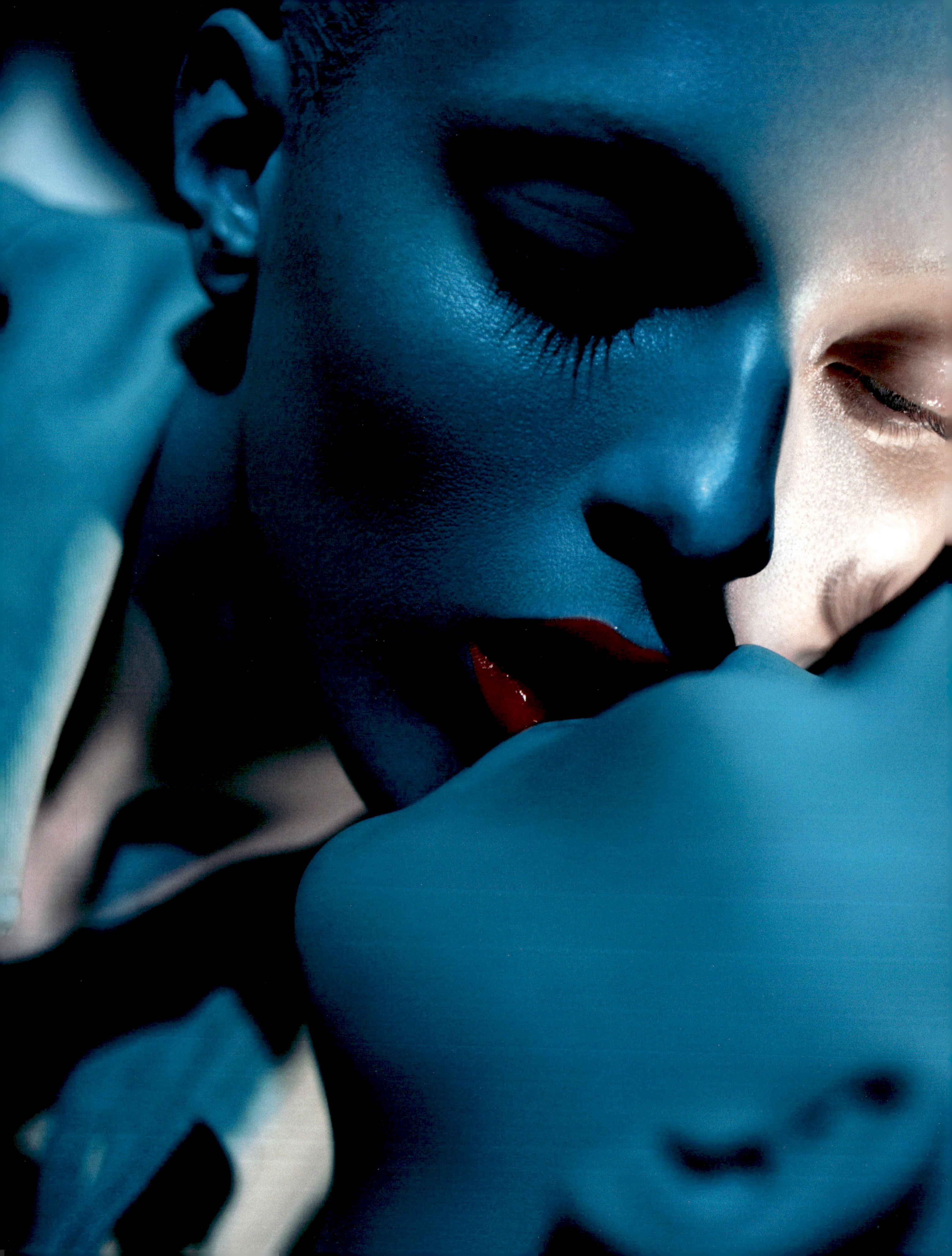

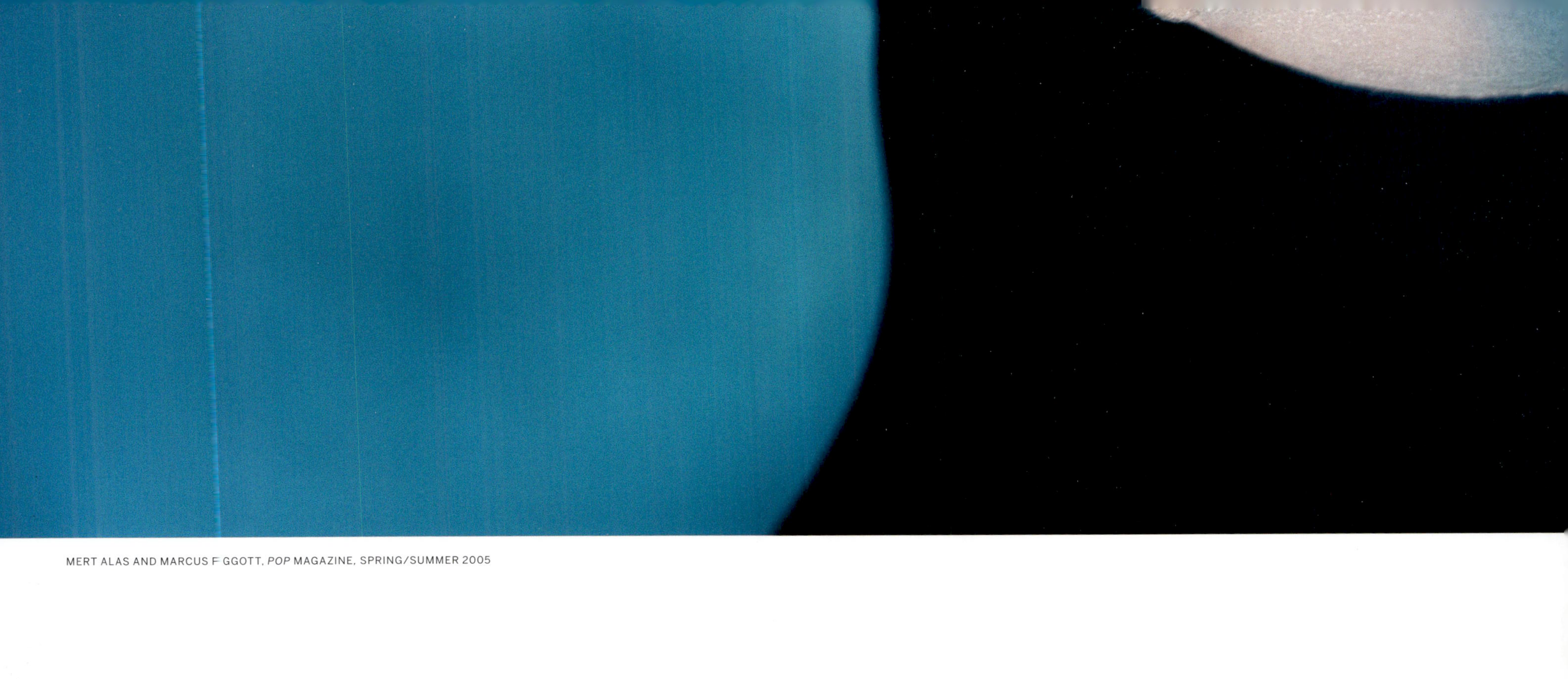

MERT ALAS AND MARCUS PIGGOTT, POP MAGAZINE, SPRING/SUMMER 2005

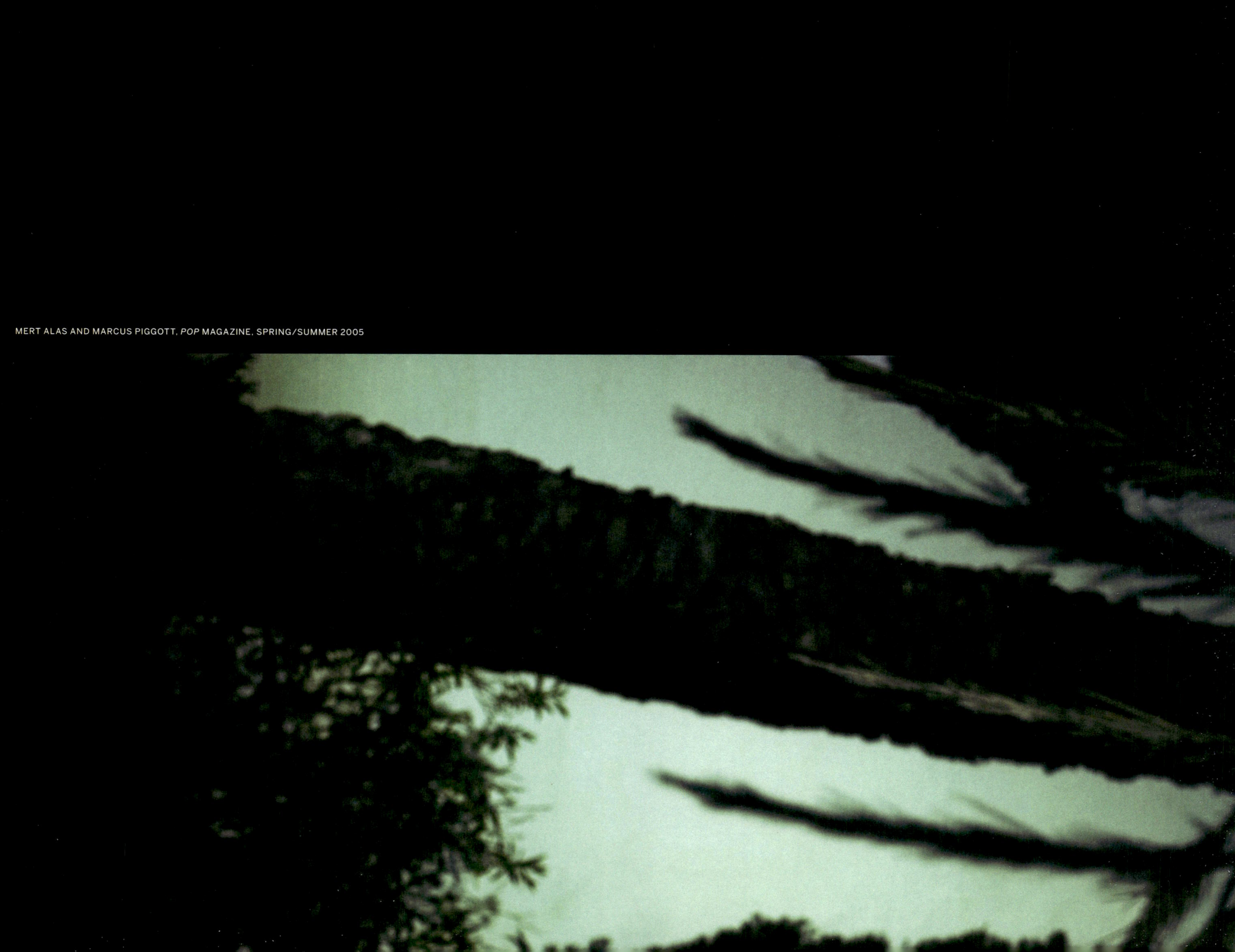

MERT ALAS AND MARCUS PIGGOTT, *POP* MAGAZINE, SPRING/SUMMER 2005

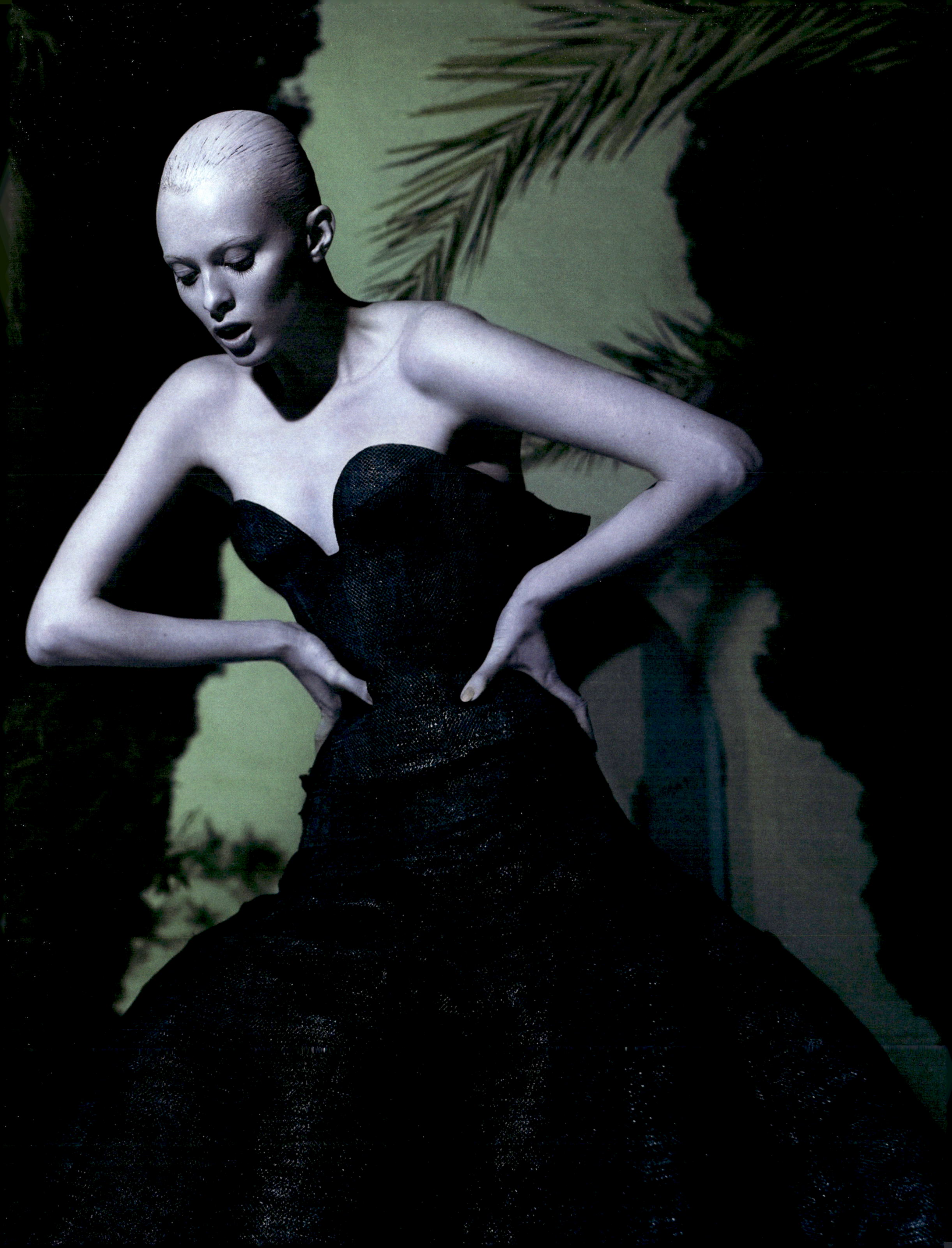

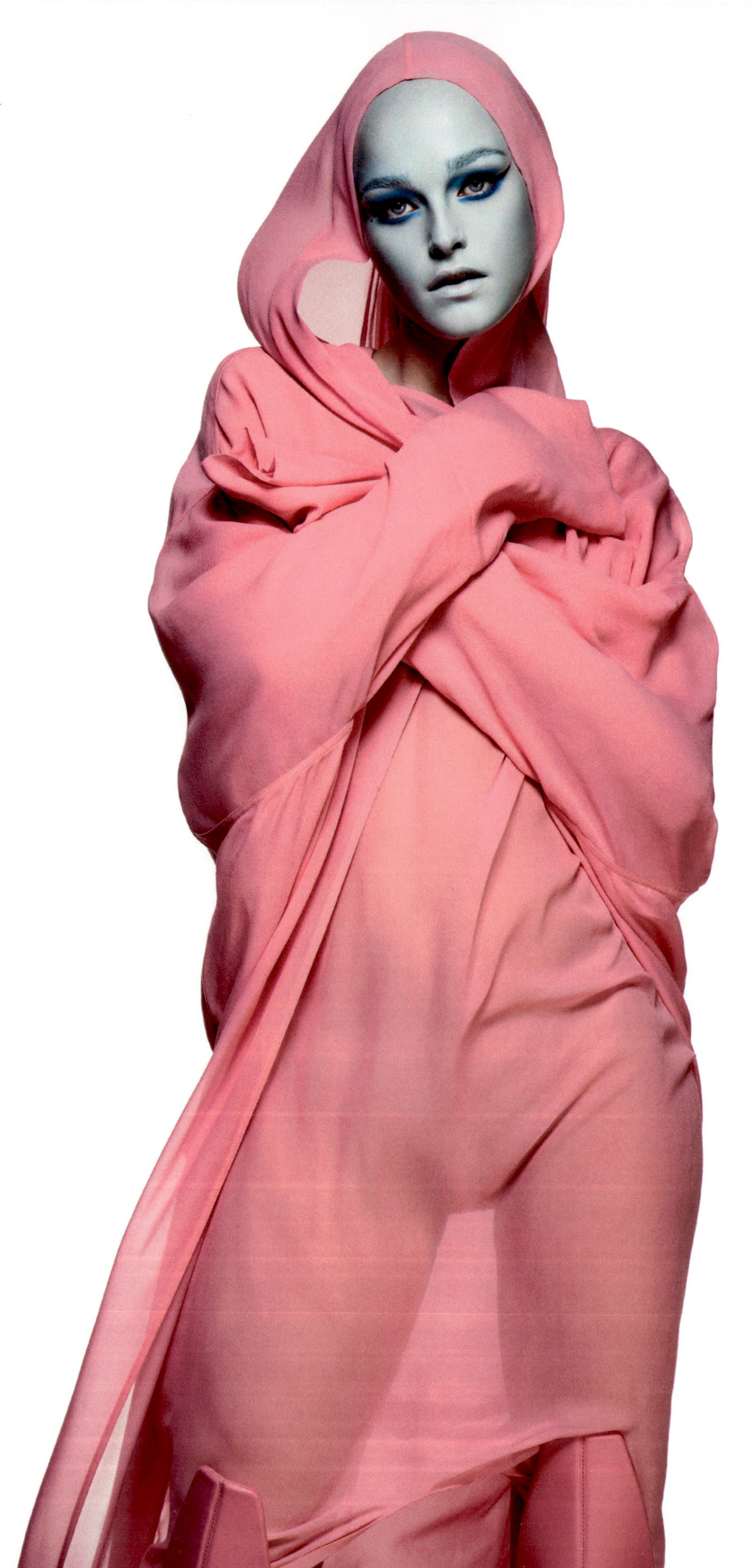

SØLVE SUNDSBØ. V MAGAZINE. SPRING 2021

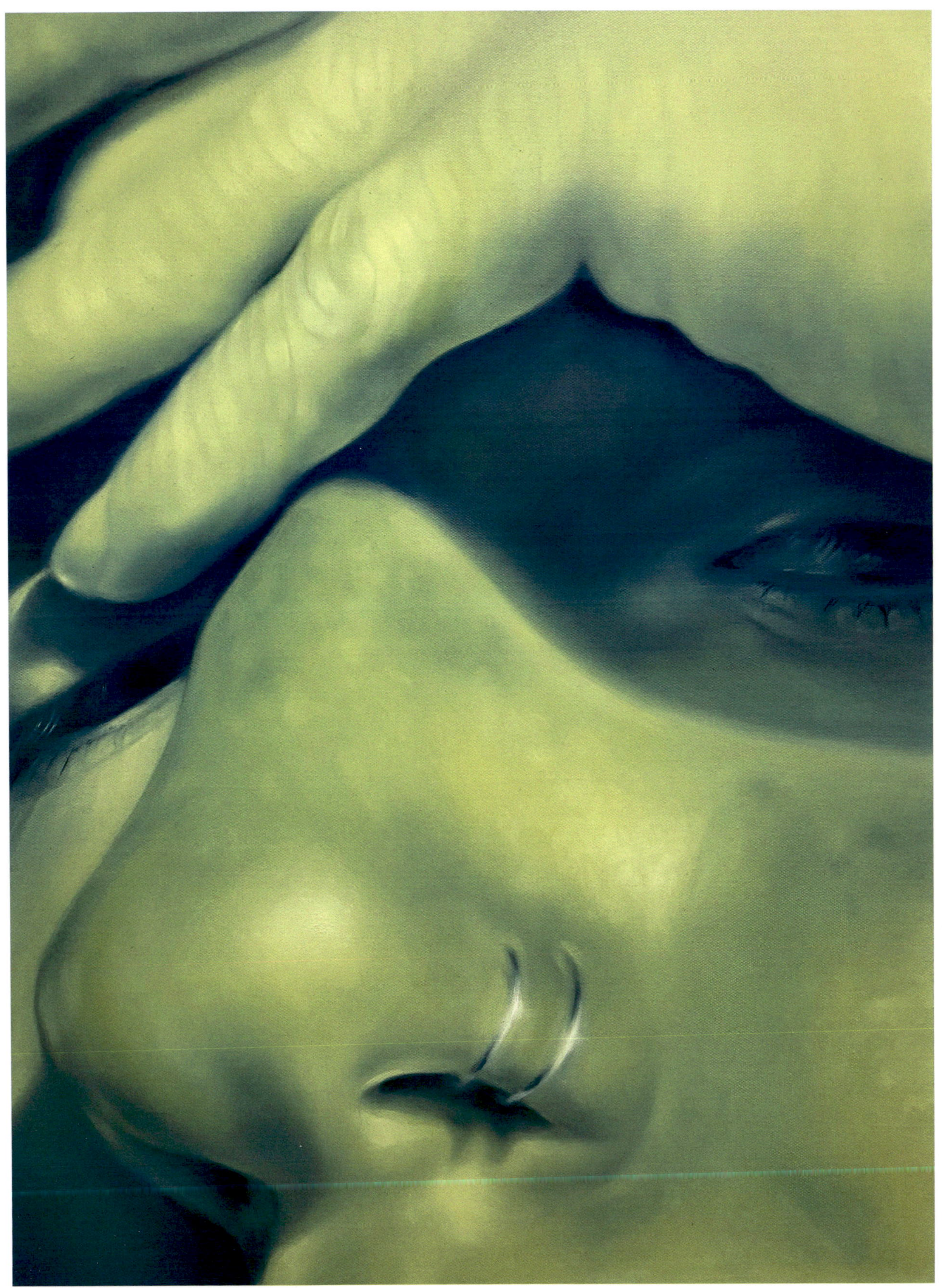

ALEJANDRA MOROS, *MI MAÑANA*, 2021

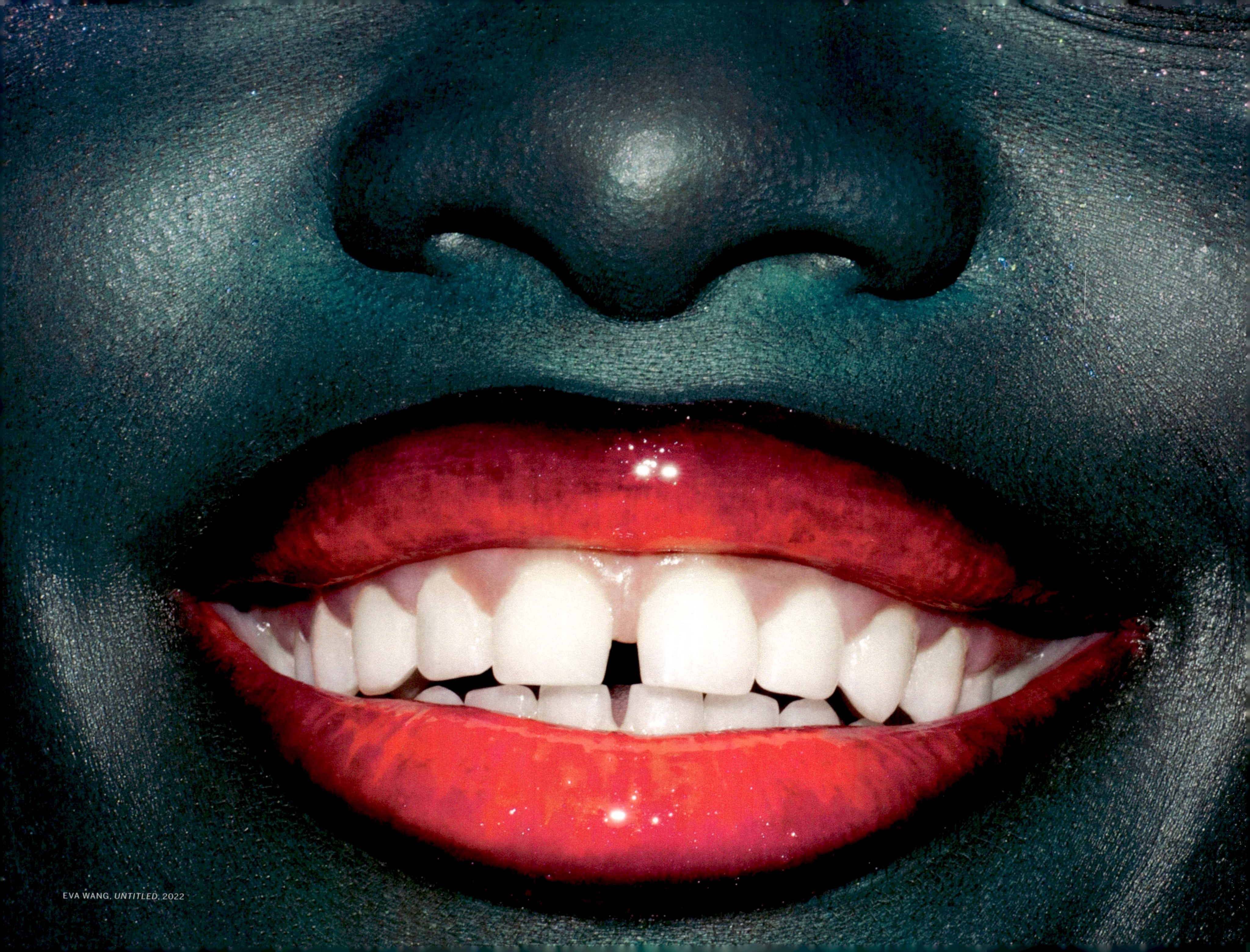

EVA WANG, UNTITLED, 2022

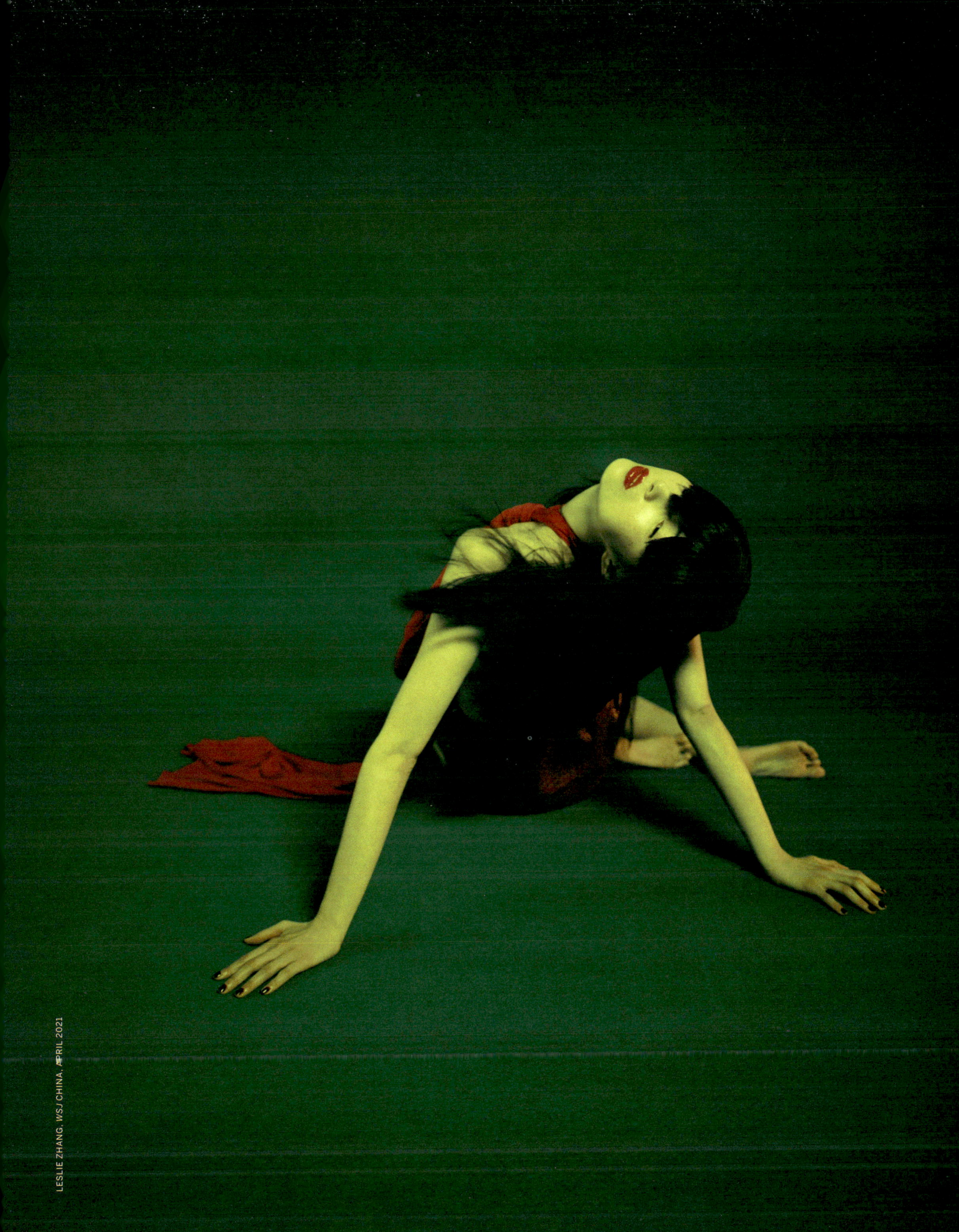
LESLIE ZHANG. WSJ CHINA. APRIL 2021

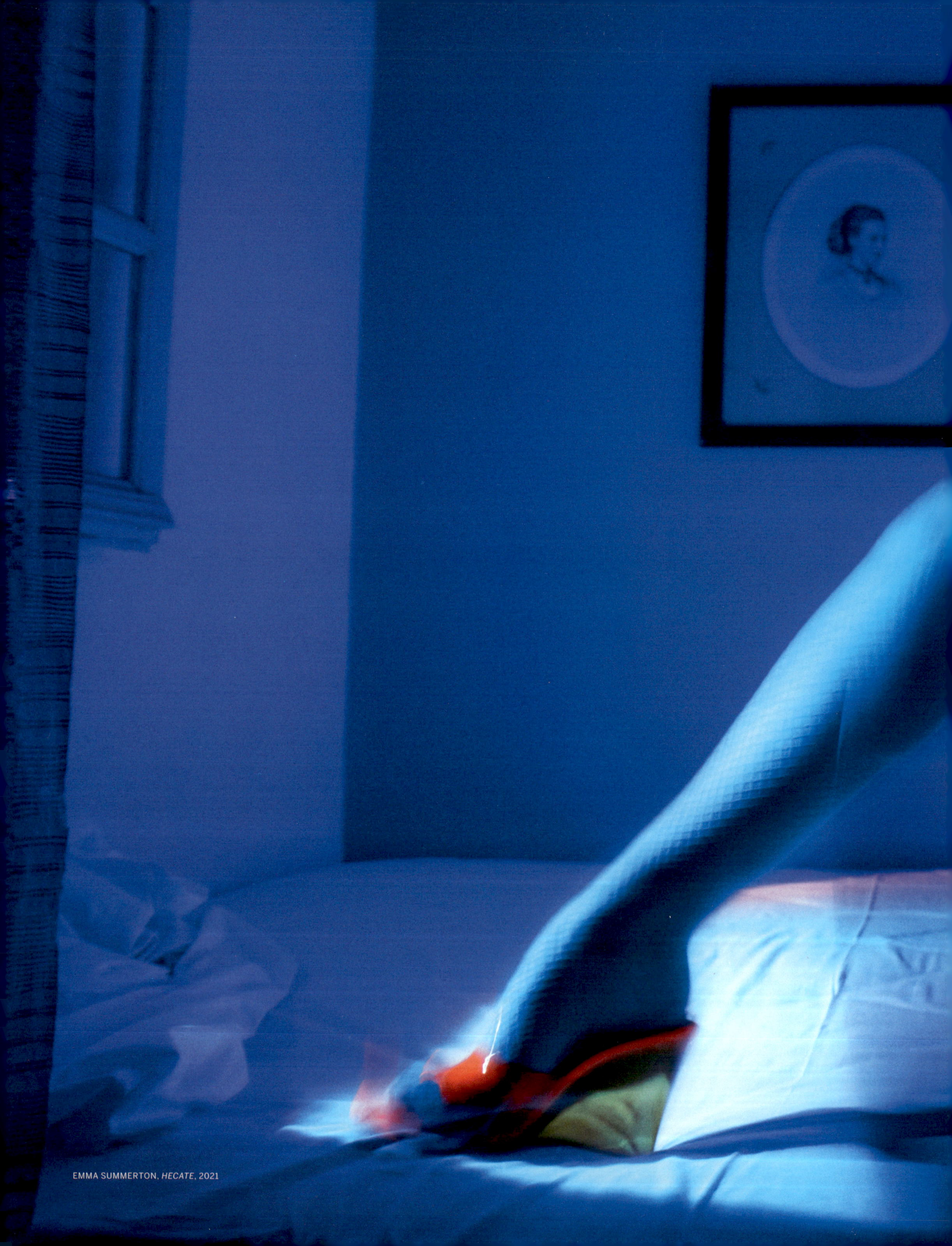

EMMA SUMMERTON, *HECATE*, 2021

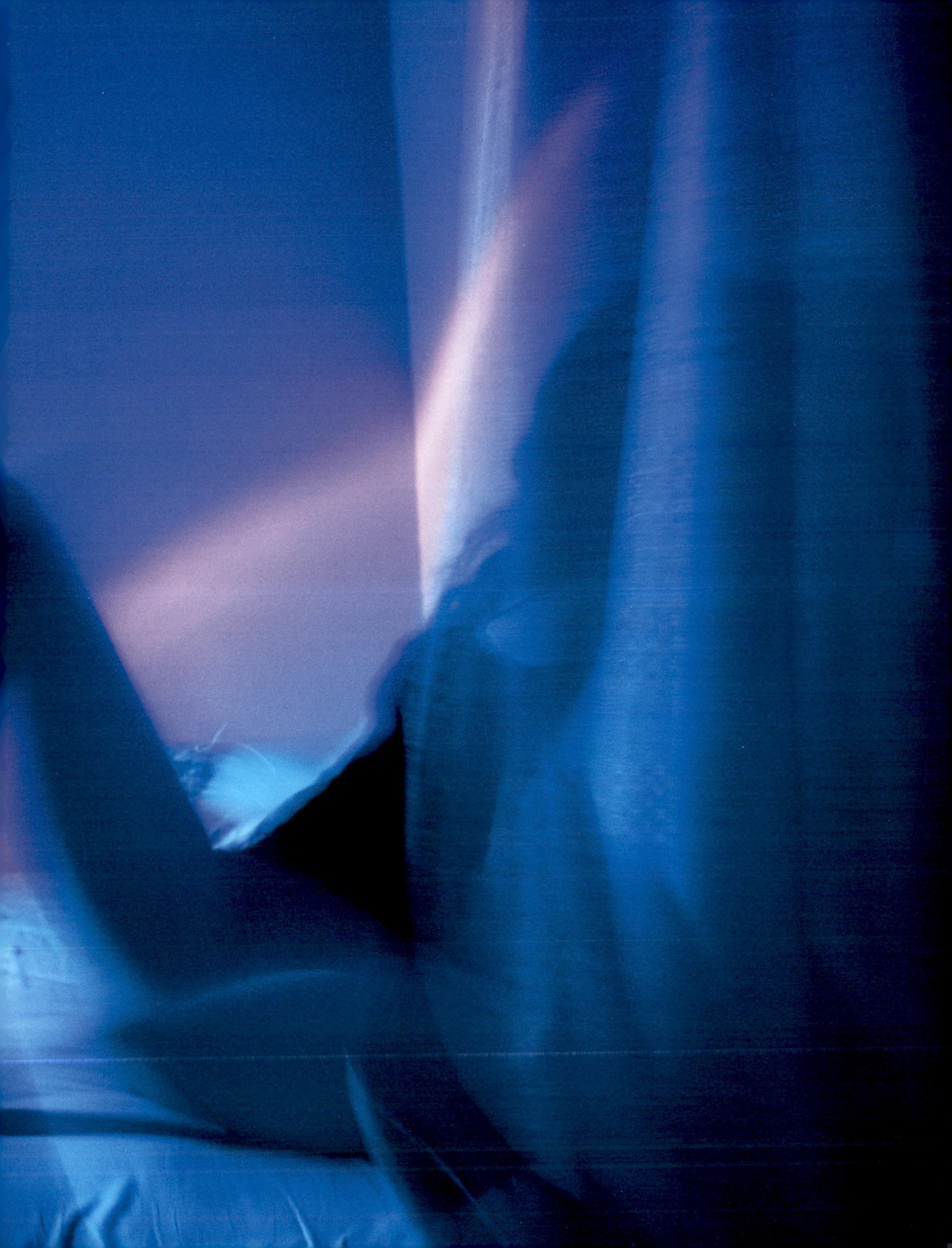

MELVIN SOKOLSKY, *LIP STREAKS*, 1967

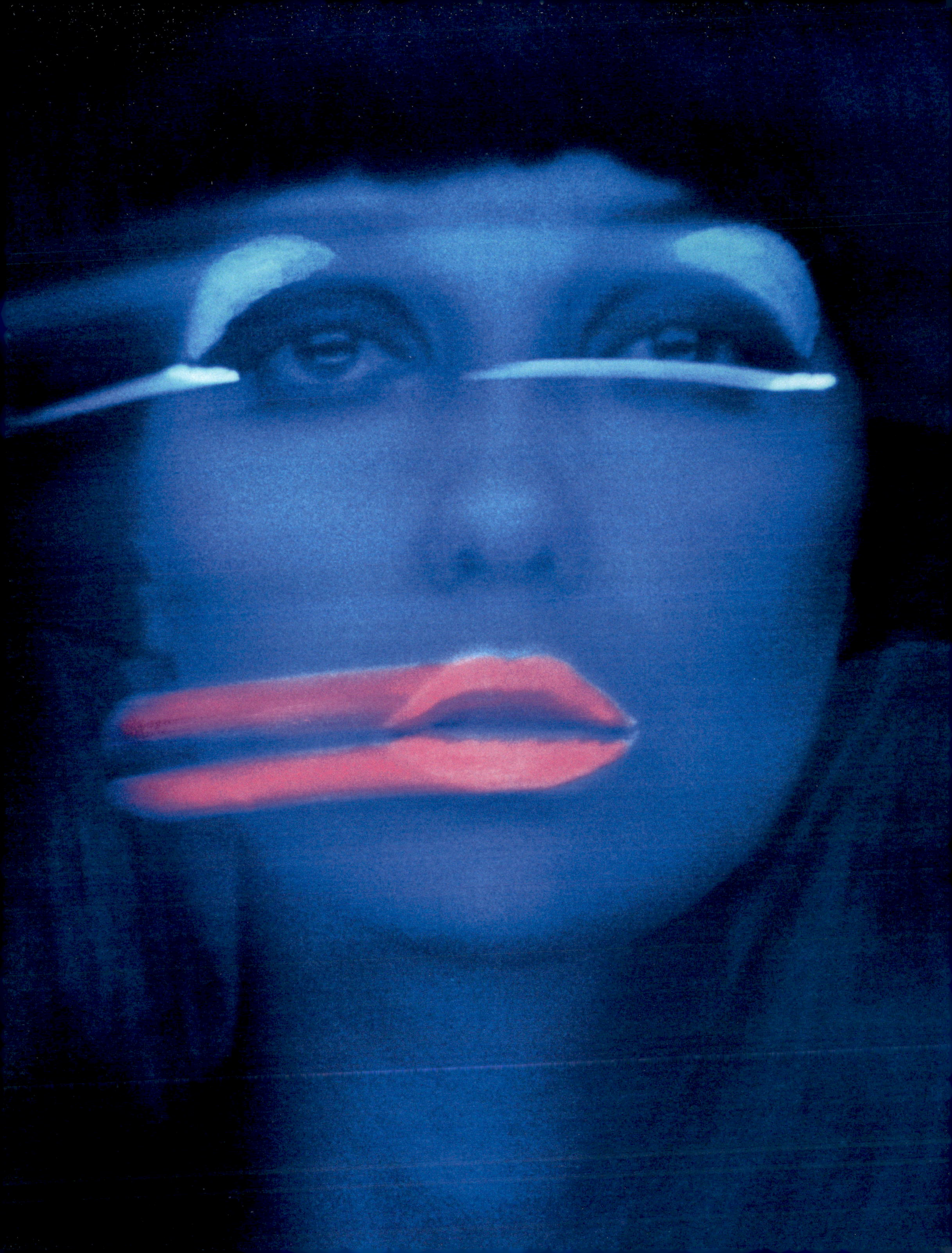

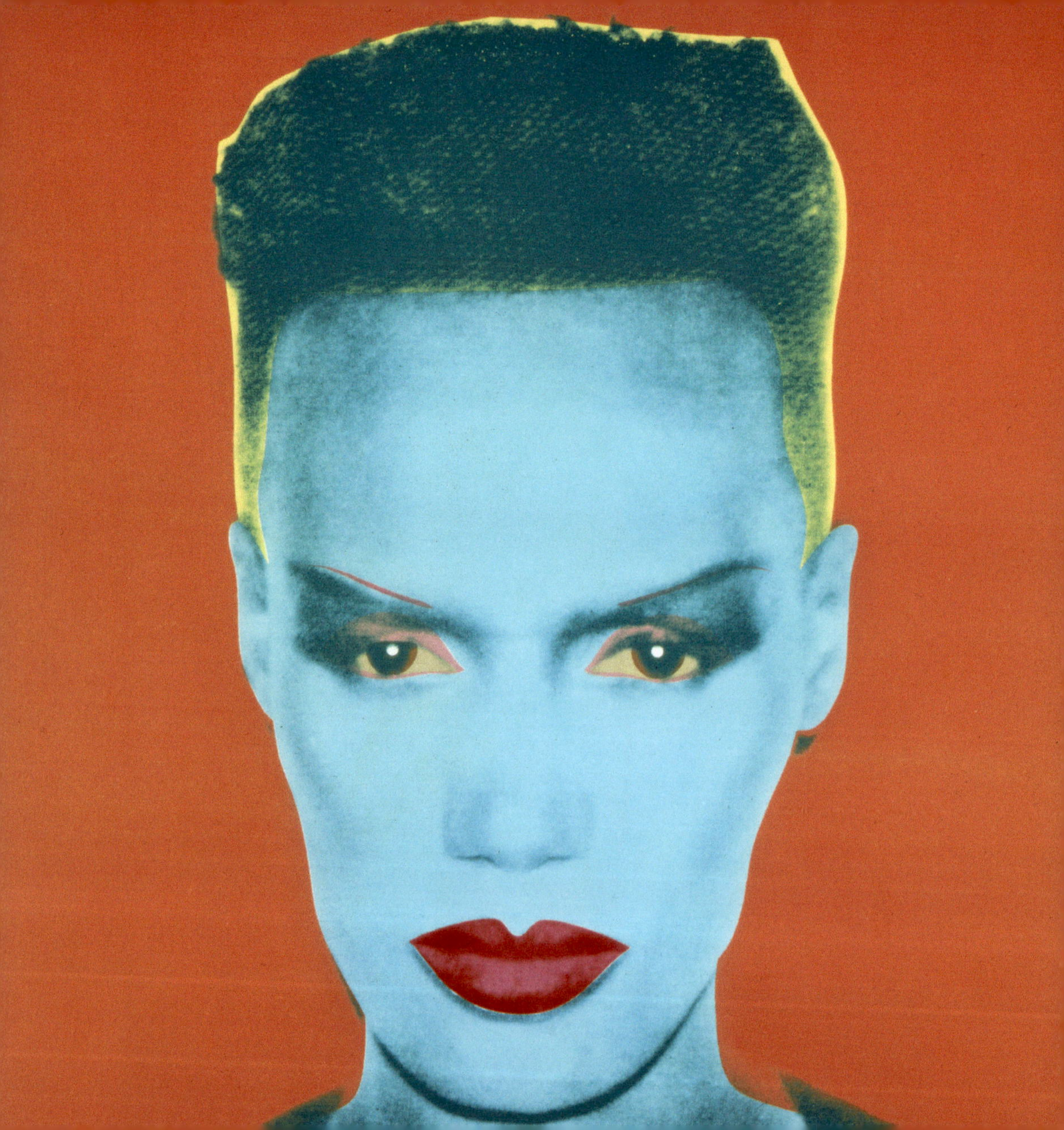

DAISY CHAIN

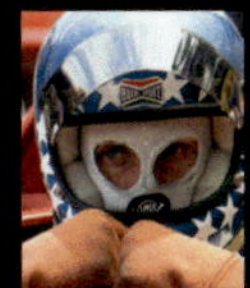

COVER

Slim Aarons, *Hans-Joachim Stuck*, 1977. © SLIM AARONS/ GETTY IMAGES, 2023.

○ VINCE ALETTI

The critic and curator recently published *The Drawer* (SPBH, 2022) a book of his collage-like arrangements of paper ephemera. All the materials came from a drawer of loose, printed matter, accumulated throughout his life. The compositions are clues to his private responses, internal thought processes, and emotional connection to public imagery and the media. These four works were created exclusively for *Daisy Chain*, and provide a visual forward that encapsulates much of the ethos of this publication. "Sometimes I think I can express myself more eloquently and poetically in pictures than in words," Aletti says. "It's a language I can share across cultures, with no need of a translator."

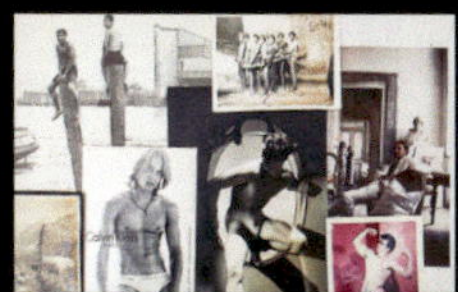

1

© Vince Aletti, 2023.
COMMISSIONED BY DAISY CHAIN.
PHOTOGRAPHER: PETE DEEVAKUL

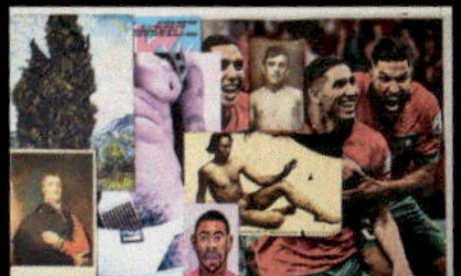

2   **3**

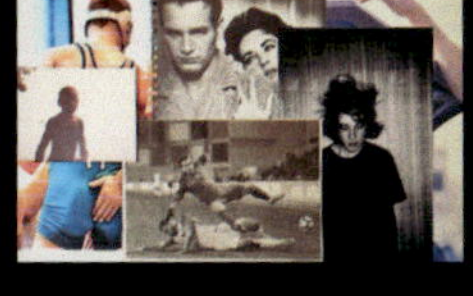

6   **7**

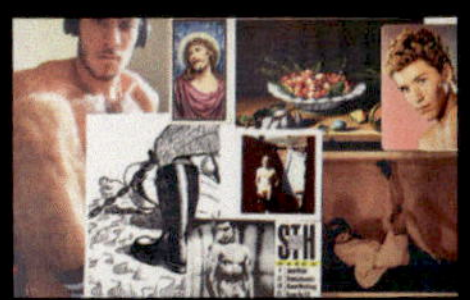

4   **5**

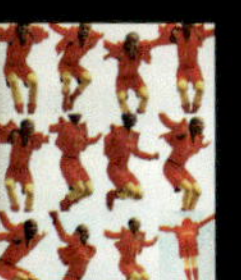

10   **11**

Hans Feurer, *Nova*, September 1971. © HANS FEURER / CAMERA WORK GALLERY, BERLIN
MODEL: unknown
ART DIRECTION: Harri Peccinotti
STYLING: Caroline Baker

◢ GOLDFISH

Goldfish can occupy a variety of spaces—from tiny jars to exotic ponds to opulent home aquariums. During the ancient Chinese dynasties, they were possessed only by the wealthy. They were markers of fortune and luck, and have survived as a glinting throughline in art history as bright tokens of contemplation and peace. The works included here present very different gazes, united by their focus on this ancient symbol of serenity. Henri Matisse was particularly spellbound: "It makes me want to become a vermilion goldfish."

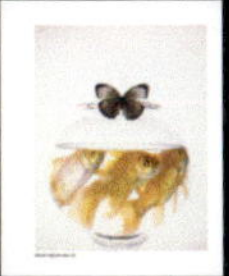

12   **13**

Irving Penn, *Goldfish*, *Vogue* cover, April 15, 1947.
IRVING PENN, VOGUE © CONDÉ NAST

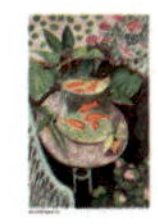

14   **15**

P14: Henri Matisse, *Goldfish*, 1912. © SUCCESSION HENRI MATISSE, C/O PICTORIGHT AMSTERDAM 2022 / PHOTO SCALA FLORENCE

P.15: © Luo Yang, Yuyu, 2019. © 2019 LUO YANG. ALL RIGHTS RESERVED.

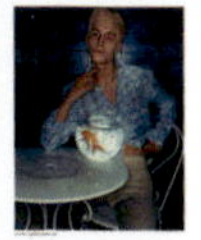

16   **17**

P.16: Nick Knight, *Jerome with Goldfish*, *Vogue Hommes*, 1994. © NK Image Ltd. c/o Nick Knight
MODEL: Jerome Lechevalier

P.17: Roy Lichtenstein, *Goldfish Bowl*, 1977. © ESTATE OF ROY LICHTENSTEIN, C/O PICTORIGHT AMSTERDAM 2022 / DIGITAL IMAGE WHITNEY MUSEUM OF AMERICAN ART / PHOTO SCALA, FLORENCE

© Erté, *Fish Bowl*, *Harper's Bazaar* cover, June 1931.
C/O PICTORIGHT AMSTERDAM 2022 / BRIDGEMAN IMAGES

Jean Baptiste Berré, *Still Life with flowers in a Vase and Goldfish Bowl*, 1800. DOROTHEUM VIENNA, AUCTION CATALOGUE 12.09.2016

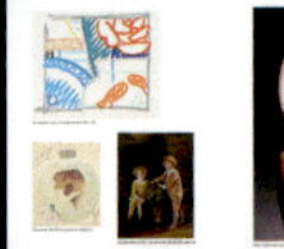
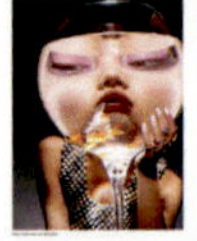
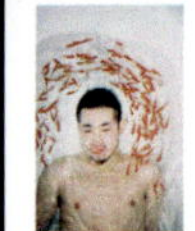
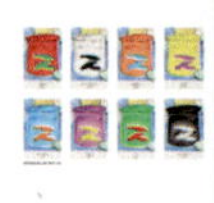

18   **19**

P.18: © Tom Wesselmann, *Still Life with Goldfish and Rose*, 1984. C/O PICTORIGHT AMSTERDAM 2022

Lydia Field Emmet, *Goldfish, a Portrait of Roland and Peter Hazard*, 1921. COLLECTION OF THE MENNELLO MUSEUM OF AMERICAN ART, MUSEUM PURCHASE

Totoya Hokkei, *Gold-Fish in a Glass Bottle*, 19th century. C/O THE METROPOLITAN MUSEUM OF ART

P.19: Carlijn Jacobs, *Vogue* Italia, January 2021.
© CARLIJN JACOBS / ART + COMMERCE
MODEL: Mao Xiao Xing
STYLIST: Imruh Asha
HAIR: Olivier Schawalder
MAKEUP: Peter Phillips

20   **21**

P.20: © Ren Hang, *Untitled*, 2012. C/O ESTATE OF REN HANG AND THE WHITE RABBIT COLLECTION, SYDNEY

P.21: John Baldessari, *Set of Eight Soups*, 2012. © 2012 JOHN BALDESSARI AND GEMINI G.E.L. LLC COURTESY OF JOHN BALDESSARI TRUST-1991 © 2022 AND SPRUETH MAGERS.

24   **25**

Guy Bourdin, *Vogue* Paris, October 1976.
© THE GUY BOURDIN ESTATE, 1976 C/O LOUISE ALEXANDER GALLERY, LOS ANGELES

2. SHANIQWA JARVIS

A master at showing both the personal and the public faces of an individual in a portrait, and the mystery and unknowable in the day-to-day. Her art and work are closely aligned—the "same love and sensitivities are put into both," she says. These images were taken during a visit to Japan in 2022, right before the borders opened. She roamed Osaka, Kyoto, and Tokyo. "This trip was different. I wasn't there for work and was able to just relax, look hard at my surroundings, and how the light would bend around things."

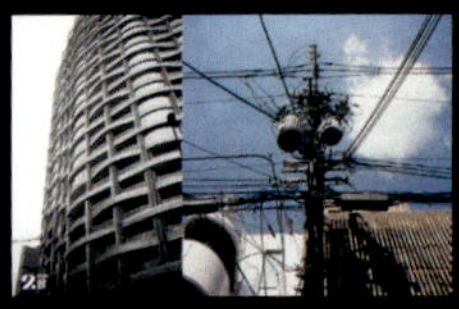
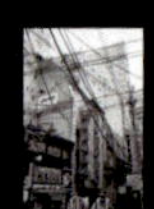
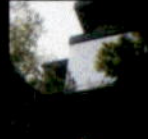

24   **25**

© SHANIQWA JARVIS, 2022. COMMISSIONED BY DAISY CHAIN.

26   **27**

30   **31**

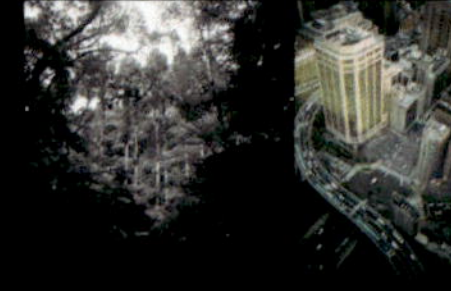
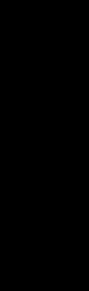
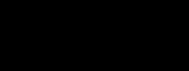

28   **29**

3. RON JUDE

His newly published *Dark Matter* (MONOGRAM, 2022) returns to the images from his 2006 book, *Alpine Star* (A-JUMP BOOKS). Those initial photographs were all pulled from the weekly newspaper of his hometown in Central Idaho, assembled and reframed to examine the impressions and stories that are created to circulate in communities. Here, years later, Ron looks again at these pictures, reassessing and reassembling them to reflect the present day, and how much our perception, mood, and sensitivities have shifted.

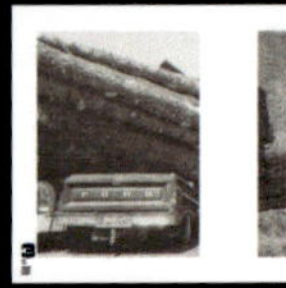

32   **33**

© Ron Jude, *Dark Matter*, 2022.

34   **35**

38   **39**

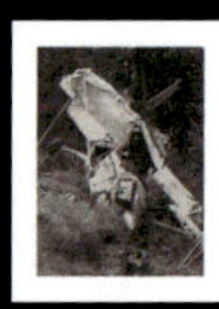
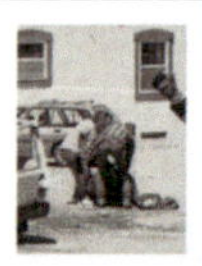

36   **37**

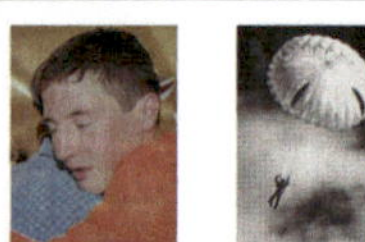

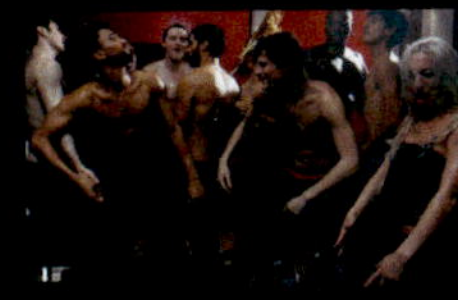

4   MARK CARRASQUILLO AND LUCIAN CLIFFORTH

A renowned makeup artist, Mark conceived this shoot around how people energize and transform public spaces. He enlisted Lucian to photograph a party of dancers who revel in each other's vitality and beauty, elevating an otherwise non-descript room into a vessel of connection and pleasure.

40   41

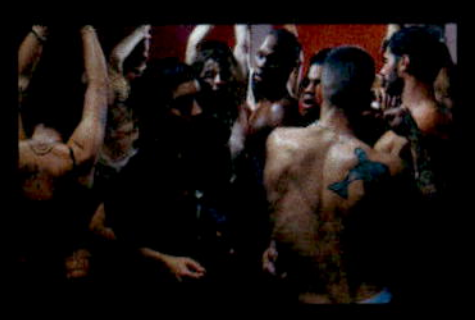

42   43

© Lucian Clifforth, 2022.
COMMISSIONED BY DAISY CHAIN.
CREATIVE DIRECTOR:
Mark Carrasquillo
PHOTOGRAPHER: Lucian Clifforth
PHOTO ASSISTANT: Matt Stejbach
MOVEMENT DIRECTOR:
Fernando Casablancas
LOCATION: Radio Nublu

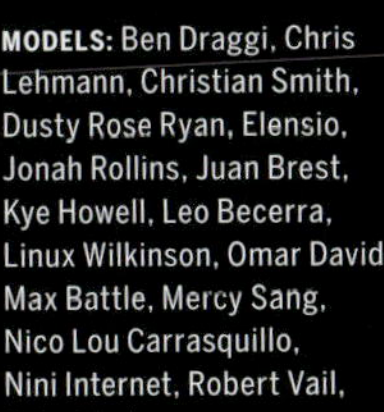

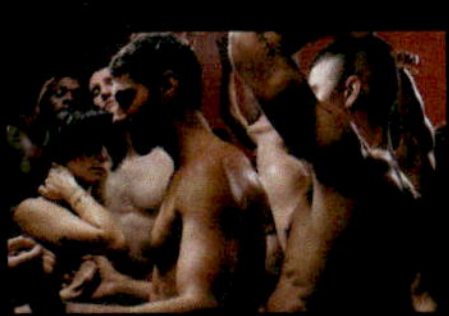

44   45

MODELS: Ben Draggi, Chris Lehmann, Christian Smith, Dusty Rose Ryan, Elensio, Jonah Rollins, Juan Brest, Kye Howell, Leo Becerra, Linux Wilkinson, Omar David, Max Battle, Mercy Sang, Nico Lou Carrasquillo, Nini Internet, Robert Vail, Zeke Lindsey

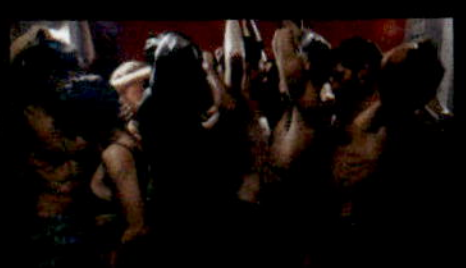

46   47

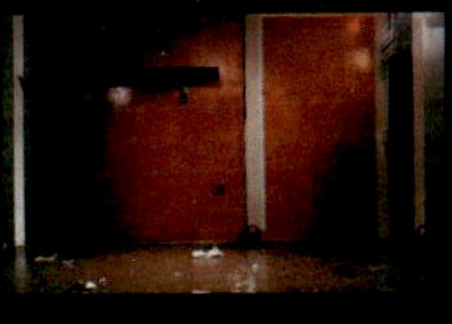

48   49

5   LIMINAL

A liminal space has an elusive, mysterious quality, a suggestion of both past and present, of transition, somehow untouched and yet full of meaning. They project a conflict of anticipation and heartbreak. These feelings are prompted not just in interior spaces (such as hallways) but also by video game backdrops, empty landscapes in horror movies, and deserted cities during lockdown. These eerie tableaux have been depicted throughout art history through painting, photography, and now digitally; their power lies in the viewer's interpretation.

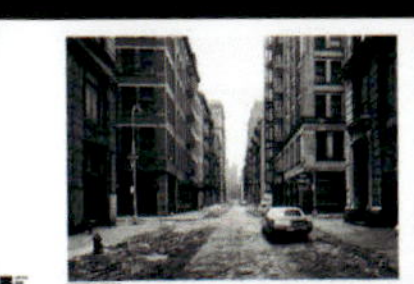

50   51

© Thomas Struth, *Crosby Street, Soho, New York*, 1978.
© THOMAS STRUTH

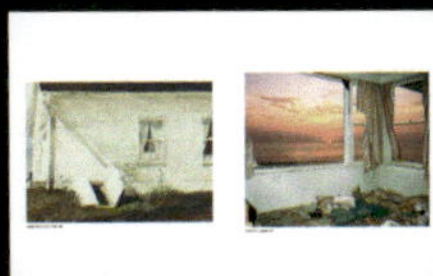

52   53

P.52: © Andrew Wyeth, *Elsie's House*, 1983. C/O PICTORIGHT AMSTERDAM 2022

P.53: © John Divola, *Zuma #85*, 1977. C/O THE JOHN DIVOLA

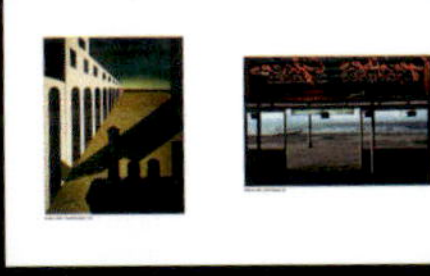

54   55

P.54: © Giorgio De Chirico, *The Morning Anxiety*, 1912.
C/O PICTORIGHT AMSTERDAM 2022 / PHOTO SCALA, FLORENCE

P.55: © Harry Gruyaert, *Ostend, Belgium*, 1988. C/O GALLERY FIFTY ONE, ANTWERP

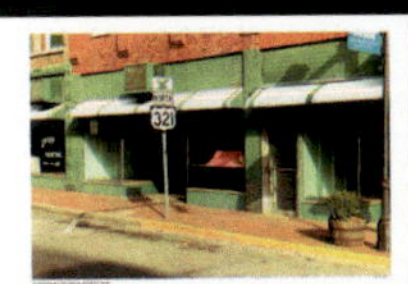

56   57

William Eggleston, *Untitled*, c.1983–1986.
© EGGLESTON ARTISTIC TRUST
C/O EGGLESTON ARTISTIC TRUST AND DAVID ZWIRNER GALLERY, NEW YORK

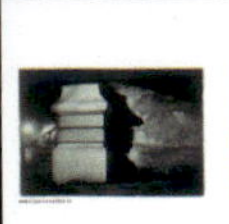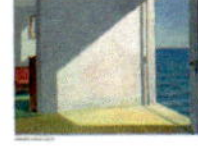

58   59

P.58: Brassaï (dit), Halasz Gyula, *Pilier de métro*, 1934. © ESTATE BRASSAÏ - RMN-GRAND PALAIS
PHOTO © CENTRE POMPIDOU, MNAM-CCI, DIST. RMN-GRAND PALAIS / JACQUES FAUJOUR

P.59: © Edward Hopper, *Rooms by the Sea*, 1951. C/O PICTORIGHT AMSTERDAM 2022 / PHOTO SCALA, FLORENCE

6   EMMY RAPPE

The model turned image-maker learned how to use a drone at her parents' Swedish dairy farm. She experimented by making films, and playing with perspective and space. She created this story in the California desert, capturing herself as a lone, alien creature in human form moving through a beautiful but forbidding landscape. In this re-contextualized view, the shapes and colors of the West provoke new feelings of remoteness; a gaze reversed, and a vulnerability and strangeness enhanced by the unexpected addition of a practical pink pool float accompanying her everywhere she goes.

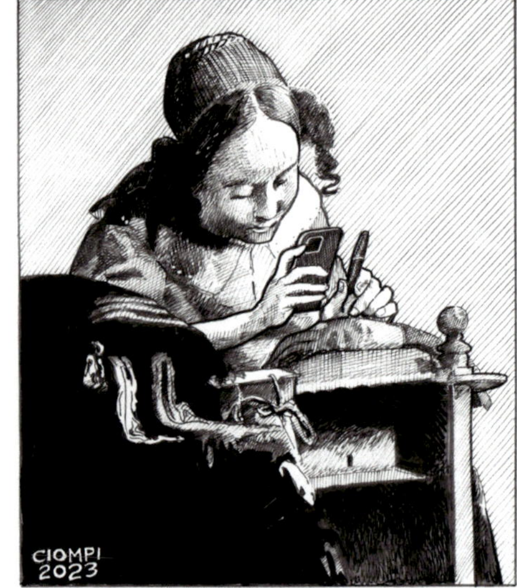

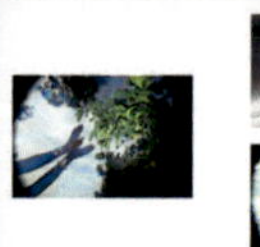

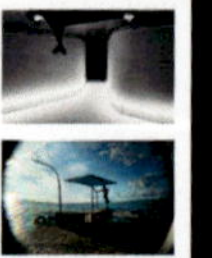

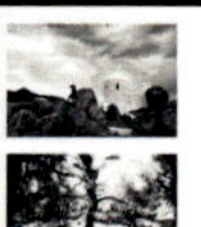

78   79   80   81

Loewe dress

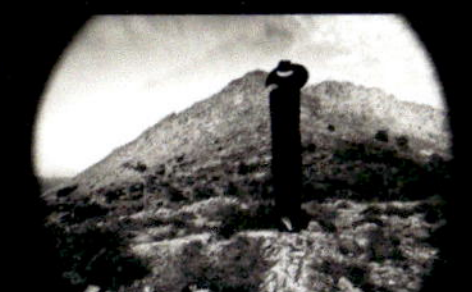

82   83

Balmain hat

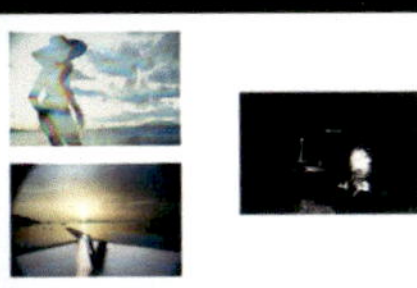

84   85

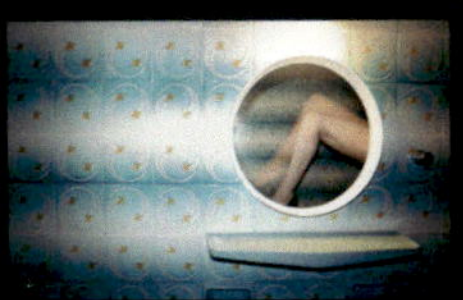

86   87

SLIM AARONS

These hyper-masculine images of the Grand Prix in Monaco during the 1970s show a tension of sportsmanship and glamor, grown men trapped in small sleek machines and constrictive fishbowl helmets. The stance of these extraordinary, risk-taking athletes at the top of their game is defensive, patriarchal, exuding an exaggerated, militaristic power; these images are a celebration not just of status, but of human achievement. Photographs that magnify obsolete stereotypes such as these have fallen out of favor, but there is no questioning their deftness and precision. The beauty is not incidental, it is controlled.

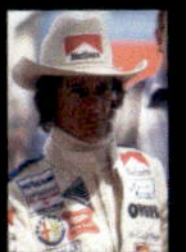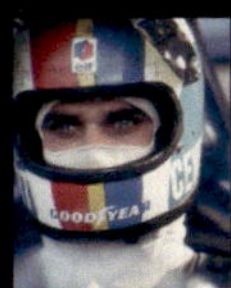

88   89

Slim Aarons, *The Monaco Grand Prix*, 1973–1977.

Arturo Merzario, 1977
© SLIM AARONS/GETTY IMAGES

Francois Cevert, 1977
© SLIM AARONS/GETTY IMAGES

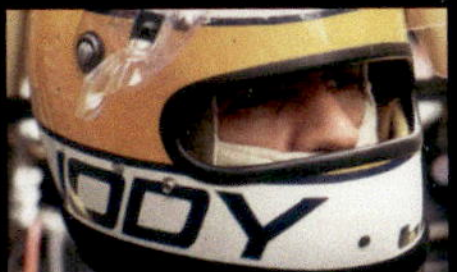

90   91

Jody Scheckter, 1977
© SLIM AARONS/GETTY IMAGES

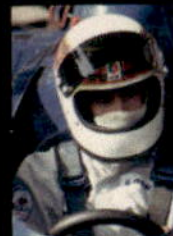

92   93

Jackie Stewart, 1973
© SLIM AARONS/GETTY IMAGES

Niki Lauda, 1977
© SLIM AARONS/GETTY IMAGES

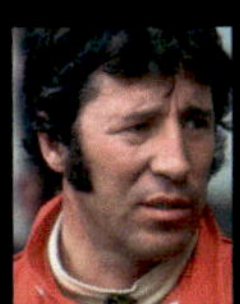

94   95

Mario Andretti, May 1977
© SLIM AARONS/GETTY IMAGES

James Hunt, 1977
© SLIM AARONS/GETTY IMAGES
Jackie Stewart, 1977
© SLIM AARONS/GETTY IMAGES

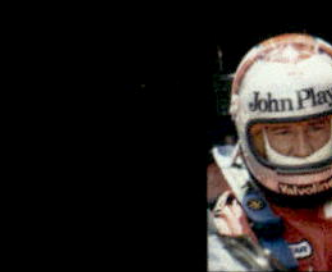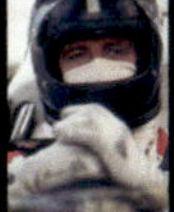

96   97

Mario Andretti , 1977
© SLIM AARONS/GETTY IMAGES

Graham Hill, 1973
© SLIM AARONS/GETTY IMAGES

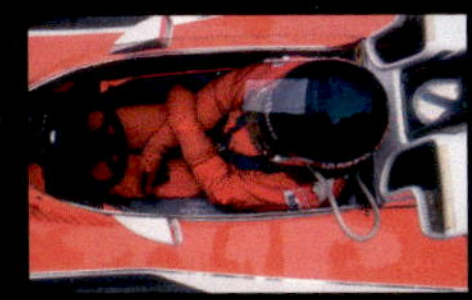

98   99

James Hunt, May 1977
© SLIM AARONS/GETTY IMAGES

KUBA RYNIEWICZ

Presenting a very personal collection of photographs from his hometown Puszczykowo in Poland, Kuba looks at the deep emotional ties that link his family life, his creative practice, and his queerness. Childhood bonds, memories, and fresh experiences are combined here; a sense of place and time, of old and new love, of minute detail and profound connection.

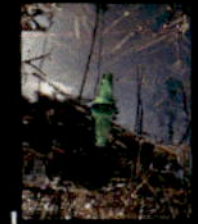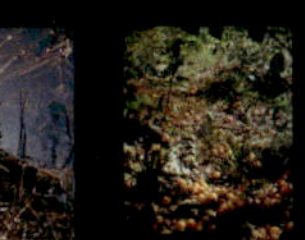

100   101

© Kuba Ryniewicz, 2022.
COMMISSIONED BY DAISY CHAIN.
C/O KUBA RYNIEWICZ
LOCATION: PUSZCZYKOWO, POLAND

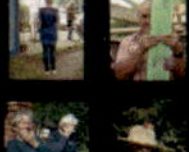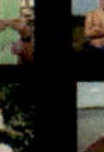

102   103

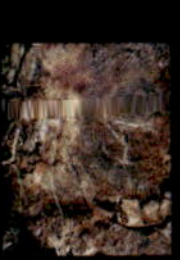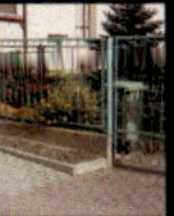

104   105

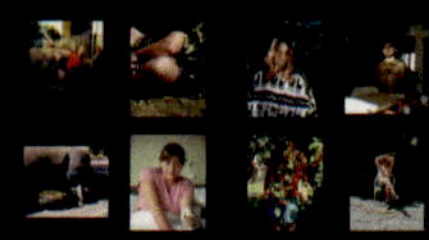

106   **107**

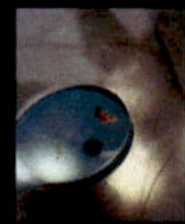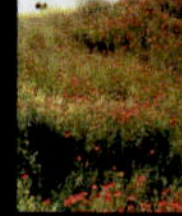

108   **109**

11 CATHERINE WAGNER

This still-life triptych comes from the series *Home and Other Stories*, 1989–91, which presents the infinitely compelling interiors of strangers—in this case, that of Christine T. in San Francisco. Catherine's work focuses primarily on contemporary culture and how it affects individuals: their habits, purchases, preferences, codes, and arrangements that form within their private living spaces, and how these choices reveal their sense of identity and place in the world.

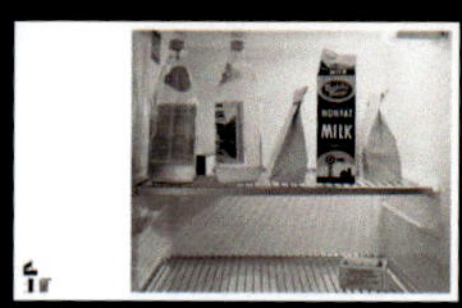

110   **111**

© Catherine Wagner, *Christine T.* from *Home and Other Stories*, 1991.
C/O GALLERY LUISOTTI, LOS ANGELES AND JESSICA SILVERMAN GALLERY, SAN FRANCISCO

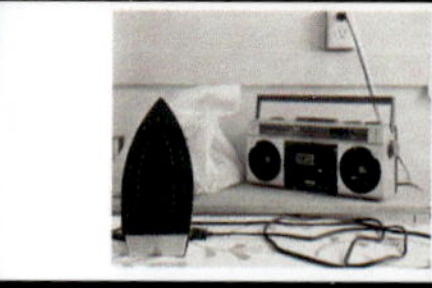

112   **113**

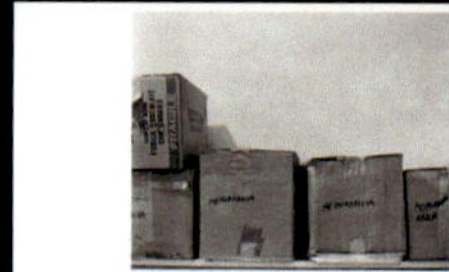

114   **115**

12 JUN AHN

The South Korean artist examines the power of gravity: she sees it as a wide angle metaphor for love and death. We are all hurtling through the universe on a rock, never in the same spot twice. Any photograph ever taken is a snapshot of a point in time and space—no matter how trivial or important—that can never be replicated. These rocks fall inevitably downwards; these images endeavor to portray the vastness of our brief moment of existence on earth and the multitude of forces that constitute our individual lives.

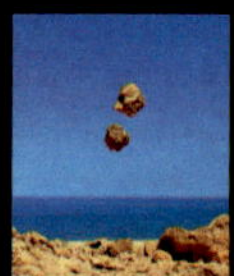

116   **117**

© Jun Ahn, 2022.
C/O JUN AHN AND CHRISTOPHE GUYE GALLERY, ZURICH
Photographed in Oman

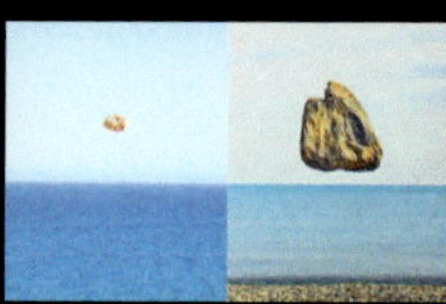

118   **119**

P.130: Photographed in Oman

P.131: Photographed in Sokcho, South Korea

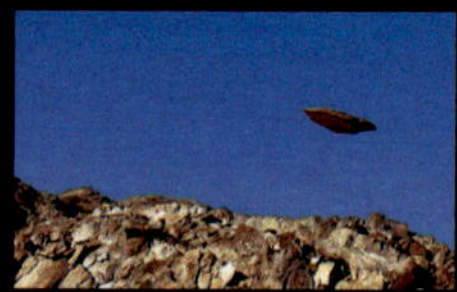

120   **121**

Photographed in Oman

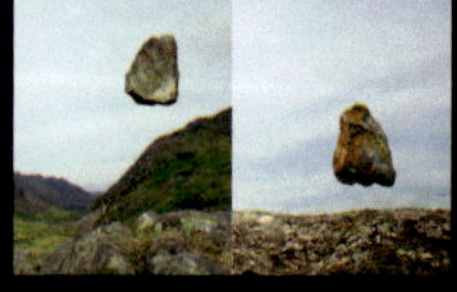

122   **123**

Photographed in Snowdonia National Park, Wales

13 PETER LINDBERGH

Aliens and science fiction were among the themes Lindbergh returned to repeatedly in his work. He possessed an uncanny grip on the otherworldly and elusive qualities of allure, glamor, and authenticity. (DAISY CHAIN CREATIVE DIRECTOR PHILLIP RECALLS THAT DURING HIS TIME AT VOGUE, THE ARRIVAL OF A NEW LINDBERGH STORY WAS CAUSE FOR EXCITEMENT, HIS STORIES WERE SO GOOD AND LOVED BY ALL: NO SMALL FEAT IN THAT OFFICE). This selection shows how the photographer imbued narrative, old Hollywood grandeur, awe, and intuition into his imagery—with his signature charm and wit—provoking wonderment and a sense of complicity with the viewer.

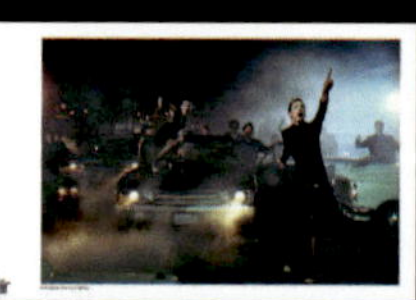

124   **125**

© Peter Lindbergh, *L.A. Report*, *Vogue Italia*, October 2000.
MODELS: Karen Elson and Milla Jovovich
STYLIST: Karl Templer
HAIR: Julien d'Ys
MAKEUP: Emmanuel Sanmartino
C/O PETER LINDBERGH FOUNDATION, PARIS

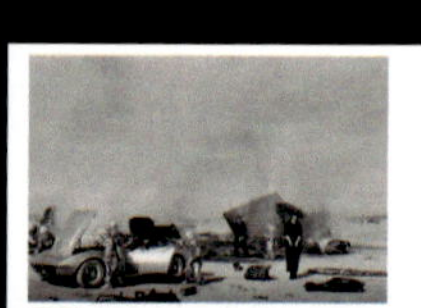

126   **127**

© Peter Lindbergh, *In a future mood*, *Vogue Italia*, March 2001.
MODELS: Guinevere van Seenus and Fred Ward
STYLIST: Nicoletta Santoro
HAIR: Julien d'Ys
MAKEUP: Gucci Westman
C/O PETER LINDBERGH FOUNDATION, PARIS

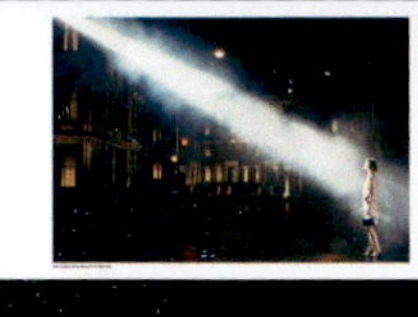
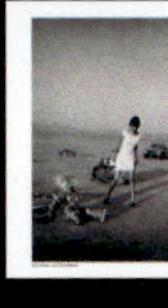
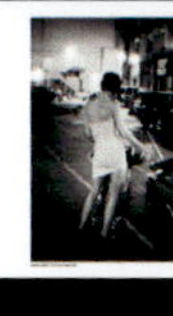
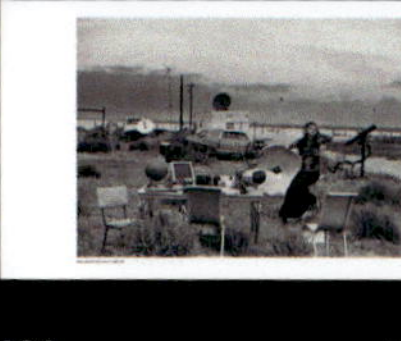
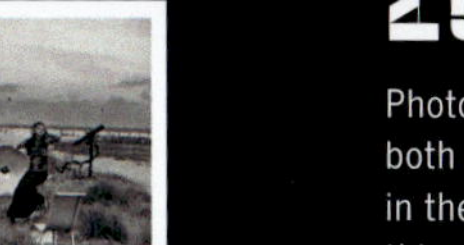

128 **129**

© Peter Lindbergh, *Leading Lady, Harper's Bazaar*, September 2002.
MODEL: Erin Wasson
STYLIST: Mary Alice Stephenson
HAIR: Odile Gilbert
MAKEUP: Stephane Marais
C/O PETER LINDBERGH FOUNDATION, PARIS

130 **131**

© Peter Lindbergh, *Femminilità Extraterrestre, Vogue Italia*, March 1990.
MODEL: Helena Christensen
STYLIST: Elizabeth Djian
HAIR: Odile Gilbert
MAKEUP: Stephane Marais
C/O PETER LINDBERGH FOUNDATION, PARIS

132 **133**

© Peter Lindbergh, *Looking Forward, Vogue Italia*, October 1998.
MODEL: Angela Lindvall
FASHION EDITOR: Nicoletta Santoro
HAIR: Odile Gilbert
MAKEUP: Stephane Marais
C/O PETER LINDBERGH FOUNDATION, PARIS

Photographed in December 2022 both in Shanghai and Zhangjiajie in the north of Hunan Province, this story was inspired by the discovery of a new lunar mineral, Changesite-(Y) collected on the Chang'e-5 mission two years ago. Named after the Chinese Moon Goddess, this mineral might be the key to producing limitless power sources on earth. Zeng's experimental and expansive style imagines this future with a dynamic, feminine energy, emanating from both the core of the earth and the outer galaxy.

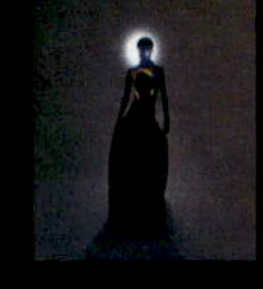
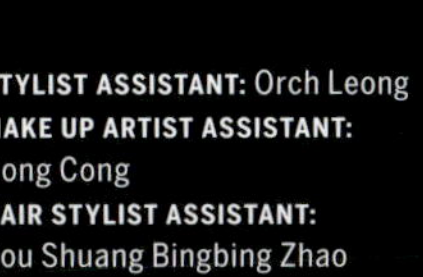
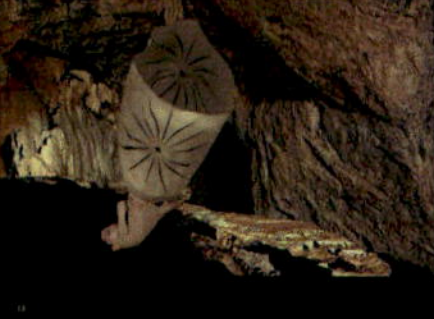
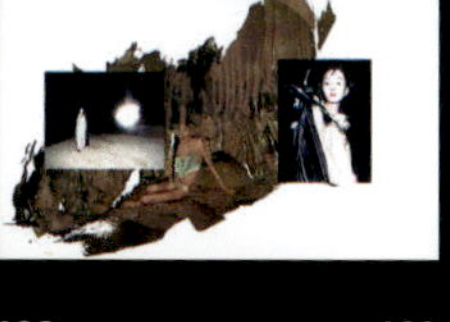

134 **135**

© Zeng Wu, *Chang'e* (嫦娥), 2023.
COMMISSIONED BY DAISY CHAIN.
PHOTOGRAPHER: Zeng Wu
MODEL: Xinye Wang
STYLIST: Alvin Yu
MAKEUP ARTIST: Clive X
HAIR STYLIST: Xueming Zhou
CO-CREATIVE: Daidai
SET DESIGNER: Jianjian
CASTING DIRECTOR: Denise Hu
EXECUTIVE SET DESIGNER: Jerry Liew
PHOTO ASSISTANT: Wu Hao, Yitian Zhang

STYLIST ASSISTANT: Orch Leong
MAKE UP ARTIST ASSISTANT: Cong Cong
HAIR STYLIST ASSISTANT: Kou Shuang Bingbing Zhao
SET ASSISTANT: Jin
PRODUCER: Wawa

P.147: Zhong Zixin skirt, Oude Waag top

136 **137**

Zhong Zixin skirt

138 **139**

Zhong Zixin dress, Cult Gaia shoes, Buerlangma geometry top

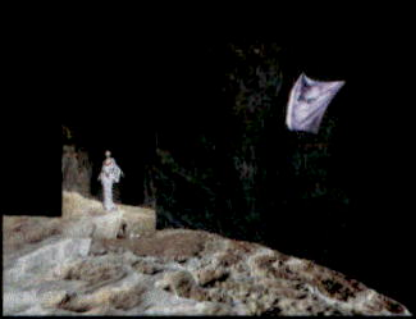
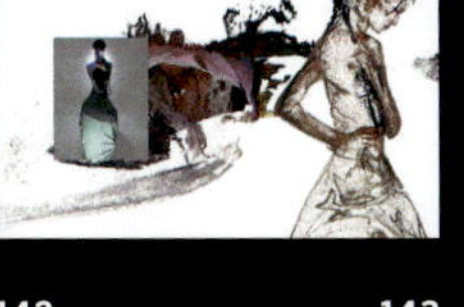
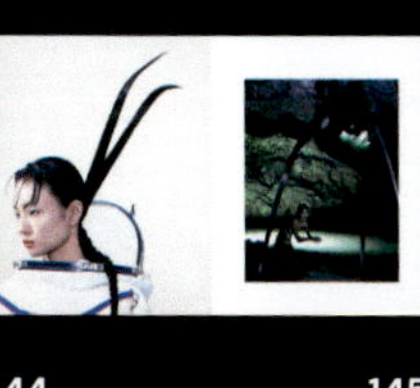
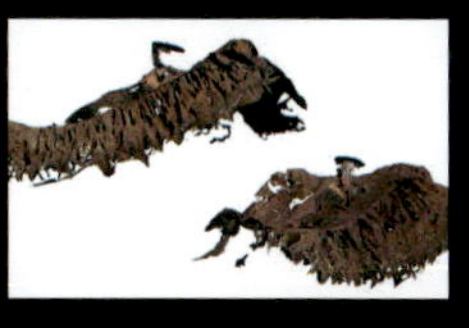

140 **141**

P.140: Nan Knits vest, dress and shawl, Cult Gaia choker and shoes

142 **143**

Zhong Zixin skirt, Oude Waag top

144 **145**

P.145: Jadeite vest by Ziwu

146 **147**

Misbhv dress and gloves, Cult Gaia shoes

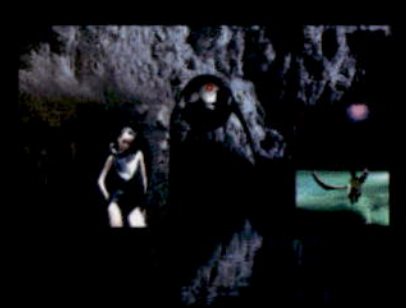
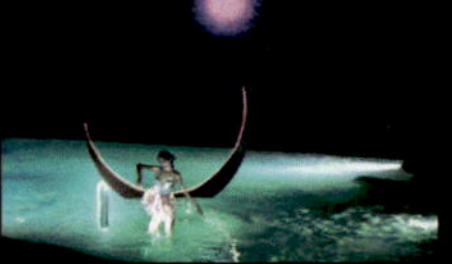
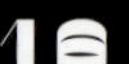

16 THIBAUT GREVET

This excerpt from his recently self-published book, *Blurred*, shows Thibaut at his most raw, even in the slickest of environments and with the most immaculate subjects. The photographer and filmmaker initially trained as a graphic designer—his bold instinct for lines, shapes, and textures resonate vividly throughout his work. Here, he captures how life flashes by at a frenetic pace, the overwhelming emotions that run fast and wild, whipping through your senses; fusing the hallucinatory imprints of these movements into his images.

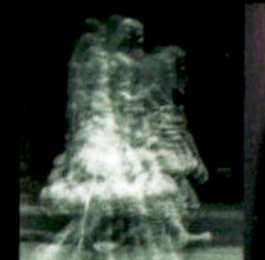
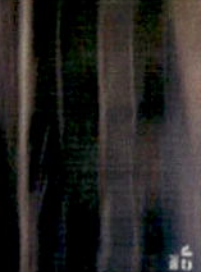

148   149

P.148: Ximon Lee tyre skin vest

150   151

Jadeite vest by Ziwu, circular piece stylist's own

152   153

© Thibaut Grevet, 2022.

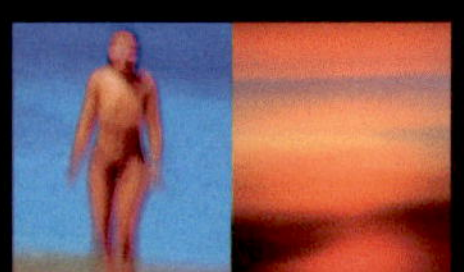
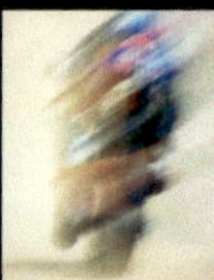
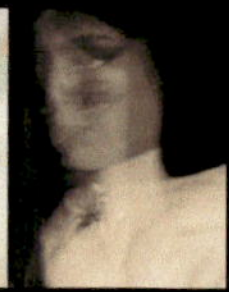
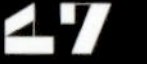

17 BLUE GREEN

When a skin tone is blue or green, it creates possibility, an opening into an individual interpretation of the status quo. The trend has recently appeared across communities and in cinema, fashion, social media, and cosplay. Spanning from the 1960s to the present, this collection highlights a delicate but strong thread that links modern imagery and progressive thought through the decades, finding strength in new directions. A mix of queer selfhood, sci-fi cliché, and the political.

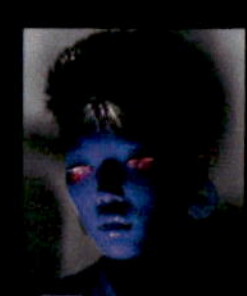

154   155

158   159

162   163

© Carlijn Jacobs / ART + COMMERCE, *Pop* Magazine, April 2021.
MODEL: Kayako Higuchi
STYLIST: Vanessa Reid
HAIR: Olivier Schawalder
MAKEUP: Cécile Paravina

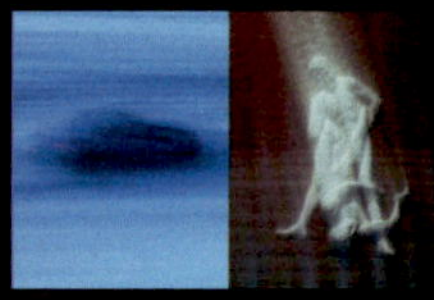
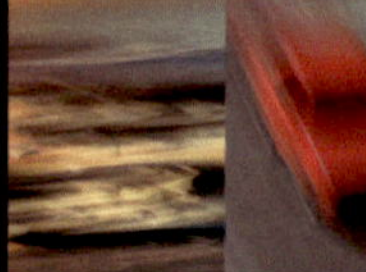

156   157

160   161

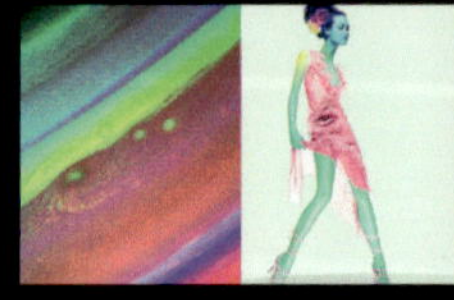
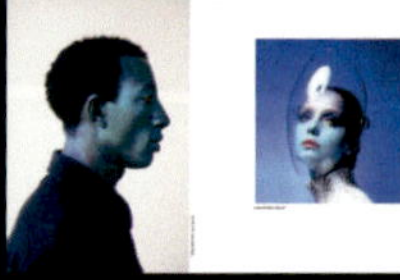
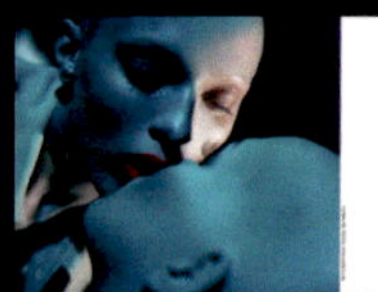
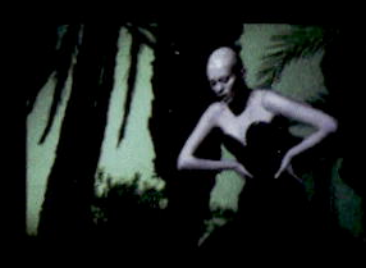

164   165

P.164: NASA/JPL-CALTECH/ ASU/MSSS, *Saturn Northern Hemisphere*, August 19, 1981, acquired December 5, 1998

P.165 : Nick Knight, *Shalom Harlow for Louis Vuitton I*, 1996.
COURTESY OF NICK KNIGHT
MODEL: Shalom Harlow
STYLIST: Lucinda Chambers
HAIR: Sam McKnight
MAKEUP: Dick Page

166   167

P.166: Viviane Sassen, *Etan / Azul 15:00*, 2013.
© VIVIANE SASSEN, COURTESY OF STEVENSON, AMSTERDAM/CAPE TOWN/JOHANNESBURG

P.167: Clive Arrowsmith, *Donna Mitchel Visor. Vogue* UK, March 1970.
© CLIVE ARROWSMITH / CAMERA PRESS
MODEL: Donna Mitchell
STYLIST: Grace Coddington
ART DIRECTOR: Barney Wan

168   169

Mert Alas and Marcus Piggott, *Pop* Magazine #10, Spring/ Summer 2005.
© MERT ALAS AND MARCUS PIGGOTT / ART PARTNER. 2005
MODEL: Karen Elson
STYLIST: Katie Grand
LOCATION: Ibiza
C/O MERT ALAS AND MARCUS PIGGOTT / ART PARTNER

170   171

Mert Alas and Marcus Piggott, *Pop* Magazine #10, Spring/ Summer 2005.
© MERT ALAS AND MARCUS PIGGOTT / ART PARTNER. 2005
MODEL: Karen Elson
STYLIST: Katie Grand
LOCATION: Ibiza
C/O MERT ALAS AND MARCUS PIGGOTT / ART PARTNER

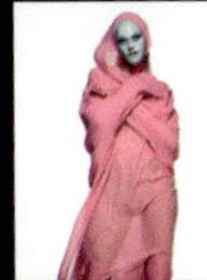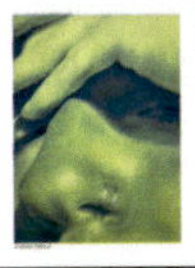

172 **173**

P.172: Sølve Sundsbø, *Spring Awakening*, *V* Magazine #128, Spring 2021.
© SØLVE SUNDSBØ / ART + COMMERCE
MODEL: Jean Campbell
STYLIST: Gro Curtis
CLOTHING: Rick Owens
HAIR: Kei Terada
MAKEUP: Val Garland

P.173: Alejandra Moros, *Mi Mañana*, 2021.
Oil on canvas, 24x18 inches

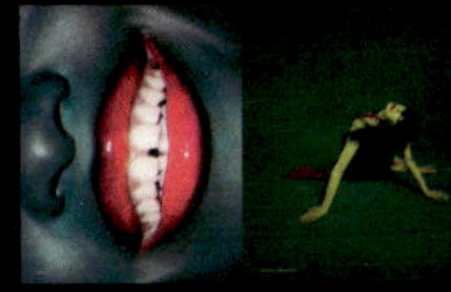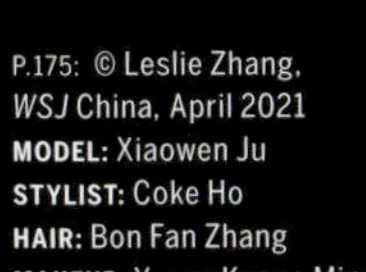

174 **175**

P.174: © Eva Wang, *Blue Green*, 2022.
COMMISSIONED BY DAISY CHAIN.
ART DIRECTOR: Adeline Gault
MODEL: Rokhaya Fall
STYLING: Gaultier Desandre Navarre
MAKEUP: Marielle Loubet
HAIR: Kazue Deki
MANICURISTS: Jessica Malige & Cecilia Abbas
LIPS: Kiko Lip Pen, Yves Saint Laurent Lipstick, Mac Gloss

P.175: © Leslie Zhang, *WSJ* China, April 2021
MODEL: Xiaowen Ju
STYLIST: Coke Ho
HAIR: Bon Fan Zhang
MAKEUP: Yooyo Keong Ming

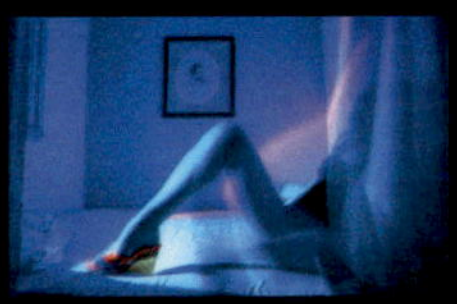

176 **177**

Emma Summerton, *Hecate*, 2021. © EMMA SUMMERTON. 2021.

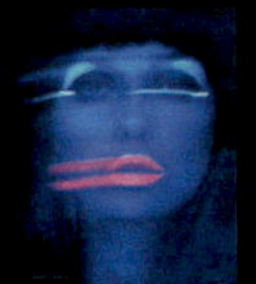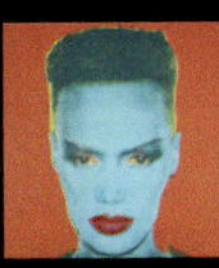

178 **179**

Melvin Sokolsky, *Lip Streaks*, 1967. © BING SOKOLKSY. 2023.
MODEL: Donna Mitchell

180 **181**

Andy Warhol, *Grace Jones*, 1986
© THE ANDY WARHOL FOUNDATION FOR THE VISUAL ARTS, INC.
C/O PICTORIGHT AMSTERDAM 2022

 **18** EXQUISITE CORPSE

First invented by the Surrealists in Paris in the early 20th century, an exquisite corpse, or *cadavre exquis*, is a simple game based in communal creativity. A group of friends take a piece of paper and take turns in drawing the part of a figure. The first begins with the head, folding down their contribution out of sight before handing it over to the next person, who then improvises. At the end, the paper is unraveled to reveal the surprise: almost always an entertaining and startling character, somehow mythological, gorgeous, and grotesque all at once.

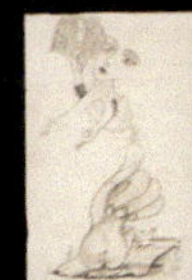

191

© André Breton, Jacques Hérold, Yves Tanguy, Victor Brauner, *Cadavre Exquis: Figure*, 1934. C/O PICTORIGHT AMSTERDAM 2023 / DIGITAL IMAGE, THE MUSEUM OF MODERN ART, NEW YORK/SCALA, FLORENCE

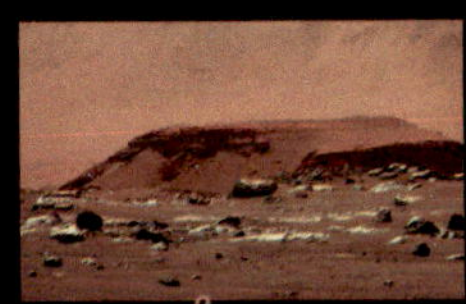

192 **LAST**

NASA/JPL-CALTECH/ASU/MSSS, *Perseverance View of the Delta in Jezero Crater from the Octavia E. Butler Landing, taken with the Mastcam-Z*, acquired February 22, 2021.

This image was a point of departure for selecting the theme of this issue: space. When Perseverance, the Mars Rover, landed on the Red Planet to begin its mission, the site was officially named by NASA as the "Octavia E. Butler Landing." As longtime admirers of the literary icon, it was inspiring to learn that her presence in the science field is as relevant as it is in the creative worlds. Groundbreaking photographs such as these signify the expanding of a public's consciousness about space and the future—just like Butler's writing.

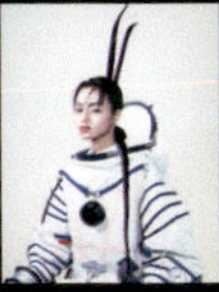

BACK COVER

© Zeng Wu, *Chang'e* (嫦娥), 2023.
COMMISSIONED BY DAISY CHAIN.
PHOTOGRAPHER: Zeng Wu
MODEL: Xinye Wang
STYLIST: Alvin Yu
HAIR: Xueming Zhou
MAKEUP: Clive X

1

The idea of creating a magazine that
functions like a game is exciting —
the game being the 1920s absurdist,
collaborative caper known as the
Exquisite Corpse, or *Cadavre Exquis*,
invented by the Surrealists in Paris
at a Left Bank café — a group sitting
around the table, each drawing part
of a figure on a piece of paper, folding
and concealing it, and passing it onto
the next. The result is never what you
imagine, and always more beautiful,
surprising, and eclectic than expected.
Welcome to *Daisy Chain*.

THE EDITORS

DAISY
CHAIN

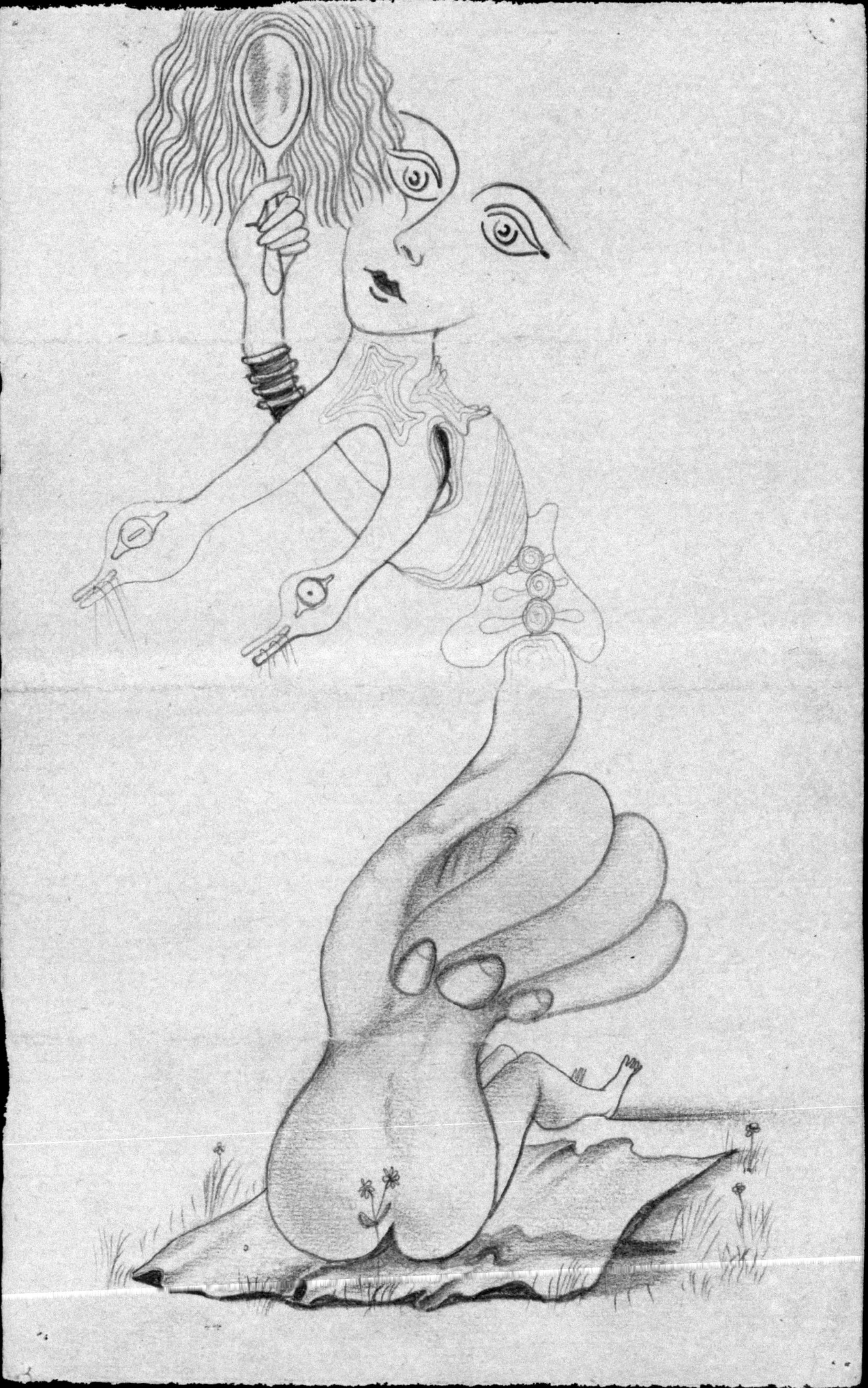

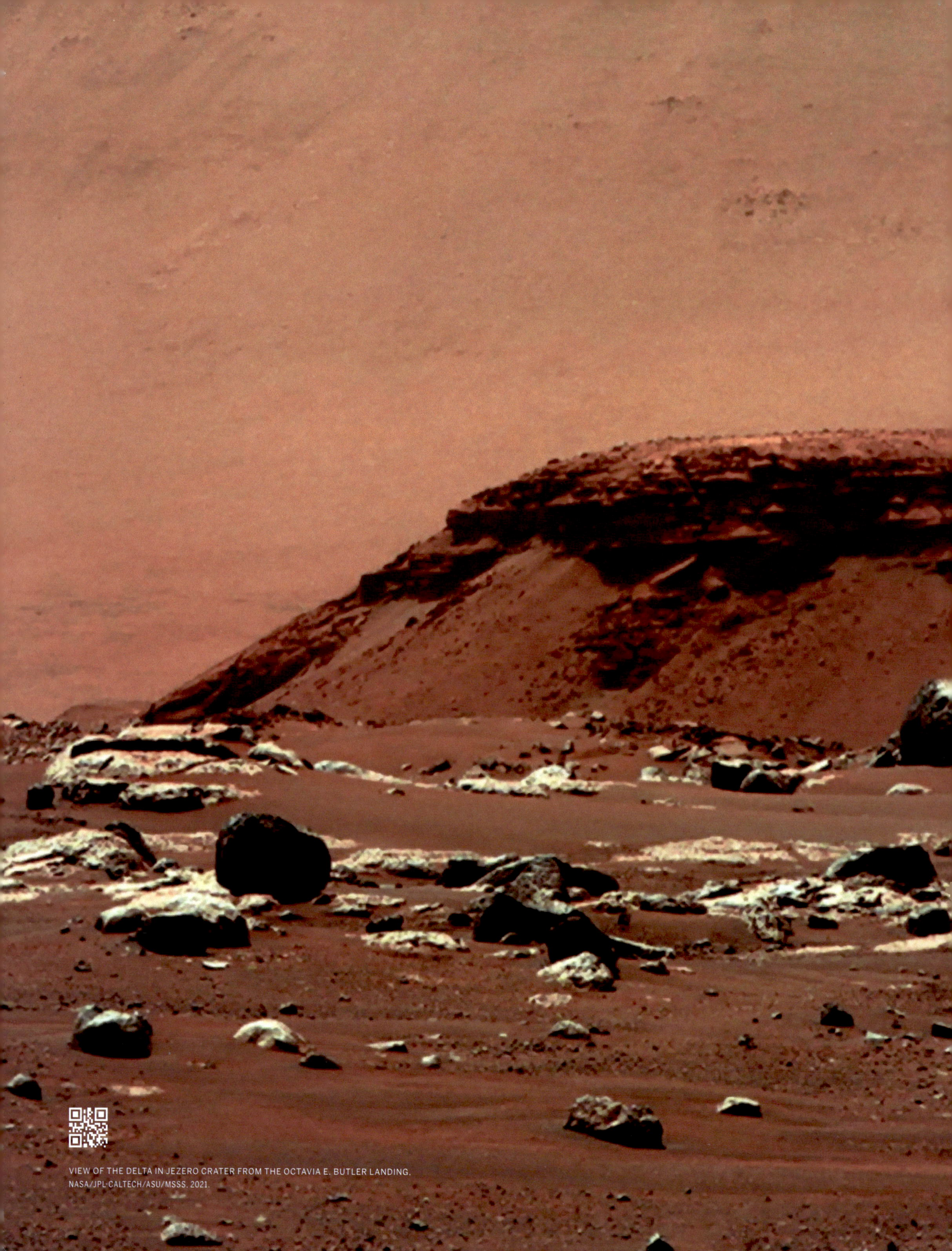

VIEW OF THE DELTA IN JEZERO CRATER FROM THE OCTAVIA E. BUTLER LANDING.
NASA/JPL-CALTECH/ASU/MSSS. 2021.